Juan de la Cierva with a C.30A Autogiro in 1935.
(O. Reder)

CIERVA AUTOGIROS

The Development of
Rotary-Wing Flight

PETER W. BROOKS

Smithsonian Institution Press
Washington, D.C.

Other books by Peter W. Brooks

The World's Sailplanes (joint editor)
The Modern Airliner: Its Origins and Development
The World's Airliners
Flight through the Ages (with C. H. Gibbs-Smith)
Historic Airships

Edited by Jeanne M. Sexton
Designed by Lisa Buck

Library of Congress Cataloging in Publication Data

Brooks, Peter W.
    Cierva Autogiros.

    Bibliography: p.
    Includes index.
    1. Autogiros—History.
2. Cierva, Juan de la, 1895-1936.
I. Title.
TL715.B75   1988   629.133'35   87–600310
ISBN 0-87474-268-4 (alk. paper)

Cover: The C.24 and C.19 Mk.IV flying together at Stag Lane, the former piloted by Juan de la Cierva and the latter by Arthur Rawson. (Courtesy O. Reder)
Frontispiece: Juan de la Cierva with a C.30A Autogiro in 1935. (Courtesy O. Reder)

To Patty

Without whose support this book could not have been written

Contents

Introduction

I first became familiar with rotary wings in the late 1930s while learning to fly de Havilland Gipsy Moth biplanes at the London Air Park Flying Club at Hanworth near London. Hanworth was then the main base of Cierva's Autogiros and these were the only practical rotary-wing aircraft anywhere in the world. My plan to learn to fly them was frustrated, however, by the outbreak of war.

The first experimental helicopters were, at that time, only just beginning to be flown successfully in France, Germany, and Scotland, but practical production helicopters were soon to emerge in Germany and the United States.

During World War II, while serving in the Fleet Air Arm of the Royal Navy, I applied to join the first helicopter pilots' course in the United States. However, I was not selected, and it was not until after the war that I first flew rotary-wing aircraft and began to understand the dominant role in their development played by Juan de la Cierva. His work was crucial during the period when the helicopter was emerging and becoming practical.

In 1955 I wrote a two-part article about Cierva's Autogiros published in the British journal the *Aeroplane*. It proved to be the starting point for this book. Later, the editor of *World Helicopter and Vertical Flight*, Basil Arkell, invited me to prepare a short history of helicopter development. This article was published in his March 1959 issue and, in updated form, is reproduced as an appendix to this book.

The data for different types of aircraft given here have been compiled from the usually incomplete and often conflicting information available. In the 1920s and 1930s dimensions, weights, and performances were by no means properly measured or recorded for experimental aircraft—which is what most autogyros were. In addition, there were, of course, many changes during development so that reliable information just does not exist. Another frequent source of inaccuracy is incorrect conversion from metric to American and British systems of measurement. To reduce such errors, I have quoted aircraft data in the units the designers originally used, giving the conversion in parentheses.

In cases where there is disagreement, for a particular aircraft type, in weight or performance figures, I have given the highest and lowest. So far as empty weights are concerned, the higher figure quoted is usually the more realistic. However, like maximum take-off weight, empty weight usually increases during the life of an aircraft type from initial design through to the most developed version in service. Quoted maximum speeds are often optimistic, design estimates being higher than actuals and actuals tending to fall still further in service and with weight increases. The quoted minimum speeds of autogyros are intended to be the lowest speed at which level flight could be maintained. However, in some cases, the figure given is probably the rather lower landing speed.

Acknowledgments

The author has had valuable and sometimes substantial assistance from the following, to whom grateful acknowledgment is made:

Miss Jean P. Alexander
S/Ldr. Basil H. Arkell
Mr. John A. Bagley
Señor D. Balaguer
Mr. N.A. Barfield
Mr. C.H. Barnes
*Prof. J.A.J. Bennett
Señor Jorge Bernabé Panós
*Mr. Harold Bolas
Mr. Jean Boulet
Mr. Peter M. Bowers
W/Cdr. R.A.C. Brie
Mr. J.M. Bruce
Mr. B.S. Campion
Mr. R.W. Cantello
Mr. P.T. Capon
Col. Bernard Chenel
*Dr. Carlos de la Cierva
    Gómez-Acebo
*Air Cdr. A.E. Clouston
Mr. S.M. Coates
*Capt. Frank T. Courtney
Mr. E. Dane
Mr. R.E.G. Davies
Señor José A. Delgado Vallina
Mr. H.W. Denny
Mr. David Dorrell
Señor Filipe E. Ezquerro
Mr. Vital E. Ferry
Mr. Hiroshi Fujisawa
Mrs. Claire S. Geller

Mr. J.D. Gillies
Mr. Hugh Gordon
Mr. Carl R. Gunther
*Mr. Raoul Hafner
Mr. W.C. Hannan
Mr. R.H. Harker
*Mr. Norman J.G. Hill
Dr. George S. Hislop
Mr. H.P.Y. Hitch
Señor Antonio Hernández-Ros
    Murcia Codorníu
*Mr. A.J. Jackson
Mr. Stuart James
*Mr. Thurstan James
Mr. Philip Jarrett
*Mr. David Kay
Mr. Masaru Kayahashi
Mr. H.F. Rex King
Mr. J.A.C. Lane
Mr. Howard Levy
*C/Capt. R.N. Liptrot
General Pierre Lissarrague
Mr. Felix Lowe
Mr. Alex S.C. Lumsden
Mr. Ralph H. McClarren
Sir Peter G. Masefield
Mr. Charles C. Miller, Jr.
General José Tomás Mora Sánchez
Mr. Kenneth Munson
Mr. Eric A. Myall
Mr. A.W.L. Nayler

Mr. Zenji Nishibori
Mr. Tadashi Nozawa
Mr. Malcolm Passingham
Mr. Stephen Pitcairn
Mr. Richard H. Prewitt
*Herr Otto Reder
Mr. Elfan ap Rees
Mr. Richard T. Riding
Señor Luis Sáenz de Pazos
Mr. David Sawers
Mr. M.P. Sayer
Mrs. Jeanne M. Sexton
*Mr. J.S. Shapiro
Mr. David R. Shepherd
*Mr. Igor I. Sikorsky
Dr. R.K. Smith
Mrs. Valerie Stedman

Mr. John Stroud
Mr. Arthur Sturgess
Mr. F.G. Swanborough
Mr. Mike Tagg
Mr. Mitsuo Tajima
Mr. John W.R. Taylor
Mr. George H. Townson
W/Cdr. N.H.F. Unwin
Mr. G.E. Walker
Dr. Ing José Warleta Carrillo
Mr. G.R.L. Weir
Mr. R.H. Whitby
Mr. L.S. Wigdor
Mr. G.H.C. Willins

*Since deceased.

John Stroud, the well-known aviation writer and historian, who has been responsible for many years for the editing of the remarkable Putnam series of historical aviation books, has contributed greatly to this volume. He checked the complete text and has helped to eliminate many errors and inconsistencies.

Miss Jean Alexander provided much of the data about Russian autogyros in Chapter 10 and also very kindly checked this chapter in draft. Mr. John Bagley helped with information about Autogiro activities at the Royal Aircraft Establishment (RAE). Señor H-Ros supplied valuable material about the early days of Autogiro development in Spain, when his father was an associate of Cierva's. Mr. Bill Hannan provided much of the information from which the three-view drawings have been prepared. The late Otto Reder loaned his unique collection of Autogiro photographs and clarified a number of points about Autogiro development in England in the 1930s, when he was a member of the design team at the Cierva Autogiro Company Limited. Mr. David Shepherd provided assistance with information about the Weir Autogiros and checked that part of the book in draft. The author is particularly indebted to the late Norman Hill for checking the entire manuscript and for the encouragement of his enthusiasm for autogyros. Vital Ferry provided most of the information about C.30 and its derivatives in France.

The Brie Papers at the RAF Museum at Hendon have been an important source of information, as have a number of files held by the Public Record Office at Kew. Mr. Mike Tagg, curator of documents at the RAF Museum, and Mr. Nicholas Pointer at the Public Record Office helped to identify this material.

Information on Japanese Autogiros largely came from the Aviation Department of the Asahi Shimbun Publishing Company to whom I am most grateful and specifically to its manager Mr. Mitsuo Tajima, and to Mr. Hiroshi Fujisawa. I am also indebted to Messrs. Tadashi Nozawa, Masaru Kayahashi, and Zenji Nishibori who very kindly supplied photographs.

Mr. Eric Myall checked the whole manuscript, corrected some errors, and filled in a number of gaps. S.M. Coates provided valuable German material.

The account of Cierva's early activities in Spain and, to a lesser extent, his subsequent work in Europe, leans heavily on material from José Warleta's excellent Spanish biography. Dr. Warleta has also generously provided a great deal of other direct help.

Acknowledgment is also due to the International Publishing Corporation Limited for permission to use an extract from H.M. Schofield's *High Speed and Other Flights*, to Sir Isaac Pitman and Sons for the extract from R.A.C. Brie's *The Autogiro and How to Fly It*, to B.H. Arkell and *Helicopter World* for the use of parts of the author's article, "The Development of the Helicopter," which originally appeared in that journal, to William Collins, Sons and Company Limited for the extract from T.H. White's *England Have My Bones* and to Cierva Rotorcraft Limited for permission to publish extracts from a Cierva Autogiro Company Limited technical report. The three-view drawings are the work of Arthur Sturgess, Jack Lane, and L.E. Bradford. Other illustrations are from the author's extensive collection. Original sources, where identified, are gratefully acknowledged. Apologies are due to those that have not been traced.

Finally, I must pay tribute to the Smithsonian Institution Press and to the National Air and Space Museum (NASM). I much appreciate all the help I have had from Felix Lowe, the Press's director, and Jeanne Sexton, who edited this book and had the onerous task of translating my English into American! My term as NASM's first international fellow in 1985–86 made possible completion of the book and I am grateful for all the help given me by the museum's enthusiastic staff and particularly by Ron E. G. Davies, the curator of air transport at NASM.

Chapter 1

Development of the Autogiro

Cierva stands out as the greatest name in the history of rotary-wing flight before Igor Sikorsky evolved the first widely used type of helicopter between 1939 and 1941. The story of how this remarkable Spaniard, Señor Don Juan de la Cierva Codorníu, developed the first practical rotary-winged aircraft—his famous Autogiro—has received little attention, yet his work was an essential preamble to the emergence of the helicopter as we know it today.

Cierva's interest in rotary wings began and ended with accidents to fixed-wing aircraft. He was born on September 21, 1895, at Murcia, in Spain, eldest son of Don Juan de la Cierva Peñafiel, a wealthy lawyer and landowner who after World War I became one of his country's most powerful political figures, being minister of education, interior, war, treasury and development in successive Conservative administrations. He retired from public life on the formation of the Spanish Republic in 1931 and died in 1938. Young Juan's mother was María Codorníu Bosch. The boy was educated first at high school in Murcia and then by private tutor in Madrid where the family had moved in 1905.

Cierva became interested in aeronautics while still a boy when he heard of Wilbur Wright's flying in France in the latter part of 1908. After Louis Blériot flew the English Channel in 1909, Cierva decided he would make his career in this new science. Enthusiasm was further stimulated by the first flights in Spain made by the Frenchman Julien Mamet on a Blériot in Barcelona on February 11, 1910, and in Madrid on March 23 where they were watched by the fourteen-year-old Cierva. With the help of his younger brother, Ricardo (born in 1897), and some young friends,[1] Cierva started by building kites and model aircraft, and, in 1910/11, two gliders. However, the first glider was not notably successful and soon crashed. The second was either not completed or was also wrecked during an early test. In 1911 with "Pepe" Barcala, Cierva enrolled at the Madrid Engineering College for Highways, Canals and Ports.

The following year the two boys and Pablo Diaz completed the construction of a powered airplane. This was the BCD-1, known as "El Cangrejo" ("Crab" or "Crayfish")—a two-seat biplane broadly similar to the Sommer and incorporating the 50-hp Gnome Omega rotary engine and other components of a crashed imported Sommer biplane. Tested by the owner of the original Sommer, a Frenchman, Jean Mauvais, at Cuatro Vientos near Madrid in August 1912, the

Juan de la Cierva's first powered aircraft, the BCD-1 "El Cangrejo," was a rebuilt and modified Sommer biplane.
(Dr. C. de la Cierva)

The BCD-2 was a small racing tractor monoplane on the lines of the Nieuport.
(Dr. C. de la Cierva)

BCD-1 flew surprisingly well and was claimed to be the first Spanish-built airplane to fly. It achieved a speed of 90 km/h (56 mph) and carried a number of passengers.

In 1913 Cierva built the BCD-2, a small racing tractor monoplane on the lines of the Nieuport with a 24-hp Anzani, later replaced by a 60-hp Le Rhône. Although flown at Getafe in December 1913 by Julio Adaro Terradillos, it did not prove as successful as its predecessor and was soon damaged in a crash. Repaired and modified, the BCD-2 was flown by Mauvais at Cuatro Vientos, but was again wrecked and further development abandoned. Both these aircraft, like the gliders which preceeded them, had been built in the carpenter's workshop of Pablo Diaz's father at no. 10, calle de Velázquez, in Madrid. For some years after this work was interrupted because the boys had to concentrate on their studies.

15

After graduating from the Madrid Engineering College in 1917 as a civil engineer, Cierva followed his father's wishes and involved himself in the family's business affairs. However, he retained his interest in aeronautics and on September 5, 1918, when Colonel Don Julio Rodríguez Mourelo, director of Spanish Air Services, announced a government military aircraft competition to be held at Cuatro Vientos in March/April 1919, Cierva found the excuse he had been seeking and returned to active involvement in aviation. Typical of the somewhat inadequate prizes offered for competition was one of 60,000 pesetas for a bomber prototype less engines. This was equivalent to about $9,600 or, say, $52,000 today. Nevertheless, Cierva was soon engaged in the design of an extremely ambitious aircraft, the C-3, to be entered in the bomber section of the competition. The project was financed, to the extent of 150,000 pesetas (then worth about $25,000, equivalent to about $130,000 today), partly by a wealthy friend, Don Juan Vitórica Casuso, Conde de los Moriles, and partly by Cierva's father. Construction, in which Cierva was much helped by Pablo Diaz, was undertaken in the Vitórica carriage workshops near Madrid, but the main components were taken to Cuatro Vientos for final erection.

The C-3 was a large 25 m (82 ft ¼ in) wing span biplane with three 225-hp Hispano Suiza 8Ba engines and a loaded weight of 5,000 kg (11,000 lb). The design was businesslike but incorporated a number of original features including several that later appeared in the better-known French Caudron C.25 transport exhibited at the 1919 Paris Salon de l'Aéronautique. Other original features included a new wing section mathematically derived by Cierva himself. The C-3 was claimed to be the first airplane to fly with three tractor engines and to be second only to an Italian Caproni in the tri-motor category. It could carry more than a ton of bombs or fourteen passengers in addition to its crew of two. Construction was completed in May 1919.

The C-3 proved to be the only entry in the bomber section of the competition and promised to have excellent flying characteristics. However, before it

Cierva's third and last airplane design was the C-3, a large three-engined biplane. (Dr. C. de la Cierva)

could take part in the competition, it crashed and was destroyed, fortunately without serious injury to the pilot, Captain Julio Ríos Argüeso, on its first flight at Cuatro Vientos on July 8, 1919. This accident—apparently caused by the pilot's overconfidence and lack of experience on large multi-engine aircraft which led to loss of flying speed while making a steep turn near the ground—was a sad disappointment. It did, however, encourage Cierva to undertake an exhaustive study of ways and means of achieving mechanical flight independent of flying speed. Meanwhile, he had to return to the family business. With his father's encouragement he also interested himself in politics. At the early age of twenty-four, Cierva became, in 1919, a member of the Spanish parliament for his native Murcia and continued to hold the seat until 1923. On December 10, 1919, he married María Luisa Gómez-Acebo Varona and set up house in Madrid at no. 34, calle de Alfonso XII. Their first child, a son named Juan, was born on July 24, 1921.

Other activities did not prevent Cierva from devoting a great deal of time and thought to his aviation interests and particularly to the problem of safe low-speed flight. These researches, which began in the latter part of 1919, not long before his marriage, were to lead to the discovery of the principles of the gyroplane, or "Autogiro" as he called it.[2] He was first led to think about rotating wings by a helicopter toy which he repeatedly launched from a balcony at his parents' home in Madrid (at no. 50, calle de Alfonso XII). From a study of the toy's behavior, he arrived at the concept of an autorotating rotor that was to be the basis of all his subsequent work.

From 1919 until his death in 1936 Cierva pursued the development of this concept with remarkable energy and success. His first idea for the application of rotating wings was for a horizontally turning windmill driven solely by the relative wind, a component of which, parallel to the axis of rotation, was to be generated by beating the wings as in an ornithopter. Cierva at first thought that the beating action would be necessary to maintain rotation of the rotor in horizontal flight. An engine would propel the machine by means of a conventional tractor airscrew and would, at the same time, furnish power for the beating movement. If the engine stopped, the windmill would act like a parachute, making possible a safe vertical descent. Practical investigation of this idea quickly established that beating the wings was unnecessary: a slight backward tilt of the rotor's axis ensured sustained rotation.

This idea of an unpowered lifting rotor which, once started spinning, was free to continue to revolve in the airflow of its own accord, was the essential concept at which Cierva arrived. It was an unexpected phenomenon, although it seems to have been proposed by Hodgson in a paper to the British Institute of Automobile Engineers in 1915 and described in a 1919 patent by Pescara (See Appendix 1). Lucien Chauvière in France also claimed to have patented the concept in 1917 based on the ideas of a Russian, D. P. Riabouchinskii. Moreover, the principle appears to have been known in the Middle Ages, when the masters of windmills understood that they could get their sails to turn into the airflow rather than out of it by setting them at a "flat" angle to the wind. Another application of the same phenomenon is the sail of a tacking ship well up into the eye of the wind.

17

In 1912, a Russian, Boris N. Yuriev, noted the work of a fellow Russian, Sorokovmovskii, who had shown that the blades of a rotor on a flying machine would keep turning of their own accord during a descent and that this could be used to provide a safe landing after a gliding descent. It seems, moreover, that these Russians understood that this principle could be used to make a safe landing after engine failure in a helicopter, as had been suggested in 1906 by G. A. Crocco in Italy.

At first sight, a freely turning rotor descending through the air might be conceived of as being "back-driven," like a windmill blown round by the wind. However, Cierva pointed out that each blade of a rotor behaves like an aircraft's wing. If the blades are set at a small positive angle to the relative airflow, they will move forward on a descending spiral path, like a gliding airplane, while continuing to provide lift and at the same time maintaining their rotational speed. Expressed more precisely, the resultant of the blades' lift and drag is always forward of the vertical axis. That is to say, as the blade goes against the wind, it is always traveling downhill or slightly away from the perpendicular axis of the whole machine. This principle of so-called autorotation is found in nature in the seedlet leaf of the maple (or sycamore) tree. The Australian aborigine's boomerang works the same way.

If the autorotating rotor is towed forward in flight by a conventional aircraft engine and propeller, the aircraft on which it is mounted can be made to maintain level flight, descend, or climb. Without an airscrew's propulsion, the aircraft with a freely turning rotor will descend in a glide like an airplane, but at a steeper angle. At lower forward speeds, the velocity downward will be greater and this angle still steeper. It is a remarkable fact that a rotor, despite its low "solidity" (ratio of blade area to disc area) descends in this way more slowly than a parachute of the same diameter carrying the same load.

An aircraft with an autorotating rotor is capable of significantly lower minimum forward speeds, and therefore of shorter take-off and landing distances, than a conventional airplane. Besides this low-speed capability it has the vital characteristic that it cannot be stalled—the rotor will always keep turning and the blades lifting while the aircraft is in flight. The drawback is, of course, that of all rotary-wing aircraft: the rotor creates more drag in translational flight than a conventional fixed wing. As a result the gyroplane was significantly slower than an airplane with the same engine, even of the 1920s. This deficiency became still more marked as faster and more efficient monoplanes took over from biplanes in the 1930s.

Cierva's initial work in Spain on rotary wings starting with models and then moving on to full-size machines, resulted in a series of Spanish patents, the first of which (no. 74,322) was applied for on July 1, 1920, and granted on August 27. On March 28, 1921, Cierva applied for an addition to his first patent, relating it to the configuration of his second Autogiro (the C.2). This addition was granted on April 20 under the number 77,569.

The two most fundamental British patents (which became particularly important when Cierva moved the center of his activities to the United Kingdom) were granted in July 1920 and April 1922. The first (Patent No. 165,748 of July 1, 1920) defined "an aircraft having the usual propelling means, and one or more horizontal airscrews supported from the fuselage and mounted to rotate freely in a plane which is slightly inclined upwards to the direction of motion." In the second British patent (no. 196,594 of April 18, 1922) covering flapping blades, discussed in Chapter 2, "rotating wings are mounted on a base plate which revolves in bearings around a shaft supported by a tubular pyramidal structure. The wings are stayed by bracing wires and fixed to the base plate by hinges which permit movement of the wings in the direction approximately in a plane passing through the shaft."

After flying his first successful Autogiro in Spain during the early 1920s, Cierva moved to England in 1925 and, on March 24, 1926, the Cierva Autogiro Company Ltd. was established there to control the development of his designs. From this date until his death, Cierva worked mainly in the United Kingdom although, during the last decade before World War II, he supervised development and construction under license of his designs in Spain, France, the United States, and Germany. The Soviet Union undertook a good deal of gyroplane development, copying as far as possible, without license, the successive steps taken by Cierva in Britain. At a relatively late stage, the Japanese also entered the picture. They developed and produced in quantity, under a license from the American Kellett Company an Autogiro based on the Kellett KD-1A, which itself had been built under Cierva license.

In the early years of development, Cierva's inventive genius and his exceptional talent as a mathematician were responsible for each successive advance that turned the gyroplane into a workable and generally accepted flying machine. He also evolved a comprehensive theoretical basis for the properties of this type of aircraft, which he confirmed by practical demonstration in flight.

Later, Cierva learned to fly and became his own experimental test pilot. During the years of intensive development between 1927 and 1936 Cierva himself did much of the difficult experimental and development flying that played an essential part in the evolution of the practical gyroplane of the 1930s. This courageous work, so ably done, was cut short by Cierva's death, ironically enough as a passenger in an airline accident.[3]

A study of Cierva's career is conveniently made in a step-by-step examination of each of his designs. His work falls naturally into a number of phases: the initial experiments in Spain, the main line of development from 1925 in the United Kingdom, and development under Cierva license in America after 1929. In addition, there is the work of a number of other experimenters in the same field. This will now be briefly considered.

From 1927, the efforts of David Kay and Raoul Hafner, in Britain, in developing gyroplanes with distinctive features were historically important, although quite separate from the main Cierva line of evolution. Similarly, the work in the same field from 1928 of E. Burke Wilford and of Gerard P. Herrick in the United States should be noted. Both made significant contributions to the subject, although also quite distinct from Cierva's work.

David Kay, a young Scotsman from Blackford, Perth, approached Cierva on April 27, 1927, with a design he had patented for varying the incidence of the rotor blades of a gyroplane. Although Cierva studied Kay's proposals, which provided for collective pitch control combined with sideways tilting of the rotor hub for lateral control, he did not adopt them for the Autogiro because he believed it went against his tenet of keeping the rotor system as simple as possible. However, some years later, Cierva did adopt the fully tilting hub for his later Autogiros. His first direct-control Autogiro, the experimental C.19 Mk.V, first flew in secret only five months before Kay's first design. Cierva publicly demonstrated direct control three months after Kay had revealed his lateral tilting and collective control system. At the time of his death, Cierva was working on collective and cyclic pitch control.

In 1929 and 1933, Kay had further discussions about his ideas with the British Air Ministry, Cierva's company, and the Weir company. With the financial backing of Lt. Col. M. Ormonde Darby, he then successively undertook the construction of two small gyroplanes to his own design. (See Appendix 3.) These prototypes, the Kay 32/1 and 33/1 (G-ACVA), were first successfully flown in August 1932 and on February 18, 1935. The Kay gyroplanes had rotors with so-called Z-hinges and had collective pitch control combined with a tilting rotor hub for lateral control. Longitudinal control was by normal elevator. In November 1933, David Kay formed Kay Gyroplanes Limited to develop his ideas. His second gyroplane, G-ACVA, was extensively tested by the Royal Aircraft Establishment at Farnborough between September 1935 and February 1936. This aircraft is still in existence. (See Appendix 3)

Raoul Hafner (1905–1980), an Austrian, had been educated in Vienna at the University and Technical College. He designed his first helicopter in 1927 at the age of twenty-two and, with the financial backing of the wealthy Scottish cot-

The Kay Type 32/1 gyroplane. Although undoubtedly originally inspired by Cierva, the Kay gyroplanes were an independent development with variable-pitch rotor blades. (Author's Collection)

20

The Kay Type 33/1 gyroplane. The Kay gyroplanes had collective pitch control, a sideways-tilting head for lateral control, and conventional elevators and rudder. (British Airways)

ton manufacturer, Major J.A. Coates, built and tested two more—the R.I and R.II—at Aspern airport near Vienna in 1930/31. Hafner moved to England in 1932 and in 1940 took British nationality. The R.II was taken to England in 1933 and used as a rotor test rig. In England, Hafner met Cierva and learned to fly C.19 and C.30 Autogiros. He decided to apply the pitch control features of R.I and R.II to his own design of gyroplane. In 1934/35 at Hanworth, he designed a small single-seat gyroplane, the A.R.III Mk.I, which was built by Martin-Baker Aircraft Ltd. (See Appendix 4.) Hafner is believed to have made use of several Cierva patents with Cierva's knowledge and permission. Development of this aircraft (G-ADMV, later DG670) was also funded by Coates. The A.R.III was first flown at Heston in September 1935 by the well-known flying instructor of the Airwork School at Heston near London and co-founder of Martin-Baker Aircraft, Captain Valentine H. "Laddie" Baker.

The A.R.III incorporated the collective and cyclic pitch methods of control studied by Cierva since 1933. Cierva had indeed suggested in June 1933, while in the United States, that the British company should switch its development efforts to this type of control while the Americans continued with the tilting head. In the event, Cierva stayed with the tilting head himself. Hafner adopted collective pitch independently and without knowledge of the earlier Kay designs that incorporated collective pitch control and a sideways tilting head. These design features not only gave the pilot complete control of his aircraft—through the rotor which, as we shall see, Cierva had already achieved in a different way by means of the fully tilting head (see Chapter 4)—but also enabled the aircraft to make "towering" take-offs similar to the jump take-offs also previously demonstrated by Cierva.

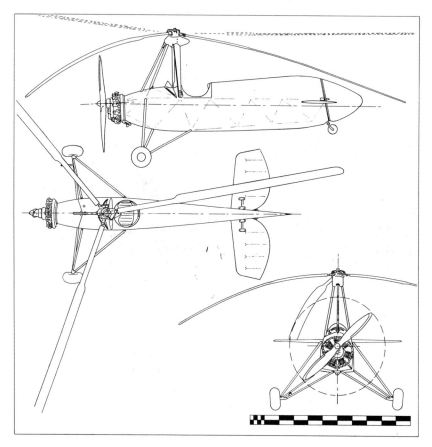

Hafner A.R.III.

"Towering" take-offs had the advantage of a positive rate of climb, sustained from lift-off. With Cierva's jump take-offs (see Chapter 9), height was usually lost momentarily at the end of the jump, before the climb-away started. The A.R.III, like the Kay gyroplanes, could go a stage further than the Autogiro in landing: collective pitch control enabled the pilot to use the kinetic energy in the rotor for a full helicopter-type autorotative landing.

The Hafner gyroplane established very clearly the advantages of combined cyclic and collective pitch control, soon to become essential features of the practical helicopter. Hafner continued to develop his designs and clearly set out his views on rotary-wing flight in a lecture to the Royal Aeronautical Society on October 14, 1937. He collaborated with the Short Brothers Ltd. subsidiary, Pobjoy Airmotors and Aircraft Ltd at Rochester from 1938, in producing a series of gyroplane and helicopter projects, of which the A.R.IV gyroplane and the P.D.6 helicopter were ordered by the air ministry in 1939. Construction of prototypes of both these designs by Pobjoy's parent company, Short Brothers Ltd., was under way at Rochester when it was stopped by the outbreak of war. In May 1940, Hafner was interned as an enemy alien, but he was released in September after applying for British nationality. (See Appendix 4)

During the war, Hafner worked on designs for rotary-winged parachutes or gliders intended for military purposes. These included the "Rotachute," and the "Rotabuggy" (see Chapter 12 and Appendix 6). Later, he again turned his attention to helicopters. In 1944 he became Chief Helicopter Designer of the Bristol Aeroplane Company Ltd. at Filton with responsibility for the Sycamore, the first British helicopter to be produced in quantity; subsequently he designed the Belvedere twin-engined twin-rotor helicopter that also saw service with the RAF. The spider system of pitch control and the tie bar blade suspension, which Hafner originally developed for his gyroplanes, became features of the Bristol helicopters. At the age of seventy-five, Raoul Hafner was lost at sea from his yacht on November 14, 1980.

E. Burke Wilford made use of ideas and patents, dating from 1926, of two Germans, Walter Rieseler and Walter Kreiser. They had built, but had not tested, a prototype in Germany in 1927. Wilford, in the United States, started the development of his gyroplane in 1929. His concept differed from Cierva's in that it employed a rigid rotor with cyclic pitch variation. This provided control and compensation for the asymmetric lift of advancing and retreating blades in translational flight. The cyclic variation of blade pitch was achieved by a system of cams. It provided control of the aircraft, at first laterally only, but later in fore-and-aft pitch as well.

Wilford's first gyroplane, the WRK (X794W), had an 85-hp American Cirrus III engine and was flown for the first time by Frank P. Brown at Paoli near Philadelphia on August 5, 1931. Initially, it weighed 1,500 lb (680 kg) and had 23 ft (7 m) span fixed wings.

Later a more powerful 165-hp Jacobs engine was substituted for the Cirrus. This aircraft was a single seater and, in developed form, had a 30 ft (9.14 m) four-blade rotor and a gross weight of 1,800 lb (816 kg). At one stage, the fixed wings were removed. It made several hundred successful flights before being destroyed in an accident, killing the pilot, J.S. McCormac.

Wilford's next gyroplane was the XOZ-1, which was built by his company, Pennsylvania Aircraft Syndicate, and first flown in 1934. It had fixed wings, a 32 ft (9.75 m) four-blade rotor and was powered by a 125-hp Kinner B5 engine, later replaced by a 155-hp Kinner R5. It employed the fuselage and tail unit of a United States Navy Consolidated (Fleet) N2Y-1 biplane trainer. Gross weight was 1,985 lb (900 kg) maximum speed 107 mph (172 km/hr) and range 150 miles (240 km) at a cruising speed of 90 mph (145 km/hr). This aircraft was later handed back to the U.S. Navy (as A8602) and was flown on floats at the Philadelphia Navy Yard during October 1936. It was also tested by the NACA before development terminated.

Gerard P. Herrick (1873–1955) pioneered the concept of what is now known as a convertiplane but which he called a Vertaplane. In 1931, with the help of Ralph H. McClarren, Herrick developed an aircraft called the HV-1 that was

The Wilford WRK with Cirrus engine. Unlike Cierva's designs, the Wilford gyroplanes had rigid rotors. Cyclic-pitch variation replaced flapping blades.
(Wilford photograph, G. Townson Collection)

Wilford XOZ-1. Wilford's second gyroplane was supplied to the U.S. Navy and tested by NACA.
(Author's Collection)

intended to fly either as a fixed-wing biplane or as a gyroplane with a fixed lower wing of 30 ft (9.14 m) span. The upper wing could be converted at will into a self-revolving low aspect ratio two-blade rigid rotor with a seesaw hinge. (Seesaw rotors are discussed in Chapter 12.)

The HV-1 (X11384) had a gross weight of 850 lb (385 kg) and was powered by a 48-hp Poyer engine. It was built, to Herrick's order, by Heath Aircraft of

The Herrick HV-1 was a fixed-wing biplane designed to convert into a gyroplane. The first attempted conversion in flight ended in a crash.
(Howard Levy)

The Herrick HV-2A. This aircraft made the first conversion from fixed-wing to gyroplane flight on July 24, 1937. Development flying continued until 1942.
(Photograph Ledger, G. Townson Collection)

Niles, Michigan. The first flight as a fixed-wing airplane was made near Philadelphia on November 6, 1931. Later, while in flight at 4,000 ft (1200 m) conversion to gyroplane flight was attempted, but the aircraft went out of control and crashed.

Herrick then got Heath Aircraft to build another aircraft, the HV-2A (X13515). Of the same basic type as its predecessor but powered by a 125-hp Kinner B5 engine, this was completed in August/September 1933. The rotor bearing now incorporated Lord Mounts instead of the ordinary ball bearing of HV-1. The rubber Lord Mounts (taking the place of bearing balls) provided some restraint to the seesaw freedom of the rotor. They also had the advantage of eliminating the need for any lubrication. The gross weight of the HV-2A was 1,700 lb (770 kg) and the fixed lower wing had a span of 28 ft (8.5 m). The upper wing/rotor had a span/diameter of 24 ft (7.3 m). Flown by George H. Townson, the HV-2A achieved the first successful conversion in flight from fixed-wing to gyroplane regimes on July 24, 1937. Testing had been delayed by lack of funds but, once started, was continued and more than one hundred conversions were subsequently made at altitudes of up to 2,500 ft (760 m). The maximum speed in fixed-wing flight was rather more that 100 mph (160 km/h), while the minimum speed as a gyroplane was less than 30 mph (48 km/h). However, development was terminated in 1942. The HV-2A is preserved in storage at Silver Hill, in Maryland, by the National Air and Space Museum, Smithsonian Institution.

The name of a Frenchman, Lucien Chauvière, the well-known propeller manufacturer, should be added to the above pioneers. In 1927/29, he built a wingless gyroplane (which he called a Giroptère). This machine had a 230-hp Renault engine and a four-blade flapping rotor 13.6 m (44 ft 7 in) in diameter. The gross weight was 1375 kg (3,030 lb). It was not successful.

Another failed design was the Odier-Bessière Clinogire (F-AJSH) of 1932/33. This had a 95-hp Renault engine and a rigid four-blade rotor 6 m (19 ft 8¼ in) in diameter mounted on a conventional looking low-wing monoplane—actually a Caudron C-193 light airplane.

In 1935, the German designer Anton Flettner, who had been working on rotary-wing designs since 1932, produced a cabin gyroplane called the Fl 184, clearly inspired by Cierva's Autogiro. This was to have been evaluated by the German navy for reconnaissance and anti-submarine duties. The Fl 184 had a three-blade 12 m (39 ft 4 7⁄16 in) rotor on a fixed spindle with cyclic and collective pitch control and a 160-hp Siemens Sh 14a engine. A single prototype (D-ADVE) was flown in November 1936. A month later it caught fire in the air and was destroyed. Flettner then produced the Fl 185, which could fly either as autogyro or as helicopter. This was briefly tested before being abandoned. Flettner next turned to conventional helicopters and later produced two successful designs with side-by-side intermeshing rotors.

Another German designer to interest himself in gyroplanes was Professor Heinrich K.J. Focke of Focke-Wulf Flugzeugbau G.m.b.H. of Bremen. Focke established a rotary-wing research laboratory in 1931 and acquired a license to build Autogiros at the end of that year. He subsequently built two types of Autogiro under license and a third type of original design before producing the first practical helicopter in 1936. (See Chapters 4, 7, 9, and Appendix 1).

Kay, Hafner, Wilford, and Herrick, with their gyroplanes, each made important contributions to rotary-wing development. However, these did not detract from Cierva's preeminent role in the invention and development of the autogyro. The Spaniard's part was dominant and his Autogiro will always be regarded as peculiarly his creation and as the most important antecedent of the helicopter.

The Flettner Fl 184. This gyroplane prototype (D-ADVE) was inspired by Cierva's work but differed in having cyclic-pitch control. Intended for the German navy, it was first flown in 1936.
(Author's Collection)

Cierva and his achievements have now passed into history but the name of his Autogiro will remain as an epitaph to the life of a talented and gallant pioneer. Only forty-one when he died, he had in less than fifteen years laid the foundations on which the practical helicopter was to be developed.

By all accounts, Cierva was a man of outstanding character and ability. He combined the talents of inventor, mathematician, practical engineer, and experimental test pilot with complete dedication to the cause of safe low-speed flight, which he made his own and which he tirelessly pursued to the day of his death. As an innovator he seems to have combined unusual resourcefulness, self-confidence, and keen powers of analysis with the patience and persistence essential for protracted development work in a difficult field. An obsessive worker, who required little sleep, he would struggle with a problem until it was solved. His energy and enthusiasm were infectious, while his modesty and charm helped him imbue many of those who worked with him with his own sense of purpose.

However, like other brilliant men, Cierva seems also to have been regarded by some as difficult to work with. His Latin temperament perhaps made him unduly hasty at times in his reaction to criticism. It was probably also partly responsible for his sometimes unreceptive attitude to important ideas like collective and cyclic pitch control. Toward the end of his life, he seems to have become so preoccupied with the development of the Autogiro, because his name had become inseparably linked with it, that he regarded this type of machine as an end

The French Bréguet-Dorand 314 made its first controlled free flight at Villacoublay near Paris on June 26, 1935. It was the first practical helicopter. (Author's Collection)

in itself. Initially, like most people, he had probably looked upon it as a step toward the ultimate development of the helicopter.

Nevertheless, there is no question that Cierva had good grounds for insisting on the greatest possible simplicity for rotor systems. Even if this made him slow to adopt such features as drag hinges and rotor blade pitch control, the basic simplicity of his designs paid off handsomely in terms of reliability and safety. Few can doubt that his genius, energy, and enthusiasm would have enabled him, had he lived, to continue to play a leading role in the development of rotary-winged aircraft after the true helicopter had become an established reality.

   As described in Appendix 1, the first helicopter to fly successfully, the French Bréguet-Dorand 314, made its first flight on June 26, 1935. This historic event took place less than eighteen months before Cierva's death on December 9, 1936. Six months before, on June 26, 1936, the even more successful Focke-Achgelis Fw 61 helicopter (D-EKRA) was flown for the first time in Germany. Within eighteen months of Cierva's death on June 7, 1938, a British helicopter, the Weir W.5, also flew successfully. This helicopter was built by G. and J. Weir Ltd., the firm which had collaborated so closely with Cierva and which had tried unsuccessfully to obtain a license from Focke-Achgelis in spring 1938. It was followed by the larger W.6 two-seat helicopter which may have been the first heli-

The German Focke-Achgelis Fw 61 helicopter made its first controlled flight a year after the Bréguet-Dorand on June 26, 1936.
(Musée de l'Air et de l'Espace)

The British Weir W.5 helicopter with the team that designed it. Left to right: *F.L. Hodgess, J.A.J. Bennett, C.G. Pullin, R.F. Bowyer, G.E. Walker, and K. Watson.*
(Weir Group, Gillies Collection)

copter in the world to carry one and then two passengers. (Ken Watson was the first passenger. Later, in February 1940, Air Vice-Marshal A.W. (Later Lord) Tedder had a flight.) The war stopped development in July 1940 and W.6 was broken up in 1941.

Although similar to the Fa 61 in overall configuration, the Weir helicopters were in fact different in several important respects. Both types had side-by-side rotors incorporating features covered by Cierva patents, but the W.5 and W.6 had two-blade rotors whereas the Fa 61 had three blades.

Of course many new problems had to be overcome in the development of both the W.5 and the W.6 helicopters. Nevertheless, a total of nearly 80 hours was flown by the former in eleven months and nearly 70 hours in nine months by the latter. The most serious problem experienced was blade breakage with the W.6. On one occasion this led to a crash, fortunately without serious consequences. To cure the problem, Weirs developed the Aerodynamically Stable Rotor (ASR), information about which James Weir passed to Pitcairns (the American Cierva Licensees) during his visit to the United States in autumn 1940. ASR principles were later applied to the design of so-called floating and full-floating hubs, which were the subject of model tests in America during 1942. Later, a type of floating hub was used in the G. and A. Aircraft XR-9 helicopter first flown in 1944.

On June 30, 1938, the United States Seventy-fifth Congress appropriated (under the Dorsey Bill H.R. 8143) $2 million (equivalent to about $15 million now) for rotary-wing and other aircraft research and development. Originally this funding had been intended for purely Autogiro development. Later the $2 million was reduced to $300,000. Toward the end of the same year, after Eugene Wilson, Senior Vice President of United Aircraft, had announced the forthcom-

The American Sikorsky V.S.300. As first tested in 1939, Sikorsky's helicopter was of the one large plus one small rotor configuration that was later to be generally adopted. The V.S.300 was initially unsuccessful in this form that was, however, finally adopted in 1941.
(Author's Collection)

The Cierva W.9. The first helicopter developed by the Weir and Cierva interests, after amalgamation in 1943, incorporated a novel anti-torque tail jet which proved unsatisfactory.
(Flight International)

ing closure of their Sikorsky Division at Stratford, Connecticut, Igor Sikorsky persuaded the board of United Aircraft to undertake a helicopter program for an expenditure of not more than $60,000 (equivalent to about $440,000 today). As a result, the Sikorsky V.S.300, which was to set the pattern for the first widely used helicopters, made its initial flights at about the same time as the W.6—the first being on September 14, 1939. Another two years were to pass, however, before the V.S.300A flew satisfactorily in definitive one-large-plus-one-small rotor form on December 8, 1941. By then, some $100,000 (currently about $750,000) had been spent on its development, excluding the cost of test flying. Development of the first Sikorsky production helicopter, the V.S.316 (XR-4), cost about a further $150,000 (or $1.125 million today).

The Cierva Autogiro Company continued its founder's work after his death. First under the technical direction of Dr. James A.J. Bennett, with H. Alan Marsh as test pilot, until its activities were interrupted by the war, and then—after amalgamation with the other Weir aviation interests in 1943—into the post-war years at Eastleigh, near Southhampton, where the Cierva Company developed the first large and small post-war British helicopters. By the time the Cierva Company suspended operations early in the war, something like £750,000 (of mainly James Weir's money—currently worth about $24.5 million) is believed to have been spent on Autogiro development in the United Kingdom. Not more than £500,000 (or $16.3 million today) of this had been recovered in sales, development contracts, and license fees.

The wartime and post-war development of helicopters by the reconstituted Cierva Company after 1943 covered three basic types (see Appendix 5). These were: the W.9 development aircraft (with single main rotor and anti-torque jet at the tail); the very large W.11 Air Horse prototypes (of three main rotor configuration); and the small W.14 Skeeter series (which was of classic Sikorsky configura-

The Cierva W.11 Air Horse. This was a very large helicopter for its time and was of three-rotor configuration. Development ended after an accident in which Alan Marsh and Jeep Cable lost their lives.
(John Stroud)

Cierva W.14 Skeeter. The last production rotary-wing aircraft developed under the Cierva name was of one large plus one small rotor configuration. Production was by Saunders-Roe Ltd.
(John Stroud)

tion with large main rotor and small anti-torque rotor at the tail). The latter was put into production by Saunders-Roe Ltd.

Six years after the war, on January 22, 1951, the Cierva organization was finally absorbed into Saunders-Roe Ltd., which in 1959 became part of Westland Aircraft Ltd., Britain's present-day helicopter group. The Cierva Autogiro Company Ltd. remained as a separate legal entity in 1951 when the first of these amalgamations took place. In 1966, the company took over Rotorcraft Ltd. and was renamed Cierva Rotorcraft Ltd. It later undertook the development of the Cierva CR Twin light twin-engine helicopter.

An assessment of Cierva's life work would not be complete without some attempt to define the scope of his contribution to the development of the practical rotary-winged aircraft as we know it today. This is also discussed in Appendix 1. His major contributions can be summarized as follows:

1. He devised, developed, and demonstrated the first truly workable rotary-wing aircraft. The example set and the practical lessons taught by the Autogiro were a major stimulus to all rotary-wing development in the 1920s and the 1930s.

2. He patiently—surprisingly quickly, considering the limited resources available to him—developed his aircraft into a practical machine quite widely employed in various roles in many parts of the world until it was superseded by the helicopter. Probably a total of something like $12 million in contemporary money (say $75 million now) was spent on Autogiro development in Europe and the United States up to the war.

3. He provided operators with a production rotary-wing aircraft about fifteen years before the true helicopter became available. Nearly 480 Autogiros were built in all up to the end of World War II. About 25 Autogiro copies seem to have been built in the Soviet Union making a total of just over 500 gyroplanes worldwide. However, despite being flown perhaps 130,000 hours in Western countries (plus an unknown number of hours in Japan during World War II), the Autogiro never fully established itself in any major practical application. To what extent this was because of its inability to offer full hovering flight would be difficult to say.

4. He rediscovered and applied the principle of autorotation of a freely turning rotor and demonstrated the high parachutal properties of the autorotating rotor with blades operating at small angles. This is made use of by all modern helicopters for engine-off descent and is an essential feature of the practical helicopter because it makes a safe landing possible after engine failure.

5. He established the advantages of articulated rotor blades and showed that the flapping blade and the use of drag hinges solved many aerodynamic and structural problems of a rotor system. These are both features of modern helicopters.

6. He invented the tilting head method of control and first tried it unsuccessfully for lateral control in the early C.4. Later he adopted it in developed form for his direct-control Autogiros and established the essential principle that effective control of a rotary-wing aircraft is best obtained through the rotor itself.

7. Although he had not reached the point of adopting cyclic or collective blade angle variation as his method of control—as used on modern helicopters—he devoted much thought to this system toward the end of his life and patented its main features.

8. His example directly stimulated development of the Kay and Hafner gyroplanes of the 1930s, which applied, respectively, the principles of collective and of combined cyclic and collective pitch control by blade angle variation to tilting head and fixed-spindle gyroplanes with flapping blades. Wilford applied cyclic pitch variation to a fixed-spindle rigid rotor. These three thus paved the way to the application of these principles to the helicopter. Herrick pioneered the convertiplane concept and the rigid two-blade rotor with seesaw hinge.

9. The direct or jump take-off development of 1933, which was the culmination of Cierva's work, was the first practical demonstration of the helicopter principle to provide vertical take-off. Although, in this case, the rotor was not engine driven during the jump, the kinetic energy previously stored in it by the engine was applied directly by a sudden automatic alteration of the blade pitch at the right moment.

10. Two of the three firms which developed the first successful helicopters, Focke-Achgelis and Weir, had previously gained rotary-wing experience building Autogiros. The Bréguet-Dorand also owed a great deal to Cierva's ideas and to the lessons he and his French licensees had learned. These three manufacturers and Sikorsky, who followed them, were all Cierva licensees and used his patents in evolving the true helicopter. Their success can thus be seen to have sprung directly from the Spaniard's pioneering work.

Cierva BCD-1 "El Cangrejo" ("Crab" or "Crayfish")

Two-seat unequal-span pusher biplane based on Sommer. One 50-hp Gnome Omega. Span 11 m (36 ft 1 $\frac{1}{16}$ in); length 11 m (36 ft 1 $\frac{1}{16}$ in); wing area 38 sq m (409 sq ft). Empty weight 300 kg (660 lb); maximum take-off weight about 400 kg (880 lb). Maximum speed 90 km/h (56 mph). First flight August 1912.

Cierva BCD-2

Two-seat mid-wing tractor monoplane based on Nieuport. One 60-hp Le Rhône (initially 24-hp Anzani). Span 9.8 m (32 ft 1 $\frac{13}{16}$ in); length probably 7.2 m (23 ft 7½ in); wing area 18.5 sq m (199 sq ft.) Empty weight about 310 kg (685 lb); maximum take-off weight about 360 kg (795 lb). Maximum speed about 106 km/h (66 mph). First flight December 1913.

Cierva C-3

Equal-span tractor biplane of original design. Three 225-hp Hispano-Suiza 8Ba. Span 25 m (82 ft ¼ in); length 18 m (59 ft ⅝ in); wing area 140 sq m (1,507 sq ft). Empty weight 3,000 kg (6,600 lb); maximum take-off weight 5,000 kg (11,000 lb). Maximum speed 160 km/h (100 mph). First flight July 8, 1919.

Chapter 2

The First Autogiros

This book covers the step-by-step evolution of the Cierva Autogiro in its successive design stages in Spain, the United Kingdom, France, the United States, Germany, the Soviet Union, and Japan. A final chapter summarizes autogyro development during and since World War II. Appendix 1 relates the autogyro story to rotary-wing development as a whole.

Cierva C.1 (60-hp Le Rhône). This aircraft, known at the time as Autogiro No. 1, was the first to incorporate Cierva's idea of freely revolving wings. It was probably built at Getafe airfield, Madrid, in the workshop of Amalio Diaz Fernandez, older brother of Cierva's old associate in building airplanes, Pablo Diaz.[4] Construction started early in 1920, possibly making use of the fuselage, landing gear, and vertical tail surfaces of a 1911 French Deperdussin monoplane. Two counter-rotating rigidly-braced four-blade rotors, 6 m (19 ft 8¼ in) in diameter of 30 cm (11.81 in) chord and Eiffel 101 symmetrical section, were superimposed on the same axis above the fuselage. A vertical control surface, mounted above the rotors, was to provide lateral control, while the normal elevators and rudder were retained for control about the other axes.

The machine weighed about 350 kg (772 lb) and was tested at Getafe in October 1920 by Cierva's brother-in-law Captain Filipe Gómez-Acebo Torre. It was not a success and did not fly because the two rotors were found to turn at different speeds. Due to the interaction between them, the lower rotor turned at only 50 rpm, less than half that of the correctly calculated speed of the upper one (110 rpm), and the unbalanced lift and gyroscopic effect thus generated rolled the machine onto its side. The C.1 did, however, confirm the autorotational properties of a freely turning rotor which were the basis of Cierva's ideas. He rejected the complication of a differential linking the two rotors so that they would turn at the same speed, but was sufficiently encouraged to try a new configuration.

Cierva C.2 (110-hp Le Rhône 9Ja). As a result of experience with C.1 and tests with a rubber-driven scale model, the second machine designed—a larger two-seater—had a single five-blade rotor 11.5 m (37 ft 8¾ in) in diameter of high solidity with rigidly braced blades. Each blade was heavily braced above and below by streamlined high-tensile steel wire. They were of Eiffel 101 symmetrical section like those of C.1 but with two duralumin spars, wooden ribs, and fabric cover-

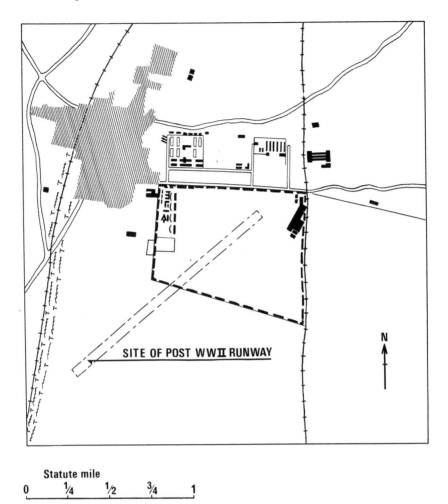

SITE OF POST WWII RUNWAY

N

The Madrid airfield of Getafe where Cierva's early Autogiros were built and tested.

Statute mile

0   ¼   ½   ¾   1

ing. Lateral stability and control about all three axes were by very large combined aileron and elevator surfaces, mounted at the rear of the fuselage, and by a normal rudder. It has been incorrectly suggested that there was also a control surface on each rotor blade. The C.2 or Autogiro No. 2—sometimes wrongly identified as C.3—seems to have incorporated either a specially built fuselage (designed to cope with the large torsional forces resulting from the differential tail control surfaces) or possibly one adapted from a biplane built by the Spanish Military Aircraft Works. Construction of C.2 was undertaken in a carpentry workshop set up by Cierva and his brother Ricardo with Pablo Diaz in calle de Luchana, in Madrid.

The Cierva C.1 was the first Autogiro design to be built.
(Ministerio del Aire photograph, courtesy H-Ros.)

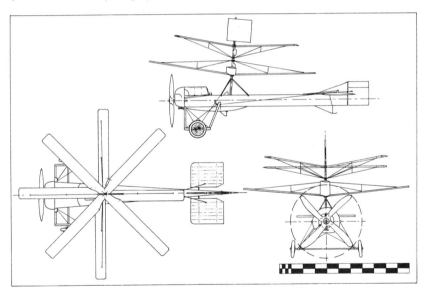

Cierva C.1.

Under an agreement signed on November 18, 1920, this workshop was formalized as a company for the manufacture of aircraft and other engineering products. Metal fittings were manufactured in the workshops of the Industrial College.

Work started on C.2 in March 1921 but was seriously delayed by a shortage of funds and by delays in delivery from France of the duralumin spars for the rotor blades. Because of this, Cierva in his impatience turned to the design and construction of his third type, C.3 (see below) completed and tested before C.2. C.2 was itself eventually completed and ready for test at the beginning of 1922. During trials conducted at Getafe by Lieutenant Gomez Spencer over the next few months, it more nearly achieved lateral balance than C.1 and C.3 but still had a tendency to sway uncontrollably and to roll over onto its side, a situation which the control surfaces were insufficiently effective to counteract completely. However, several hops to a height of about 2 m (6 ft) were made. The machine was damaged and rebuilt three times in the course of tests. The trials were abandoned in April 1922.

Cierva C.3. (50-hp Gnome Omega later replaced by 80-hp Le Rhône 9C.) Construction of C.3, known as Autogiro No. 3 but sometimes incorrectly identified as C.2, started in the spring of 1921, when it became clear that there was going to be a delay in the completion of C.2. C.3 was completed well before C.2 and was thus the second Autogiro to be tested—a fact which has often led to confusion between the two types. C.3 was ready for trial at Getafe airfield in June 1921. It employed a single rigid rotor of high solidity with three thick symmetrical-section broad-chord cantilever blades, rather like the wings of a Fokker airplane, mounted on what was possibly the modified fuselage of an old 1911–12 French Type E Sommer monoplane, probably originally imported into Spain by Jean Mauvais in 1913. It retained its normal engine and landing gear but was fitted with new elevators and rudder. The aim was to provide lateral control—and to compensate for the unbalanced lift from the advancing and retreating blades—by means of a patented system of manual incidence control. Cierva's theory, applied in C.2, called for a "compensated rotor" which, by a choice of appropriate sections and incidences along the blades, would balance the lifts of the advancing and retreating blades. In the case of C.3, by collective pitch variation, he believed he could

The C.2 was the third Autogiro completed. This was in early 1922. C.2 had a rigidly braced five-blade rotor and differential tail control surfaces.
(British Airways)

The C.3 at Getafe.
(Courtesy H-Ros.)

achieve lateral control. This would be done by varying the blade incidences by equal amounts each side of their balanced-lift settings. Cierva applied for a patent to cover this concept on May 30, 1921.

The incidence of the broad-chord fabric-covered wooden blades was altered collectively by warping. This was achieved by struts to the trailing edge of each blade from a flange and bearing mounted above the rotor head on a coaxial shaft that passed through the hub from the pilot's control below. However, the system proved impractical because the incidence variation could not allow for the effect of changes in aircraft speed.

First trials, conducted by Lieutenant José Rodríguez y Diaz de Lecea, were encouraging because the rotor attained its calculated rotational speed and lift during taxying. However, the control system was inadequate so that the aircraft rolled onto its side before, or soon after, leaving the ground. Although the machine was extensively tested, successively damaged and repaired on several occasions, and tried in nine different forms—some with a more powerful 80-hp Le Rhône 9C engine—it did not achieve more than brief hops a few inches off the ground. Cierva concluded that the ineffective control was due to torsional instability of the cantilever blades as a result of shifts in the center of pressure. The first successful rigid rotor on a gyroplane was to be developed in America about ten years later by E. Burke Wilford. Also, at about that time in 1931, Ralph H. Upson in the United States proposed cyclic pitch control by flaps on the trailing edges of the blades.

Cierva C.4 (80-hp Le Rhône 9C). While the tests with C.2 were proceeding during the first part of 1922, Cierva started to receive financial assistance from the

The C.4 in its early forms had a sideways-tilting rotor hub for lateral control. Control loads proved to be too great to be practical.
(Courtesy H-Ros.)

Spanish government. Some of the funds were spent on wind-tunnel tests on Autogiro models performed at the Aeronautical Laboratory at Cuatro Vientos, by its head, Lieut. Col. Emilio Herrera Linares.[5] Sometime earlier, in December 1920, while on holiday on the family's estate in Murcia, Cierva had undertaken a series of tests with a small model Autogiro of C.2 configuration powered by twisted rubber. Helped by his brother Ricardo and his cousin Antonio Hernández Ros Murcia Codorníu, who built the model, Cierva repeated the tests many times and established that the model, with its rotor with five flexible blades made of thin pliable palm wood (rattan), was perfectly stable. The full-size machines were not.

After he returned to Madrid, the model was successfully demonstrated in March 1921. The idea of articulating the blades of a full-size rotor to overcome the unbalance between the advancing and retreating blades, and thus achieving the same effect as the flexible blades of the model, first came to Cierva at the beginning of January 1922 while he was attending a performance of the opera at the Theater Royal in Madrid. A windmill on the stage had hinged blades. Cierva was later to claim that his other great Autogiro concept, that of direct control by tilting the rotor hub, also came to him at the opera but this was almost exactly ten years later in London.

The freely flapping blades concept had been first suggested by Charles Renard in 1904 and patented by Louis Bréguet on October 28, 1908 (French Patent No. 395,576). Bréguet subsequently incorporated the idea in his 1908 helicopter. However, the primary intention then had been to reduce the stresses in the blades and the rotor's gyroscopic effects rather than to overcome the rolling tendency resulting from the unbalanced lift of advancing and retreating blades in translational flight. The rediscovery of this principle and its application by Cierva

Close-up of C-4 tilting rotor hub.
(Author's Collection)

was the decisive factor which made possible the successful Autogiro. On April 18, 1922, Cierva applied for a Spanish patent to cover the concept—no. 81,406 was granted on November 15, 1922.

Construction of a new design incorporating this feature was started in March 1922 while tests with C.2 continued. The latter confirmed that, although short hops to a height of about 2 m (6 ft) were possible, the configuration was incapable of controlled flight. Apart from the rolling tendency, the gyroscopic action of the rigid rotor seriously interfered with control. Nevertheless, the limited success of the C.2 convinced Cierva of the practicability of the Autogiro.

41

The new design, later identified as C.4, but known at the time as Autogiro No. 4, had a single four-blade rotor, 8 m (26 ft 3 in) in diameter. The rotor blades were of Eiffel 101 symmetrical section 70 cm (28 in) wide and were articulated at their roots and braced downwards with cables and upwards by rubber shock absorbers allowing them a vertical flapping motion. These restraints prevented the blades rising too high or dropping too low while at rest or when rotating at less than flying speed. The flapping hinges were below the plane of the blades with bent blade roots so that the blades flew flat rather than coned. Blade construction was of tubular steel spars, wooden ribs, and fabric covering. Normal speed of rotation was about 140 rpm. As in the C.3, the fuselage probably came from a Sommer monoplane; indeed, the fuselage, the Le Rhône 9C engine—even the tail surfaces and landing gear (in modified form)—may have been the very ones used in the C.3. The C.4 had only an elevator and no fixed stabilizer. Lateral control was to be provided by a sideways-tilting rotor hub.

The C.4 was completed in April/May 1922. José María Espinosa Arias tested it at Getafe from June onward, for many months.[6] It crashed several times and was tried in fifteen different forms, plus three or four lesser modifications. Changes included shortening the fuselage, increasing the track of the landing gear, and substituting a larger 9.75 m (31 ft 11 $2\frac{7}{32}$ in) diameter rotor with blades of Eiffel 106 section. The last change was made after a hinge had failed on one of the blades of the original rotor, fortunately without catastrophic results.

The freely flapping blades were found to have overcome the problem of the unbalanced lift of the advancing and retreating blades. The rising advancing blade automatically reduced its incidence to the relative airflow, and hence its lift, while the retreating blade did the opposite. Because the centrifugal forces acting on the blades were about ten times the lift that they generated, the blades took up a mean coning angle of about one in ten with the plane of rotation. Articulation of the blades had also completely removed any gyroscopic effect from the rotor.

These tests established, however, that the pilot's lateral control by tilting the rotor head, as then designed, was too heavy to be practical. The pilot was unable to restrain violent oscillations of the control column transmitted from the rotor. Therefore, as the fifth modification of the C.4, the rotor hub was fixed. At a later stage still, despite Cierva's reluctance to use airplane-type controls, ailerons on outriggers were added to provide control in roll. Actually, the C.4 was found to fly quite well in calm conditions without any lateral control at all, although the rotor head had to be permanently offset somewhat to prevent the aircraft from rolling over on the ground. Ailerons were needed in certain circumstances and these lateral control surfaces were to remain a feature of all Cierva's designs until 1932. Later they were incorporated into fixed wings. In its final configuration, the C.4 had a fixed, slightly offset rotor head and ailerons. It had its first tests in this form on January 10, 1923, when, encouragingly, it rolled over on the ground the opposite way to all previous accidents. It took a week to repair the damage.

There is some controversy about the first flight date of the C.4 but the most reliable evidence is that on January 17, 1923, in its latest form the C.4 made the first controlled gyroplane flight in history, a flight which has been described as the

The C.4 in its later form with fixed rotor hub, larger 10-meter diameter rotor, and ailerons on outriggers. This was the form in which the first flights were achieved on January 17, 1923.
(Author's Collection)

most significant since the first flight of the Wright brothers. Piloted by Cavalry Lieutenant Alejandro Gómez Spencer, a flying instructor at the Spanish Flying Corps flying school at Getafe and "a Spanish gentleman whose surname and appearance both indicate an English ancestry," it made a steady straight flight of 183 m (600 ft) at a height of about 4 m (13 ft) across Getafe airfield. A further series of similar flights after engine trouble on January 20 were repeated before official military and Aero Club observers on January 22. The latter included General Francisco Echague Santoyo, director of Air Services, and Don Ricardo Ruiz Ferry, president of the Spanish Royal Aero Club Commission. The C.4 was then transported to Cuatro Vientos military airfield and on January 31 was flown again by Spencer on an officially observed circular flight of 4 km (2½ mi) in 3½ minutes at a height of more than 25 m (80 ft). The speed range of this aircraft in level flight was estimated at between 65 and 95 km/hr (40 and 60 mph) and the rate of descent, at low forward speed without power, at 2 to 3 m/s (6 to 10 ft/sec), although it was, in fact, almost certainly considerably higher than this.

The excellent low-speed characteristics of the Autogiro were effectively demonstrated on January 20 when the C.4 accidentally got into a steep nose-up altitude (nearly 45 degrees to the horizontal) after engine failure at a height of about 8–10 m (25–35 ft). The Autogiro's reaction to this situation was to descend vertically quite slowly, and to land undamaged without running more than 1 m (3 ft).

Juan de la Cierva with Alejandro Gomez Spencer who made the first successful flight in an Autogiro.
(Musée de l'Air et de l'Espace)

Cierva C.5. (110-hp Le Rhône 9Ja). Construction of C.5, probably the first Autogiro to bear the "C" designation at the time, was put in hand at Cierva's expense in the workshops of the Industrial College early in 1923 as soon as the success of C.4 had been established. C.5 was larger than C.4 and probably used the same Le Rhône engine and two-seat fuselage as C.2, although if so, the latter was considerably modified. C.5 had a three-blade articulated but cable-braced rotor about 11.5 m (37 ft. 8¾ in) in diameter and ailerons on outriggers for lateral control. It was completed in April and was flown successfully at Cuatro Vientos by Gomez Spencer in the spring of 1923, but proved to be over-sensitive on the controls and particularly on the elevator. It was destroyed in July in an accident on the ground after it had made only a few flights. A blade failed in fatigue from excessive twisting attributed to movement of the center of pressure on the highly cambered blades, which were of Gö 430 section. After this experiment, although he already considered three to be the ideal number of blades for a rotor, and although two-blade and three-blade rotors were tested on the C.8R Autogiro in 1927, Cierva employed four blades on all his successful designs until he introduced his first completely cantilever three-blade rotor in 1931.

Cierva C.6 (110-hp Le Rhône 9Ja). Cierva had built his first five Autogiros with private money—mainly, or even entirely, provided by his father, who had also been supporting his son with an allowance. Juan was now married with two children (his second child, Jaime, was born on May 10, 1923, and five more were to be born during the following ten years). He clearly had to consider carefully the

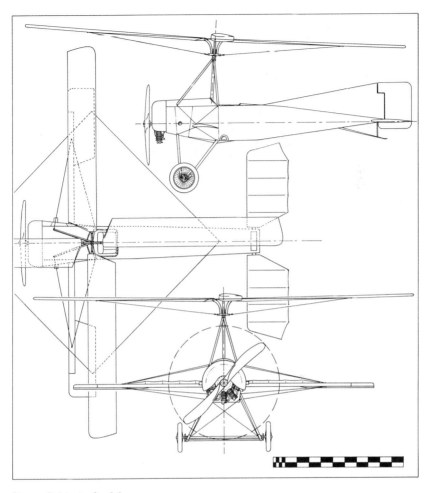

Cierva C.4 in its final form.

continued spending of his family's resources on his experiments. In this connection, it is interesting to note that Cierva wrote to the British aircraft manufacturers, Westland, in September/October 1923 to enquire whether they would be interested in the Autogiro. The reply was negative at this time, but Westlands were to build Autogiros in the 1930s and, after World War II, they became the United Kingdom's main helicopter manufacturers.

The rotors of C.2, 3, 4 and 5 had all turned in a clockwise direction (seen from above). As a result, each of these Autogiros tended to roll to the right because of the greater lift generated on the left side by the higher relative speed of the advancing blades. The French engines used in the earliest Autogiros all turned anti-clockwise (seen from the front). Reaction to a propeller turning in this direction tends to roll an aircraft to the left. With these Autogiros therefore, this effect reduced the tilting tendency due to the rotor.

*The C.5 Autogiro had a three-blade rotor which suffered fatigue failure.
(Ministerio del Aire photograph, courtesy H-Ros.)*

C.6 was the first Autogiro with anti-clockwise rotor and propeller. This must have increased the tilting tendency due to the rotor. However, the effect was small. Later successful Autogiros—starting with the C.8L series—had rotors that turned sometimes in one direction and sometimes in the other, irrespective of that of their engines. The flapping hinges on C.4 and on all later Autogiros were the important antidote to the rolling tendency. Direct-control Autogiros also had "differential" tailplanes, that is with inverted camber on one side.

Government funded tests at the Aeronautical Laboratory at Cuatro Vientos, made with a one-tenth scale model with freely flapping blades, had demonstrated the promise of Cierva's latest concept. General Echague accordingly agreed that the government should meet the cost of a new full-scale machine that was to be named C.6.

The wind-tunnel tests, because of scale effects, did, in fact, exaggerate the Autogiro's potential. They rather misleadingly suggested that, theoretically, an Autogiro could have a speed range three times that of an equivalent airplane, as well as a higher maximum speed, this being as much as 8.5 times the minimum. Nevertheless, the decision to proceed with development was a sound one.

A single-seater, C.6, was built at the Spanish Military Aircraft Works also at Cuatro Vientos under the supervision of Captain Luis Sousa Peco. It incorporated the wooden wire-braced fuselage, tail unit, engine, and slightly modified wider-track landing gear of the well-known British Avro 504K trainer. C.6 was fitted with a four-blade 11 m (36 ft 1 1/16 in) articulated but cable-braced rotor and had Bristol Fighter ailerons attached at the rear of small fixed surfaces on outriggers. The rotor, requiring a minimum of 70/80 rpm for take-off, turned at 130/140 rpm in normal flight. The blades of Gö 429 symmetrical section gave an almost stationary center of pressure and, hence, a minimum of torsional forces in the blades. Each blade had a chord of about 75 cm (30 in) and weighted 40 kg (88 lb). The blades had wooden ribs mounted on a single tubular metal spar (curved in

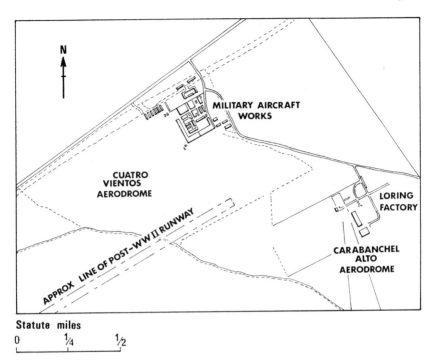

N

MILITARY AIRCRAFT
WORKS

CUATRO
VIENTOS
AERODROME

LORING
FACTORY

APPROX LINE OF POST-WW II RUNWAY

CARABANCHEL
ALTO
AERODROME

Statute miles

0   ¼   ½

Cuatro Vientos and Carabanchel Alto airfields near Madrid.

elevation) and were fabric covered. The spar was strengthened in tension by an internal steel cable attached at each end. Lead weights were fixed as necessary at the outer ends of the blades for balancing purposes.

The C.6 started flying at Cuatro Vientos with the Experimental Squadron of the Aeronautical Laboratories in the first half of February 1924 with Captain José Luis Ureta Zabala as pilot. It was soon clear that C.6 was a marked improvement on its predecessors. Test flying for the military authorities by Ureta continued for two or three months. Fourteen years later, during the Spanish Civil War, Ureta was to command a Heinkel He 111 bomber squadron of the Nationalist Air Force.

In mid-April 1924, the British aircraft manufacturers, Vickers Ltd. arranged through their Spanish agent, Ignacio Fuster, to send a representative, Captain Oliver Vickers, to see a demonstration of the C.6. In May, Captain P.D. Acland, managing director of the Vickers Aviation Department, wrote to Cierva offering to test a model of the Autogiro in the Weybridge wind tunnel if Cierva would supply the necessary data.

Cierva visited France and England at the end of October 1924 but this was probably primarily on his father's business, and it is not clear that he had any useful discussions about the Autogiro.

Meanwhile, there had apparently been a hiatus in Autogiro activity following Ureta's demonstration to Vickers. The Spanish Air Services were much preoccupied during 1924 with the Rif war in North Africa. Ureta was posted away from Cuatro Vientos and no suitable pilot was available to fly the Autogiro. However, a new pilot, who became enthusiastic about the Autogiro, Captain Joaquín Loriga Taboada, was posted to Cuatro Vientos in August as commanding officer of the rating squadron and, after briefing by Cierva, he started flying the C.6 on December 9. He made another flight on the eleventh when he made a complete circuit and climbed to 175–200 m (575–660 ft) followed by an almost vertical descent and landing. On his third flight on December 12, Loriga made the first cross-country flight in an Autogiro, from Cuatro Vientos to Getafe, covering 12 km (7½ miles) in 8 minutes 12 seconds at an average speed of 77 km/h (48 mph) (see map). Cierva followed the flight in a Fokker C.IV piloted by Julio de Rentería.

The IXth Paris Aeronautical Salon took place from December 5 to 21, 1924. Loriga went to Paris with a film of the C.6 in flight and during the Salon showed it to a meeting of the Société Française de la Navigation Aérienne (SFNA) where the Autogiro aroused great interest. Georges Lepère, a distinguished French aeronautical engineer, who was destined to play a major role in the Autogiro story (see Chapter 3), showed particular enthusiasm and argued strongly in its favor.

On January 16, 1925, the C.6 was demonstrated again to Vickers, this time to a technical team led by Rex Pierson, chief designer of the Aviation Department at Weybridge. During these demonstrations, after take-off from Cuatro Vientos and while climbing steeply over buildings at the edge of the airfield, Loriga suffered sudden complete engine failure. Although he was at only 45–60 m (150–200 ft), he was able to turn back to the airfield and land safely downwind, running less than 19 m (60 ft). A rotor blade was damaged in the landing, but such a maneuver would have almost certainly been fatal in an airplane. It provided convincing evidence of the safe flying characteristics of the Autogiro. Despite this, however, Vickers did not take up the Autogiro. This may have been because of differences between the results of the wind-tunnel tests in Spain and others undertaken at Weybridge in January/February, following the Spanish visit. Vickers were not to reconsider the possibility of an Autogiro manufacturing license until 1935.

Just before the Vickers team arrived in Madrid, the Commercial Attaché at the British Embassy wrote to Cierva's father asking for details of the Autogiro's performances in the previous month. These had received considerable publicity, and this was the first sign of official British interest in the Autogiro.

The C.6 had accumulated a total of more an than hour of flying in numerous short flights by February 1925. Only short flights were possible at this time because of the need for frequent greasing by hand of the various bearings in the rotor head. In March 1925 the C.6 was damaged in an accident at Cuatro Vientos while being flown by Loriga.

As a result of Loriga's visit to Paris, Cierva himself went there, gave a talk,

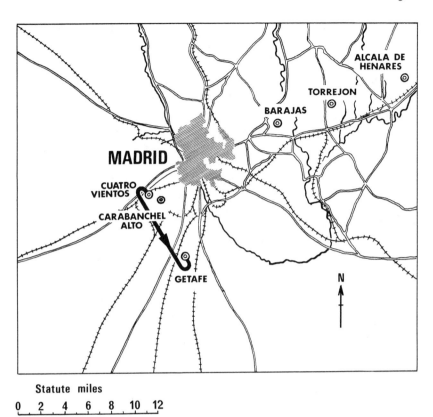

Statute miles

0   2   4   6   8   10   12

The first of the C.6's made the first cross-country flight by a rotating-wing aircraft near Madrid in 1924. The pilot was Captain Joaquín Loriga Taboada.

and showed films of the Autogiro to the SFNA on April 4, 1925. From Paris he went on to London and, while in England, had a meeting with the Vickers people at Weybridge. The results were disappointing. However, H.E. Wimperis, director of research at the British Air Ministry, was more encouraging and the Royal Aeronautical Society suggested that Cierva give a lecture on the Autogiro.

On his way back from London, Cierva stopped off in Paris and had talks with the French Under Secretary of State for Aeronautics, Victor Laurent-Eynac, and Director of the Service Technique de l'Aéronautique (STAé), General Fortant. The French agreed to an Autogiro demonstration at Villacoublay or Étampes.

On his return to Madrid late in April 1925, Cierva accordingly sought permission from General Jorge Soriano Escudero, who had succeeded General Echague as director of Air Services, for use of a C.6 for demonstrations in France and England, these to be given in May and June respectively with Loriga as pilot.

The C.6, repaired after the accident in March, was exhibited at the IVth Automobile and Aero Show at Montjuich near Barcelona from May 20 to 31, 1925. It was probably not flown again after the accident.

Cierva C.6bis (C.6A) (110-hp Le Rhône 9Ja). A second somewhat modified example of the C.6, originally called C.6bis, but later referred to as C.6A, was completed at the Military Aircraft Works under the supervision of Captain Rafael Llorente Sola in late May or early June. It was first flown on June 6 or 8 by Loriga, who claimed a maximum speed of 108 km/h (67 mph) and a rate of climb of 1.14 m/s (225 ft/min). At this time, incidentally, Cierva was claiming that the Autogiro had the same performance as an equivalent airplane. This was to be disproved late in the year following the tests in England. The Autogiro was then found to be both slower and with a lower rate of climb than a comparable airplane.

The C.6bis differed from the original C.6 in having a slightly larger rotor (which turned at 140–160 rpm and ran much more smoothly), pegs on the undersides of the blades (onto which a starter rope to spin-up the rotor could be wound), a slightly wider landing gear track, a rotor pylon of greater height, a smaller stabilizer but a balanced elevator that was larger than the standard Avro 504 control surface and had a greater range of movement. The new rotor had 29 instead of 24 ribs per blade and had its leading edge covered with wood and the rest with fabric. Each blade was 5.15 m (16 ft 10¾ in) long giving a rotor diameter

The second C.6, the C.6bis, at Cuatro Vientos having its rotor spun-up by car tow. The alternative early method was to use a team of men or a horse. (Photograph Kadel & Herbert; courtesy Peter Bowers)

*The C.6bis—now known as the C.6A—in flight at Farnborough in October 1925.
Note the changed tailplane and elevator compared with the standard Avro 504 unit on
the first C.6 (above).*
(W/Cdr N.F.W. Unwin)

of 10.5 m (34 ft 5¾ in). Loriga very effectively demonstrated the new machine before King Alfonso XIII of Spain, numerous officials, and foreign attachés at Cuatro Vientos on June 24, 1925. King Alfonso took a keen interest in aviation development and became a strong supporter of the Autogiro. Cierva was appointed a Caballero of the Civil Order of Alfonso XII at this time in recognition of his services to Spanish aviation. On July 15 the Spanish government approved a grant of Pta. 200,000 ($34,000, equivalent to about $175,00 today) for further Autogiro development.

When the original C.6 was sent to the exhibition in Barcelona, Cierva planned to complete the C.6bis for the demonstrations in France and England. These had originally been scheduled for May and June but, in the event, the C.6bis did not fly until early June. It was then used for the demonstration before the king. Meanwhile, there were other developments. An American, Harold F. Pitcairn (1897–1960), who was destined to play a major role in the history of the Autogiro (see Chapters 3 and 5), wrote to Cierva on April 25, 1925, while on a visit to England. He enclosed a letter of introduction from Heraclio Alfaro (see Chapter 5) and asked for a meeting. Pitcairn and his engineering associate Agnew E. Larsen visited Madrid briefly in May, had a discussion with Cierva through an interpreter, and saw films of the Autogiro in flight. The C.6 was not available for inspection—it was dismantled and under repair—but they were probably shown the C.6bis, then still under construction.

The delay to the completion of the C.6bis led to the French informing Cierva's representative in France (Raoul Ricci) early in June that a demonstration of a C.6 in France would not be worthwhile. The STAé suggested instead that Cierva demonstrate a more advanced dual control two-seat Autogiro with a 180-hp-Hispano-Suiza engine that would be suitable for manufacture in France. Cierva had apparently mentioned this project during his earlier discussions. Presumably this was the design which eventually emerged as the Loring C.VII but which was not to fly until November 1926.

With the French demonstration indefinitely postponed, Cierva visited England in late July/early August and again in September to make arrangements for the Autogiro's presentation in October. When the aircraft was ready it was shipped by sea from Bilbao to London.

In his lecture given to the Royal Aeronautical Society in London on October 22, 1925, Cierva stated that there was a third (probably somewhat further modified) example of the C.6 which like its predecessors was built by the Spanish Military Aircraft Works at Cuatro Vientos. However, apart from Cierva's lecture, the balance of evidence suggests that it was the C.6bis, renamed C.6A, and not a third aircraft that was demonstrated in England and that no third C.6 was built in Spain. The absence of a C.6B remains unexplained, the next C.6's being designated C.6C and C.6D.

By the time of the demonstrations in England, Cierva had tried out no less than thirty-two distinct configurations of the Autogiro as approximately tabulated below. Up to October of that year, 400/500,00 Pta or about £12,000 (equivalent to more than a quarter of a million dollars now) had been spent on Autogiro development.

Type	Number of Configurations
C.1	1
C.2	4
C.3	9
C.4	15 + 4 lesser modifications
C.5	1
C.6	2
	32 + 4

Regardless of whether there was a third Spanish C.6, there seems to have been little difference between the first C.6 and the machine demonstrated in England. The rotor blades fitted to the aircraft which arrived in England were reported to be 5.5 m (18 ft) long, which suggests that the C.6A had a somewhat larger rotor than the C.6. On the other hand, the rotor diameter was measured at Farnborough at 10.8 m (35 ft 6 in), which is smaller than the earlier version.

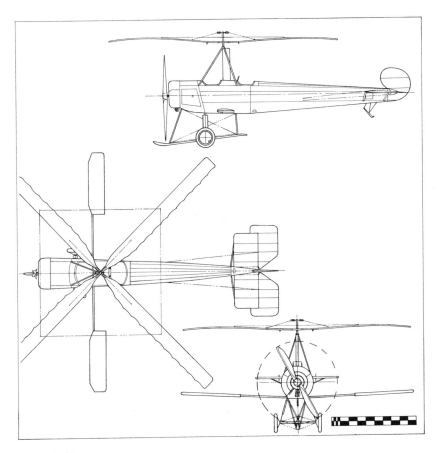

Cierva C.6A.

The Avro 504 landing gear fitted to the first C.6 was inadequate for Autogiro landings. Accordingly a gear with improved shock absorbers was fitted to the second C.6.

The visit to Britain, at the invitation of H.E. Wimperis, the Air Ministry's director of Scientific Research, began on October 1. Cierva himself arrived on the fourth. The Autogiro was taken to the Royal Aircraft Establishment (RAE) at Farnborough where it was assembled. Captain Loriga, who had expected to undertake the demonstrations in England developed pleurisy and, much against his will, had to be replaced, at short notice, by the well-known British test pilot Captain Frank T. Courtney. (Loriga was to lose his life in a fixed-wing aircraft accident at Cuatro Vientos on July 18, 1927.)

In his book *Flight Path* Courtney recalls how he got the job. He had delivered an airplane from England to Madrid in the summer of 1925 and, while there, had been shown the "crazy looking" C.6 in a hanger at Cuatro Vientos, reportedly "built by a nut called Cierva." Back in England a few weeks later, he received

The C.6A *at Farnborough after a new oleo landing gear had been fitted.*
(O. Reder)

a telephone call from Cierva, who had meanwhile arrived in London. When he called on him at his hotel, Courtney found that the Spaniard had been given his name by Wimperis at the Air Ministry as a suitable pilot for the tests to which the Autogiro was to be subjected by the British authorities. Courtney had the advantage from Cierva's point of view that he spoke some French. Cierva had no English at this time but spoke French fluently.

Courtney first tried the Autogiro on October 10, when he spent about thirty minutes taxying the aircraft and making a number of short straight hops. Two days later, he made his first proper flight (of ten minutes) in rather bumpy conditions after about another thirty minutes of taxying. From this time until February, 1927, Courtney continued to act as Cierva's test pilot of the various Autogiro designs, accumulating a total of about ten hours flying spread over about forty flights.

On October 2, a week before the first tests of the C.6A in England, an officially sponsored British helicopter, the Brennan, crashed. The Air Ministry had reportedly by then spent about £55,000 (about $930,000 today) since 1919 on the development of this helicopter, which had been undertaken by Louis Brennan, CB, at the Royal Aircraft Establishment, Farnborough. Although it made about 200 flights of an average duration of about three minutes in 1924–25 for a total of about ten hours flying, these were all hovering flights near the ground. The Brennan helicopter proved to be unstable in translational flight. Its longest flight covered 600 ft (183 m) and the greatest height reached had been about 8 feet (2.4 m).

Development of this helicopter at RAE between 1919 and 1925 was evidence of the British Air Ministry's long-standing interest in the possibilities of rotary-wing flight. It had shown this interest also by the offer, in March 1922, of £50,000 worth of prizes (about $1 million now) for a successful helicopter. The requirements for the prizes were that the helicopter should carry a pilot, fuel for one hour, and a 150 lb (68 kg) military load. It was required to rise vertically to 2,000 ft (600 m), remain hovering over one spot for thirty minutes, attain a speed of 60 mph (96 km/h), descend from 500 ft (150 m) undamaged without using its engine, and alight within a hundred foot (30 m) circle. There were thirty-four entries for the competition but no actual attempts at the prizes and so these were reoffered in March 1925. There were a number of further entries, including one from the American Harold Pitcairn, who was soon to become interested in the Autogiro, but again no attempts were made to win the prizes and these were finally withdrawn in April 1926. Other governments (notably the French and American) made similar attempts at this time to stimulate helicopter development.

The crash of the Brennan helicopter, as the culmination of six years of development, followed so closely by the successful demonstrations of the Autogiro, swung interest in Britain away from the pure helicopter and focused it instead on the gyroplane. Compared with the complexities of the helicopter, the basic simplicity of the Autogiro impressed everyone.

First demonstrations of the Autogiro by Courtney were given at Farnborough to Sir Philip Sassoon, under secretary of state for air on October 14, and to Sir Samuel Hoare, secretary of state for air, Sir Hugh Trenchard, chief of the air staff, and a large number of other interested people including Sir Sefton Brancker, director of civil aviation, and the press on October 19. The distinguished visitors were received at RAE by the Superintendent, Mr. W. Sydney Smith. The aircraft was again demonstrated at Farnborough, (on October 28) this time before the Queen of Spain. Six days earlier, on October 22, these practical demonstrations had been amplified by Cierva in a paper, "The Development of the Autogiro," read in translation on his behalf before a large audience at a meeting of the Royal Aeronautical Society in London by its Chairman, Sir Sefton Brancker.

Extensive tests of the Autogiro were undertaken at RAE where it was flown on one occasion for about fifteen minutes by an RAF pilot, Squadron Leader Rollo A. de Haga Haigh, AFC, but most of the time by Courtney. The trials included flights without use of the ailerons. Absence of lateral control was found to be largely compensated by the machine's pendulum stability. However, ailerons were required in rough conditions. In landing tests, very steep angles of descent (more than thirty degrees) were achieved. The Autogiro was finally damaged in a landing accident on October 31 after decending almost vertically at 16 ft/sec (4.88 m/s) with the engine switched off. It was, however, soon repaired. Sometime after its arrival in England the C.6A was fitted with an oleo landing gear of Avro 504N type. This was an obviously desirable modification to cope with the higher rates of descent of the Autogiro compared with an airplane. Autogiro landings sorely taxed the original bungee shock absorbers. The Autogiro was flying again before representatives of the Patent Office on November 11.[7]

Drawing of C.6A, showing rotor structure and other details.
(Illustrated Newspapers Group)

Before this, the tests, which evaluated the C.6A against Specification 14/25 and were conducted by H.M. Garner to a program approved by the director of scientific research, had found that the Autogiro had a maximum speed of 67 mph (108 km/h)—about 20 mph (32 km/h) slower than the standard Avro with the same engine. It had a lower rate of climb—250 ft/min (1.27 m/s), compared with 650 ft/min (3.3 m/s)—but a significantly steeper angle of climb (up to about four degrees more). The landing run was shorter—between 15 and 75 ft (5 and 23 m). At low forward speeds, the rate of descent was 10-13 ft/sec (3–4 m/s). The mean of four level low speed runs gave 39 mph (63 km/h); the Avro stalled at 45 mph (72 km/h). The smallest radius of turn measured was 207 ft (63 m). Difficulties were experienced with take-offs, where correct rotor rpm and airspeed were found to be critical. In any case, a run of 600-650 ft (180-200 m) was required. The flying weight was 1,934 lb (877 kg), 80 lb (36 kg) more than the standard Avro 504K. Each rotor blade weighed 88 lb (40 kg).

The results of the program of tests were sufficiently encouraging for the Air Ministry to decide to sponsor further development of the Autogiro. Accordingly, in January 1926, a machine similar to the C.6A was ordered from A. V. Roe & Co. Ltd., to be built under Cierva license. A second similar machine was ordered by Cierva from Avro. This was the start of a long association between Cierva and the Avro Company. The Air Ministry also proposed that development of two or three more Autogiros of new improved design should be undertaken, and an announcement to this effect was made by Sir Samuel Hoare on November 9, 1925. The types envisaged were to include one similar to the C.6A but with the more powerful Armstrong Siddeley Lynx engine and a rotor spin-up drive; a second to be a single-seater of the smallest practical dimensions, and a third for research, its design to be agreed with the Aeronautical Research Committee.

Early in the new year, another attempt was made to interest the French in the Autogiro. The C.6A was taken to France by surface transport. Reassembled, it was demonstrated by Frank Courtney at Villacoublay, near Paris, over a period of two weeks in January and February 1926. On January 26, Courtney made a flight of fifteen minutes but on the twenty-seventh he had a spectacular crash when he was blown over by a sudden 68 km/h (42 mph) gust of wind while landing on muddy ground. The aircraft was quickly repaired and was flying again on February 2. The demonstration included flights by two Frenchmen, Ingenieur Cousin and Adjudant Moutonnier. Generally speaking the performance measured at Villacoublay was as good as, or better, than at Farnborough. However, the French apparently decided against involvement in Autogiro development at this time. Three years were to pass before Weymann-Lepère were to start work on the C.18, the first French Autogiro.

Despite this setback, Cierva was awarded the Grand Prix Scientifique de l' Air for 1925 by the Société Française de la Navigation Aérienne. The C.6A is believed to have been subsequently returned to Spain where it was used for a certain amount of further development flying, although the main stream of progress shifted to England. Before it went back to Spain, C.6A was probably the Autogiro demonstrated at Farnborough to Harry Guggenheim and Rear Admiral Hutchinson Cove during their visit to the United Kingdom in March/April 1926. Guggenheim and Cove were visiting Europe, on behalf of the Daniel Guggenheim Fund for the Promotion of Aeronautics, to study aeronautical developments in Europe. They were most impressed by the Autogiro and had discussions in Spain with Cierva and Emilio Herrera of the Aeronautical Laboratory at Cuatro Vientos. As a result, they recommended that the Guggenheim Fund should sponsor a demonstration tour by an Autogiro in the United States. In the event, this was not followed up.

Cierva C.1

60-hp Le Rhône. Rotor diameter 6 m (19 ft 8 1/4 in); rotor blade section Eiffel 101; fuselage length 7.57 m (24 ft 10 in). Maximum take-off weight 350 kg (772 lb). No other data available.

Cierva C.2

110-hp Le Rhône 9Ja. Rotor diameter 11.5 m (37 ft 8 3/4 in); fuselage length 8.5 m (27 ft 1 5/8 in). Empty weight 538 kg (1,186 lb); maximum take-off weight 788 kg (1,737 lb). Maximum speed 125 km/h (78 mph); minimum speed 12 km/h (7.5 mph); absolute ceiling 4,250 m (13,950 ft). Performance estimated. No other data available.

Cierva C.3

50-hp Gnome Omega, later replaced by 80-hp Le Rhône 9C. No other data available.

Cierva C.4

80-hp Le Rhône 9 C. Rotor diameter 8 m (26 ft 3 in) and later 9.75 m (31 ft 11 13/16 in); rotor blade section Eiffel 101 and later Eiffel 106; fuselage length 6.88 m (22 ft 4 3/4 in); span of ailerons 7.67 m (25 ft 2 in). Empty weight 400–430 kg (881–948 lb); maximum take-off weight 500–600 kg (1,102–1,322 lb). Maximum speed 88 km/h (55 mph); minimum speed 56–61 km/h (35–38 mph); rotor speed 140 rpm. Tested in 16 different forms.

Cierva C.5

110-hp Le Rhône 9Ja. Rotor diameter about 11.5 m (37 ft 8 3/4 in); rotor blade section Gö 430; fuselage length 8.5 m (27 ft 10 5/8 in). No other data available.

Cierva C.6, C.6bis,C.6A

110-hp Le Rhône 9Ja. Rotor diameter 10 m (32 ft 9 11/16 in) (C.6), 10.5-11 m (34 ft 5 3/8 in–36 ft 8 15/16 in) (C6bis and C.6A); rotor blade section Gö 429; overall length 10.47m (34 ft 4 1/8 in). Empty weight 655 kg (1,444 lb); maximum take-off weight 780–1,090 kg (1,720-2,400 lb). Fuel 73 litres (16 Imp gal). Maximum speed 100–108 km/h (62–68 mph); minimum speed 55–63 km/h (34–39 mph); initial climb 1.0–1.3 m/s (200–250 ft/min) rotor speed 130/140 rpm (C.6), 140/160 rpm (C.6A).

Chapter 3

Cierva Moves to Britain

Among those who watched Frank Courtney's demonstrations of the Autogiro at Farnborough in October 1925 was James G. Weir, younger brother of Viscount Weir of Eastwood (1877–1959), the prominent Scottish industrialist and former secretary of state for air. Jimmy Weir had been interested in aviation since its earliest days—he had been a spectator at the famous pioneer aviation meeting at Rheims in 1909 and took his Aviator's Certificate (no. 24) on a Blériot monoplane at Hendon on November 8, 1910. At the end of World War I, with the rank of Brigadier-General, he had held the important appointment of technical controller at the ministry of munitions. After the war, be became honorary air commodore of one of the first squadrons of the Auxiliary Air Force.

James G. Weir (1887–1973) was largely responsible for the development of the Autogiro in the United Kingdom. (Weir Group, Gillies Collection)

Weir was enormously impressed by the C.6 flights and thereafter became a lifelong advocate of the Autogiro. Indeed, it is not too much to say that it was his enthusiasm and drive that induced Cierva soon afterward to establish himself in Britain. There, Cierva pursued his life's work on the development of rotary-wing aircraft, largely assisted by Weir's continuing interest and support.

When the British authorities began to show interest in the Autogiro, Cierva's father, who had had previous dealings in Madrid with the well-known London commercial bankers, Lazard Brothers & Co. Ltd., wrote to Sir Robert M. Kindersley of Lazards (later Lord Kindersley and a director of the Bank of England, 1914–46) suggesting that the bank might be interested in the commercial potential of his son's invention. Sir Robert's son, Hugh K.M. Kindersley (also of Lazards) knew Spain and spoke Spanish, having worked in the bank's Madrid Branch. He was therefore put in touch with Cierva and they soon became good friends.

Within a few days of seeing the flights at Farnborough, James Weir had convinced his brother of the promise in Cierva's design. The brothers thereupon constituted themselves as a committee, in association with Frank Courtney and Hugh Kindersley, to study ways and means of developing the Autogiro. The committee negotiated through Spanish representatives of Lazards with Cierva's father. The Cierva Autogiro Company Ltd. was established in England on March 24, 1926. With James Weir as chairman, Juan de la Cierva as technical director, and Hugh Kindersley as a director, this new British company was formed "to exploit the world patents of the Cierva machine, including the English patents." The company was not itself intended to manufacture aircraft but merely to "negotiate the selling outright of patents and the granting of licenses and royalties." However, it was soon involved in development work. Capital of £30,000 (then equivalent to $145,000) was put up by James Weir, Hugh Kindersley, J.J. Astor, and several financial institutions. Cierva was allotted 20,000 £1 preferential shares for his patents. Lord Weir himself did not participate because he did not want to prejudice his position as independent advisor to the British government. He thought he might do so if he became financially involved in a development in which the Air Ministry was already interested.

Cierva C.6C (130-hp Clerget 9Bb). As recorded in the last chapter, the Air Ministry had, indeed, sought a license from Cierva and in January 1926 had ordered (under Contract no. 680624/26) an Autogiro to Specification 3/26 from A.V. Roe & Co. Ltd. This aircraft, which was built at Hamble near Southampton, was to be basically similar to the Spanish-built C.6A, but had a more powerful Clerget rotary engine instead of the Le Rhône. Also known as the Avro Type 574, the C.6C was a single-seater and was given the military serial J8068. A second similar Autogiro was ordered by Cierva. The Avro 575 (C.6D) was a two-seater and bore the civil registration G–EBTW.

Test flying of the C.6C started on June 19, 1926, and was undertaken at Hamble by Frank Courtney, who had been appointed technical manager of the new company. The C.6C had an 11 m (36 ft 1 $\frac{1}{16}$ in) cable-braced four-blade constant-chord rotor of similar design to that of the C.6bis. It was 34 ft 4$\frac{1}{8}$ in

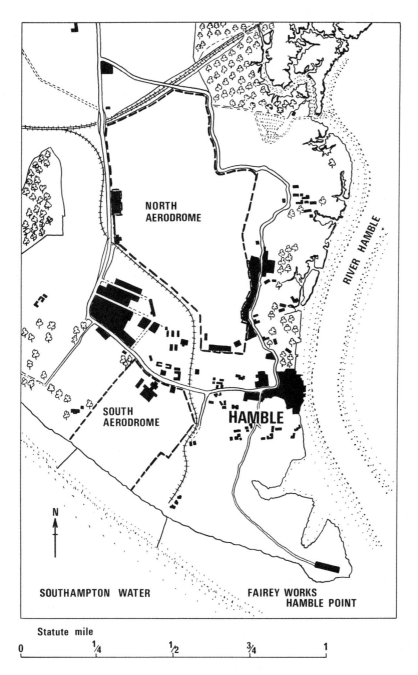

The airfields at Hamble on Southampton Water where the Cierva Autogiro Company was first established.

(10.46 m) long and weighed 1,490 lb (676 kg) empty. It had ailerons on out-riggers and the standard Avro 504K landing gear. The performance in the air seems to have been a distinct improvement on the Spanish C.6s but the take-off run was still about 650 ft (200 m) and the landing run 40–60 ft (12–18 m) in a 5 mph (8 km/h) wind.

The Royal Air Force decided that the C.6C (J8068) should be demonstrated before George V and Queen Mary, the King and Queen of Spain, and a number of other prominent people at the Seventh RAF Display at Hendon on July 3, 1926. Three days before the Display a fitting broke during a test flight allowing four cables, designed to hold up the blades when at rest, to come adrift. As a result, the blades dropped lower and lower as the rotor slowed down after landing. They proceeded to foul the airscrew and rudder before finally coming to rest with a resounding crash against the fuselage side. Frank Courtney, who had hurriedly jumped from the cockpit, narrowly escaped decapitation. Fortunately, the damage could be repaired in time for the show, and the Autogiro received considerable publicity following its participation in the Display. As a result, some people seem to have jumped to the conclusion that rotary-wing aircraft were already proven practical vehicles suitable for commercial operations.

Thus, even in distant New Guinea, a Mr. Frederick Fairburn was to suggest in August 1926 that Autogiros would be a solution to the transport problem between the coast and the remote inland goldfields. Despite the difficulties of constructing airfields, this role was, in fact, soon to be undertaken with outstand-ing success by fixed-wing airplanes.

There was little appreciation in 1926 of the further intensive development that would be required before the first production Autogiros, still of extremely limited capability, could enter service in 1930.

The first British Autogiro, the C.6C, being demonstrated [before King George V] by Frank Courtney at the RAF Pageant at Hendon on July 3, 1926.
(R.T. Riding)

Frank Courtney with Juan de la Cierva.
(Flight International)

Late in 1926, after being damaged in a crash at the Royal Aircraft Establishment on September 25, the C.6C was fitted with stub wings, like those which had already been fitted to the C.6D. These incorporated ailerons and served to unload the rotor in forward flight. They were the outcome of a new fixed-wing theory that Cierva was evolving at this time. He predicted that there would be a substantially constant rotor speed throughout the translational speed range, as well as improved high speed efficiency if a fixed-wing was fitted that would carry approximately 30 percent of the total weight at high speed. The wings also had less drag than the booms which previously carried the ailerons. Other changes made to the C.6C during its repair included a much wider-track landing gear and a more rigid attachment of the rotor blades at the hub.

Soon after this modification, while the C.6C was being tested by Courtney at Hamble on February 7, 1927, a rotor blade broke off while the machine was at a height variously estimated as between 60 and 220 ft (20 and 70 m). The aircraft fell to the ground and was destroyed. Courtney was fortunate to escape with comparatively slight injuries. The cause of the accident was found to be the rigidity of the blades in the plane of rotation. Stresses induced in the blade roots by the drag-reversal that occurred as the blades rotated (the "Coriolis Effect") caused fatigue failure at the root of one blade. A second adjacent blade became detached before the aircraft hit the ground. This weakness was overcome in subsequent designs by

The C.6C (right) *seen in developed form at Hamble alongside the later C.8V.* (H.F. King)

the adoption of drag hinges at the blade roots with cables and damping devices to restrain excessive movement of the blades in the drag plane. The blades were thus allowed to move slightly in relation to each other in the plane of rotation, as well as being free to flap vertically.

Before introduction of drag hinges, flexing of the blades in relation to each other was intended to be limited by inter-blade bracing cables tensioned by small weights that were acted on by centrifugal force. These mass-loaded cables were replaced by rubber cords after the introduction of drag hinges and these served to prevent excessive angular displacement of the blades. Drag hinges significantly reduced the general level of vibration, which was high in all early Autogiros. Specifically, it removed a certain roughness in flight due to a whipping action of the rotating blades.

Difficulties had been experienced prior to the accident with distortion of blade spars at the roots. It had been apparent for some time that the blades tended, under aerodynamic loads, to bend backwards in the plane and in relation to the direction of rotation. After the accident, Courtney said he had pointed this out to Cierva some time previously. The obvious cure was to put some flexibility into the blade attachments in the plane of rotation. However, nothing had been done about it because Cierva considered the additional complication unjustified. Even after the accident, Cierva showed some reluctance to adopt drag hinges and, indeed, two unsuccessful further Autogiros (the C.10 and the C.11) were built without them in 1927/28.

Relations between Cierva and his test pilot had not always been happy. They deteriorated after the accident, and Courtney, who had a reputation for being "difficult", left the company. A contributing factor to his departure may have been that Cierva himself gained his Royal Aero Club Aviator's Certificate (no. 8077) on January 20, nearly three weeks before the accident, with the obvious intention of undertaking test flying. He had begun to learn to fly on Avro Avian light airplanes with the Hampshire Aeroplane Club at Hamble the previous summer and he obtained his "A" license (no. 1035) on February 28, 1927. By the middle of the year he started to fly Autogiros.

Although the Avro chief test pilot, H.J.L. (Bert) Hinkler (1892–1933) was officially responsible for Autogiro testing from February 1927 until January 1928, Cierva, despite his inexperience as a pilot, seems to have taken over an increasing share himself from the latter part of 1927. He was probably not "approved" by the Air Ministry as a test pilot until at least mid-1928.

Cierva and Courtney were not to meet again for nine years. Courtney had moved to the United States but was on a visit to London in 1936 when he accidentally ran into Cierva. They talked, and parted friends. The following morning Cierva was killed in the DC-2 crash at Croydon.

Cierva C.6D (130-hp Clerget 9Bb). On July 29, 1926, seven months before the C.6C crash, Courtney had first flown the C.6D (the Avro 575). It had a similar 11 m (36 ft 1 ⅟₁₆ in) rotor to its predecessor but was a two-seater—the first successful Autogiro able to carry a passenger.

On July 30, 1926, Courtney carried Cierva himself in the C.6D as the first passenger ever to fly in a gyroplane. Bert Hinkler was his second passenger. After these flights, new stub wings incorporating ailerons were fitted, the landing gear was modified into a new wide-track configuration, and the rotor was exchanged for a new 12 m (39 ft 4 ⅞₁₆ in) type with four cable-braced paddle blades. This rotor was similar to that first tried on the C.8V earlier in the summer (see under C.8V).

The modifications incorporated, this Autogiro was shipped to Germany and, on September 5, 1926, was demonstrated by Courtney at Tempelhof, Berlin. On this occasion Cierva and a journalist called Kleffel, who was a friend of Ernst Udet, the First World War fighter ace and later leading figure in the Luftwaffe, were given rides in the Autogiro. It has sometimes been wrongly stated that Udet himself flew in the Autogiro on this occasion. He was not to do so until October 1928 when the C.8L-II visited Berlin.

After its return to England, the C.6D seems to have been tried at one point without ailerons or other type of lateral control. The C.6D may have been tested in this form by Bert Hinkler in October 1926. Later, the stub-wings were restored and C.6D with C.8V was demonstrated to the press at Hamble on the twentieth of that month. On this occasion, James Weir is believed to have flown an Autogiro for the first time although, according to one report, he made an earlier brief flight in the C.6A during the first demonstrations at Farnborough. About twenty pilots (including several from RAE) had flown Autogiros by this date. C.6D may have been flown in its latest configuration by both Hinkler and Courtney at Worthy Down in January 1927. Autogiro test flying had been temporarily moved there in January—probably because of flooding at Hamble. The maximum speed of the C.6D was increased by 20 mph (32 km/h) when fitted with the improved rotor. There was also a marked improvement in rate of climb.

After Courtney's crash in the C.6C and the grounding of Autogiros by the British Air Ministry for three months, C.6D was fitted with a modified rotor

C.6D *fitted with stub wings plus new rotor and landing gear, flying over Berlin, September 5, 1926.*
(Author's Collection)

C.7 *in modified form with rotor moved aft.*
(D. Balaguer)

incorporating drag hinges and probably became known as the C.8R (see below). Much of the flying on this aircraft was undertaken by Cierva himself—his first flight as an Autogiro pilot was probably on C.8R at Worthy Down on August 2. Cierva made a substantial contribution to the thirty-five hours of test flying completed on the C.6C, C.6D, C.7, C.8V, C.8L-I and C.9 in that year despite poor weather. This was a notable advance on the fourteen hours flown in 1926.

Cierva C.7 (Loring C.VII) (300-hp Hispano-Suiza Model 8Fb). This was a new design of Autogiro, the largest, heaviest and most powerful yet attempted. A single example was built under Cierva license at Carabanchel Alto, near Cuatro Vientos, by the Spanish aircraft constructor Dr. Jorge Loring Martinez in the latter part of 1926, presumably to the order of the Spanish government. The C.7 was funded out of the Pta 200,000 government grant of 1925. It was completed in October and, unflown, was exhibited at the First Madrid Aero Show, which opened on October 27 in the Glass Palace at the Retiro Park. The exhibition closed on November 7 and on the 15th, the C.7 was flown for the first time by Commandante Ureta at Carabanchel. Its performance was disappointing.

Cierva had estimated in 1925 that an Autogiro with a 450-hp Hispano-Suiza engine could be designed to achieve a maximum speed of no less than 300 mph (480 km/h), while retaining a landing speed of only 40 mph (64 km/h). Such a performance would, of course, have completely eclipsed that of contemporary fixed-wing aircraft. Although less powerful than the 1925 proposal, with 300 hp, C.7 should have offered a spectacular improvement in performance that was not achieved. Vibration limited maximum speed to 180 km/h (112 mph).

The C.7 had the fuselage of a Loring T-1 airplane, cable-braced four-blade 12 m (39 ft 4 $\frac{7}{16}$ in) rotor without drag hinges (similar to that of the C.6D), stub wings with full-span ailerons and wide-track four-wheel landing gear. The ailerons were extended in to the fuselage so that they were in the propeller slipstream, thus improving lateral control. The C.7 was a two-seater with tandem open cockpits and had ventral radiators for its large water-cooled engine. Like the slightly earlier C.8V in Britain, it did not have an air-cooled rotary engine. The latter type of engine had the advantage for Autogiros that its rotation helped cooling at low airspeeds. When initially tested, the C.7 was found to be tail heavy and, after the first tests, the rotor axis was moved aft about 60 cm (2 ft) by tilting the rotor pylon backwards.

After Courtney's accident, Cierva used the C.7 to develop a new 12.6 m (41 ft 4 $\frac{1}{16}$ in) rotor with drag hinges and of wider chord at the roots. The aircraft was also fitted at this time with a new two-wheel landing gear. The first flight of the C.7 in its modified form was made at Carabanchel by Loring's test pilot, Reginald Truelove,[8] on May 19, 1927. Both before and after its first flight, this aircraft was used by Cierva to study the problem of the vibrations experienced with inter-blade bracing. He flew as a passenger in this aircraft on a number of test flights. A second C.7 may have been ordered by the Spanish government but was apparently not completed. The original C.7 probably ended its days with the experimental unit at Cuatro Vientos.

Tests of autogiro rotors at this time were made on a specially constructed ground rig, erected at Hamble. Rotors were mounted on the top of a tower, their rotation generated by the natural wind so that their behaviour in motion could be studied. This rig anticipated the helicopter rotor test towers of a later era. Much of the work on the rotor tower was conducted by H.M. Yeatman, who had joined the Cierva team in 1926.

There had been considerable vibration at first with the double hinges on the C.7, and tests on the rotor tower made a significant contribution to its reduction.

Cierva C.8V (180/200-hp Wolseley Viper). Ordered by the Cierva company from Avro in the spring and built in the summer of 1926, this machine initially had a new cable-braced four-blade 12 m (39 ft 4 $\frac{7}{16}$ in) rotor with paddle blades but still without drag hinges. The rotor was mounted on the fuselage of an Avro 552A—the designation of the Avro 504 trainer when fitted with a Wolseley Viper water-cooled engine. The C.8V was a two-seater and had stub wings with ailerons, a wide-track landing gear and (later) a fixed fin. It bore the Avro drawing office designation of Type 586. Clearance considerations restricted the diameter of the propeller to less than required to absorb the power of the Viper engine.

The C.8V may have been test-flown partly by Bert Hinkler and partly by Frank Courtney as early as July 1926. In the course of development, it was fitted with a rotor with blades of reduced chord, which greatly improved performance. Later still, in January 1927, a substantial four-wheel landing gear was fitted. This modification was probably intended to reduce the Autogiro's sensitivity to winds while on the ground. The more "draggy" gear was not, however, found to be satisfactory and the C.8V was probably not flown a great deal in this form. In August 1927, the C.8V was fitted with a modified two-wheel landing gear with central skid. At the same time, the rotor was replaced with the new C.8 rotor with drag hinges (probably of the type known as no. 2A). This rotor was already fitted to the C.8R and probably derived from that developed on the C.7. The C.8V was registered as G-EBTX in September and, on October 20, Hinkler flew it from Hamble to Croydon and back a total of 128 mi (206 km) for a demonstration at Croydon arranged by John Lord of Avro's. This was the second cross-country flight by an Autogiro in the United Kingdom, the first having been made by Cierva three weeks earlier in the C.8L-I.

An RAE pilot tested the C.8V at Hamble on November 11, 1927. At a take-off weight of 2,700 lb (1225 kg) a rate of climb of about 260 ft/min (1.32 m/s) was measured.

In February 1928, Cierva had an accident while flying the C.8V at Hamble, similar to the one he had had only a few days earlier in the C.11 at Yate near Bristol (see Cierva C.11). Both accidents were attributed to attempting to take-off with insufficient rotor rpm but that to the C.8V is more likely to have been simply due to being blown over by the high wind—which could all too easily happen to the early Autogiros. Soon after this accident, G.I. Thomson, the chief flying instructor of the Hampshire Aeroplane Club, was appointed part-time test pilot to the Autogiro company, Bert Hinkler having resigned as Avro's chief test pilot in Janu-

First rotor hub with flapping and drag hinges mounted experimentally on C.7. (J. Warleta)

C.8V in its later form, with fixed fin, flying over the C.8R and a de Havilland D.H.60 Moth.
(Author's Collection)

ary. In 1930, the C.8V was reconstructed once more as the Avro 552A fixed-wing airplane.

Cierva C.8R. (130-hp Clerget 9Bb). Early in 1927, after the C.6C crash and while Autogiros were still grounded in England, Cierva designed a new cable-braced four-blade rotor with flapping and drag hinges. This was developed on the rotor tower and tested on the Spanish C.7. The rotor had tapered paddle-shaped blades (known as Type 2A) instead of the constant-chord ones of the C.6s and was 12 m (39 ft 4 7⁄16 in) in diameter. It was probably basically a modification of the new rotor (without drag hinges) first fitted to the C.8V the previous summer and to the C.6D in October.

The first C.8 rotor with drag hinges seems to have been fitted in May/June 1927 to the C.6D, which thus became the C.8R, although there is some debate about this designation. If used at all, it was probably first applied to the earlier modification in October. The C.8R was known by Avro as their Type 587. This machine, like the C.6C, in its last configuration, and all the C.8s except the C.8L-1, had its ailerons incorporated in narrow-chord stub-wings braced by inverted vee struts. These stub-wings not only provided a mounting for the ailerons and the wide-track landing gear but also unloaded the rotor in flight by providing some lift. The C.8R was first flown with drag hinges by Bert Hinkler in the spring of 1927.

As part of a program to try out a variety of rotor configurations, the C.8R was tested with a large-area cable-braced three-blade rotor early in June 1927—the first to be tried by Cierva since the C.5 in 1923. In September, it was also tried with a two-blade rotor, but this was found to be unacceptably rough in flight. That same month, the C.8R was registered G-EBTW. It was loaned to the Air Ministry in the summer of 1928 and on July 3 was flown from Hamble to the RAE by Flight Lieutenant H.C.A. ("Dizzy") Rawson who was shortly to join the Cierva Company (see below). C.8R remained at RAE for tests at least until September 20, when Flight Lieutenant D.W.F Bonham-Carter had a forced landing in it. The C.8R was scrapped in 1929.

Cierva C.8L-I (180-hp Armstrong Siddeley Lynx). The British Air Estimates, published in March 1927, stated that three new Autogiros had been ordered by the Air Ministry. These were the C.8L, the C.9, and the C.10, the first two from Avro to be designed by Roy Chadwick and the last from George Parnall and Company Ltd. to be designed by Harold Bolas. The C.8L had a stationary air-cooled radial engine and made use of the wooden wire-braced fuselage of an Avro 504N but with a special wide-track landing gear without central skid. It had horn-balanced elevators and ailerons on outriggers. One aircraft, which came to be known as the C.8L-I (J8930), was ordered by the Air Ministry to Specification 11/26 (under Contract No. 698109/26) late in 1926. It was built at Hamble by Avros as the Avro 611 during 1927 and completed in July. The C.8L-I had a new 12 m (39 ft 4⁷⁄₁₆ in) cable-braced four-blade rotor with paddle-type blades (known as Type No. 6) which were first tried on the C.8V. The blades had steel spars, spruce ribs, and fabric coverings and weighed 87 lb (39 kg) each. They were of wider chord—36 in (91 cm) mean—than those (known as Type No. 2A) on C.8R and C.8V. The C.8L-I was sometimes flown fitted with the rudder of the C.6C, bearing that aircraft's serial number J8068, which has sometimes caused the two types to be confused.

Initial test flying was done at Hamble in July or August 1927 by Bert Hinkler. Cierva himself made the first cross-country flight by a rotary-winged aircraft in the United Kingdom on September 30, 1927, when he delivered the C.8L-I the 44 miles (70 km) to Farnborough from Hamble via Worthy Down. On arrival, he commented on the C.8's poor performance. This was about three weeks before Hinkler's flight from Hamble to Croydon and back in the C.8V.

The C.6D with new rotor and stub wings came to be known as the C.8R. It was apparently first flown with a new rotor (without drag hinges) by Bert Hinkler in October 1926. First flight with a redesigned rotor, incorporating drag hinges, was in spring 1927.
(S.A. Chandler)

The C.8R with three-blade rotor in June 1927.
(National Air and Space Museum, Smithsonian Institution)

71

The C.8R flying with two-blade rotor in September 1927. (Author's Collection)

C.8L-I, photographed at the Royal Aircraft Establishment, Farnborough, October 1, 1927.
(Crown copyright photograph, courtesy RAE)

From now on Cierva undertook an increasing share of the testing of his machines. Test flying had been mainly done by Hinkler since Courtney's crash early in the year. After Hinkler's resignation in January 1928, testing was undertaken part-time by G.I. Thomson from February until Arthur Rawson joined Cierva full-time as demonstration and test pilot in July 1928. Rawson had accumulated 200 hours on Autogiros by February 1930 and was later to become the first pilot to achieve 1,000 hours on rotary wings. He left the company in 1932.

At Farnborough, after a test flight on October 6 in the condition in which it arrived, the C.8L-I was fitted with C.8V type (Type No. 2A) narrower and lighter rotor blades (of 21 inches, 53 cm mean chord weighing 69 lb (31 kg) each) with which it continued to fly for some time before reverting to its original rotor blades in January 1928. These tests were made by Cierva, who is recorded as having flown the aircraft at RAE on November 9 and 10. He reported the performance with the different rotor as no better or worse than it had been with the original. An attempted test flight on November 25 by an RAE pilot, Flight Lieutenant Barbour, carrying E.T. Jones as passenger, was unsuccessful in that the Autogiro could not be induced to take-off and was damaged. They were more successful on January 11, 1928, after the original rotor blades had been refitted. The same crew then made a flight of 1 hour 5 minutes. However, this also ended in a crash following fatigue failure of the turnbuckles securing the bracing between two opposite pairs of blades.

The C.8L-I was apparently not repaired for about a year and was not flown again at RAE until February 20, 1929, when it was damaged once more while being taxied by Barbour. The rough surface of Farnborough airfield—this was, of course, in the days before hard runways—made it difficult to spin-up the rotor to flying speed by the fast taxying required and on this occasion the rotor blades hit the rudder.

For the next series of tests, the C.8L-I was accordingly taken by road to Andover where the airfield had a smoother surface. Flying at Andover started on March 7, 1929. Four different military pilots flew a total of seven hours during twenty-three flights, spread over the next four months. On July 17, 1929, the C.8L-I was flown from Andover to Farnborough by Flight Lieutenant Rogenhagen, but it was apparently again returned to Andover by road for the next series of tests starting in January 1930. Over the following five months, three pilots flew a total of twelve hours on some nineteen flights. The C.8L-I was then again damaged, probably on May 8, and finally written-off in about June of that year.

Cierva C.8L-II (180-hp Armstrong Siddeley Lynx IV). This was a civil version of the C.8L-I and, like its predecessor, made use of an Avro 504N fuselage but with stub wings, incorporating ailerons, added. The landing gear was wide-tracked like the military version, but attached to the winds and with a central skid, the rotor blades had improved bracing, and the direct-drive engine was more effectively cowled. The C.8L-II was built by Avros at Hamble in the first part of 1928 as the Avro 617 to the order of James Weir.

The C.8L-II (registered G-EBYY) was first flown at Hamble early in May 1928. It was damaged by Cierva in a landing accident at the Hampshire Air Pageant at Hamble on May 28—he landed with drift and broke the landing gear—but, flown by Rawson, was entered by J.G. Weir in the King's Cup Air Race on July 20. Rawson retired from the race after a forced landing from fuel shortage in a field at Nuneaton too small for take-off. From August 7, based on Northolt, he undertook a 3,000 mi (4,800 km) tour of Great Britian and visited many civil and RAF airfields as well as James Weir's estate at Dalrymple near Edinburgh.

The C.8L-II apparently had a speed range of from 25 to 106 mph (40 to 170 km/h) and was thus about 10 mph (16 km/h) slower than an equivalent airplane. It would take off in about 300 ft (90 m) and land with about 6 ft (2 m) of ground run.

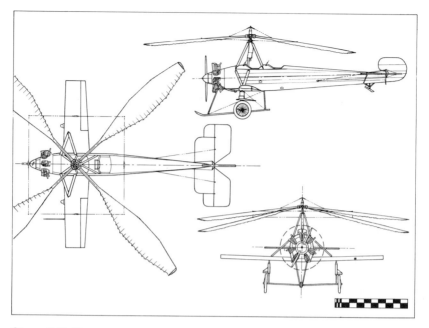

Cierva C.8L-II.

Left to right: *"Bud" Taylor, A.V. Roe, Arthur Rawson, and Juan de la Cierva in front of the C.8L-II at Hamble.*
(Author's Collection)

On September 17, Cierva flew the well-known British aviation journalist, Major C.C. Turner, from Hamble to Croydon in the C.8L-II. The following day, now with Henri Bouché, editor of *l'Aéronautique*, as passenger, he flew from London (Croydon) to Paris (Le Bourget) with stops at Saint-Inglevert and Abbeville. The first leg crossing the sea was flown at a height of 4,000 ft (1200 m) in 66 minutes. This was the first international flight by an Autogiro and resulted in Cierva being awarded the 1928 Grand Prix de l'Académie des Sports (worth 25,000 francs) presented by Henri Deutsch de la Meurthe. The Aéro Club de France later also presented him with the 1929 Lahm Prize (worth 50,000 francs) for this flight. The Union pour la Sécurité en Aéroplane awarded him a further 20,000 francs.

Cierva damaged the C.8L-II during a demonstration at Le Bourget a few days later. While taking off, the landing gear hit an obstruction damaging one wheel. As a result, he crashed in landing but the damage was soon repaired. Accompanied by Rawson, Cierva then flew the C.8L-II to Brussels on October 4 where he demonstrated it on October 12 before continuing to Cologne. From there, Rawson made a continental tour of some 1,200 mi (1930 km) on to Berlin where the aircraft was demonstrated to Ernst Udet and then back to Amsterdam and Paris. The C.8L-II was sold in France later that year where it was studied by the Weymann-Lepère Company which was about to acquire an Autogiro license

Juan de la Cierva and Henri Bouché, editor of L'Aéronautique, *in the C.8L-II at Croydon before the first rotary-wing flight across the English Channel on September 18, 1928.*
(Royal Aeronautical Society)

and, in collaboration with Cierva, to design the C.18 Autogiro. The C.8L-II was demonstrated at Orly and at the Vincennes Air Display in May 1929. After being stored for many years, it was exhibited at the 1950 Brussels Aero Show and is now preserved by the Musée de l'Air et de l'Espace in Paris.

Cierva C.8L-III (180-hp Armstrong Siddeley Lynx IV). Similar to the C.8L-II, except that it had a fixed fin in front of the rudder, this machine was built by Avros at Hamble apparently as another example of their Type 617 to the order of the Italian government. It was first flown by Rawson in September 1928, then shipped to Italy and demonstrated by Cierva at Monte Cello airfield near Rome in January 1929. Cierva trained the first Italian pilot to fly the Autogiro (Captain Gramda) in twenty minutes flying time with three landings. While in Italy, Cierva read a paper about the Autogiro (in French) to the Associazione Italiana di Aerotecnica. Among the distinguished audience was General G.A. Crocco, director general of manufacture at the Air Ministry, who in 1906 had suggested cyclic pitch control and wind-milling of the rotor as a method of safe descent and landing for a helicopter after engine failure. Crocco later had a flight in the Autogiro.

Cierva C.8 Mk.IV (or C.8W) (220-hp Wright Whirlwind J-5). A Wright Whirlwind-engined version of the C.8 was built for the Cierva Company in the Avro works at Hamble and flown in November 1928. (Although Avros moved their design organization and experimental shops out of Hamble and back to their main works in Manchester in spring 1929, an Autogiro design team was retained there, and Avro continued Autogiro manufacture at the Hamble works until 1932.) The C.8 Mk.IV was built for and sold to the wealthy American aviation enthusiast, Harold F. Pitcairn, who had first become interested in the Autogiro more than three years earlier. He had visited Madrid in May 1925, about four months after Vickers from Britain had evaluated and turned down the Autogiro. However, that was five months before the C.6A was demonstrated in England and ten months before the Cierva Autogiro Company was formed there. If Pitcairn had reached an agreement with Cierva at this time, he might have diverted the mainstream of Autogiro development to the United States.

The Pitcairn family were heirs to the Pittsburgh Plate Glass fortune and Harold Pitcairn had founded Pitcairn Aviation Inc. in the autumn of 1923 to build fixed-wing aircraft. However, he had been interested in helicopters since 1916 and had made numerous tests with rotary-wing models. These had established that fixed vanes in the rotor down-wash were not an effective anti-torque device with a single rotor. Tests with a toy helicopter (in his case the "Hi-Flyer", which had been on the market since about 1912) convinced him, as they had Cierva some years earlier, that a single rotor helicopter was inherently stable and that, if a means could be found of controlling a single rotor, helicopter flight would be practical. It seemed to him that Cierva had discovered such means. Pitcairn filed his first rotary-wing patent on March 1925 shortly before his Madrid visit. A separate Pitcairn company—Pitcairn Aeronautics Inc.—was formed early in 1926 to undertake rotary-wing development. In 1927, this company successfully

*The C.8 Mk.IV, or C.8W, had an American Wright Whirlwind engine and was
specially built for Cierva's American licensee, Harold F. Pitcairn.
(S. Pitcairn)*

flew a tip jet-driven model helicopter using compressed carbon dioxide gas as the
propelling agent.

In 1925 and again in 1926, Pitcairn considered obtaining a license from
Cierva to build Autogiros in the United States. He was deterred only by the fact
that, at that time, the Autogiro required more space to take-off than an equivalent
conventional airplane. This seemed to deprive it of any practical value.

However, during a visit to England in the summer of 1928, Pitcairn had a
flight in the C.8L-II and dinner with Cierva that same evening. He returned to
London in August and, following discussions with James Weir, ordered an example of the C.8 design fitted with an American engine for evaluation in the United
States. The Wright Whirlwind engine turned in the opposite sense to the Lynx,
and it was thought that there might be some lateral imbalance at high forward
speeds as a result. A device to tilt the whole apex of the rotor pylon was accordingly incorporated in this C.8 and this proved helpful in trimming the aircraft for
low-speed or high-speed flight. When the C.8W was completed, Harold Pitcairn
himself flew it before it was crated for shipment. The C.8 Mk.IV (NC418)
became the first Autogiro and the first practical rotating-wing aircraft to fly in the
Western Hemisphere when Rawson tested it after reassembly, on December 19,
1928, at Pitcairn Field, Bryn Athyn, Pennsylvania.

Subsequently, this aircraft was extensively demonstrated to United States
authorities and the National Advisory Committee for Aeronautics (NACA). It
was also used for comparative flight tests against the Pitcairn PA-5 Mailwing

biplane. In a series of tests of take-off, climb, speed, and other characteristics, the C.8 Mk.IV was flown by Pitcairn himself for comparison with a Mailwing flown by the Pitcairn test pilot, James C. Ray. The results were analyzed by Agnew Larsen and Paul Stanley.

Except for deficient lateral and directional stability, the C.8 proved to have generally good flying and handling characteristics. However, at high diving speeds, it was found that the rotor began to lose revolutions and excessive blade flapping developed with considerable roughness. Later, toward the end of 1929, this fault was largely eliminated by reducing by three degrees the incidence of the fixed wing. This improved the aircraft's handling throughout the speed range. (Cierva took out a British patent, no. 330,665 of June 19, 1930, covering the best use of auxiliary fixed wings on Autogiros.) Well before this, the C.8W had been used for tests on various rotor combinations and also for tests of a deflector tail for rotor spin-up.

The C.8 stood up to its comparison with the Mailwing well enough to confirm Pitcairn in his decision to acquire the American license for the Autogiro. Following successful negotiations with Cierva, the Pitcairn-Cierva Autogiro Company of America Inc. was formed in February 1929 to license the manufacture of Autogiros in the United States. Cierva himself became a director of the American company. Negotiations on behalf of Cierva were conducted by Colonel John Josselyn, by then managing director of the Cierva Autogiro Company Ltd. (He continued to hold this office until 1933.) Under agreements signed on February 14, 1929, Pitcairn obtained U.S. rights to all Cierva's patents and inventions for $300,000, equivalent to $1.8 million now.

The rotary wing patents acquired by Pitcairn from Cierva and others registered directly in his name include eleven that were to prove of controlling importance to the modern helicopter. These patents were the subject of a remarkable legal action against the United States government taken by the Autogiro Company of America between 1951 and 1977. This action related to use of these patents without license by the whole of the American helicopter industry with the notable exception of Sikorsky. During the period 1945 to 1954, production model helicopters had been supplied by these companies to the U.S. government without payment of any license fees. The plaintiff won his case and on July 23, 1977, was awarded $32 million in royalties and compensation by the United States Supreme Court.

On May 13, 1929, Harold Pitcairn used the C.8 Mk.IV to make the first extended cross-country flight by Autogiro in America. This was from Pitcairn Field to Langley Field, Virginia, via Washington, D.C., and was followed by a demonstration to the NACA at Langley and to the United States Navy at Norfolk before returning to Pitcairn Field. At Langley, Orville Wright, the first man to fly in an airplane, inspected the Autogiro.

Shortly after the Langley trip, covering a distance of more than 500 mi (800 km), Pitcairn flew the C.8W to Washington, D.C., to give a demonstration to members of the administration and Congress and to a large number of other important people, including the Spanish Ambassador.

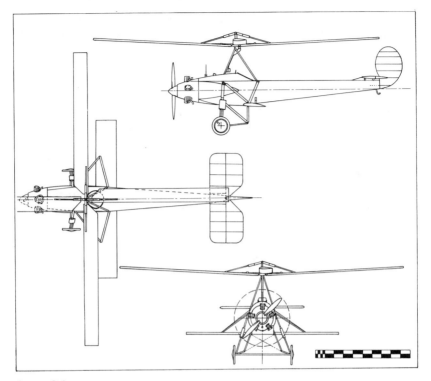

Cierva C.9.

Prior to these flights, in the spring of 1929, at Cierva's suggestion, the C.8W had been given enlarged vertical tail surfaces and upturned tips to its fixed-wings, which had a length approximating to the tip chord inclined upwards at a 45 degree dihedral. These modifications improved the C.8W's lateral stability and followed unsuccessful tests with a large auxiliary high fin mounted above the cockpits. Upturned wing tips had been first tried on the European C.12 and C.17 in late 1928 to early 1929. The C.18 and C.19, examples of which arrived in America in August/September 1929, also had this feature. It became standard on almost all fixed-wing Autogiros. The C.8W is preserved in what is now the Silver Hill Facility (located in Maryland) of the National Air and Space Museum, Smithsonian Institution in Washington, D.C. Its last flight was on July 22, 1931, when Jim Ray landed it in front of the Smithsonian Castle on the Mall in central Washington.

Cierva C.9 (70-hp Armstrong Siddeley Genet I). According to a Royal Aircraft Establishment report by H. Glauert (BA.577 of March 1926), Cierva studied the design of an ultra-light Autogiro early in 1926 at about the same time as he was first scheming the C.8L-I. This small Autogiro was to have had a rotor 25 ft 6 in (7.77 m) in diameter, a 30-hp Bristol Cherub engine, and to have used the fuselage of the Avro Avis ultra-light aeroplane. However, RAE concluded that

Cierva's estimates of a top speed of 59 mph (95 km/h) and a rate of climb of 190 ft/min (0.96 m/s) were optimistic and that this Autogiro would not have left the ground. Cierva did more inconclusive project work on a small single-seater while in Spain in 1927.

Probably partly for this reason the C.9, intended to be of the smallest practical size, was finally built with more than double the power and with a loaded weight greater by about a third than the earlier project. Even so, it proved to be under-powered. Late in 1926 this small experimental single-seat Autogiro (J8931) was ordered by the Air Ministry (under Contract no. 698108/26) to Specification 4/26 at the same time as the C.8L-I. It was built in 1927 by Avro at Hamble as their Type 576.[9] It incorporated a wooden plywood-covered fuselage specially designed by the Avro chief designer, Roy Chadwick, a design closely similar to that used for the Avro Avian I light airplane prototype. The C.9 had a wide-track oleo landing gear and out-rigged "winglets" as ailerons braced by inverted V-struts, projecting directly from the lower longerons. The empty and loaded weights were about half those of the C.8. The cable-braced four-blade rotor, which was of new design with untapered blades, was 30 ft (9.14 m) in diameter—the smallest yet on a practical Autogiro. It operated in the opposite sense to previous British-built Autogiros (clockwise from above). The C.9 was first flown by Hinkler and later by Cierva at Hamble in September 1927, but there must have been problems because the aircraft does not seem to have been delivered to the Air Ministry until the following year.

Flight Lieutenant Bonham-Carter flew the C.9 at Hamble on May 24, 1928, and it was apparently delivered to RAE by road after this test because Bonham-Carter flew it again at Farnborough on July 18 when he made two 10-min flights. He made another flight, this time of 45 min, on July 19. This was followed by two short flights by Cierva at RAE on the last day of the same month. The C.9 could land in 36–45 ft (11-14 m) in a 5 mph (8 km/h) wind but required 660–780 ft (200–238 m) to take-off. The C.9 was flown with a new type of rotor with "half-length" untapered blades on September 18, 1928. It was finally deposited in the Science Museum at South Kensington in London in January 1930 and is now in storage.

Cierva C.10 (70-hp Armstrong Siddeley Genet I). A small experimental single-seat Autogiro (J9038) ordered by the Air Ministry from Parnall late in 1926, at the same time as the C.8L-I and C.9 were ordered from Avro. Designed by Harold Bolas to Specification 4/26 like C.9 and built at Yate, the C.10 was completed in January 1927. Like C.9, it was originally designed with the 30-hp Bristol Cherub engine. The rotor pylon was a complicated six-strut structure in front of the cockpit, which was probably intended to make possible changes in the rotor spindle's fore-and-aft position. The cable-braced four-blade 30-ft rotor was without the drag hinges that had been adopted for all Autogiros following the C.6C accident. Cierva was still keen to avoid the complication of drag hinges if he could—hence this further experiment which provided a direct comparison with the C.9 with its drag hinges. Like the C.9, the C.10's rotor turned in the opposite

The C.9, with new rotor with half-length blades, photographed at RAE, Farnborough, on September 6, 1928.
(W/Cdr. N.F.W. Unwin)

C.10 after its crash at Yate on April 26, 1928. Note the unexplained control rods between fuselage and rotor hub that may have been part of a tilting rotor control system but were more probably a trimming mechanism.
(H.F. King)

sense to previous Autogiros. The strut-braced ailerons projected directly from the lower longerons of the fuselage. The C.10 never flew. Like the C.11 two months before, it overturned and was damaged at Yate while attempting to take-off on its first flight on April 26, 1928. The pilot was Flight Lieutenant H.A. Hamersley. The accident was attributed to gyroscopic action but was probably due to an incorrect hub setting or to ground resonance caused by lack of blade damping and

81

insufficient stiffness in the rotor pylon. The C.10 was repaired and modified in several respects, including fitment of a wider track landing gear and a 5 degree tilt to the right of the rotor pylon. It was decided to try again on a smoother airfield. The C.10 was accordingly taken by road to Andover and, piloted by Rawson, another attempt to take-off was made on November 5, 1928. It failed: the aircraft again rolled over onto its side before leaving the ground. Further tests were abandoned.

C.10 and C.11 (below) apparently had control rods between rotor hub and pilot's cockpit. Their purpose is unknown but may have been part of a hub-tilting mechanism for control through the rotor or for adjusting the rotor spindle's fixed tilt setting. The latter seems the more likely explanation. Cierva did not achieve direct control by tilting the rotor for another four years.

Cierva C.11 (120-hp A.D.C. Airdisco). A larger experimental two-seater Autogiro (G-EBQG) was also built by Parnalls but to the order of the Cierva Company. It was completed in November 1927. This machine, also mainly designed by Bolas, was known as the Parnall Gyroplane. Like the C.10, the C.11 had a rather complex six-strut pylon carrying the rotor over the front cockpit and a cable-braced four-blade rotor without drag hinges. Unfortunately, the C.11 also overturned and was wrecked on its first attempted take-off in February 1928 at Yate with Cierva as pilot.

In October 1928, the C.11 was reconstructed at Hamble with a new smaller rotor. The fixed wings were moved forward, given marked dihedral and altered in profile, their original single bracing struts to the fuselage being replaced by inverted-V struts. The landing gear was now braced to the wings. The C.11 is

C.11 in October 1928 as reconstructed. Unexplained control or trimming rods between fuselage and rotor hub are again visible.
(H.F. King)

believed to have flown successfully in this form. The control rods and curiously complex rotor pylon first seen on the C.10, which may have been part of the trial installation of a system whereby the fixed tilt setting of the rotor hub and its fore-and-aft position could be altered, reappeared on both the original and on the first reconstruction of the C.11.

More than a year after the first reconstruction, C.11 was again rebuilt at Hamble, this time with a massive but simpler diagonally braced pyramid-type rotor pylon and a rotor spin-up drive from the engine. The latter is reported to have been designed by Frank B. Halford, designer of the Airdisco engine and later famous as designer of the Cirrus and Gipsy engines. The aircraft was then tested at Hamble but does not seem to have been flown very much in this final form—if at all. It was handed over to Air Service Training as an instructional airframe in 1931 when that organization took over the old Avro works at Hamble. Cierva did not attempt any further designs without drag hinges.

The accident at Yate was said to have been due to Cierva attempting to take-off with insufficient rotor rpm. However, the overturning accidents suffered by both C.10 and C.11 are more likely to have been due to an incorrect rotor hub tilt setting or to ground resonance which was imperfectly understood at that time. Many years later Bolas considered ground resonance to be the most likely explanation. All the early Autogiros were susceptible to this phenomenon, particularly when landing out of wind. In those days, the mathematics of the self-exciting dynamic system, involving blade and hub oscillations, had not been developed so that rotor systems were often designed with unsatisfactory characteristics.

The rotor spin-up drive tried on the C.11 was demonstrated on the ground to RAE representatives on January 8, 1930. It weighed about 165 lb (75 kg) and proved to be too heavy to be acceptable. However, a satisfactory lighter drive was to be developed in the United States in 1930. (It first appeared on the PCA-2 prototype in March of that year.) Meanwhile, in 1929, as discussed below, Cierva was to try aerodynamic methods of rotor starting.

Cierva C.12 (Loring C.XII) (225-hp Wright R-760 Whirlwind J-5). A large experimental Autogiro ordered by the Spanish Aeronáutica Militar, the C.12 was built in Spain in 1929 under Cierva license and to Cierva's design by Dr. Jorge Loring's factory at Carabanchel Alto near Cuatro Vientos, Madrid. Funding probably came from the remainder of the Pta 200,000 grant. This last Loring Autogiro had a 12 m (39 ft 4$\frac{7}{16}$ in) cable-braced rotor, supplied from England, which was similar to that on the C.8. The fixed wings had tips upturned at an angle of about 45 degrees. C.12's performance, powered by the excellent American Wright Whirlwind engine, represented a significant advance on all previous Autogiros. The C.12 was to be used by Cierva to develop the deflector tail for slipstream rotor starting.

Up to this time, Autogiros had suffered from the serious defect of requiring, for starting, a team of men with a rope. Ever since 1924 on the C.6bis, a rope had been wound onto knobs on the underside of the roots of the rotor blades near the hub and pulled to start the rotor, rather in the manner of spinning a top. The aircraft then had to be taxied across the airfield until the airflow had speeded up the

The rotor spin-up drive demonstrated on the C.11 at Hamble, probably early in 1930. This drive is said to have weighed about 165 lb and was not successful. (J.A.C. Lane drawing)

The Loring C.12 as originally built at Carabanchel Alto in 1928–29 and first flown on May 23, 1929. The simple monoplane deflector tail for rotor spin-up proved to be ineffective. (AISA)

rotor to the 120-130 rpm required for take-off. Alternatively, after starting the rotor by turning it by hand, it could be brought up to speed by even more prolonged taxying.

This drill had been a serious objection to the Autogiro's practicability. Until a more efficient method of spinning up the rotor was devised, the Autogiro, although it could be landed in small fields, required a large—and smooth—airfield for some uncomfortably fast and wobbly taxying before take-off. Much effort was therefore devoted by Cierva to solution of this problem. One modification of the standard procedure (originally patented on July 1, 1920) was tried early on by Frank Courtney with one of the C.6's. His scheme involved tying one end of the starting cable to a stake fixed in the ground and then taxying the aircraft away from it, thus spinning up the rotor. The method proved too drastic. On the first trial, the rotor speeded up satisfactorily but the cable came off the rotor knobs with a giant whip-crack and neatly cut the rudder in two. Had Courtney's head been a few inches higher it might have done the same to his skull. This ingenious idea was abandoned.

As already mentioned, a mechanical rotor drive had been retrospectively fitted late in 1929 to the Parnall-built C.11 of 1927. It was not satisfactory, at least partly because of its excessive weight.

A year earlier, in January 1929, the Cierva company had been granted a patent for another rotor-starting system employing compressed air, steam, or water fed under pressure from jet reaction nozzles at the tips of some or all of the blades. Cierva had been contemplating such a system for a number of years. Although tested, the idea had once again proved impractical.

The deflected slipstream rotor-starting system that Cierva developed on the C.12 was a marked advance on previous methods and was a characteristic solution: Cierva always preferred aerodynamic to mechanical ways of doing things. However, the system was still not the complete answer. The deflected airstream would spin up the rotor to about 85 rpm. Thereafter, particularly when there was little wind, taxying was still required to work up the rotor to full flying rpm of about 120. But the final solution of the problem—a satisfactory mechanical drive—soon appeared. A practical clutch and drive shaft between the engine and the rotor were to be developed in the United States early in 1930. They were fitted to production PCA-2s delivered from April 1931 and a British version on production C.19 Mk.IVs from March 1932.

Meanwhile, during 1929, Cierva developed his aerodynamic solution on the C.12. As first completed, this aircraft had a monoplane deflector stabilizer and elevator with small end-plate fins mounted on an unusually long fuselage. It was found that the amount of slipstream from the propeller deflected by this arrangement was inadequate. The design was accordingly modified with a shortened fuselage and a large and complex box deflector tail which both channeled and deflected the slipstream onto the rotor. After a lot of experiment, this was found to be the most effective arrangement although, as already explained, it was still not entirely satisfactory. It came to be known in Spain as the "scorpion tail" and was soon to be used on the C.19 series in England (see Chapter 4).

The C.12 in final form with larger scorpion deflector tail. Piloted by Luis Rambaud (left), this Autogiro flew from Madrid to Lisbon nonstop in four hours on July 11, 1929. (AISA)

The C.12 in its initial form was first flown by Cierva in May 23, 1929, at Carabanchel Alto. He demonstrated it to the press later that month. After tests with the first box tail, starting on June 11, Cierva appears to have flown the final version, with its somewhat heavier and larger box tail, at Cuatro Vientos toward the end of the month. Both scorpion tail versions had a shorter fuselage than the original design. During one flight at this time, Cierva achieved a height of 12,000 ft (3660 m) then a record for Autogiros. (It was to be nearly two years before Autogiro altitude records of the order of 20,000 ft (6,100 m) were to be established in the United States.)

In early July, Cierva again demonstrated the C.12 to the press. On another day at Getafe, he showed it off to his wife and children and gave his mother a flight. He had intended to make a long-distance demonstration flight to Seville in the C.12 but he ran out of time—he had to go to England to make the first flights of the C.19 Mk.I and to supervise its exhibition at the Olympia Aero Show in London, starting on July 16. On July 11, 1929, Luis Rambaud Goma, the Loring test pilot, flew the C.12 350 mi (563 km) nonstop from Madrid to Lisbon in four hours.[10] This was a distance record for an Autogiro at that time and was made possible by the C.12's large fuel capacity—about double that of the C.8. Rambaud demonstrated the C.12 at Amadaroc near Lisbon but the aircraft was unfortunately slightly damaged. On the return flight to Madrid excessive vibration, attributed to an inadequate repair, forced him down at Tancos. The flight was resumed after several days when Talavera was reached. Finally, late in July, a landing on poor ground near Caceres led Rambaud to abandon the flight and return the C.12 to Madrid by road.

Luis Rambaud was later to have a distinguished career in the Nationalist Air Force during the Spanish Civil War. He commanded both fighter and bomber squadrons and finally lost his life on October 29, 1938, in an accident to a Dornier Do 17 subsequently attributed to sabotage. In 1941, Commandante Rambaud was posthumously awarded the Military Medal. A second C.12 is believed to have been originally ordered but was not completed.

Cierva C.13. (485-hp Bristol Jupiter VIII). Sometimes referred to as the C.14, this was a project by Short Brothers (Rochester & Bedford) Ltd. to Air Ministry Specification 31/26 for a single-engine Autogiro flying boat. This design was studied by Cierva and Arthur Gouge (Short's chief designer) between late 1926 and August 1927 but was not built. The 31/26 was to have had a two-blade rotor, 52 ft 6 in (16 m) in diameter, mounted on a pylon above a metal flying boat hull, which was to be stabilized on the water by sponsons. It is not surprising that this ambitious project was not pursued. The stability and vibration problems for such a large and powerful Autogiro would almost certainly have proved insuperable at this period. After a few model tests in the seaplane tank at Rochester early in 1927, the project was abandoned. Four years later, in March 1931, Shorts were reported to be interested in a new Autogiro flying boat but nothing came of this later project either. Shorts were not to become involved with gyroplanes until 1939 when they received an order from the Air Ministry for two or three Hafner AR.IVs, which were later canceled because of the war.

Cierva C.14, C.15, and C.16. These are believed to have been projects of which no details have survived.

Cierva C.17 Mk.I. (95-hp ADC Cirrus III). Avro-built at Hamble, as their Type 612, the C.17 was intended for production for the private owner or flying club pilot. Originally projected early in 1928 with the 85 hp Cirrus II motor, it was to have sold for £900 (then equivalent to $4,400). Designed by Roy Chadwick, it incorporated the wooden wire-braced fuselage of the Avro 594 Avian IIIA light airplane and had a cable-braced paddle-type four-blade rotor, 33 ft 3¼ in (10.14 m) in diameter mounted on a tripod above the front cockpit. The C.17 carried two people and 50 lb (23 kg) of baggage at a maximum speed of 90 mph (145 km/h). The minimum speed was 28 mph (45 km/h). Only one machine, G-AABP, is believed to have been built. It was first flown by Cierva on October 23, 1928, but was found to be underpowered. The design incorporated a feature Cierva was anxious to test: the propeller's thrust line was arranged to pass through the aircraft's center of gravity. This was expected to improve longitudinal stability. (See British patent no. 330,513 of June 4, 1930). G-AABP was dismantled in December 1931 shortly before the Cierva Company left Hamble.

Cierva C.17 Mk.II (100-hp Avro Alpha). Designed late in 1928 as the Avro 620, but similar to the C.17 Mk.I except for the more powerful engine, stub wings with upturned tips and no fixed fin, the Mk.II was first flown by Cierva probably in

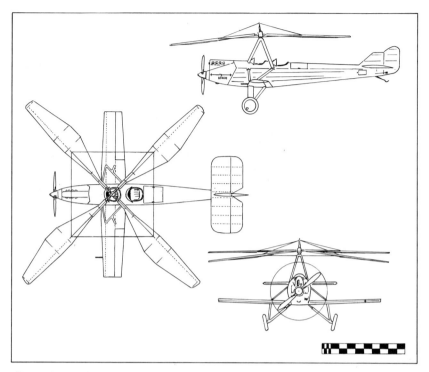

Cierva C.17 Mk.I.

April or early May 1929. Tests continued in the hands of Rawson. It was as a result of tests with upturned wing tips on the C.12 in Spain and on this aircraft that Cierva recommended this feature to Pitcairn in the spring of 1929 for incorporation on the C.8W and PCA-1. The C.17 Mk.II was found to be still underpowered. Nevertheless, four of these aircraft were laid down by Avro as a private venture late in 1928/early in 1929 (as G-AAGJ, G-AAGK, G-AAGL and G-AAHM), although probably only the first was completed as a C.17. G-AAGJ was rebuilt as a fixed-wing Avian in 1935. The Alpha radial engine was an unsuccessful attempt by Avro to enter the light aero-engine business. It did not go into full production. G-AAGK, G-AAGL and G-AAHM were later used as C.19 Mk.I registrations and G-AAHM finally became the first production C.19 Mk.IV.

Cierva C.17 Hydrogiro. (100-hp Avro Alpha). This machine is incorrectly described in some records as the C.12. The Hydrogiro was the first floatplane Autogiro to be built and seems to have been assembled at Hamble early in 1930, probably because of reported interest in Autogiros by the French navy. It may also be significant that D.R. Pye, assistant director of scientific research at the Air Ministry, pointed out the advantages of an Autogiro seaplane at Cierva's lecture to the Royal Aeronautical Society on February 13, 1930. The Hydrogiro appar-

The first seaplane Autogiro, the so-called Hydrogiro, which was reported to have borne the designation C.12 but was, in fact, a variant of the C.17.
(Author's Collection)

ently had the same Avro 594 Avian IIIA light airplane fuselage as the first C.17 Mk.II (G-AAGJ). However, the rotor pylon was changed, apparently being at first a single forward-leaning wide-chord strut. Later it reverted to a tripod over the front cockpit like the earlier C.17s. The rotor itself had four cable-braced paddle blades and was probably the same as the landplane's. The stub wings had up-turned tips like the C.17 Mk.II and again there was no fixed fin.

On April 25, 1930, Cierva himself first tested this Autogiro as a seaplane on Southampton Water, after launching from the Avro slipway on the South airfield at Hamble. It is probable he did not leave the water. It was reported that the Hydrogiro was subsequently flown by Arthur Rawson and that it took off easily and alighted well even in "rather rough water." It must, in any case, have been seriously underpowered when fitted with its twin Avian metal floats, so that it is not surprising that development of the C.17 Hydrogiro was not continued. The first seaplane Autogiro with an adequate power-to-weight ratio was probably the second XOP-1 of the United States Navy, which is believed to have made its first flight in 1932.

The French navy's interest in Autogiros crystalized in May 1930: their requirement for two Autogiro floatplanes was taken up with Avions Weymann-Lepère, the Autogiro licensees in France. Captain Georges Lepère prepared a number of design studies to meet this requirement, which he discussed with Cierva in June, and these led to the design and development of the CTW.200 (see later).

Weymann-Lepère C.18 (225-hp Wright R-760 Whirlwind J-5 and later J-6). This was a large two- to four-seat cabin Autogiro built under Cierva license in

France by the Weymann-Lepère Company to the designs of Cierva and Captain Georges Lepère. The C.18 was ordered by the Cierva Company for Loel Guinness, probably early in 1929 for entry in the Guggenheim Safe Aircraft Competition announced in Washington in April 1927, with entries being accepted from September 1, 1927. The competition was to be held in November 1929.

The designer of the C.18, Lepère, was an experienced aircraft engineer who had been responsible for a number of successful airplanes in France and the United States during and after World War I. Returning to France, he had worked until 1928 in the Schneider armaments firm, where he was involved in the development of the prototype of an all-metal stressed-skin twin-engine bomber. With the formation of the new company, Lepère was able to develop a new type of stressed-skin all-metal construction in which the skin consisted of duralumin sheets riveted together by means of edge-flanges, the sheets being stiffened by widely spaced extruded semicircular grooves. The internal wing and tail structures consisted of single-plate spars and plate ribs, while the fuselage had bulkheads built up of duralumin channels. This advanced form of construction was used for the prototypes of two airplane designs as well as for the C.18. It had similarities with the earlier Wibault system of metal construction quite widely used in the 1920s and '30s for a variety of successful French airplanes and, under license, by Vickers in England.

The C.18 was thus notable in a number of respects: its all-metal stressed-skin structure was advanced for its day; it was the first cabin Autogiro; and it had a rather ineffective monoplane deflector tail for rotor starting very similar to the first type fitted, at about the same time, to the Loring C.12 prototype in Spain. Other innovations on the C.18 were the rotor brake—one of the first on a rotary-

The French-built Weymann-Lepère C.18 in its original form. The rotor brake drum is visible below the rotor head.
(Pitcairn photograph)

wing aircraft—and the upturned wing tips, which were like those on the Spanish C.12. The landing gear incorporated Messier shock-absorbing struts.

The C.18, like the C.12, was fitted with a four-blade cable-braced rotor of similar diameter and technology to that of the C.8 (with Avro F.1017 paddle blades). Later, as we shall see, the C.18 was fitted with an American PCA-1 rotor hub and probably "planked skin" blades supplied from England (Type RB-55). Completed in June 1929, the C.18 was first flown at Villacoublay on August 12, possibly by Cierva just before his departure for his first visit to the United States. In late August or early September, the Autogiro itself was shipped to the United States, probably without its engine. This was about the same time that the first C.19 Mk.II was taken to America by Cierva and nine months after the C.8W had introduced the Autogiro to North America.

Pitcairn had intended to enter the PCA-1, the first American Autogiro, in the Guggenheim Safe Aircraft Competition. However, he realized that it would not be ready in time and decided to enter the C.18 instead.

When the C.18 arrived at the Pitcairn plant at Willow Grove, Pennsylvania, Pitcairn installed one of the new seven-cylinder R-760 geared J-6 versions of that light and efficient air-cooled radial, the American Wright Whirlwind of 225 hp, which he was also proposing to use on the PCA-1B. He fitted a cable-braced rotor with one of the new PCA-1 hubs designed and built by the Machine and Tool Designing Co. In this form and with a higher rotor pylon and other changes, the C.18 was first flown in America probably by Cierva in September 1929, some of the flights being witnessed by James Weir and Hugh Kindersley, who were on a visit to the United States. Earlier the C.18 had been given the British registration G-AAIH on June 5, 1929, but it was struck off the United Kingdom Register at the end of 1930. In spite of being flown in America and later fitted with an improved landing gear, its high vibration levels (also experienced with the PCA-1s) and poor performance meant that it was still not ready by the September 1 closing date for entries in the Guggenheim Competition.

The Autogiros would, in any case, have been at a decisive disadvantage in the competition. Under the rules, an arbitrary and, for Autogiros, irrelevant gliding angle requirement would have unfairly penalized them. The competition was held at Mitchell Field, Long Island, in November 1929 and the $100,000 prize (equivalent to about $600,000 now) was won by a specially designed conventional airplane, the Curtiss Tanager. There is no record of the ultimate fate of the C.18, although it is believed not to have flown after November 1929.

The C.18 designation was originally used for a projected small single-seat Autogiro schemed by Cierva in Spain in 1927. It was to have been powered with a 30-hp Bristol Cherub or 56-hp Siemens-Halske five-cylinder radial engine. This Autogiro was not built.

Weymann CTW.200. (One 95-hp Renault 4Pb). Georges Lepère left Avions Weymann-Lepère during 1930 and the company was thereupon renamed Établissements Aéronautiques Weymann. Before he left, Lepère launched the design of an Autogiro for the French navy, which had issued a requirement in May 1930. This was later ordered under Contract no. 921/0 of February 7, 1931,

The Weymann CTW.200 Autogiro was an open cockpit side-by-side two-seater similar in several respects to the British C.19 Mk.III. (Cierva Rotorcraft Ltd.)

modified by Amendment no. 1 of September 28, 1932. The CTW.200 or WEL.200 as it was first known, was considerably smaller than the C.18 and was, in fact, of similar weight and power to the C.19 (see Chapter 4). A side-by-side two-seater, with an open cockpit and dual control, the CTW.200 had a conventional fabric-covered welded chromemolybdomen steel tube structure similar to that of later Weymann airplanes. The cable-braced four-blade rotor was 11 m (36 ft 1 ¹⁄₁₆ in) in diameter and was mounted on a four-leg pylon. It was apparently of C.19 technology built by Avro while the wooden wings, landing gear with Bendix brakes, and deflector tail built-up of steel tubes seem to have been similar to those of the C.19 Mk.III. The CTW.200 was exhibited in mostly mocked-up form at the XII Paris Salon (November 28–December 14, 1930) and was first flown by Cierva during Easter week in 1931. It was subsequently flown on a number of occasions by Pierre Martin, the Weymann test pilot, who also flew the first production aircraft—the CTW.201 at Villacoublay in April 1931. A 95-hp Salmson A.C.7 radial was offered as alternative power plant and a cabin top over the cockpit was also an option.

It is not known whether both Autogiros ordered by the French navy were completed and delivered. It seems that at least the CTW.200 prototype and the first production aircraft, the CTW.201 no. 1 (F-ALLA), were completed and flown.

Weymann CTW.210. (One 100/145-hp Hispano-Suiza 6Pa). This was a cabin development of the CTW.200 with the gross weight increased from 640 kg (1,410 lb) to 750 kg (1,653 lb) and a more powerful engine. A Weymann brochure offered the CTW.210 as a touring Autogiro that could be alternatively fitted with the 95-hp Renault 4Pb, the 90-hp Salmson A.C.7, or the 130-hp Renault radial engine. The first CTW.210 (F-ALQX) was fitted with an engine-powered

Juan de la Cierva about to fly the first production CTW.201.
(Musée de l'Air et de l'Espace)

The CTW.210 prototype may have been the second European Autogiro to fly with an
engine-powered rotor spin-up drive.
(Musée de l'Air et de l'Espace)

rotor drive and was probably the second European Autogiro to fly with this important device, having done so less than a year after the British C.19 Mk.IV, which first flew in June 1931.

Georges Lepère maintained his interest in rotary wings after leaving Weymann. He soon joined the Lioré-et-Olivier company where he was responsible for the design of other Autogiros (see Chapter 6).

The Autogiros described in this chapter were either entirely designed and developed under Cierva's supervision at Hamble or, if built elsewhere, incorporated rotors that had been designed there. Design and construction work at Hamble was undertaken under contract to Cierva by Avros in their experimental design office and works on Hamble South airfield. This arrangement continued from the spring of 1926, when Cierva set up his base there, until the spring of 1929 when Avro moved their design and development organization back to Manchester. Thereafter, as we shall see in the next chapter, Autogiro design and development work, while continuing at the same place, became a more direct Cierva responsibility.

The rapidity with which successive Cierva types were turned out by the small team at Hamble is evidence that the design, manufacture, and test cycle for rotary-wing aircraft at this time was as short as it was for fixed-wing aircraft. This was mainly because the relatively simple designs of those days could be done on a trial-and-error basis and did not have to be right first time. Design of a particular item could be tackled in the sure knowledge that it could always be easily modified or changed later if it did not work: the designer only had to "nip down to the shops" for a quick alteration. Because of this, and because of the depth and range of experience quickly accumulated as a result, a new rotor head and transmission, for example, could be designed and manufactured in a few weeks and at correspondingly little cost. The contrast with a later era is striking.

While the design of a modern helicopter requires typically three years from start of design to first flight by a team of at least several hundred design engineers, the Autogiros of the 1920s and early '30s were designed by a handful of people in perhaps four to six months.

From early 1932 the technical and drawing offices of the Cierva Company, after they left Hamble, were located at Bush House, Aldwych, in London. They moved to Hanworth later that year. At that time the offices had a strength of about twelve people of whom seven were draftsmen. From mid-1932, a partly independent Autogiro design team was also active at Weirs in Scotland.

Cierva C.6C (Avro 574)
130-Clerget 9Bb. Rotor diameter 36 ft 1 $\frac{1}{16}$ in (11 m); rotor blade section Gö 429; overall length 34 ft 4⅛ in (10.47 m). Empty weight 1,490 lb (675 kg); maximum take-off weight 1,915–2,275 lb (868–1,031 kg). Fuel 16 Imp gal (73 liters). Maximum speed 87 mph (140 km/h); minimum speed 15 mph (24 km/h); rotor speed 140 rpm.

Cierva C.6D (Avro 575)
130-hp Clerget 9Bb. Rotor diameter 36 ft 1 $\frac{1}{16}$ in (11 m) and later 39 ft 4½ in (12 m); rotor blade section Gö 429; overall length 34 ft 4⅛ in (10.47 m). Maximum take-off weight 1,915 lb (868 kg). Fuel 16 Imp gal (73 liters). Maximum speed 87 mph (140 km/h); minimum speed 15 mph (24 km/h); rotor speed 140 rpm.

Cierva C.7 (Loring C.VII)
300-hp Hispano-Suiza Model 8Fb. Rotor diameter 12 m (39 ft 4½ in) and later 12.6m (41 ft 4 in); rotor blade section Gö 429. Empty weight about 900 kg (1,985 lb); maximum

take-off weight 1,350–1,407 kg (2,976–3,102 lb). Maximum speed: 180 km/h (112 mph); cruising speed 128 km/h (80 mph); rotor speed 120 rpm.

Cierva C.8V (Avro 586)

180/200-hp Wolseley Viper. Rotor diameter 39 ft 4½ in (12 m); rotor blade section Gö429; overall length 36 ft 3 in (11.05 m). Empty weight 2,005 lb (909 kg) or 1,994 lb (904 kg) with four-wheel landing gear; maximum take-off weight 2,768 lb (1,255 kg). Maximum speed 100 mph (160 km/h); initial climb 270 ft/min (1.37 m/sec). Rotor speed 120 rpm.

Cierva C.8R (Avro 587)

130-hp Clerget 9Bb. Rotor diameter 39 ft 4½ in (12m); rotor blade section Gö 429; overall length 34 ft 4⅛ in (10.47 m). Empty weight 1,637 lb (724 kg) or 1,676 (760 kg) with larger area three-blade rotor; maximum take-off weight 2,212 lb (1,003 kg). Fuel 16 Imp gal (73 liters). Maximum speed 107 mph (172 km/h); rotor speed 120 rpm.

Cierva C.8L-I (Avro 611)

180-hp Armstrong Siddeley Lynx. Rotor diameter 39 ft 4½ in (12 m); rotor blade section Gö 429; overall length 36 ft 1 ¹⁄₁₆ in (11 m). Empty weight 1,650 lb (748 kg); maximum take-off weight 1,980–2,535 lb (898–1,150 kg). Fuel 24 Imp gal (109 liters). Maximum speed 68–70 mph (109–113 km/h); minimum speed 25–40 mph (40-66 km/h); initial climb 110 ft/min (.55 m/sec); rotor speed 125 rpm.

Cierva C.8L-II (Avro 617)

210-hp Armstrong Siddeley Lynx IV. Rotor diameter 39 ft 4½ in–39 ft 8 in (12-12.09 m); rotor blade section Gö 429; overall length 36 ft 1 ¹⁄₁₆ in (11 m); span of fixed wing 26 ft (7.9 m). Empty weight 1,650–1,750 lb (748–793 kg); maximum take-off weight 2,380–2,470 lb. (1,080–1,120 kg). Fuel 24 Imp gal (109 liters). Maximum speed 100–106 mph (161–170 km/h); minimum speed 25 mph (40 km/h); initial climb 500–650 ft/min (2.5–3.3 m/sec); range 255 miles (410 km) at 85–91 mph (136–145 km/h); rotor speed 115–120 rpm.

Cierva C.8L-III (Avro 617)

210-hp Armstrong Siddeley Lynx IV. Rotor diameter 39 ft 4½ in (12 m); rotor blade section Gö 429; overall length 36 ft 1 ¹⁄₁₆ in (11 m); span of fixed wing 26 ft (7.9 m). Empty weight 1,750 lb (793 kg); maximum take-off weight 2,240 lb (1,016 kg). Fuel 24 Imp gal (109 liters). Maximum speed 106 mph (170 km/h); minimum speed 25 mph (40 km/h); initial climb 750 ft/min (3.8 m/sec); rotor speed 120 rpm.

Cierva C.8W (C.8 Mk.IV)

220-hp Wright Whirlwind J-5. Rotor diameter 39 ft 4½ in (12 m); rotor blade section Gö 429; overall length 36 ft 1 ¹⁄₁₆ in (11 m); span of fixed wing 26 ft (7.9 m). Empty weight 1,735 lb (787 kg) (estimated); maximum take-off weight 2,470–2,500 lb (1,120–1,134 kg). Fuel 24 Imp gal (109 liters). Maximum speed 112 mph (180 km/h); minimum speed 25 mph (40 km/h); initial climb 1,000 ft/min (5.08 m/sec); rotor speed 120 rpm. The span was 28 ft 4 in (8.63 m) after the addition of upturned tips.

Cierva C.9 (Avro 576)

(See note 9)

70-hp Armstrong Siddeley Genet I. Rotor diameter 30 ft (9.14 m); rotor blade section Gö 429; overall length 24 ft 6 in (7.46 m); span of fixed wing 16 ft (4.87 m). Empty weight 816 lb (370 kg); maximum take-off weight 1,073 lb (486 kg). No other data available.

Cierva C.10

70-hp Armstrong Siddeley Genet I. Rotor diameter 30 ft (9.14 m); rotor blade section Gö 429; fuselage length about 22 ft 8 in (6.9 m); span of fixed wing about 17 ft (5.2 m). Maximum take-off weight probably about 1,100 lb (500 kg); rotor speed 135 rpm. No other data available.

Cierva C.11

120-hp ADC Airdisco. Rotor diameter probably about 35 ft 3¼ in (10.75 m), rotor blade section probably Gö 429. No other data available.

Cierva C.12 (Loring C.XII)

225-hp Wright R-760 Whirwind J-5. Rotor diameter 12 m (39 ft 4½ in); rotor blade section Gö 429. Empty weight 840 kg (1,850 lb). Maximum take-off weight 1,135–1,161 kg (2,500–2,560 lb). Fuel 200 liters (44.5 Imp gal); rotor speed 120 rpm. No other data available.

Cierva C.17 Mk.I (Avro 612)

90-hp ADC Cirrus III. Rotor diameter 33 ft 3¼ in (10.15 m); rotor blade section Gö 429; overall length 28 ft 9 in (8.76 m). Empty weight 970–1,010 lb (440–458 kg); maximum take-off weight 1,455 lb (660 kg). Fuel 17 Imp gal (77 liters). Maximum speed 90 mph (145 km/h); minimum speed 25–29 mph (40–45 km/h); initial climb 500 ft/min (2.54 m/sec); range 210 miles (337 km) at 70 mph (112 km/h); rotor speed 130 rpm.

Cierva C.17 Mk.II (Avro 620)

100-hp Avro Alpha. Rotor diameter 33 ft 3¼ in (10.15 m); rotor blade section Gö 429; overall length 28 ft 9 in (8.76 m). Empty weight 970 lb (440 kg); maximum take-off weight 1,455 lb (660 kg). Minimum speed 25 mph (40 km/h); rotor speed 130 rpm.

Cierva C.17 Hydrogiro (Avro 620)

100-hp Avro Alpha. Rotor diameter probably 33 ft 3¼ in (10.15 m); rotor blade section probably Gö 429; overall length 28 ft 9 in (8.76 m). Maximum take-off weight 1,455 lb (660 kg). No other data available.

Weymann-Lepère C.18

225-hp Wright R-760 Whirlwind J-5 and later J-6. Rotor diameter 12.0 m (39 ft 4½ in) later 12.6 m (41 ft 4¹⁄₁₆ in)—unconfirmed, rotor blade section Gö 429. No other data available.

Weymann CTW.200 and CTW.201

95-hp Renault 4Pb. Rotor diameter 11 m (36 ft 1 ¹⁄₁₆ in); rotor blade section Gö 429; length 5.5 m (18 ft 0 ½ in); span of fixed wing 6.5 m (21 ft 4 in). Empty weight 430–450 kg (948–

992 lb); maximum take-off weight 636-650 kg (1,402–1,433 lb). Fuel 48 liters (10.7 Imp gal). Maximum speed 150 km/h (93 mph); minimum speed 30 km/h (19 mph); absolute ceiling 2,800 m (9,185 ft); range 400 km (248 miles) at 125 km/h (77 mph).

Weymann CTW.210

100/145-hp Hispano-Suiza 6Pa. Rotor diameter 11 m (36 ft 1 1⁄16 in); rotor blade section Gö 429; length 5.5 m (18 ft 0 ½ in); span of fixed wing 6.8 (22 ft 3¾ in). Empty weight 570 kg (1,257 lb); maximum take-off weight 750 kg (1,653 lb). No other data available.

Chapter 4

Production Autogiros

The C.17, described in the previous chapter, seems to have been the first Autogiro developed specifically with the intention of quantity production. In the event, it proved unsatisfactory and only prototypes were completed.

A keen private airplane pilot, James Weir visualized in 1928 a small, low-powered Autogiro as a means of personal transport, from, say, his home to his office in Glasgow, a distance of less than forty miles. He persuaded the Cierva board that such an aircraft had a significant potential market now that private flying was increasing rapidly in the United Kingdom following formation in 1925 of the first government-subsidised flying clubs. The C.19 was accordingly designed with this objective—to be sufficiently inexpensive to buy, and economic and straight-forward enough to operate for the private owner and flying club pilot.

Cierva C.19 Mk.1. (80-hp Armstrong Siddeley Genet II). Designed to meet the above specification, the C.19 became the first successful production Autogiro. However, it did not achieve this status immediately. A bulky box deflector tail, based on experience gained with the larger experimental Spanish C.12 and French C.18, for the first time provided a method of rotor starting that was reasonably practical except when there was little or no wind. However, it also contributed excessive weight and drag to which such a small, low-powered aircraft was particularly sensitive. Cierva had probably foreseen the difficulty but hoped that it would be offset by the fact that the C.19 was not adapted (as most of its predecessors had been) from an existing design of airplane but was designed from the start as an Autogiro. In the event, as originally conceived, the C.19 proved to be seriously underpowered, particularly as the empty weight came out to about 60 lb (27 kg) heavier than the original 750 lb (340 kg) estimate. Only in developed form with the large Genet Major engine were its deficiencies sufficiently overcome for it to become the first widely used Autogiro. However, despite its deficiencies, the C.19 Mk.I was judged "pleasant to fly and easy to handle" by the RAE pilots who tested it for its Certificate of Airworthiness (C of A).

The C.19's were built to Cierva's order in the old Avro works at Hamble, work starting on them there during the first half of 1929. The Avro company's design office, under Roy Chadwick, with Jim Turner as chief draftsman and Harold Rogerson as chief technician, moved from Hamble to Newton Heath,

The first Cierva C.19 Mk.I (G-AAGK) being inspected by HRH the Prince of Wales, later King Edward VIII, at Hamble.
(H.W. Denny)

Manchester, in June, 1929. This followed the Avro company's takeover in May 1928 from Crossley Motors, their principal shareholders (apparently for £270,000, about $8.0 million today) by the Armstrong Siddeley Development Company Ltd. In July 1935, the latter was to become part of Hawker Siddeley Aircraft Co. Ltd., and later of the Hawker Siddeley Group. However, some of the Avro design staff remained behind after the move and from May 20, 1929 were contracted by Avro to the Cierva Company.

The new Autogiro design office team of about twelve people was headed by Charles Saunders with Reg Calvert, who had been in charge of Avro's Autogiro work under Chadwick, as chief designer, and Henry Dyer as chief draftsman. The works and experimental shop at Hamble, still managed by Avro, continued to manufacture Autogiros while development work continued there under Cierva's personal direction until he finally moved out of Hamble in May 1932. Because Avro retained control of the shops at Hamble until 1932, all C.19's except the last (the Mk.V prototype) were given Avro construction numbers. First flown in April 1929, the C.17 Mk.II was, however, the last Hamble Autogiro design to be given an Avro type number (Avro 620). Starting with the C.19 Mk.I, design became the responsibility of the Cierva technical office at Hamble.

The C.19 Mk.I was a two-seat aircraft with fixed rotor spindle, conventional airplane controls and strut-braced stub wings with upturned tips to unload the cable-braced 30 ft (9.14 m) four-blade rotor in flight. The rotor blades (of Avro

RB-53 type) were still of Gö 429 profile but introduced a new form of construction. They had "planked skins" consisting of two thicknesses of mahogany planking at 90 degrees to each other for each blade surface. This type of blade had been first tried on the C.17 Mk.II. The new Autogiro's loaded weight was 1,300 lb (590 kg) and its top speed 85 mph (137 km/h). The third C.19, G-AAHM, was exhibited at the VII International Aero Exhibition at Olympia between July 16 and 27, 1929, eight weeks after the start of the design. It was shown there with a long-chord NACA engine cowling, but this was later removed after flight trials by Cierva during July when the first aircraft had shown that the engine tended to overheat. The first C.19 was awarded a British Certificate of Airworthiness without the engine cowling on August 2.

Three machines of the C.19 Mk.I type were laid down at Hamble—G-AAGK, G-AAGL and G-AAHM—but only the first two gained Certificates of Airworthiness as Mk.Is. These machines had Bendix brakes that were needed to hold the aircraft stationary on the ground while the rotor was started and brought up to speed. The deflector tail on the C.19 brought the rotor up to a speed of between 100 and 130 rpm in about forty-five seconds. Thereafter, particularly if there was no wind, taxying was needed to reach the full flying 150 rpm, requiring a run of at least a hundred feet (30 m).

Being designed from scratch as an Autogiro, The C.19 had a shorter and lighter fuselage than previous designs. It was built of welded steel tubes faired with wood stringers to give a rounded shape. It was hoped that this would help to give a better performance on 80 hp than was, in fact, achieved. A decision was therefore taken to re-engine the Mk.I with the 105-hp Genet Major I five-cylinder engine, thus creating the C.19 Mk.II. However, despite this change, which gave some improvement, the C.19s continued to be underpowered and overweight.

Cierva C.19 Mk.II. (105-hp Armstrong Siddeley Genet Major I). With a more powerful engine, the Mk.II had its loaded weight increased to 1,400 lb (635 kg) and the maximum speed rose to 95 mph (153 km/h). Three of these machines were built (G-AAKY, G-AAKZ and G-AALA), the first, G-AAKY, being taken to the United States by Cierva on the *Majestic* shortly after it was completed on August 3, 1929, less than two weeks after the Mk.I had gained its Certificate of Airworthiness. On arrival in America, the new Autogiro was assembled at Pitcairn's works at Willow Grove and flown by Cierva on August 20. Cierva demonstrated it before a crowd of about 500 on August 22. G-AAKY thus became the first Autogiro to be publicly demonstrated on the other side of the Atlantic, previous demonstrations by the C.8W having been to selected audiences. Cierva then showed off the C.19's capabilities before a daily crowd of about 100,000 spectators at the 1929 National Air Races meeting at Cleveland, Ohio, held between August 24 and September 2. While in Cleveland, he read papers to the Society of Automotive Engineers and the American Society of Mechanical Engineers.

Cierva was on a three-month's first visit to the United States at this time, (August to November 1929). During his stay, with the technical assistance of Paul H. Stanley of Pitcairns, he put into final form the first edition of his "Engineering

C.19 Mk.II landing and showing why the bottom of the fins were cut away on later models of the C.19.
(Courtesy H-Ros.)

Theory of the Autogiro," which covered the theoretical aspects of gyroplane performance. At this time, his calculations were in two distinct parts, one covering low incidence, high speed flight and the other high incidence, low speed flight and vertical descent. Although the results of the two sets of calculations could be joined by smooth curves there was, in fact, a small gap in the theory between the two conditions. Practical verification of Cierva's theory was very close.

Cierva later (1934–35) wrote another standard text, "Theory of Stresses in Autogiro Rotor Blades." Although neither of these works was published, both were widely read by rotary-wing aircraft designers and had a considerable influence on future development. Nevertheless, some other experimenters in the rotary-wing field undoubtedly felt that Cierva should have made his results more widely available than he did. No doubt he was secretive for perfectly legitimate commercial reasons. Ahead of all others, he naturally wanted to keep the benefits of his work primarily for his own company and its licensees. As we shall see later (Chapter 10), at least the Russians and probably others were trying hard to copy his designs without permission.

As a result of the British Air Ministry's sponsorship of Autogiro development, the Royal Aircraft Establishment also undertook numerous investigations into the Autogiro's characteristics. This work was notably done by H. Glauert, C.N.H. Lock, J.A. Beavan, P.A. Tufton, J.B.B. Owen, and a number of others, their findings being fully written-up in official RAE and Aeronautical Research Committee R & M reports. On January 20, 1927, Glauert also read an important paper before the Royal Aeronautical Society on the theory of the gyroplane. Despite the fact that this paper correctly defined the mechanism, performance, and fundamental limitations of rotors with flapping blades, Cierva publicly took strong exception to almost every point Glauert made. He rather unfortunately gave the impression that he resented other investigators in the field he had made his own. This attitude, in its turn, probably contributed to the antagonism toward the Autogiro which seems to have existed in certain official circles and in at least part of the British technical press—specifically in *The Aeroplane*, under its controversial and astringent editor, the formidable C.G. Grey.

The second C.19 Mk.II (G-AAKZ) gained a British Certificate of Airworthiness on September 26, 1929. Rawson demonstrated it before the French authorities at Le Bourget on October 8. The third Mk.II (G-AALA), piloted by James Weir, was demonstrated at Hanworth and several other United Kingdom airfields early in January 1930. Piloted by Rawson, it carried the British director of civil aviation, Sir Sefton Brancker, on his first flight in an Autogiro at Heston on January 7. Brancker was characteristically enthusiastic, having long been a strong supporter of the Autogiro. In the following month, on February 13, Cierva read his second paper before the Royal Aeronautical Society. This time, instead of Brancker doing it for him, Cierva was able to read his paper in English himself. In it, he recorded progress made in the development of the Autogiro since his first lecture in October 1925. Summing up the stage reached, Cierva said that the Autogiro was 5 to 10 percent slower than an equivalent airplane; rate of climb, 20 percent less; angle of climb, 50 percent greater; and minimum horizontal speed, 50 percent less. He claimed that, with proper handling, the Autogiro could be landed without forward run, even in still air. At an angle of descent of 45 degrees, the vertical speed of the latest Autogiros was no more than 12 to 13 feet per second (3.66 to 3.96 m/s).

The C.19 Mk.II's, G-AAKZ and G-AALA, were used as development and demonstration aircraft. G-AAKZ was sent to France in spring 1930 where it was used by Avions Weymann-Lepère for several demonstrations, including one to the French Air Ministry on April 28 and another, piloted by the Weymann test pilot Pierre Martin, at an air show at Orly on May 18. A month later Martin had an accident during a demonstration to the French naval authorities who had placed an order with Weymann-Lepère for two Autogiros in May. This led to the design and construction of the CTW.200 (see Chapter 3). G-AAKZ was returned to Hamble for repair.

The C.19 Mk.II, G-AALA, was lent to the Air Ministry during March–April 1930, being flown by Rawson to RAE from Hamble on March 13. While at Farnborough, G-AALA was tested for a total of about 18½ hours during seventeen flights by two pilots—Flight Lieutenants Rogenhagen and Maitland. They found that the deflector tail would spin-up the rotor to about 50 percent of normal rpm, requiring a take-off run of 600 ft (183 m) in an 8 mph (13 km/h) wind. The landing distance in this wind was about 60 ft (18 m). The speed range was 31 to 82 mph (50 to 132 km/h) and the rate of climb 540 ft/min (2.74 m/s).

Cierva with the C.19 Mk.IIA in Spain.
(Ministerio del Aire photograph, courtesy H-Ros.)

Cierva C.19 Mk.IIA. (105-hp Armstrong Siddeley Genet Major I). This was an interim development of the C.19 Mk.II pending the appearance of the Mk.III production version. It had increased tankage, longer travel landing gear, and rotor-hub modifications. The sole example, G-AAUA, appeared in January 1930 and was demonstrated by Rawson at Hamble in May by which time it had been fitted with a larger 35 ft (7.6 m) cable-braced rotor with four blades of a new form of construction but still of Gö 429 profile. Instead of the "planked skin" blades used on previous C.19s, Cierva now employed a single tubular spar with wooden ribs at approximately a 3-inch spacing. The leading edge was covered with thin plywood but the rest of the covering was fabric. The inter-blade cables incorporated friction dampers instead of the elastic cord used previously. This type of blade was to remain standard for a couple of years. The larger rotor (it was of 16 percent greater diameter) reduced the disc loading and considerably improved performance—particularly at the lower end of the speed range.

Also during May, Rawson flew G-AAUA to Glasgow where a number of demonstrations were given before returning to Hamble early in June. On June 28, 1930 the C.19 Mk.IIA took part in the Eleventh RAF Display at Hendon flying alongside the Handley Page Gugnunc, slotted and flapped biplane, and the tailless Westland-Hill Pterodactyl. G-AAUA gained a C of A on August 1, 1930, and, departing from Croydon on August 8, was taken by Cierva on a tour of France and Spain in August and September 1930. During some 200 hours of flying, with demonstrations at almost every stop, Cierva made over 300 landings and visited many places in his homeland. He convincingly demonstrated that, expertly handled, the latest version of his invention was a practical flying machine. He made one landing, to refuel, in a small field in high mountains and another, on a fairway of Santander Golf Course, measuring only 150 ft (45 m) in length. In neither case was any difficulty experienced in taking the machine off again: a quite impossible feat for any conventional airplane. This C.19 was claimed to have a speed range of 25 to 95 mph (40 to 153 km/h) and to be therefore only slightly slower than equivalent contemporary airplanes. As a result of the tour, Cierva took the first steps toward the establishment of a Spanish Autogiro Company. Unfortunately, nothing was to come of this for political reasons following the ending of the Spanish Monarchy in 1931. Cierva was awarded the Medalla de Oro del Trabajo by the Spanish government in 1930.

G-AAUA was sold to the Campania Española de Aviación in March 1931 but was damaged in an accident soon afterward and shipped to the United Kingdom on May 22.

Cierva C.19 Mk.III. (105-hp Armstrong Siddeley Genet Major II). This was really the definitive version of the Mks. II and IIA and thus the first true production Autogiro. It differed principally from the earlier models in that it had the new enlarged 35 ft (7.6 m) four-blade cable-braced rotor, first tried on the Mk.IIA, and was fitted with a rotor brake. Nine Mk.III's were built at Hamble,[11] plus one aircraft (G-AALA) converted from a Mk.II. The first Mk.III, destined for Pitcairn, was flown by Cierva in the first half of July 1930. The second gained its C of A on September 10.

In August 1930, the first Mk.III went to the United States, where it was demonstrated alongside the prototype Pitcairn PCA-2 and the experimental PCA-1B at the 1930 National Air Races in Chicago held between August 23 and September 1. In the United States, G-AAYN became X3Y. Another of the type (G-AAYP) was flown by Rawson on a trip to Germany in September. The following year, in the summer of 1931, Rawson made another tour of Germany and Switzerland in a C.19 Mk.III (G-ABGB) giving demonstrations. During this visit much of the flying was undertaken by the Junkers test pilot, Fritz Loose. On neither of these expeditions was any serious difficulty experienced with the aircraft—both were satisfactory in terms of reliability and economy of operation.

From April to October, 1931, the C.19 Mk.III (G-AALA), flown by Reginald A.C. Brie, toured the United Kingdom with C.D. Barnard's Air Display on the "Daily Mail" Air Tour. (Brie had joined Cierva originally on a temporary basis as a demonstration pilot in November 1930. A tireless worker, he accumulated more than 400 hours of flying on Autogiros during the first nine months of 1931.) During the tour, he visited 108 towns and flew through every sort of weather. On some occasions, the Autogiro was able to demonstrate when conventional airplanes were grounded. About 20,000 mi (32,000 km) were covered, 528 separate demonstrations given, and 245 passengers carried. The same Mk.III G-AALA was fitted experimentally with one of Cierva's 34 ft (10.36 m) three-blade cantilever rotors, which did away with all external bracing of the blades. (See later under C.19 Mk.IV prototype).

Another Mk.III (G-AAYP) was the first Autogiro to compete successfully in a race when it won second place at 93 mph (150 km/h), piloted by Reginald Brie, in the Skegness Air Race on May 14, 1932. Two Mk.III's (K1696 and K1948) were supplied to the Air Ministry. They had previously been G-AAYO and G-ABCM. The latter, delivered from Hamble on January 5, 1930, was used at least until the end of that year for experimental purposes at RAE, Farnborough.

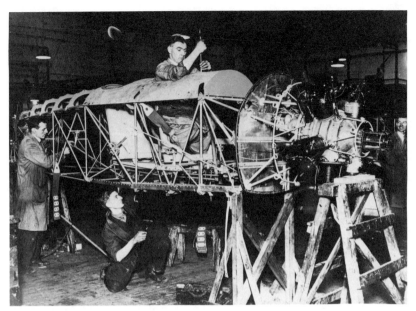

C.19 Mk.III *fuselage assembly at Hamble.*
(H.W. Denny)

Final assembly of C.19 Mk.III G-ABCM at Hamble.
(H.W. Denny)

C.19 Mk.III K1948 at RAE Farnborough.
(Crown copyright photograph, courtesy RAE)

K1696 appeared in a flying display at Croydon on October 24 and 25, 1930, and K1948 at the Thirteenth RAF Display on June 25, 1932. One Mk.III (G-ABCK) went to New Zealand where it was registered ZK-ACL, its owners being Garland and Grant Ltd. of Wellington. It crashed in May 1931 at Oamaru and the wreck was returned to the United Kingdom. On March 4, 1931, Rawson and Brie demonstrated a C.19 Mk.III at Heston before representatives of the Admiralty's Air Division.

H.M. Schofield in his book *High Speed and Other Flights* gives some revealing impressions of flying a C.19 Mk.III in 1931.

"My first commission was to fetch an Autogiro from the base at Hamble ready for a display at Leicester the next day. — It was a boisterous day, and I felt a trifle strange as we taxied out across the tiny aerodrome beside the sea. — Well away from the hangars we turned gently around and stood half out of the wind to start the 'revving-up' procedure before take-off. I say gently advisedly, for taxying an Autogiro is no small part of the art. Due to the huge disc area of the rotors utmost consideration must be given to the wind until sufficient rotor speed has been gained and centrifugal force is induced in large quantities by fast 'revving'. When turning slowly there is a risk that the wind will sling the blades up and away and thus particularly finish off the machine; for in their oscillating departure they are apt to carve chunks out of all parts of the outfit and the pilot concerned would be well advised to duck inside and wait until silence betokens the cessation of hostilities. How terrible it all seems, but a little experience is enough to safe-guard against the terror and it does not happen often nowadays.

"Ready to get off, I locked the lever which turns the tailplane and elevators upwards and thus diverts the stream of air from the propeller up to the rotors and starts them rotating, pushed the wheels brakes hard on with my feet, and gently opened the throttle. The rotors slowly responded, at first turning laboriously, but gradually speeding up until their indicator showed that they were doing a nice eighty revs a minute.

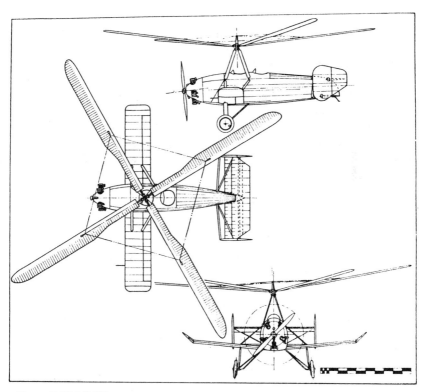

Cierva C.19 Mk.III.

"The throttle was now full open, so releasing the tailplane and elevators which fell back into their normal position, and still keeping her straight with the brakes, for the rudder is ineffective at the slow take-off speed, we ran along half a dozen yards, turning into wind at the same time, shifted feet from brakes to rudder as she left the ground, and we were on our way. —

"Our landing was not one of the best. A high wind had sprung up at Heston, and the gusts near the ground gave me plenty to think about. The initial effort resulted in a tremendous uplifting just as we touched, we suddenly found ourselves at about sixty feet with no forward speed at all, and the upturned faces of the crew that had been sent to catch us and bring us in, in anticipation of our trouble, made an amusing picture with their mouths and eyes wide open in amazement.

"I gave her a burst of engine as we went down on the lift, but just as the landing party put out their hands to catch us, the performance started all over again, up we went a second time.

"By this time, we were getting perilously near the hangars, but it was very apparent that only by utilizing the screen provided by the aforesaid hangars would we ever be able to park ourselves, so I kept straight on, and fortunately my guess was a lucky one; we sat down right on the tarmac and, heading straight for the hangar doors, came to rest with a hymn of praise in our hearts.

"For several weeks I took the windmill all over the country, and nothing untoward transpired until the occasion of a trip to Nottingham for a display.

"I had learned all about a curious characteristic which occurred towards top speed. The rotor revolutions decrease as forward speed increases until a state may be reached where with a high speed, the supporting revolutions are insufficient to keep the machine up, and she loses height. I believe the trouble has been overcome in later models, and it was never a critical state of affairs in itself, but could be awkward if suddenly induced by a bump or some atmospheric disturbance.

"I had revved up for a few seconds to see that the engine was still in form, when we stuck a colossal bump, and in a twinkling the bus turned herself into a Nautch dancer. Rotors waved themselves like a bunch of angry snakes, a horrible shuddering shook us to such an extent that the whole world appeared to be shimmying, and we fell like a brick out of the sky.

"I closed the throttle and pulled back the stick, and the phenomenon died as rapidly as it had started, but it left something to think about."

An RAE handling report on K1696 (one of the RAF Mk.IIIs) stated that this Autogiro handled normally at speeds above 45 mph (72 km/h). Lateral control was normal and effective and longitudinal control "very sensitive" but not difficult. Below 45 mph (72 km/h), the aircraft was "very stable" but lateral and longitudinal control remained fair down to 35 mph (56 km/h). Below 27 mph (43 km/h) on the ASI, the aircraft yawed slowly to starboard on a level keel and could not be stopped with rudder or ailerons. Landing was not difficult in normal conditions. It was another matter in strong or gusty winds. The deflector tail enabled the rotor to be spun up to about 70 percent of normal speed, requiring a take-off run of about 270 ft (82 m)—a significant improvement over the C.19 Mk.II.

However, Pitcairn was critical of the rotor spin-up arrangements on the C.19 Mk.III. The Americans found that, in still air, the deflector tail would give only about 60 rpm so that a relatively long take-off run was still required. Clearly, the engine-powered drive on the PCA-2 was much more satisfactory (see Chapter 5).

From a commercial point of view, production of the C.19 Mk.III apparently covered its costs. The average cost for these aircraft was reported as £1,200, while they were sold for £1,250. However, the market proved limited and, as a practical vehicle, the C.19 Mk.III clearly still had limitations.

Cierva C.19 Mk.IV prototype. (105-hp Armstrong Siddeley Genet Major I). Cierva visited the United States again in November/December 1930. One development there obviously represented an important step forward. This was the light (48 lb, 22 kg) and effective clutch and engine drive for rotor starting designed by A.E. Larsen of Pitcairn's with the assistance of Heraclio Alfaro and Jean Nicol of the Machine and Tool Designing Company. This drive was fitted initially to the Pitcairn PCA-2 prototype first flown in March 1930 (see Chapter 5). It was a far more effective development than the slipstream-deflecting stabilizer and elevators introduced in Europe the previous year and Cierva realized that it would have to be adopted for the next British version of the Autogiro.

The C.19 Mk.IV prototype at Hamble. Juan de la Cierva is seen standing behind the dorsal fin which was enlarged in production aircraft.
(Author's Collection)

While he was in the United States, Cierva had also been analyzing Autogiro rotor performance and had satisfied himself about the considerable potential increase in efficiency that would result if the parasite drag of blade suspension and inter-blade bracing cables and friction damper arms could be eliminated. Tests were conducted at Willow Grove on a C.19 in which damping was by means of felt blocks at the wing roots. Inter-blade cables were eliminated. Short flights were made with both four-blade and two-blade rotors with this arrangement.

Cierva returned to Europe in December 1930 and first went to Paris to take part in the First Congress on Air Safety (December 10–23) at which G-AAYP was demonstrated, having been brought over from England by Reginald Brie. Cierva went to Spain in late December and stayed until March 1931. During this period, he devoted much thought to the development of his rotor theory. This led him to the adoption of a cantilever rotor (that is one without external bracing cables) of lower solidity (ratio of blade area to disc area) with three blades of RAF 34 section to replace the four-blade configuration and symmetrical Gö 429 section on which he had standardized since the C.6. Before leaving Madrid, he gave a lantern slide lecture to the Spanish Royal Aero Club illustrating the history of the development of the Autogiro.

On his return to England in March 1931, Cierva launched a vigorous development program on a new rotor. He proposed to use it on the C.24, a new cabin Autogiro being designed in association with the de Havilland Aircraft Company (see Chapter 6). The new rotor was first tried on the C.19 Mk.III, G-AALA, and later on G-AAHM, which became the Mk.IV prototype.

This prototype had originally been laid down as a C.17 Mk.II and was then converted into the first C.19 Mk.I. It was not awarded a C of A in this form but was employed as a Cierva Company development aircraft. When first flown at

Hamble in Mk.IV form in June 1931, it was fitted with the new 34 ft (10.36 m) three-blade cantilever folding rotor and a monoplane tail unit. The latter was neater and lighter than the complicated box structure of previous C.19s. At first, G-AAHM had a vertical tail surface of rather smaller dimensions than later production aircraft but it was supplemented by side fins. These were later removed and a larger vertical tail became standard. A number of other modifications were progressively incorporated in G-AAHM. These included the engine-powered rotor spin-up drive designed by F.L. Hodgess and manufactured in collaboration with Mollart Engineering Co. Ltd. and Armstrong Siddeley.

The three blades of the revolutionary new cantilever rotor, like those of the previous cable-braced type, were manufactured at Hamble using techniques developed by Avros. They had tubular steel spars at about quarter chord. Initially, light spruce ribs were bolted to the spar by steel clips ("scrivets"). There was an ash leading edge member and a much lighter spruce strip at the trailing edge. The blades were fabric covered. By late 1931, however, Cierva had decided on a new structural design of blade for the C.19 Mk.IV. It consisted essentially of a solid balsa wood fairing to the tubular spar with a spruce core, the whole assembly being covered with fabric. This type of blade remained in use until the introduction of the C.30 direct control Autogiro which reverted to built-up blades with spruce ribs and plywood covering.

The engine-powered spin-up drive would accelerate the rotor to flying speed (180 rpm) in 30 seconds and the take-off run was reduced to about 90 feet (27 m). The angle of climb was 8 degrees. The Mk.IV would descend at an angle of 40 degrees at a vertical speed of 13 ft/sec (3.96 m/s).

On November 19, 1931, soon after the rotor spin-up drive had been installed, the Mk.IV prototype was publicly demonstrated by Cierva, alongside the new cabin C.24 Autogiro. This took place at Hanworth, where the Cierva Company was soon to set up its headquarters. The C.19 Mk.IV gained a Certificate of Airworthiness on March 22, 1932. G-AAHM was finally wrecked while attempting to take-off from the White City Stadium in London on September 29, 1932. Reginald Brie had previously made a demonstration landing in the stadium at the instigation of General Critchley of the Greyhound Racing Association.

Experimental flying, including that on the direct control C.19 Mk.V, continued at Hamble until mid-1932. Reginald Blake, the company's secretary, became general manager at this time, and G.B. Ellis, chief designer. Colonel Josselyn ceased to be managing director in 1933, although continuing as a member of the board of directors.

Cierva C.19 Mk.IVP. (105-hp Armstrong Siddeley Genet Major I). The Mk.IVP designation probably covered three preproduction aircraft of the new type converted from Mk.IIIs at Hamble in 1932—G-ABFZ, G-ABGA, and G-ABGB—although some records suggested it was used for the first nine Mk.IVs and, according to another authority, for all production Mk.IVs. All these Autogiros, like the prototype, had the rotor-starting clutch and drive, new folding three-blade cantilever rotor, and monoplane tail unit. Maximum speed was 102 mph (164 km/h) and cruising speed 95 mph (153 km/h). Rate of descent at minimum forward speed was about 13 ft/sec (3.96 m/s) which the landing gear was designed to absorb. The take-off run was about 150 ft (45 m) while no ground roll was required in landing.

G-ABFZ was used for an attempted flight from London to Cape Town in 1932. J.N. Young left Hanworth on April 25 and reached Tunis in North Africa on May 19. He abandoned the flight on May 23, a hundred miles west of Cairo, at Mersa Matru, after a heavy landing on one wheel. This aircraft and another C.19 Mk.IVP (G-ABGB) were later used by Sir Alan Cobham's National Aviation Day Displays in the United Kingdom and in South Africa.

Cierva C.19 Mk.IV. (105-hp Armstrong Siddeley Genet Major I). This was the ultimate production version of the C.19 which had all the features already incorporated in the Mk.IVP. One Mk.IV (G-AAYP) was converted from a C.19 Mk.III and thirteen[12] were built from scratch at Hamble to the new standard. The first production C.19 Mk.IV (G-ABUC) was ferried from Hamble to Hanworth by Cierva on May 25, 1932.

The French Lioré-et-Olivier and the German Focke-Wulf companies acquired licenses to build the C.19 Mk.IV. The Germans may have built only one of these aircraft (see below), while the French are believed to have not made any use of their license. In August 1932 three Mk.IVs went to Japan. Two were purchased through Okura and Company for the Japanese navy and a third for the Asahi Shimbun newspaper. Another (G-ABUD) was hired by London's Metropolitan Police and flown by their own pilot, Flight Lieutenant R.E.H. Allen, who learned to fly Autogiros for that purpose. This aircraft was used in May and June 1932 for experiments in observing and directing road traffic from the air. On Derby Day (June 1), it was used to control traffic before and after the racing. Later in June, Brie flew G-ABUD to Denmark for a sales demonstration.

It was reported that more than 70 different pilots flew the C.19 Mk.IV solo, including 6 who were not fixed-wing pilots and 6 women. The maneuverability of the C.19 Mk.IV was convincingly demonstrated by Reginald Brie in a "dog fight" with Chris Clarkson in a Moth at the Household Brigade Flying Club meeting at Heston on May 18, 1932.

One C.19 Mk.IV (G-ABXG) was sold for £1,050 to J.A. McMullen who had been the Autogiro School's first pupil. Others went to Singapore, Germany, Sweden, Australia, Japan, and Spain.

In an informal discussion with representatives of the British Air Ministry in August 1932, Brie stated that the cost of the C.19 Mk.IV prototype had been of the order of £15/20,000 and £5,000 for, presumably, the first production aircraft. In today's values, these costs were equivalent to about $330/440,000 and $110,000 respectively. C.19 Mk.IVs were being sold at a price of £1,085–£1100 at this time which suggests that a production run of several hundred was anticipated.

In May 1932, an Autogiro flying school was started by the Cierva Company at Hanworth under the management of Reginald Brie. Equipped initially with a C.19 Mk.IV, G-ABUD, and later with a second aircraft, G-ABUF, the school, with H.A. Marsh as chief flying instructor, trained large numbers of Autogiro

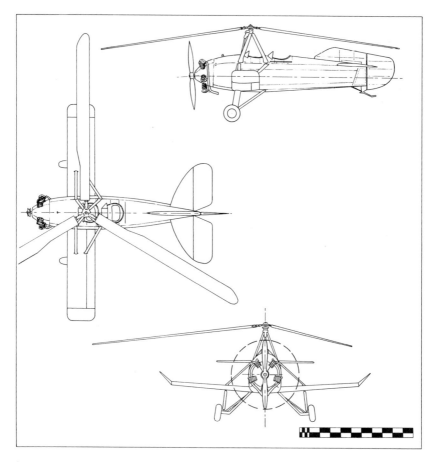

Cierva C.19 Mk.IV.

pilots in the years that followed. (Previously with the Hampshire Aeroplane Club as an instructor, Alan Marsh had met Cierva at Hamble and had taught him to fly. He joined the Cierva Company as assistant to Brie on April 5, 1932, and served the company faithfully for 18 years, becoming probably the world's most experienced rotary-wing test pilot by the time of his death in the crash of the large Cierva Air Horse helicopter on June 13, 1950. By then, 4,000 of his total of 6,400 hours as pilot had been on rotary wings.)

The first pupil at the Autogiro school was J.A. McMullen, aged sixty-eight. Dual instruction was given for £3 (then equivalent to about $10.50) per hour, which was about double the cost on a light airplane. The school had a standing offer at this time to train qualified airplane pilots to fly the Autogiro and to give them one hour's solo flying on it—all for five pounds ($17.50). Six men and five women (including Mrs. J.G. Weir, the first woman to get an Autogiro endorsement on her current "A" license) had gone solo by the end of 1932. By September

Alan Marsh and Reginald Brie in front of an Autogiro school C.19 Mk.IV at Hanworth. Low-pressure tires are fitted.
(W/Cdr. R.A.C. Brie)

1934, the school was flying about 200 hours per month. It had re-equipped with C.30A direct-control Autogiros in June of that year. By the end of 1935, it had trained no less than 298 pilots, 37 of the ab initio on the Autogiro. Thereafter it became less busy and finally closed down on the outbreak of war in 1939. By then, 9,330 hours had been flown and 368 people had been trained on the Autogiro, including about 90 without previous flying experience.

The first pilot to obtain a British commercial pilot's license (the "B" license) ab initio on Autogiros was Jack Richardson. He did this on the C.19 Mk.IV and later had his license endorsed to include C.30's. Max Stoker was the first to obtain a "B" license ab initio on the C.30.

Adoption of Hanworth as the center of Cierva's activities led to this attractive London airfield, with its then rural setting and country house atmosphere, becoming the spiritual home of practical rotary-wing flight. There, up to World. War II, a band of enthusiasts, with all the zeal of early Christians, practiced the cult and championed the cause of the Autogiro. T.H. White put it well in his delightful book *England Have My Bones.*

Writing in thinly veiled terms of a flight in February 1935, with Alan Marsh in a C.30 at Hanworth, White recorded: "We went over to Handley today, to see the Autogiros, and I was given a flight in one: the pilot being Sedge. There is an urge about these tree-pipit machines which must captivate any moderately sensi-

A *Cierva C.19 Mk.IV flying over the Thames near Hanworth.*
(Charles E. Brown)

tive person. Mouse said to me, as we walked to the hangars: 'For God's sake don't say anything against Autogiros. They are all unbalanced about them.' And so they were, but in an infectious way. It is the urge of the pioneer. I have sometimes reproached myself for not being on the surface of the globe in time to come in with the lunacies of Blériot and Grahame White. Here was something remotely comparable; although I was too late to catch the bus, even here. They were people with a mission, people believing in things, touchy and enthusiastic to the last degree. It was a heart movement of the first magnitude when I said to Sedge in the air: 'What happens if you contrive to turn it upside down?' and he answered 'Nobody knows.'[13] If I learned to fly an Autogiro next summer, would they let me go with a parachute and try? There was another thing which gave me a proud feeling, Cierva had hawked his invention all over the continent before the British offered him finance. However much we may have been behind the world, however much we may have been apathetic and unpoetical at the birth of aviation, we have snapped into it with this at any rate. The race has its streak of lunacy, its itch for the still-vexed Bermoothes."

Focke-Wulf C.19. (110-hp Siemens Sh 14). Early in 1931, the German Professor Heinrich K.J. Focke established a special section to study rotary-wing aircraft in the design office of his company, the Focke-Wulf Flugzeugbau A.G. of Bremen. A license to build the Cierva C.19 Mk.IV was also acquired toward the end of the same year and a larger Autogiro of similar technology was designed but not built. Thereafter Focke, who was technical director of the company, concentrated on rotary-wing developments. Kurt Tank (who later became famous as the designer of the enormously successful Fw 190 fighter of World War II) joined the

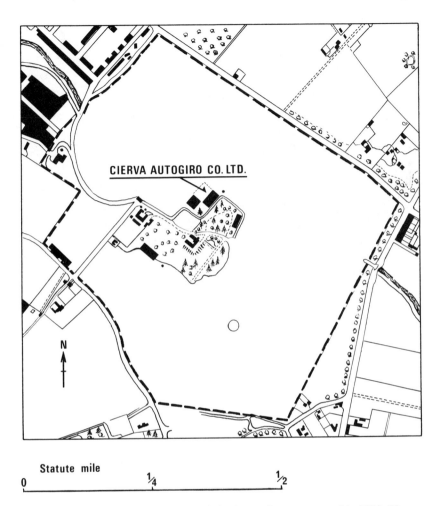

Hanworth airfield near London to which the Cierva Company moved in 1931–32.

company to look after fixed-wing design in November 1931. In the latter part of 1933, after a disagreement in the board of directors, Focke left Focke-Wulf to found a new company to specialize in the development of rotary-wing aircraft. This was the Focke-Achgelis G.m.b.H. at Hoyenkamp bei Delmenhorst near Bremen. Tank then succeeded Focke as technical director of Focke-Wulf, although the latter continued as an ordinary director of his old company.

Late in 1931, the French Lioré-et-Olivier company also acquired a license to manufacture the C.19 Mk.IV but this was not taken up. Although it has been reported that the French C.19 Mk.IV was to be designated C.21, this seems unlikely.

German-built Focke-Wulf C.19 with Siemens engine.
(O. Reder)

The C.19 license agreement with Focke-Wulf was signed by Cierva Autogiro G.m.b.H. in December 1931. The German Cierva Company had been formed by O.J. Merkel in Berlin in July to act as agent of the parent British company. The first German Autogiro was completed in mid-May 1932 and first flown by Rawson and Cierva in Bremen in June. Cierva was in Bremen at this time having stopped off on his European tour in the C.24. Known as "Don Quichote" (Don Quixote), it has been suggested that the German C.19 may have borne the Cierva designation C.20, but this seems doubtful. It is believed to have been the only Autogiro of C.19 type completed in Germany, although a small batch is reported to have been planned. Don Quichote appears to have been projected with an 80-hp Siemens Sh11 radial. However, it would certainly have been underpowered with this engine (like the first British C.19s) and it was apparently only flown with the 110-hp Siemens Sh 14. D-2300 was crashed in 1934.

Arthur Rawson left the Autogiro company after his visit to Berlin. Reginald Brie then became chief pilot.

Cierva C.19 Mk.I

80-hp Armstong Siddeley Genet II. Rotor diameter 30 ft (9.14 m); rotor blade section Gö 429; overall length 30 ft (9.14 m); span of fixed wing 20 ft 6 in (6.24 m). Empty weight 750–810 lb (340–367 kg); maximum take-off weight 1,300 lb (589 kg). Fuel 13 Imp gal (59 liters). Maximum speed 85–95 mph (136–153 km/h); minimum speed 25 mph (40 km/h); initial climb 400–500 ft/min (2.03–2.54 m/sec); range 160–280 miles (257–450 km) at 70–80 mph (112–129 km/h); rotor speed 140/160 rpm.

Cierva C.19 Mk.II and IIA

105-hp Armstrong Siddeley Genet Major I. Rotor diameter 30 ft (9.14 m) and later 35 ft (10.66 m); rotor blade section Gö 429; fuselage length 17 ft 8½ in (5.39 m); span of fixed wing 20 ft 6 in–21 ft 6 in (6.24–6.55 m). Empty weight 850–964 lb (385-437 kg); maximum take-off weight 1,400 lb (635 kg). Fuel 23 Imp gal (104 liters). Maximum speed 82–95 mph (132–152 km/h); minimum speed 25-31 mph (40–50 km/h); initial climb 500–540 ft/min (2.54–2.74 m/sec); service ceiling 8,000 ft (2,438 m); range 300 miles (482 km) at 70 mph (112 km/h); rotor speed 180 rpm.

Cierva C.19 Mk.III

105-hp Armstrong Siddeley Genet Major I. Rotor diameter 35 ft (10.66 m); rotor blade section Gö 429; fuselage length 18 ft 3 in (5.56 m); span of fixed wing 20 ft 6 in (6.24 m). Empty weight 930–1,075 lb (421–488 kg); maximum take-off weight 1,400–1,552 lb (635–704 kg). Fuel 15½–18 Imp gal (70-81 liters). Maximum speed 82–95 mph (132–153 km/h); minimum speed 25–28 mph (40–45 km/h); initial climb 480–500 ft/min (2.43–2.54 m/sec); absolute ceiling 13,000 ft (3,962 m); service ceiling 7,500 ft (2,286 m); range 175–250 miles (281–400 km), at 75 mph (120 km/h); rotor speed 125 rpm.

Cierva C.19 Mk.IVP

105-hp Armstrong Siddeley Genet Major I. Rotor diameter 34 ft (10.36 m); rotor blade section RAF 34; fuselage length 19 ft 9¾ in (6.03 m); span of fixed wing 20 ft 6 in (6.24 m). Empty weight 1,032–1,075 lb (468–488 kg); maximum take-off weight 1,450–1,550 lb (657–703 kg). Fuel 16½ Imp gal (75 liters). Maximum speed 102 mph (164 km/h); minimum speed 25 mph (40 km/h); initial climb 465 ft min (2.3 m/sec); ceiling 11,200 ft (3,413 m); range 250 miles (402 km) at 90-95 mph (145-152 km/h); rotor speed 180 rpm.

Cierva C.19 Mk.IV

105-hp Armstrong Siddeley Genet Major I. Rotor diameter 34 ft (10.36 m); rotor blade section RAF 34; fuselage length 19 ft 9¾ in (6.03 m); span of fixed wing 20 ft 6 in (6.24 m). Empty weight 975–1,050 lb (442–476 kg); maximum take-off weight 1,450–1,550 lb (657–703 kg). Fuel 16 Imp gal (73 liters). Maximum speed 100–102 (160–164 km/h); minimum speed 25 mph (40 km/h); initial climb 630 ft/min (3.2 m/sec); absolute ceiling 14,000 ft (4,267 m); service ceiling 11,000 ft (3352 m); range 230 miles (370 km) at 80–90 mph (128–144 km/h); rotor speed 180 rpm. Price £1,100.

Focke-Wulf C.19 Don Quichote

110 hp Siemens Sh 14. Rotor diameter 10.36 m (34 ft); rotor blade section RAF 34; overall length 6.92 m (22 ft 8½ in); span of fixed wing 6.24 m (20 ft 6 in). Empty weight 520 kg (1,146 lb); maximum take-off weight 705 kg (1,554 lb). Maximum speed 115 km/h (96 mph); cruising speed 140 km/h (87 mph); minimum speed 35 km/h (22 mph) ceiling 2,500 m (8,202 ft); rotor speed 180 rpm.[14]

Chapter 5

American Autogiros

Such widespread interest was aroused in America by the arrival of the C.8 Mk.IV late in 1928 that James Weir and Cierva seem to have actually hoped for a time that the booming U.S. motorcar industry might take up the Autogiro as a potential private vehicle for general public use. Indeed, Lord Weir wrote to Henry Ford on this subject on November 25, 1928. Unfortunately, nothing came of the idea and American Autogiro development had to go forward on the comparatively modest resources of Harold Pitcairn and three licensees. Nevertheless, it is said that these Americans were to invest no less than $4.5 million in the Autogiro, significantly more than the total of £750,000 (then equivalent to about $3.5 million) reported to have been spent by the Cierva Company in Great Britain.[15]

British-built Cierva C.8W (C.8 Mk.IV) flying in the United States in modified form with fixed fin, up-turned wingtips, and low-pressure tires.
(S. Pitcairn)

It is clear with hindsight—although it was not so obvious at the time—that the Autogiro, as then available and even as subsequently developed, lacked certain fundamental characteristics essential for widespread public adoption. In addition, by late 1928, Ford was, in any case, heavily committed financially to the Ford Tri-Motor program—his first venture in aviation and one about which he may already have been having second thoughts. 1928 had also seen the abandonment of his proposed "airplane for the masses" program. Under the circumstances, it was unlikely that he would have been attracted to another aviation venture at this time.

The Pitcairn-Cierva Autogiro Company of America was accordingly formed in February 1929 as a subsidiary of Pitcairn Aviation Inc., to license the manufacture of Autogiros in the U.S.A. The Pitcairn Aircraft Company itself was licensed by Pitcairn-Cierva to undertake the design and manufacture of the first American Autogiro. Before doing so, Harold Pitcairn, Agnew E. Larsen, one of his senior engineers, and Jean Nicol of Jos. S. Pecker's office (later the Machine and Tool Designing Company and the Autogiro Specialities Company) visited England and France in April 1929 to acquire helpful design information.

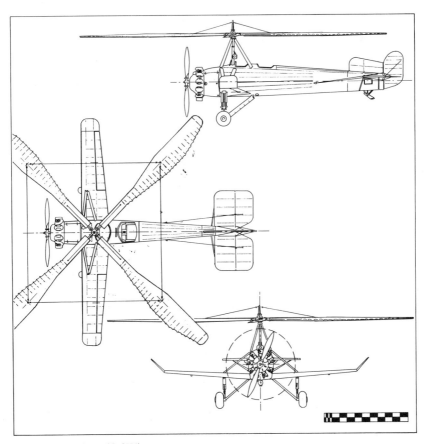

Cierva C.8 Mk.IV (C.8W).

In France, they had discussions with Georges Lepère who, in cooperation with Cierva, was at that time designing the C.18 cabin Autogiro. It had been ordered by the Cierva Company for Loel Guinness for entry in the Guggenheim Safe Aircraft Competition due to be held in the United States during the latter part of 1929 (see Chapter 3).

Pitcairn PCA-1. (300-hp Wright R-975-EG Whirlwind J-6). The Americans' original intention was to fit the latest Cierva rotor to a modified Pitcairn PA-5 Mailwing fuselage rather on the pattern of previous development in Europe. However, later an entirely new larger three-seat design with a four-blade 43 ft. (13.1 m) rotor of C.19 Mk.I technology was decided upon instead. Work started at Bryn Athyn in mid-July 1929 on the design and construction of the first American Autogiro, known at first as the PC-1 and later as the PCA-1. This aircraft (X94N) was flown for the first time by Juan de la Cierva on about October 8, 1929. The PCA-1 had a loaded weight of 2,600 lb. (1179 kg), about the same as the C.8s, the Spanish C.12, and the French C.18. Not only was it considerably larger than the C.19 Mk.II which Cierva had brought to the United States in August, it was also considerably more powerful, having the nine-cylinder Wright R-975-EG Whirlwind geared engine of 300 hp.

The PCA-1 showed clear signs of its Pitcairn lineage with a welded square-section steel tube fuselage, which may have been partly adapted from that of a Mailwing airplane. A novel long-travel wide-track (13 ft 3 in, 4.04 m) Praying Mantis landing gear had little, if any, side travel when loaded so that landings could be made with little or no forward roll and no damage would result to the wheels or tires. (Side travel tends to pull the tires from the wheels at zero ground speed.) There were relatively large (33 ft, 10.05 m span) plywood-covered strut-braced fixed wings with upturned tips for lateral stability (as had recently been fitted to the C.8W on Cierva's recommendation). It also had Frise ailerons and a boxlike deflector tail, like the C.12 and C.19 Mk.I, for aerodynamic rotor starting.

The rotor hub (known as the Model 300) was designed by the Joe S. Pecker Company—later the Autogiro Specialities Company—and weighed only about 75 lb (34 kg) (3.1 percent of the empty weight) compared with nearly 200 lb (90 kg) for the C.8 (11.5 percent of the empty weight). The RB-55 rotor blades were supplied from England by the Cierva Autogiro Company and were of planked-skin construction, that is to say they had two thicknesses of mahogany planking at 90 degrees to each other for each blade surface. This type of blade was manufactured by Avro and had been first introduced on the C.19 Mk.I in England in mid-1929. There was rubber-cord shock-absorbing bracing between the blades, as on previous British Autogiros, but friction dampers on the inter-blade cables (of Cierva design) were also tried. The rotor was mounted on a pylon consisting of four tubular struts with the front two-seat cockpit below and between the two rear struts.

The PCA-1 had been entered, while under construction, in both the National Air Tour and the Guggenheim Safe Aircraft Competition. It was com-

The first American Autogiro. PCA-1 had a steel tube fuselage, deflector tail for rotor spin-up, and strut-braced wings.
(Author's Collection)

PCA-1A with duralumin tube fuselage and deflector tail for rotor starting.
(Pitcairn photograph)

pleted too late to participate in either of these events, which started on October 10 and in November respectively.

In any case, the first PCA-1 did not survive long. It was badly damaged in a crash landing on about October 12, while being flown by Cierva, a few days after its first flight. Cierva himself was fortunate to escape unhurt. The aircraft was not rebuilt because the remains were destroyed in the fire that, on November 18, 1929, burnt out the old Pitcairn factory at Bryn Athyn. Fortunately, Pitcairn had wisely decided to build three development aircraft and Cierva was able to fly the second aircraft in late October.

121

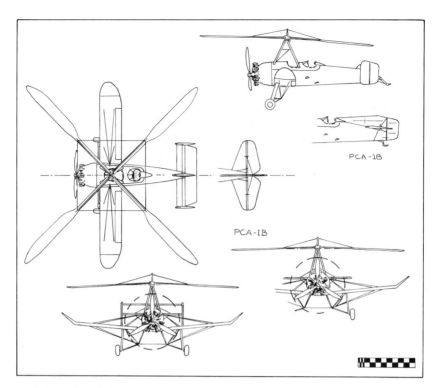

PCA-1A and PCA-1B.

Pitcairn PCA-1A. (225-hp Wright R-760-E Whirlwind and later the 300-hp R-975-EG Whirlwind). The other two PCA-1's differed from the first in having fuselages of very light duralumin tube construction manufactured by the Charles Ward Hall Aluminum Aircraft Company of Buffalo, New York. The wings were also of different construction to the first aircraft, with fabric covering, and were braced by numerous cables. The landing gear was of new design and had low-pressure Akron balloon tires. The PCA-1A retained the box tail of the original aircraft. This machine seems to have been flown in the latter part of October 1929, not long after the crash of the PCA-1.

A maximum take-off weight of 2,900 lb (1315 kg) has been quoted for the PCA-1A (X95N), but this would almost certainly have been with a more powerful engine than that initially fitted.

At first, the PCA-1A had the 225-hp direct drive seven-cylinder R-760 Whirlwind J-6 engine. Later, this was apparently replaced by the larger geared 300-hp R-975-EG Whirlwind with nine cylinders. The geared engine was more efficient at the Autogiro's low airspeeds but was not adopted for production aircraft, presumably for reasons of cost and weight.

Details of PCA-1A's contribution to Pitcairn's development activities are not known. In addition to being re-engined, it seems that the box tail was removed quite soon and replaced by a simple monoplane surface and single fin and rudder. At the end of its flying career, the PCA-1A was presented by Pitcairn to the Franklin Institute in Philadelphia. In 1955 it was transferred to the National Air and Space Museum of the Smithsonian Institution in Washington where it is still preserved at their Garber facility at Silver Hill.

Pitcairn PCA-1B. (225-hp Wright R-760-EG Whirlwind and later the 300-hp Wright R-975-EG Whirlwind). The PCA-1B (X96N) was similar to the PCA-1A with duraluimin tube fuselage and cable-braced fabric-covered wings. It was painted black and was usually known as the "Black Ship." The loaded weight was 2,700 lb (1225 kg) and the rotor was initially the same as that on the PCA-1 and -1A. The box deflector tail of the PCA-1 and -1A was discarded in the PCA-1B, to be replaced by a lighter simple tail unit. This type of tail unit was later fitted (retrospectively) to the -1A as well. The engine seems at first to have been a geared R-760 of 225 hp but this was later replaced by the larger R-975 of 300 hp. The PCA-1B was extensively used for test, development and demonstration flying. This aircraft was flown by Cierva before his return to Europe early in November 1929.

When he first flew the aircraft Cierva noted that it was badly down on performance, having a maximum speed of 87 mph (140 km/h). This was improved to 105 mph (169 km/h) (Cierva claimed 115 mph, 185 km/h) by fitting a more efficient propeller and ultimately to 120 mph (193 km/h) with the larger engine. The PCA-1B was publicly demonstrated for the first time, together with the first of the production versions (the prototype PCA-2) and the British Cierva C.19 Mk.II, G-AAKY, at the 1930 National Air Races held at the Curtiss-Reynolds Airport in Chicago from August 23 to September 1. The PCA-1B and the PCA-2 prototype were flown to Chicago, the total flying time for the journey being 6 hours 50 min-

The PCA-1B with R-760 engine, stiffened rotor pylon, and high-pressure tires. (Howard Levy photograph)

utes, giving an average speed of about 100 mph (160 km/h). The C.19 was taken by road. Pitcairn had hoped to also have the Alfaro PCA-2-30 Autogiro at Chicago, but it was destroyed in a crash on its way to the meeting.

The PCA-1B was extensively employed in the testing of a whole series of rotor blades. Pitcairn first manufactured a set of blades for the PCA-1's that Paul Stanley designed after he and Childs had visited England in May 1930. These were based on blades fitted early in 1930 to the C.19 Mk.IIA and later adopted as standard for the C.19 Mk.III. The new American blades (known as Type AB-3) proved to have spars of insufficient torsional rigidity with the result that, when tested on the PCA-1B on June 17, 1930, excessive torsional deflection occurred. This led to slowing down of the rotor and an emergency landing causing considerable damage to the aircraft but fortunately no injury to the pilot. As a result of this accident, criteria were established for adequate torsional rigidity of rotor blades.

The next step in this development was when, as a result of the accident, a set of blades was rebuilt with a somewhat reduced diameter than had been used previously. At the same time, it was decided to balance dynamically the four blades of this rotor. (In other words, to ensure that the pendular periods of all the blades were identical). When fitted to the aircraft and tested in July 1930, these blades greatly improved qualitative performance and, indeed, made it as good as, or even better than, that of the C.8W. Dynamic balancing of rotor blades was therefore adopted by Pitcairns as standard practice until a form of construction, giving a much more uniform weight distribution than plank-skin blades, could be introduced.

Meanwhile, Pitcairns had designed and built their own set of planked-skin blades (Type AB-2). When tested, these were found to give flying characteristics which were qualitatively less satisfactory than had been expected. Investigation of the causes, and comparisons between the C.8 and PCA-1 rotor hubs led to the conclusion that the dimensional relationship of the drag-hinge offset and the centroid of inertia of the blades was critical. Experiments, in which the drag-hinge offset was increased by use of extension blocks, improved the flying characteristics of the PCA-1 and later of the C.19. As a result of the investigation, Cierva derived his pendular theory of proper drag-hinge offset.

The PCA-1B was also used for experiments on the effect of altering the angle of incidence of the fixed wings. In this way, the most efficient setting was determined. Other tests were directed, as a preliminary to putting the Autogiro into production in the United States, at establishing the aircraft's likely acceptability to potential users.

Pitcairn's old factory at Bryn Athyn had been destroyed by fire on November 18, 1929—just three weeks after the U.S. stock market crash started a period of worldwide economic recession. Toward the end of the year, the company moved all its operations to Willow Grove, Pennsylvania, where Pitcairn had established an airfield shortly after purchasing land in February 1926 and where a new factory had been under construction since May 1929. The last five Mailwing airplanes (the PA-8's for Eastern Air Transport) were built at the new factory until, after almost two years, all work ceased on fixed-wing aircraft.

Cierva and Harold Pitcairn with a C.19 Mk.II.
(Pitcairn photograph)

Pitcairn PCA-2 prototype. (225-hp Wright R-760-E Whirlwind J-6-7). Construction of the PCA-2 prototype (X760W) with the direct drive 225-hp seven-cylinder Whirlwind was started late in 1929. Painted green, it was first flown in March 1930. Similar to the PCA-1B with a gross weight of 2,750 lb (1247 kg) (which was, however, to be increased to 3,000 lb (1360 kg) in production aircraft), it had British-supplied rotor blades and, like previous Pitcairn airplanes, a fuselage of welded steel tubes that was easier to modify and repair than the duralumin structures of the PCA-1A and -1B. The PCA-2 differed from the PCA-1s in being designed so that all the disposable load in the side-by-side two-seat front cockpit was close to the aircraft's center of gravity. There was thus no change of balance with change of load. A number of other small improvements were incorporated. The span of the fixed wing had been reduced from 33 to 30 ft (10.06 to 9.14 m) and the wing bracing cables and been reduced in number. The rotor pylon was a tripod and the rotor diameter had been increased from 43 to 45 ft (13.11 to 13.72 m). The tail unit was of the simplified type first used on the PCA-1B but without the fin extension forward to the cockpit headrest. Most important of all was the engine drive for rotor spin-up, designed in the later part of 1929 or early in 1930, and manufactured by the Machine and Tool Designing Company. Initially, this drive would spin-up the four-blade 45 ft (13.72 m) rotor to 80/90 rpm in 30/40 seconds (taking 15/20 hp), which meant that a short run

125

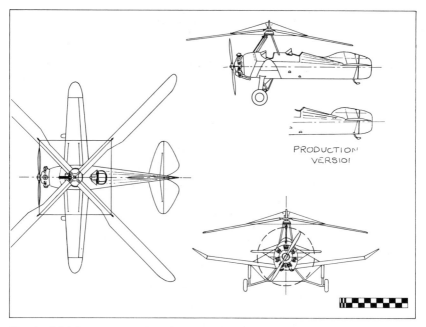

PRODUCTION
VERSION

Pitcairn PCA-2 prototype and production versions.

was still required to accelerate the rotor to take-off speed. However, later development of this same gear-box and clutch (which weighed only 48 lb (22 kg) or 65 lb (29 kg) for the complete installation) enabled it ultimately to spin-up 50 ft (15 m) rotors to the full 125 rpm needed for take-off—which required about 55 hp.

The delivery flights of the prototype PCA-2 and PCA-1B to Chicago from Philadelphia for the 1930 National Air Races were the longest cross-country flights (650 mi, 1050 km) by Autogiros up to that time. As a result, they highlighted a number of problems—in particular, fatigue difficulties with the blade suspension cables. These were found to suffer fatigue failures every few hours so that several blades were broken as rotors slowed down on the ground after landing, and dropped until they hit some other part of the structure. The failures were cured by means of elastic links at the hub attachment of the blade suspension cables arranged so as to take up the slack of the cables in flight.

Another improvement to the blade-bracing was tried out on the PCA-2. As already mentioned, friction dampers of Cierva design on the inter-blade bracing cables (mounted at about 40 percent of the blade radius) had been introduced on the PCA-1. These were a distinct improvement on the earlier elastic cord or bob weight systems but there was reason to believe that hydraulic damping would give even better results. A set of hydraulic dampers was accordingly designed and manufactured at Pitcairns in the summer of 1930 and tested on the prototype PCA-2. These Pitcairn dampers were later redesigned by Houdaille-Hershey who produced an oil damper subsequently used on all American Autogiros with externally braced blades. The oil dampers proved entirely satisfactory except for some sensi-

PCA-2 prototype and PCA-1B flying over Manhattan.
(Author's Collection)

tivity to weather conditions. They reduced the so-called wobbling or Autogiro feeling, an irregular rocking motion caused by horizontal oscillations of the blades.

Pitcairn PCA-2. (300-hp Wright R-975-E Whirlwind J-6-9). Production of the PCA-2 was announced on October 30, 1930. The production version (the first

*James Ray, the Pitcairn test pilot, and Thomas Edison
in front of the PCA-2 prototype.
(Author's Collection)*

was NC784W) was manufactured by a newly formed company, the Pitcairn
Autogiro Company, a licensee of the Pitcairn-Cierva Autogiro Company of
America which changed its name to Autogiro Company of America in January
1931. The PCA-2 had the more powerful 300-hp nine-cylinder J-6-9 direct-drive
engine. The four rotor blades were American-manufactured but were of similar
construction to those first tried by Cierva on the C.19 Mk.IIA and had chrome
molybdenum steel spars with wooden ribs and plywood and fabric covering. The
rotor diameter and fixed-wing span were the same as those of the prototype. The
fin was reduced in area and was of more pleasing shape.

Performance of the production aircraft with the more powerful engine was a
considerable improvement on the prototype. Maximum speed increased from 98
to 118 mph (158 to 190 km/h), cruising speed from 87 to 98 mph (140 to 158
km/h) and rate of climb from 650 to 800 ft/min (3.3 to 4.06 m/s). All this despite
the increase in weight.

The prototype PCA-2 had been publicly demonstrated at the National Air
Races at Chicago in August 1930. The first production aircraft flew on Novem-

Production PCA-2 with welded steel tube fuselage.
(Author's Collection)

ber 1. After several of the type had been built and sufficient flying time had been accumulated, the PCA-2 was submitted for certification and became the first Autogiro to gain a United States Department of Commerce approved Type Certificate (no. 410). This was awarded on April 2, 1931.

In January of that year, the Pitcairn test pilot James C. Ray had made a 2,500 mile (4000 km) round trip from Willow Grove to Miami. He made landings on the way at many small and unprepared fields, under a wide variety of weather conditions. In Miami, Ray attended the All-American Air Races and the dedication of the New United States Navy airfield.

On April 22, 1931, James Ray landed a PCA-2 on the south lawn of the White House in Washington. The occasion was the presentation of the Collier Trophy to Harold Pitcairn and his associates (including Edwin Asplundh, Agnew Larsen, and Geof Childs) by President Herbert Hoover. Hoover himself became very interested in the Autogiro. The Collier Trophy is awarded annually by the American National Aeronautic Association for the greatest achievement in aviation in the United States, the value of which has been thoroughly demonstrated by actual use during the preceding year. Juan de la Cierva had been prevented by political events in Spain from attending the presidential presentation. However, he received the British Royal Aeronautical Society Silver Medal in that year.

Pitcairn built 51 Autogiros during 1931 of which 46 were sold. Of these, 21 were PCA-2's (plus three of the XOP-1 naval variant, see below). PCA-2's were supplied to a wide range of operators, many of whom used the aircraft for advertising. Purchasers included Beech-Nut Packing Company, Coca-Cola, Standard Oil of New York (SOCONY) and of Ohio and other states, Texas Air Transport, Champion Spark Plugs, Detroit News (which placed the first order on February 12, 1931), Morgan Oil Company, Sealed Power Piston Rings, Silverbrook Coal

Company, and a number of others. It is recorded, in fact, that PCA-2's were flown in all the then forty-eight states of the United States. The highest utilization of an Autogiro in 1931 was achieved by the Horizon Company, which flew 550 hours in 7½ months—equivalent to an annual rate of 880 hours.

In 1932, Captain Lewis A. Yancey, the Autogiro pilot for Champion Spark Plugs, made a notable flight in a PCA-2 from Florida to Cuba and then from Cuba to Yucatan over the Gulf of Mexico. He followed this with a spectacular landing on the summit of the great Maya pyramid of Chichén Itzá.

In 1931, one PCA-2 was purchased by the National Advisory Committee for Aeronautics (NACA) for research at Langley Field, Virginia. A test program extending over five years was carried out at Langley with Bill McAvoy and Melvin Gough as pilots. This produced the "first authoritative information on Autogiro performance and rotor behaviour"—to quote from the NACA report on the investigations.

Tests on May 27, 1931, showed that increasing the gross weight from 3,225 lb (1463 kg) to 3,625 lb (1644 kg) increased the take-off distance in still air from 350 to 400 ft (107 to 122 m), the rate of climb was reduced from 650 ft/min to 450 ft/min (3.3 to 2.3 m/s) and the rate of descent was increased from 18 to 20 ft/sec (5.49 to 6.1 m/s). The rotor rpm increased from 140/145 to 145/150. Flight measurements on this aircraft were compared with test data obtained while running the aircraft's rotor full-scale in a large wind tunnel. Other flight tests with the NACA PCA-2 included measurements during violent maneuvers (up to 4.3g) and a series of tests with the fixed-wing set at several angles of incidence to vary the proportion of the load which it carried. A maximum speed of 140 mph (225 km/h) was achieved and a best lift/drag ratio of 6.7 was measured. For blade motion and later for blade-stalling studies, a hub-mounted camera was developed—a technique applied much later to helicopters.

Pilots' growing confidence in the Autogiro is emphasized by the first loop (actually the first two) to be performed by an Autogiro made by a Canadian, Godfrey W. Dean, at Willow Grove on October 13, 1931. He was flying Fairchild Aircraft Ltd. of Canada's PCA-2, CF-ARO. John Miller also repeatedly looped a PCA-2 (NC10781) at about this time during flying exhibitions at country fairs.

The first Autogiro accident caused by icing occurred in the United States late in 1931. This led to research into rotor blade icing and to consideration of solutions to a problem which, many years later, had to be solved before all-weather flying became possible with helicopters. Pitcairn had made unsuccessful attempts to explore the effect of icing conditions during the 1930/31 winter. Following the accident, a program was launched in 1931. During these tests on November 28 severe icing conditions were found to cause a slowing down of the rotor with possible catastrophic loss of lift and coning of the rotor. A warning bulletin to Autogiro pilots was accordingly issued suggesting immediate landing in the event of loss of 10/15 rotor rpm in icing conditions.

At about this time it was realized that Autogiros normally had a rather uncomfortable sideways tilt in forward flight. After a series of tests, the tilt was reduced by offsetting the rotor bearing about one inch sideways and also by giving it a sideways inclination of about one degree.

Tests were also conducted by Pitcairns into allowable fore-and-aft loading limits. These followed a series of minor landing accidents, attributed to improper longitudinal balance reducing control effectiveness in landing.

The famous pilot, Amelia Earhart, was the first woman to fly an Autogiro solo. She established, on her second attempt, an altitude record of 18,415 ft (5613 m) in a PCA-2 on April 8, 1931, after taking off from Willow Grove. Captain Lewis L.A. Yancey increased this to 21,500 ft (6553 m) over Boston, Massachusetts, on September 25, 1932. In May, John M. Miller flew a PCA-2 across the continent, leaving Willow Grove on the fourteenth and landing at San Diego on the twenty-eighth. Between May 29 and June 6, 1931, in another PCA-2 (NC10781), Amelia Earhart also flew across the United States coast to coast (Newark to Oakland). She attempted the return crossing but, on June 22, having flown 11,000 mi (17,700 km) in 150 hours, she crashed at Abilene, Kansas, when hit by a "dust devil" while taking off. Miss Earhart continued flying a PCA-2 for Beech-Nut for several years.

About 100 pilots had flown Autogiros in America by the end of 1931. In November of that year, the first two Autogiro-only private pilots' licenses were awarded in the United States. These went to E.E. Law and Nathan Pitcairn, nephew of Harold Pitcairn.

In October 1934, a PCA-2 was presented to the Georgia School of Technology for a program of flight research. Flown for 60 hours by a pilot on the staff of the school, the Autogiro was used to study general aerodynamic and stability characteristics of rotary-wing aircraft.

The XOP-1, PCA-3 and PA-21 (see below) were developments of the PCA-2. The basic PCA-2 fuselage was also used for the later direct control PA-33 (YG-2) and PA-34 (XOP-2). In many cases, these later Autogiros were, in fact, earlier aircraft rebuilt to the later standard.

Pitcairn XOP-1. (300-hp Wright R-975 Whirlwind J-6-9). Three modified PCA-2s (8850, A8976-7) were supplied to the United States Navy, under the designation XOP-1. They were two-seaters with dual control and a special radio installation. The first was sent to Anacostia Field near Washington early in 1931. Piloted by Lieutenant (later Rear Admiral) Alfred M. Pride, USN, this aircraft made three landings on and take-offs from the aircraft carrier, U.S.S. *Langley* off Norfolk, Virginia, on September 23, 1931. These were the first landings on a ship by a rotary-wing aircraft.

The first XOP-1 was probably also flown by David Ingalls, assistant secretary of the navy for aeronautics, on the occasion when he was invited by President Herbert Hoover to bring an Autogiro to the president's retreat at Rapidan for a weekend. Ingalls, a former U.S. Navy pilot, flew the Autogiro to Rapidan and demonstrated it to the president, also making flights with the president's son, Herbert Hoover, Jr., as passenger.

The second XOP-1 was mounted on twin floats and tested as a seaplane. The third was shipped to Nicaragua in the spring of 1932. It was to have been

131

Rotor hub and spin-up drive of the XOP-1.
(S. Pitcairn)

evaluated by the United States Navy during operations against insurgents under the guerrilla chief Augusto Cesae Sandino who had started a revolt the previous year.

The intention had been to try out the Autogiro on actual operations, flying from short primitive strips to drop supplies and ammunition; evacuate the wounded; and bomb and straf pinpoint targets. In the event, instead of using it on operations, a board of review was set up to supervise comparative trials of the Autogiro and a Vought O2U-1 fixed-wing airplane. These tests were to show that the 300-hp Autogiro could take-off in 200 ft (60 m) carrying its crew of two and 50 lb (23 kg) of payload and could climb to 1,000 ft (300 m) in two minutes. In contrast, the 425-hp O2U-1 could take-off in the same distance carrying two crew and 200 lb (90 kg) of payload and had a higher rate of climb. On the other hand, the Autogiro landed in much shorter distance—never more than 50 ft (15 m). The XOP-1 could cruise at 70 mph (113 km/h) for three hours, giving a still air range of 210 miles (338 km) but this was substantially less than the airplane. The board of review concluded that the Autogiro's ability to climb more steeply and, when required, to fly much more slowly than the airplane provided insufficient advantages in the proposed roles to offset its lower cruising speed, smaller disposable load, and reduced rate of climb.

It seems that the navy's verdict on the results of these tests set the pattern,

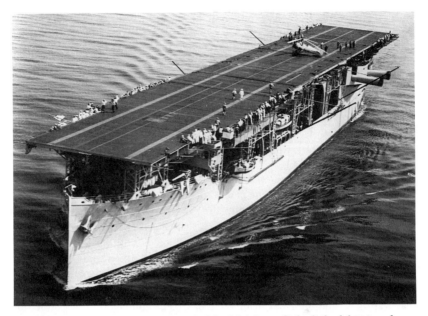

Pitcairn XOP-1, the U.S. Navy version of the PCA-2, on flight deck of the aircraft carrier U.S.S. Langley, *September 23, 1931. These were the first operations from a ship by a rotary-wing aircraft.*
(U.S. Navy photograph)

even in the longer term, for the generally unfavourable attitude of the United States military services to the Autogiro. However, the XOP-1 as a Spanish development aroused great enthusiasm among the local population of Nicaragua—with its past Spanish connections—when it was seen at Zacharias Field near the capital, Managua, on June 28, 1932.

The United States Army also considered Autogiros at this time but no orders were placed. The army had conducted wind-tunnel tests on a model four-blade Autogiro rotor at Wright Field in 1930 and had followed this in 1931 with a full aerodynamic investigation.

Pitcairn PCA-3. (300-hp Pratt & Whitney R-985 Wasp Junior). This was a version of the PCA-2, fitted with a Pratt & Whitney engine. It was manufactured to the special order of United Airports, a subsidiary of the United Aircraft and Transport Corporation, another of whose subsidiaries was the Pratt & Whitney engine company.

The PCA-3 gained Department of Commerce Approved Type Certificate No. 446 on August 25, 1931, and the first (NC11671) was delivered by James Ray to Hartford, Connecticut, where it was to be used for engine and propeller development. It had the distinction of being the first Autogiro to be fitted with a variable pitch propeller. This aircraft was destroyed by fire in September 1931 and in December was replaced by a second aircraft (NC11612). The latter had accumulated some 60 hours of flying up to July 1933 when it was sold. No other examples of the PCA-3 were built.

Pitcairn PCA-4. This was a design study, undertaken by Pitcairn during 1931, of a twin-engine Autogiro. It is interesting that Cierva was also thinking in terms of a twin-engine design at this time (see Cierva C.26 in Chapter 6) and it seems probable that design information was exchanged between the two companies.

Kellett K-1X. (45-hp Szekely later exchanged for a 65-hp Velie M-5). The Kellet Aircraft Corporation of Philadelphia, Pennsylvania, was founded in July 1929 by W. Wallace Kellett, his brother Rodney, C. Townsend Ludington, and his brother, Nicholas. The business had originally started in 1923 as an aircraft dealership at Pine Valley airport. The new corporation concentrated from the first on the development of rotary-wing aircraft. Fred Seiler, the chief engineer, was responsible for their first design, the K-1X, which was taxied at speeds of up to about 60 mph (96 km/h) late in 1930, but proved incapable of flight. The K-1X was a small single-seat gyroplane with a 40-hp Szekely three-cylinder engine, a gross weight variously reported at 775 and 900 lb (350 and 408 kg) and a teetering (or seesaw) two-blade cantilever rotor 27 ft 6 in (8.38 m) in diameter made of laminated spruce. The rotor was made all in one piece and tapered toward the tips from a thick Gö 449 section at the center. The fuselage, built by the Budd Company of Philadelphia, was of spot-welded strip steel construction, covered with fabric. There was no fixed-wing but the large horizontal tail, 19 ft 6 in (5.94 m) in span, had control surfaces which combined the action of elevators and ailerons. Development of this design ran into difficulties and was discontinued. Meanwhile, during 1931, Kellett had obtained an Autogiro license from the Pitcairn-Cierva Autogiro Company of America and the company turned to a more conventional Autogiro development.

The Kellett K-IX gyroplane designed by R.H. Prewitt and tested but not flown late in 1930. (C.C. Miller, Jr.)

134

Kellett K-2. (165-hp Continental A-70-2 or 210-hp Continental R-670). The K-2 (sometimes at first referred to as the KA-1) was Kellett's first Autogiro and was designed in close cooperation with Autogiro Company of America engineers by a team under W. Lawrence Le Page as chief engineer. Le Page had previously been with Pitcairn and had worked on the PCA-1's and the C.18. The K-2 was a side-by-side two-seater with an open cockpit that could be fitted with a coupé top if desired. It had a conventional Cierva four-blade cable-braced 41 ft (12.5 m) rotor and low-aspect-ratio fixed-wing made of wood, braced by inverted V-struts and with upturned tips. The characteristic Kellett rotor pylon had one main rearward leaning strut braced by two lighter struts to behind the cockpit. The K-2 was fitted with a mechanical engine-powered spin-up drive, including clutch and gear box, produced by the Autogiro Specialities Company of Philadelphia. It weighed 45 lb (20.4 kg). There was also a rotor brake and a Heywood compressed-air starter on the engine.

The K-2 was first flown by Jim Ray on April 24, 1931, and it obtained U.S. Department of Commerce Approved Type Certificate No. 2-431 in Group 2 on May 27, 1931. This was upgraded to ATC No. 437 on July 17, 1931. Early effective public demonstration of the new Autogiro was made with take-offs and landings from Philadelphia's Hog Island Airport. Cierva himself flew a K-2 at Philadelphia on December 30, 1931.

The K-2 went into production and immediately attracted sales. Twelve were built. One was demonstrated to the U.S. Army at Wright Field in autumn of 1931. From July 1932, some of the K-2s were modified (as K-2-As) to take the 210-hp Continental R-670 engine.

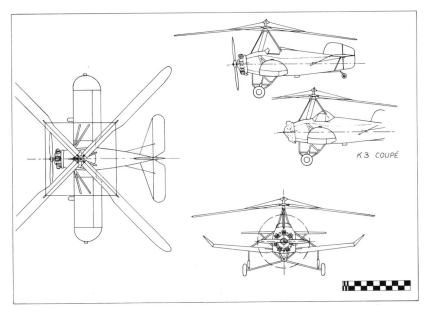

Kellett K-2 with cabin K-3 inset.

135

The Kellett K-2 prototype.
(J.W.R. Taylor)

Out of a total empty weight of 1,518 lb (689 kg) the K-2's rotor weighed 331 lb (150 kg) (21.8 percent), of which the blades weighed 278 lb (126 kg) and the hub 53 lb (24 kg) (3.5 percent of the empty weight—a similar percentage to that of the Pitcairn PCA-1B). The hub (known as the Model 400) was a product of the Autogiro Specialities Company.

Kellett K-3. (210-hp Kinner C5). This was a re-engined and slightly improved model of the K-2 which, like the K-2 itself, could be fitted with a steamlined cabin enclosing the two side-by-side seats. It could take off in 165 ft (50 m) in still air and land in 5 to 35 ft (1.5 to 10 m) depending on the wind. It was exhibited at the 1932 Detroit Air Show and gained U.S. Department of Commerce Approved Type Certificate No. 471 on March 26, 1932. At least six of the type were built, the first two being conversions of K-2's.

One K-3 was delivered to Buenos Aires, Argentina, in 1932 and became the first Autogiro in South America, demonstrated there by E.E. Denniston of Philadelphia. It was followed by three others in 1933. Two K-3's were exported to Japan, having been ordered in December 1932 through Okura & Company for Japanese army evaluation. The type was also used for towing advertising banners in the United States. Like the K-2, the K-3 was demonstrated in 1932 to the U.S. military authorities at Wright Field. It was, however, considered to have too low a performance for military use.

A K-3 (NR12615), with a 210-hp Continental R-670 engine (sometimes incorrectly referred to as a K-4) was given the name "Pep Boys Snowman." The Pep Boys automotive store chain of Philadelphia lent it to Rear Admiral R.E. Byrd's (second) Antarctic Expedition of 1933/35. The Autogiro had previously been used by the store for advertising and promotion. The K-3 was thus the first rotary-wing aircraft to be operated in the polar regions. The Autogiro left Boston

The Kellett K-3 Autogiro used by the Second Byrd Antarctic Expedition of 1933–35. (Author's Collection)

in October 1933 in Byrd's supply ship *Ruppert*. It was unloaded in the Bay of Whales on January 28, 1934, and flown the same day by W.S. McCormick to the expedition's base at Little America.

Byrd himself flew in the Autogiro with McCormick on a reconnaissance of the sea ice before the end of January, and throughout February it continued to be used for short range reconnaissances. Byrd commented: "I was greatly impressed with the virtues of the autogiro. With its singular hovering instincts and its nearly vertical landings, it is a perfect instrument for short-range reconnaissance in the polar regions."

On March 24, the Autogiro, flown by McCormick with Byrd as passenger, set out on a search for one of the expedition's fixed-wing aircraft which had force-landed away from base. Despite a strong wind, the Autogiro found the missing machine and landed nearby. Later, it took the two leaders of the rescue dog teams on short flights to show them the position of the airplane. Although the Autogiro subsequently suffered engine trouble, this episode brought it much credit. Previously, the K-3 had been the subject of good-natured disparagement from the two airplane pilots whom it had now rescued.

On September 1, 1934, nine days after the return of the sun at the end of winter, the Autogiro made the first flight of the season. It was then used for daily temperature soundings of the upper air whenever the weather permitted, the best height reached being 9,000 ft (2750 m). There was some concern about flying in very low temperatures because of the risk of rotor blade dampers becoming solid at below -50 degrees C.

On September 28, the Autogiro crashed from about 75 ft (25 m) shortly after take-off and was destroyed. McCormick was knocked unconscious, had an arm broken, and suffered from shock. Later it was established that drifting snow had filled the rear fuselage before take-off, thus shifting the center of gravity dangerously far aft.

The Kellett Aircraft Corporation was renamed the Kellett Autogiro Corporation in April 1932 when the company was reorganized.

Kellett K-4. (210-hp Continental R-670). This was a prototype two-seater that appeared in June 1933 as an improved version of the K-3 and was, in fact, a rebuilt K-2. It was certificated (Approved Type Certificate No. 523) on December 27, 1933. It had smaller tapered wings than the earlier K-types and these were without upturned tips having a continuous marked dihedral from root to tip. The strut-braced landing gear had wheel brakes and low-pressure tires; there was a wider dual-control cockpit (for which a canopy was an optional extra); the fuselage was lengthened by 9 in (23 cm), the rotor pylon was redesigned to consist of one main member braced by three streamlined tie rods; and there was a steerable tailwheel. The pilot had a better view from the cockpit. The cable-braced four-blade rotor was slightly improved over earlier models. There was a Heywood compressed-air engine starter. The new 225-hp Jacobs L-4 engine was offered as an alternative power plant but was probably not fitted. A second K-2 may, however, have been converted into a K-4.

About twenty-five Kellett K-2 and K-3 series Autogiros were built in all, the K-4 prototype being the last of the pre-direct-control types. The next production Kellett Autogiro was the direct-control KD-1, which first flew on December 9, 1934, and appeared in production form early in 1935. (See Chapter 8.)

Pitcairn-Alfaro PCA-2-30. (110-hp Warner Scarab). This was a one-off experimental light tandem two-seat open-cockpit sporting Autogiro, originally ordered

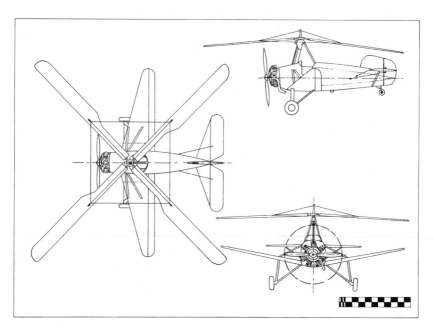

Kellett K-4.

by Pitcairn on January 12, 1929. Design started on July 17 and construction followed in November. It was completed on July 18, 1930, having been built to Pitcairn's order by Heraclio Alfaro of Cleveland. As first designed, the PCA-2-30 (X759W), like the PCA-1, had a deflector tail. This feature was, however, replaced in November 1929 by a mechanical rotor starter designed by Alfaro. The drive weighed only 37½ lb (17 kg), well within Cierva's definition of 40 lb, or at most 50 lb (18 or at most 23 kg), as the acceptable limit for such a device. The PCA-2-30 was the first Autogiro fitted with a spin-up drive, although it seems that the PCA-2 prototype may have been the first to fly with this device, which it did in March 1930.

Alfaro was a distinguished Spanish engineer who had learned to fly in France in 1911. He designed a fighter which, built by Hereter S.A. in Barcelona,[16] was entered in the 1919 Military Aircraft Competition for which Cierva had built his C-3 bomber. Later in 1919, Alfaro worked with Raul de Pateras Pescara in Barcelona on the development of the latter's helicopter. A later version achieved a flight of 10 min 10 sec in January 1924. Alfaro then moved to the United States where he set up an aircraft design engineering and development business in Cleveland.

The PCA-2-30, originally called the PC-2-30 and said to have been later named PA-11, was first flown as a prototype on August 18, 1930. The designation is believed to have been derived from the concept of a small equivalent to the PCA-2, but with a 30-ft (9.14 m) rotor like the C.19 Mk.I. As built, the rotor diameter was increased to 34 ft (10.36 m). The rotor, mounted on a tripod pylon, was of advanced design incorporating friction dampers at the blade roots. The PCA-2-30 was of novel construction making extensive use of bakelite or Formica (an early type of plastic). The four rotor blades, designed and manufactured by the Formica Company, were covered in Micarta. The fuselage had a conventional structure of welded steel tubes with fabric covering. Wings and ailerons were covered in Formica while the stabilizer and rubber were of wood with Micarta covering. The vertical fin was of welded steel tubes, fabric covered.

The Alfaro Autogiro, apparently unflown, was delivered by truck to Pitcairn Field in July 1930. During preliminary tests, this Autogiro behaved very well having the smoothest running rotor of any yet tested. However, even at a minimum flying weight of 1,385 lb (628 kg), it did not have adequate performance or disposable load for commercial use, being both underpowered and overweight. In an attempt to improve its performance, the diameter of the four-blade rotor was increased to 38 ft (11.58 m) and the rate of rotation reduced from 155 to 135 rpm, but this resulted in undesirable vibrations. On its way to the National Air Races in Chicago in August 1930, flown by J. Paul Lukens, the PCA-2-30 was wrecked attempting to take off on August 21 at Butler, Pennsylvania. Further development of the type was then abandoned. The accident was said to have been caused by the weight of condensed moisture that accumulated inside the Micarta covered blades preventing them from attaining the proper rotor revolutions for take-off. In 1931 Pitcairn produced the more powerful PAA-1 to meet the same requirement as the PCA-2-30.

Pitcairn-Alfaro PCA-2-30 light Autogiro prototype.
(Author's Collection)

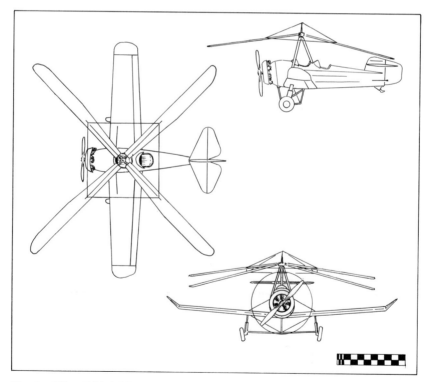

Pitcairn-Alfaro PCA-2-30.

Line-up of Autogiros at Willow Grove, Philadelphia. Left to right: *the British C.19 MK.II, Pitcairn PCA-1B, PCA-2 prototype, PCA-2-30, and the British C.8W before a fixed fin was added.*
(Author's Collection)

As vice president and chief engineer, Heraclio Alfaro later joined the L.W. Steere Company, the fourth American Autogiro licensee. However, no further Autogiro developments resulted.

Pitcairn PAA-2 prototype. (120-hp Martin-Chevrolet 4-333, later replaced by 125-hp Kinner B5). The first American Autogiros of the PCA series were relatively large three-seat aircraft of rather greater weight, power, and rotor diameter than the earlier British Cierva C.8. The first Kellett Autogiros were rather smaller side-by-side two seaters. By the time the PCA-2 entered service in April 1931, the much lighter and lower-powered C.19 model had been in production in Britain for more than a year and a half. A C.19 Mk.II had been in the United States since August 1929 and a Mk.III since August 1930.

Harold Pitcairn foresaw a requirement for a similar less expensive Autogiro in the United States. After the failure of Alfaro's PCA-2-30, the alternatives of building the C.19 or of developing an entirely new, smaller Autogiro, the PAA-1, were considered. Although a full set of C.19 drawings was purchased, it was decided to go ahead with the new PAA-1. This was an open-cockpit tandem two-seater, development of which was undertaken in the spring of 1931 by Walter C. Clayton, Pitcairn Aircraft's chief engineer.

Tests at Willow Grove of both Warner Scarab (as fitted in the Alfaro Autogiro) and Kinner radial engines in Pitcairn PA-4 airplanes showed that the latter had the better power-to-weight ratio. This engine was therefore selected as the power plant for the PAA-1. Before the first machine (X10756) was completed, however, a decision was taken to convert it into a modified version fitted with a new Martin inverted four-cylinder air-cooled inline engine designed by Louis Chevrolet. This version was named PAA-2, the designation PA-11 was also, probably incorrectly, reported. The PAA-2 differed from the original design only in the engine and in being fitted with a nosewheel landing gear. Some flying was done with the PAA-2 from February 1931, but trouble with the power plant and with the landing gear led to a decision to revert for production to the PAA-1

The Pitcairn PAA-2 light Autogiro prototype with 120 hp Martin-Chevrolet engine.
The nosewheel landing gear was also tried on the PAA-1.
(Pitcairn photograph, G. Townson Collection)

configuration. The one and only PAA-2 is believed to have later been converted to PAA-1 standard.

Pitcairn PAA-1. (125-hp Kinner B5). The prototype of the production-type aircraft (X10770) appeared in March 1931. First displayed at the 1931 Detroit Aircraft Show, the production PAA-1 gained Department of Commerce Approved Type Certificate No. 433 on August 7, 1931. The PAA-1 proved to be somewhat underpowered and overweight but, despite the Great Depression soon to be at its height, quickly achieved sales and a total of twenty-one were built—seventeen in 1931. The PAA-1 had a 37 ft (11.28 m) rotor with four cable-braced rotor blades and hub, wings, tail unit and landing gear all geometrically similar to those of the PCA-2, making it effectively a two-thirds size replica of the earlier design but still significantly larger than the British C.19. The PAA-1, like its predecessor, had a mechanical rotor spin-up gear but of different design, in this case by the Autogiro Specialities Company and of a type originally produced for the first Kellett Autogiro. It weighed 45 lb (20 kg). The rotor hub came from the same supplier.

The rotor blades of the PAA-1 were designed for easy production with a single steel tubular spar, stainless steel ribs and leading edge, and fabric covering. These blades were tested on the PAA-2 and on the first PAA-1 but a fatigue study indicated that they were probably under design strength and they were abandoned after only a few hours flying. The definitive PAA-1 production blades had a new spar but used the same structure as the first design aft of the spar. This type of blade was also used on the later PA-18.

A production PAA-1 with rotor spin-up drive.
(Pitcairn photograph, G. Townson Collection)

Pitcairns devoted considerable attention to fatigue at this time. The work was largely done by A.V. de Forest, who developed a type of "scratch recorder" to record flight stresses in Autogiro rotor blades. A series of tests were conducted which produced useful information as to the proper and safe location of spot-welds on Autogiro rotor blade spars. These tests showed that spot-welds were as detrimental to fatigue life as holes of the same diameter. Spot-welds were finally located on the ventral axis with respect to bending in the lift plane. These tests also highlighted the importance of surface finish. A draw-filing operation was therefore introduced to remove any radial scratches on the spars that might act as stress raisers.

Fatigue testing on the ground was done on the tuning fork principle. Electro-magnets were used to excite vibrations on the specimen at the 60-cycle electric current frequency (3,600 reversals per minute). The effects of large numbers of reversals could thus be determined in a relatively short time.

In 1931 metal tabs were experimentally fitted to the trailing edges of the blades of a PAA-1 rotor. Such tabs were found to be a powerful means of adjustment of the tracking of each blade. Another set of experiments with the PAA-1 at about this time related to an investigation of the possibility, suggested theoretically, of improving the longitudinal stability of an Autogiro by having a fixed wing, of a profile which gave an unstable travel of the center of pressure, instead of one with the symmetrical section usually used. To check the theory, two PAA-1's of the same loaded weight were tested using the same rotor speed at 85 mph (137 km/h). The ailerons of one machine were drooped (to simulate an aerofoil with an

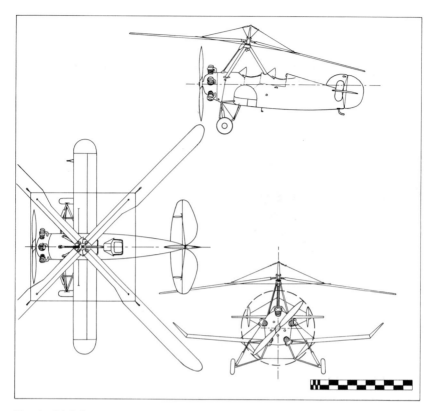

Pitcairn PAA-1.

unstable travel of the center of pressure) while the fixed wing of the other machine was of the normal symmetrical section. The PAA-1 with the drooped ailerons showed better stability.

All American Autogiros produced up to 1933 had four-blade cable-braced rotors despite the fact that the C.19 Mk.IV had been flying in the United Kingdom with a fully cantilever folding three-blade rotor since June 1931 and production versions were in service from March 1932. Pitcairn accordingly purchased a cantilever C.19 Mk.IV rotor hub and blades late in 1931 and fitted these to a PAA-1, NC10771. A significant improvement in performance resulted but the flying characteristics proved to be qualitatively inferior to those with the cable-braced rotor. A low-frequency vertical vibration, known as "bouncing," proved an intractable problem with cantilever rotors which was reduced to an acceptable level only after much development work.

Cierva made a detailed analysis of the problem during 1933 and produced recommended solutions that were partially successful. However, it was not until the introduction of much more flexible rotor blades from the mid-1930s that the problem was largely overcome.

Pitcairn PAA-1 with experimental cantilever three-blade rotor. (Pitcairn photograph)

As numerous accidents had occurred when Autogiros landed with drift, a fully castoring landing gear was designed and built for the PAA-1. This was tested on NC10771 during 1934 with excellent results so that a similar gear was later used on the AC-35 and PA-36 Autogiros.

The PA-18, PA-20, and PA-24 were all developments of the basic PAA-1. In many cases, these later Autogiros were, in fact, airframes of earlier aircraft modified up to the later standard. Fuselages of second-hand PA-18's were used for jump take-off PA-39s.

On January 15, 1932, Cierva and Pitcairn were jointly awarded the John R. Scott Medal and $1,000 Premium[17] by the Board of Directors of City Trusts of the City of Philadelphia "for the invention of the Autogiro, its improvement and development as a propelling and stabilizing force for heavier-than-air craft, and its introduction into America." The citation further stated: "This apparatus derives its lift from the rotary movement of its support surfaces through the air and differs from the aeroplane in that its supporting surfaces or blades are free to move at a speed independent of the machine as a whole. The application of this apparatus to this character of craft will, in a large measure, make for safety and convenience not to be otherwise secured."

Buhl Autogiro. (165-hp Continental A-70). The third American Autogiro licensee (granted a license in March 1931 by the Autogiro Company of America) was the Buhl Aircraft Company of Marysville near Detroit in Michigan. This company was related to the large financial, manufacturing, and real estate organization of the same name, based in Detroit. The aircraft company had originally

145

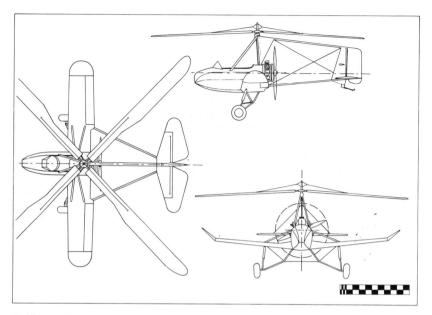

Buhl Autogiro.

been formed in March 1925 with Lawrence D. Buhl as president and A.H. Buhl as vice president. It was then known as the Buhl-Verville Aircraft Company and devoted itself to the manufacture of fixed-wing light aircraft. Later it produced a range of commercial biplanes collectively named Airsedan. In April 1931, Buhl's chief engineer, Etienne Dormay, started the design of an unusual type of Autogiro with a pusher engine. It had similarities with Cierva's C.21 design study of the previous year (see Chapter 6) and pioneered a configuration not to be tried again until the Pitcairn YO-61 of 1942, post–World War II. However, the pusher layout has been widely used for small "aerial motor-bike" autogyros (see Chapter 12).

Buhl's design team under Dormay consisted of R.V. Doorn as assistant chief engineer and nine other engineers.

The Buhl Pusher Autogiro had a loaded weight of 1,850 lb (839 kg), later increased to 2,000 lb (907 kg), and a conventional cable-braced four-blade Cierva rotor 40 ft (12.19 m) in diameter. The rotor, landing gear, and fixed wing were taken straight from the PA-18. The rotor—which had an engine-powered spin-up drive—was mounted on a tripod to which was also attached the upper of the three booms that supported the tail unit. Pilot and passenger were accommodated in tandem in a nacelle built up of steel tubes to which strut-braced fixed wings, with upturned tips, and the landing gear were attached.

The Buhl Pusher was first flown by the manufacturer's test pilot, Jimmy Johnson, on December 15, 1931. It proved to be underpowered. Cierva flew the aircraft himself when he visited Buhl Airport near Detroit on December 28. He is

The Buhl Autogiro prototype which was the first Autogiro with pusher engine. (Howard Levy)

said to have later given flights to General Billy Mitchell, Edsel Ford, and other prominent people in this aircraft, of which only one example was built. Buhl ceased building aircraft in 1932 after getting into financial difficulties.

Pitcairn PA-16. Design study undertaken for Pitcairn by Heraclio Alfaro in 1931. This was of a two-seat cabin Autogiro with fixed wings, airplane-type control surfaces, and cable-braced four-blade fixed-spindle rotor. The tail unit consisted of a fixed central fin with twin fins and rudders mounted on the tips of the horizontal tail surfaces. This design was not proceeded with. The PA-16 designation was probably adopted because there had been seven Pitcairn Autogiro types with PA numbers since the PA-8 airplane of 1930.

Pitcairn PA-17. Design study in 1931 of a development of the PAA-1. This was a two-seat fixed-rotor spindle Autogiro with tandem open cockpits like its predecessor. It also had a four-blade cable-braced rotor and differed mainly in having side fuel tanks between the fuselage framework structure and the outer faired lines of the rounded fuselage profile. This design was later evolved into the PA-18, which incorporated the results of much development work on the PAA-1.

Pitcairn PA-18. (160-hp Kinner R5). An improved and enlarged version of the PAA-1 which benefited greatly from the increased power of its Kinner engine and from its enlarged 40 ft (12.19 m) diameter rotor. The rotor pylon consisted of two struts, both on the center line of the fuselage. The PA-18 had a larger fixed wing, better fuselage shape, and higher weights than the PAA-1. It was designed to elim-

Pitcairn PA-18, the developed version of the PAA-1, of which at least eighteen were sold in 1932–33.
(Pitcairn photograph)

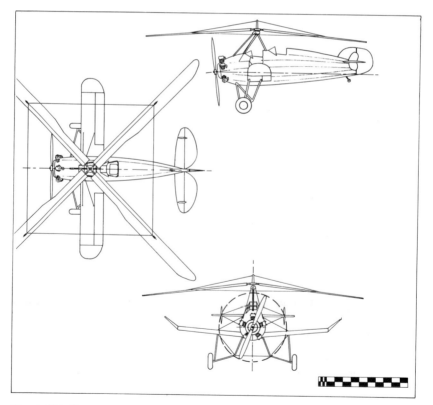

Pitcairn PA-18.

inate various undesirable features of the earlier design. These included the necessity of ballasting the PAA-1 for certain load distributions, poor longitudinal stability due to type and location of the fixed wing, etc. The PA-18 made its first flight on March 1, 1932, and was exhibited at the 1932 Detroit Air Show. It gained U.S. Department of Commerce Approved Type Certificate No. 478 on April 7, 1932. At least nineteen were sold in eighteen months and possibly as many as twenty-three were built by Pitcairn Aircraft at Willow Grove. (The name of the company was changed to Pitcairn Autogiro Company in January 1933.) A slowdown in sales of the PA-18 led to its being offered at a reduced price of $4,940 from March 1933 so that it replaced both the PA-20 and the PA-24 for the remainder of the time that Pitcairn continued to do business in the civil market.

Pitcairn PA-19. (420-hp Wright R-975-E2). A report in the London *Times* of February 10, 1931, said a five-seat cabin Autogiro was planned. This materialized in the United States as the PA-19 designed by a team under R.B.C. Noorduyn who joined Pitcairn in February 1932 to take charge of the project. The PA-19 was the largest Autogiro so far built when first flown by Jim Ray in September 1932.

A big cabin four-to-five seater, with a large (50 ft 7½ in, 15.43 m) cable-braced four-blade rotor, the PA-19 had its rotor axis arranged so that it could be moved fore and aft in the first aircraft or tilted in the subsequent machines. This so-called pilot assistor was for trimming purposes under different loading conditions and was operated by a control in the cockpit. Unusually large plywood-covered cantilever fixed wings were of mixed construction and incorporated ailerons. The fuselage was a fabric-covered welded steel tube structure of typical Pitcairn design. The cabin had two individual seats in front with dual controls. There was a large bench-seat at the back of the cabin which was soundproofed and luxuriously furnished. Test flying was largely complete by November 1932, although certification required another seven months. Performance was quite impressive with a top speed of 120 mph (193 km/h) and a cruising speed of 100 mph (160 km/h). Take-off required 270 ft (82.3 m) with no ground run in landing.

It is interesting to note that no completely satisfactory later technology (direct control or jump take-off) Autogiro as large as the PA-19 was to be developed. The French C-34 of comparable size was flown in 1939 but it had poor flying characteristics.

A total of five PA-19's were built. Certification was achieved on June 23, 1933 (ATC No. 509), and one aircraft was retained as a company demonstrator. The first sale, in February 1933, was to the Year-Round Club in Florida. This aircraft continued to fly until 1935. Two PA-19's were sold to the Hon. A.E. Guinness and exported to the United Kingdom in 1935 where they were registered G-ADAM and G-ADBE. The first is believed to have crashed at Newtonards in Northern Ireland in 1935. The second crashed later at Gatwick and was finally broken up in 1950, having been stored during World War II. Its C of A had expired on September 30, 1939. The fifth PA-19 was sold to Colonel R.L. Montgomery.

The Pitcairn PA-19, a large five-seat cabin Autogiro.
(Pitcairn photograph)

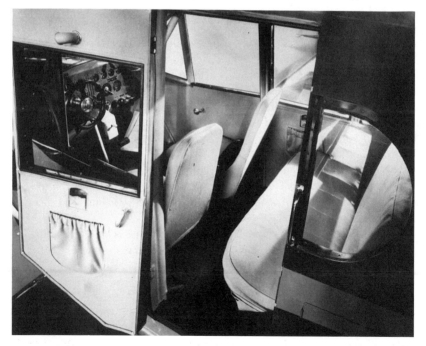

PA-19 cabin.
(Pitcairn photograph)

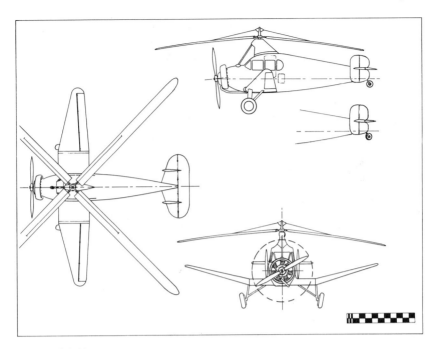

Pitcairn PA-19.

The Pa-19 was also offered with the 420-hp Pratt & Whitney R-985-T3A Wasp Junior engine but was never flown with this power plant. A Hamilton-Standard variable-pitch propeller was also an optional extra and was said to increase the cruising speed by seven mph (11 km/h).

Since 1931, Cierva had been studying the phenomenon known as bouncing and had made a number of suggestions to overcome the problem. While in the United States during 1933, he made recommendations that were incorporated in the design of a cantilever three-blade rotor for the PA-19. However, when tested on the PA-19, qualitative performance was not entirely satisfactory so that the cable-braced rotor was retained on these aircraft.

Tests were also made on the PA-19 cantilever rotor of rotor hub fairings aimed at reducing blade-root losses. The results of these tests were also disappointing.

During this American visit, Cierva received an outstanding award for his "development of the theory and practice of the Autogiro." This was the Daniel Guggenheim Gold Medal for 1932, presented to him during a ceremony at Soldier's Field in Chicago. The only previous recipients had been Orville Wright, Prandtl and Lanchester.[18] In connection with this ceremony, on June 28, 1933, Jim Ray landed a PA-19 at Soldier's Field—an operation which the pilot judged more difficult than the PCA-2's landing on the White House lawn in 1931. Another important award to Cierva at this time was the 1932 Fédération

151

Aéronautique International (FAI) Gold Medal made on January 11, 1933. In October 1933, the Franklin Institute of Philadelphia awarded him the Elliott Cresson Medal[19] "in consideration of the original conceptions and inventive ability which have resulted in the creation and development of the Autogiro."

During his 1933 visit to the United States, Cierva indicated that he was thinking of switching his development effort from the tilting rotor head to cyclic and collective pitch control. He suggested that Pitcairn should continue to concentrate on the tilting head presumably to avoid an overlap in the two companies' activities. In the event, Cierva did not get very far toward these new objectives. It was Raoul Hafner, working independently but using, with permission, some of Cierva's patents, who was to produce the first gyroplane to fly with cyclic and collective pitch control two years later. Toward the end of 1933 (November 16) Pitcairn did, however, file an American patent (no. 2,380,582) covering a fixed spindle rotor with all cyclic and collective pitch functions performed by varying the pitch angles of the individual blades while rotating at high speed. This patent was not granted until July 31, 1945.

Pitcairn PA-20. (125-hp Kinner B5). This was an improved version of PAA-1 of cleaner aerodynamic form and better performance. It had the same 37-ft (11.28 m) rotor as the PAA-1. A tailwheel replaced the PAA-1's tailskid. One or two PA-20s were built from scratch and at least six PAA-1's were modified to PA-20 standard. This model and the PA-24, a higher-powered version, with the larger 40 ft (12.19 m) rotor, appeared in August 1933. Production of the PA-20 was, however, terminated on about April 14, 1933, and that of the PA-24 in January 1934, and they were replaced by the PA-18. The PA-24 is discussed in Chapter 8.

Experience in service with the PA-18, PA-20, and PA-24 led to the conclusion that the control characteristics of the Autogiro in the stage of development then reached were inadequate for the larger numbers of less-experienced pilots by whom it was now being flown. Many minor accidents occurred, causing broken rotor blades, damaged landing gears, propellers, or tail surfaces, etc., although there were few injuries and no fatalities. The accidents were caused by loss of control at low speeds near the ground when the airflow over control surfaces was often insufficient, particularly in turbulence. It was also apparent that there were difficulties in achieving acceptable levels of vibration with cantilever rotors and direct control.

As a result, at the end of 1933, the Pitcairn Company stopped manufacture of its current types and decided to concentrate instead, with a reduced staff, on the development of improved models and particularly on the direct-control development with cantilever rotor that Cierva had started in England in 1931. At the same time they would seek to overcome the various vibration difficulties. Direct control, in due course, overcame the deficient control characteristics of the early Autogiros but, meanwhile, American winged Autogiros are said to have continued to be produced up to 1935–36—probably usually as rebuilds of PAA-1s.

Pitcairn PA-21. (420-hp Wright R-975-E2 Whirlwind). This was an improved version of the PCA-2 and differed only in being fitted with a more powerful Mark of Whirlwind engine. This model was announced in 1932 and was intended to bear much the same relationship to the PCA-2 as the PA-20 and PA-24 did to the smaller PAA-1. However, the Pitcairn decision at the end of 1933 to stop manufacture of Autogiros of fixed-rotor spindle pre-direct-control technology affected the PA-21 and it seems that none were built. Probably, however, a small number of PCA-2's were modified to PA-21 standard, fitted with the 420-hp R-975-E-2 Whirlwind engine. The maximum speed of the PA-21 at 125 mph (201 km/h) was the highest of any Autogiro flown up to 1934.

Pitcairn PCA-1, PCA-1A, PCA-1B

300-hp Wright R-975-EG Whirlwind J-6-9 (PCA-1 and later PCA-1B) or 225-hp Wright R-760-E Whirlwind J-6-7 (PCA-1A and PCA-1B initially). Rotor diameter 43 ft (13.11 m); rotor blade section Gö 429 (modified): Pitcairn No. 4; fuselage length 21 ft 8 in (6.6 in); span of fixed wing 33 ft (10.05 m). Empty weight 2,200 lb (998 kg)—estimated; maximum take-off weight 2,600 lb (1,180 kg) (PCA-1), 2,900 lb (1,317 kg) (PCA-1A), 2,700 lb (1,225 kg) (PCA-1B). Fuel 52 US gal (195 liters). Maximum speed 105 mph (169 km/h); minimum speed 20 mph (32 km/h).

Pitcairn PCA-2

225-hp Wright R-760-E Whirlwind J-6-7 (prototype) or 300-hp Wright R-975-E Whirlwind J-6-9 (production). Rotor diameter 45 ft (13.72 m); rotor blade section Gö 429 (modified); fuselage length 22 ft 1 in (6.73 m); span of fixed wing 30 ft 3⅝ in (9.22 m). Empty weight 2,025–2,093 lb (918–949 kg); maximum take-off weight 3,000–3,225 lb (1,360–1,463 kg). Fuel 52 US gal (195 liters). Maximum speed 118 mph (193 km/h); minimum speed 20–24 mph (32–38 km/h); initial climb 800 ft/min (4.06 m/sec); service ceiling 15,000 ft (4,572 m); range 290 miles (466 km) at 87–98 mph (140-157 km/h).[20] Price $15,000.

Pitcairn PCA-3

300-hp Pratt & Whitney R-985 Wasp Junior. Rotor diameter 45 ft (13.72 m); rotor blade section Gö 429 (modified); fuselage length 23 ft 1 in (7.03 m); span of fixed wing 30 ft 3⅝ in (9.22 m). Empty weight 2,121–2,148 lb (962–974 kg); maximum take-off weight 3,063 lb (1,389 kg). Fuel 52 US gal (195 liters). Maximum speed 120 mph (193 km/h); minimum speed 20 mph (32 km/h); initial climb 800 ft/min (4.06 m/sec); service ceiling 15,000 ft (4,572 m); range 300 miles (482 km) at 100 mph (160 km/h). Price $15,000.

Kellett K-2

165-hp Continental A-70-2 or 210-hp Continental R-670 (K-2-A). Rotor diameter 41 ft (12.49 m); rotor blade section Gö 429; fuselage length 19 ft 6 in (5.94 m); span of fixed wing 26 ft (7.92 m). Empty weight 1,551 lb (703 kg) coupé version, 1,518 lb (688 kg) open cockpit version; maximum take-off weight 2,200–2,265 lb (997–1,027 kg). Fuel 35 US gal (132 liters). Maximum speed 100 mph (160 km/h) coupé version 95 mph (152 km/h) open cockpit version; minimum speed 20–24 mph (32–38 km/h); initial climb 650 ft/min (3.3 m/sec); service ceiling 9,000 ft (2,743 m); range 250 miles (402 km) at 82 mph (131 km/h) coupé version, 78 mph (125 km/h) open cockpit version; rotor speed 130 rpm. Price $8,255 coupé version, $7,885 open cockpit version. (Weights and performance with A-70-2 engine.)

Kellett K-3

210-hp Kinner C5. Rotor diameter 40 ft 6 in–41 ft (12.34–12.49 m); rotor blade section Gö 429; fuselage length 10 ft 6 in (5.94 m); span of fixed wing 26 ft (7.92 m). Empty weight 1,647 lb (747 kg); maximum take-off weight 2,300 lb (1,043 kg), increased to 2,400 lb (1,088 kg). Fuel 35 US gal (132 liters). Maximum speed 110 mph (177 km/h); minimum speed 20–24 mph (32–38 km/h); initial climb 980–1,200 ft/min (4.97–5.08 m/sec); service ceiling 10,000 ft (3,048 m); range 250 miles (402 km) at 90–93 mph (144–149 km/h); rotor speed 130 rpm. Price $8,135/$6,250.

Kellett K-4

210-hp Continental R-670 or 225-hp Jacobs L-4. Rotor diameter 40 ft 6 in (12.34 m); rotor blade section Gö 429; fuselage length 19 ft 11 in (6.07 m); span of fixed wing 24 ft 7 in (7.49 m). Empty weight 1,620 lb (734 kg) Continental and 1,770 lb (774 kg) Jacobs; maximum take-off weight 2,362 lb (1,071 kg) Continental, 2,400 lb (1,088 kg) Jacobs. Fuel 45 US gal (170 liters). Maximum speed 110 mph (176 km/h) Continental and 114 mph (183 km/h) Jacobs; initial climb 940 ft/min (4.77 m/s) Continental, 1,000 ft/min (5.08 m/s) Jacobs; absolute ceiling 13,500 ft (4,114 m); range 335 miles (540 km) at 93 mph (149 km/h) Continental and 95 mph (152 km/h) Jacobs.

Pitcairn-Alfaro PCA-2-30

125-hp Warner Scarab. Rotor diameter 34 ft (10.36 m), later 38 ft (11.58 m); rotor blade section probably Gö 429; fuselage length 19 ft (5.79 m); span of fixed wing 30 ft 6 in (9.3 m). Empty weight 1,050–1,283 lb (476-582 kg); maximum take-off weight 1,384–1,813 lb (628–822 kg). Rotor speed 155 rpm (34-ft rotor), 135 rpm (38 ft rotor). No other data available.

Pitcairn PAA-1

125-hp Kinner B5. Rotor diameter 37 ft (11.28 m); rotor blade section Gö 429 (modified). Fuselage length 18 ft 7 in (5.66 m); span of fixed wing 22 ft 9 in (6.93 m). Empty weight 1,148–1,178 lb (520–534 kg); maximum take-off weight 1,648–1,750 lb (747–793 kg). Fuel 27 US gal (102 liters). Maximum speed 90 mph (144 km/h); minimum speed 20 mph (32 km/h); initial climb 550 ft/min (2.79 m/sec); service ceiling 10,000 ft (3,048 m); range 250 miles (402 km) at 75 mph (120 km/h). Price $6,750.

Buhl Autogiro

165-hp Continental A-70. Rotor diameter 40 ft (12.19 m); rotor blade section Gö 429; fuselage length 21 ft 6 in (6.55 m); span of fixed wing 25 ft 3 in (7.69 m). Empty weight 1,400 lb (635 kg); maximum take-off weight 1,850–2,000 lb (839–907 kg). No other data available.

Pitcairn PA-18

165-hp Kinner R5. Rotor diameter 40 ft (12.19 m); rotor blade section Gö 429; fuselage length 19 ft 4½ in (5.9 m); span of fixed wing 21 ft 3 in (6.47 m). Empty weight 1,310–1,354 lb (609–614 kg); maximum take-off weight 1,900–1,950 lb (861–884 kg). Fuel 30 US gal (113 liters). Maximum speed 100 mph (160 km/h); minimum speed 20–26 mph (32–41 km/h); initial climb 680–700 ft/min (3.45–3.55 m/sec); service ceiling 12,000 ft (3,657 m); range 250 miles (402 km) at 80–85 mph (128–136 km/h). Price $6,750, reduced to $4,940 in March 1933.

Pitcairn PA-19

420-hp Wright R-975-E2 Whirlwind. Rotor diameter 48 ft–50 ft 7½ in (14.63–15.43 m); rotor blade section probably Gö 429; fuselage length 25 ft 9 in–26 ft (7.84–7.92 m); span of fixed wing 30 ft 8 in (9.34 m). Empty weight 2,675–2,690 lb (1,213–1,220 kg); maximum take-off weight 4,032–4,640 lb (1,829–2,104 kg). Fuel 90 US gal (340 liters). Maximum speed 120 mph (193 km/h); minimum speed 30–35 mph (48–56 km/h); initial climb 850 ft/min (4.31 m/sec); service ceiling 12,500 ft (3,810 m); range of 365 miles (587 km) at 100 mph (160 km/h); rotor speed 125 rpm. Price $14,500–$14,950.

Pitcairn PA-20

125-hp Kinner B5. Rotor diameter 37 ft (11.28 m); rotor blade section probably Gö 429; fuselage length 18 ft 7 in (5.66 m); span of fixed wing 22 ft 9 in (6.93 m). Empty weight 1,198 lb (543 kg); maximum take-off weight 1,770–1,800 lb (802–816 kg). Fuel 27 US gal (102 liters). Maximum speed 88–93 mph (141–150 km/h); cruising speed 70–79 mph (112–127 km/h); minimum speed 26 mph (41 km/h); initial climb 550 ft/min (2.49 m/sec); service ceiling 7,150 ft (2,180 m). Price $3,900–$4,940.

Pitcairn PA-21

420-hp Wright R-975-E2 Whirlwind. Rotor diameter 45 ft (13.71 m); rotor blade section probably Gö 429; fuselage length 23 ft 1 in (7.03 m); span of fixed wing 30 ft (9.14 m). Empty weight 2,029 lb (920 kg); maximum take-off weight 3,000 lb (1,361 kg). Fuel 52 US gal (195 liters). Maximum speed 125 mph (201 km/h); minimum speed 28 mph (45 km/h). Price $15,750.

Chapter 6

Direct Control

By the early 1930s the various unsatisfactory mechanical features of the first production Autogiros were being overcome so that the type could be more widely used. At the same time, Autogiros were being increasingly flown by run-of-the-mill pilots. In these circumstances, the lack of control, particularly at low speeds, of Autogiros with conventional airplane-type controls became more evident and provided Cierva with the incentive to look again at the control problem.[21] The result proved to be of crucial importance in turning the Autogiro into a fully practical aircraft. It was perhaps the outstanding example of Cierva's genius as pragmatic innovator and engineer.

The development (covered by British Patent No. 393,976, applied for on December 16, 1933) was apparently undertaken entirely with private money. Assistance from the British government to Autogiro development had, in any case, been only modest up to this point—a total of some £16,000 since 1925 (equivalent to about $440,000 today).

Cierva realized that only a system that operated through the rotor could provide adequate control at low airspeeds and in such situations as cross-wind landings. Just as the solution of the original flapping blade problem had come to him ten years earlier at the opera in Madrid, so too the concept of direct control, came to him when attending the opera—in this case, one rainy night in London. The sight of a long line of umbrellas suggested to him later, as he enjoyed the music, that a rotor's disc might be arranged to be tiltable from below much as an umbrella's canopy can be tilted in all directions by means of its handle.

Cierva C.19 Mk.V. (105-hp Armstrong Siddeley Genet Major I). An experimental single-seat version of the C.19, the Mk.V (G-ABXP) was converted by Avro to Cierva's requirements out of the last production Mk.IV. Work started at Hamble in the latter part of 1931. (Hamble was in process of being taken over by Air Service Training Ltd. at this time.)

Many changes were made to G-ABXP, the most important being the fitting of a universally mounted rotor hub that could be tilted in all directions by the pilot. He exercised control through a column linked to the tilting head at the top of the rotor pylon by two push-pull rods that emerged from the fuselage in front of the cockpit in a manner reminiscent of the C.10 and C.11. After his return from

The Cierva C.19 Mk.V direct-control prototype with tilting head operated by push-pull rods. In early form without tailplane.
(Museo de Aeronáutica y Astronáutica)

America in February 1932, Cierva used this aircraft first at Hamble and later at Hanworth to establish the effectiveness of control through the rotor and then to refine the details of the mechanical system by which he achieved it. The first test flights were made in the period March 5 to 22 without wings or tailplane.

Cierva had tried a sideways-tilting rotor head on the first version of the C.4 in 1922, but had later abandoned it as a means of lateral control and had adopted ailerons instead, because of excessive control loads. As far as is known, Cierva did not revert to tests with a tilting rotor hub until 1932. However, it is just possible, although unlikely, that the unexplained control rods between fuselage and rotor hub visible in photographs of the experimental C.10 and the original and first reconstructed versions of the C.11 are evidence of unsuccessful experiments with direct control during 1927 and 1928. (See Chapter 3.) A more likely explanation is that the control rods and curiously complex rotor pylons on the C.10 and C.11 were to make possible experimental changes to the fore-and-aft and lateral setting of the rotor spindle and the spindle's position in relation to the aircraft's center of gravity.

Probably on grounds of excessive complication, Cierva had previously rejected the laterally tilting head combined with variable-incidence rotor blades patented by David Kay. He now returned to the tilting head and carried its development to a logical conclusion by making the rotor free to tilt in all directions. He thus obtained both fore-and-aft and lateral control without separate control surfaces and–most important—the improved control he needed quite independently of forward speed and without the complication of variable-incidence rotor blades. Although the experimental C.19 Mk.V retained a rudder, it emerged that this control could also be dispensed with for most purposes.

The early flights at Hamble of the experimental C.19 Mk.V without wings were kept secret as long as possible but could not remain so for long, particularly as this was not a government-sponsored program and was therefore unprotected by

157

the Official Secrets Act which, between the Wars, kept many aeronautical developments in the United Kingdom from being reported in the press. Sure enough, the story broke in the *Sunday Express* of March 27, 1932, and was widely reported elsewhere over the following few days. The impression given by the reports was that satisfactory direct-control Autogiros would soon be available. As might be expected, this had serious adverse effects on sales of existing types of fixed-spindle Autogiros, particularly the Pitcairn PA-18 and Kellett K-3, recently launched on the market in the United States. James Weir was similarly concerned about its likely effect on sales of the C.19 Mk. IV.

Of course, at this stage, the C.19 Mk.V was purely experimental. Its handling characteristics were still unsatisfactory and considerable refinement would be required before direct-control Autogiros could be put into production. Production C.30As did not, in fact, appear until July 1934. Cierva first gave details of direct control in a lecture delivered to the Aero-Technical High School at Cuatro Vientos in Madrid on April 12, 1932. He had previously, in January of that year, explained the direct-control concept to his Pitcairn American licensees—to whom he had also propounded his further idea of collective pitch variation for jump take-off. (See Chapter 9.)

Pitcairn took out an American patent (no. 2,380,580) covering control by tilting the rotor disc and jump take-off by collective pitch variation. Zero pitch gave no lift for rotor spin-up; steep pitch gave the jump, and autorotative pitch was used for climb out.

The C.19 Mk.V in later configuration.
(Author's Collection)

In the course of extensive experiments over the following year, Cierva developed and refined this latest step. The C.19 Mk.V was flown with two- and three-blade rotors and with various types of tail unit, including a biplane arrangement. The C.19 Mk.V prototype suffered from a rolling tendency caused by reaction to engine torque. This undesirable feature was overcome in later direct-control Autogiros by fitting asymmetrically cambered "differential" stabilizers with fixed tabs, adjustable on the ground.

The C.19 Mk.V was tested at Farnborough between August 2 and 5, 1932, when it was flown by three pilots for a total of six hours. Their conclusions were: "The take-off is improved and the landing run reduced compared with the C.19 Mk.IV. The lack of stability and the lag in the controls make flying unpleasant while the behaviour when using rudder alone and when the stick is pulled right back might make it dangerous." Speed was limited to 80 mph (129 km/h).

The C.19 Mk.V was first demonstrated in public at Hanworth on November 14, 1932. In the spring of 1932 the C.19 Mk.V had been flown by Pitcairn and Ray who had come over specially from the United States. They were of the opinion that the aircraft still required much development, vibration levels and stick forces being excessive.

An important development, first tried in a rather different form on the French C.L.10 in November 1932 (see below) was adapted to the C.19 Mk.V late in January 1933. This was literally the adoption of the umbrella handle concept in the form of a hanging stick—the pilot's control column was suspended into the cockpit from the top of the rotor pylon and was linked directly to the universally-tilting rotor hub. This arrangement replaced the previously used conventional stick, mounted on the cockpit floor, which had required a more complicated linkage, with two long push-pull rods from the rotor hub to the fuselage in front of the cockpit. This had proved unsatisfactory in the original configuration of the C.19 Mk.V because of excessive play and elasticity. Possibly there were earlier experiments in direct control with the C.10 and C.11 in 1928 but if so these were unsuccessful for the same reason. The new design consisted of a simple suspended stick free to move both fore-and-aft and sideways. It had been proposed by Otto Reder, an engineer who joined the Cierva Company at the end of October 1932. The hanging stick became a feature of many later direct-control Autogiros. Reder apparently got the idea from a similar arrangement on the Arado L.11 high-wing monoplane in Germany.

The Mk.V prototype, which had been used for these important experiments, was finally scrapped in 1935 although some reports say it was rebuilt as the C.30 prototype.

Cierva's direct-control development work on the C.19 Mk.V in the first part of 1932 led to the design later that year of the C.L.10 referred to below. It was followed, in due course, by the W.1 (C.28) and C.30 prototypes in the spring of the following year. The first American direct-control Autogiro, the PA-22, first flew successfully in the summer of 1933, Cierva himself making the first flights.

The successful development of direct control proved to be a real breakthrough in turning the Autogiro into a practcal vehicle. The main criticism of the handling characteristics of all earlier Autogiros, with separate control surfaces, had been that this form of control became ineffective at the low speeds of which these aircraft were capable. This lack of control was particularly serious in rough conditions when approaching to land. Pilots of the early Autogiros always had to be on their guard under such circumstances. It was all too easy to run out of lateral control in the final stages of the approach and then strike the ground in a banked attitude with disastrous consequences to the revolving rotor.

The direct-control Autogiro did away with all this. For the first time the pilot exercised control of his aircraft through the rotor and was thus no longer dependent on airflow over fixed surfaces. The Autogiro had reached a new level of practicability. In developed form, direct-control worked very well in Autogiros of up to about 2,500 lb (1134 kg) gross weight, which included types like the Kellett KD-1. In the smaller sizes like the Cierva C.30 it was, if anything, even better. However, it became progressively less satisfactory in larger aircraft.

Moreover, all direct-control Autogiros suffered from one persistent problem that was reduced to acceptable levels only after protracted investigation. This was the uncomfortable characteristic of vertical bouncing in flight: with three blades, there was a three-per-revolution vibration of the whole aircraft. The greater rigidity of the cantilever rotor blades, which went with elimination of the droop support and inter-blade cables used on earlier rotors, caused the problem.

A test program involving a total of twenty-six different types of rotor tested in England, France, and the United States over a period of three or four years was required before a solution was found. The most flexible rotor blades gave the smoothest ride and step-tapered rotor blade spars had to be developed to achieve the necessary flexibility in bending.

The C.19 Mk.V development aircraft led to the C.30 series Autogiros which form the subject of the next chapter. The C.30 was the first production direct-control Autogiro and it was to prove the most successful and widely used type of gyroplane up to that time or indeed ever since. Direct control in the C.30 provided a new level of practicability—control was independent of flying speed and the level of vibration was quite acceptable, although less satisfactory than the C.19 with airplane-type controls. The main penalty, from the pilot's point of view, was a rather heavy and unfamiliar feel to the control column, which hung down from the rotor pylon.

Cierva C.20. (230-hp Armstrong Siddeley Lynx). Design study for the British Air Ministry undertaken late in 1929. No details available. The design was not proceeded with.

Cierva C.21. Design study of side-by-side two-seat Autogiro with pusher engine installation. Rotor spin-up was to have been by a deflector tail mounted on tail booms. The configuration was patented on February 11, 1930, but the design was not proceeded with. (See Buhl Autogiro in Chapter 5.)

Cierva C.22. (450-hp Armstrong Siddeley Jaguar). This was a 1930 design study for the British Air Ministry of a large Autogiro with a gross weight of 5,000 lb (2,270 kg), a fixed wing and conventional controls. It was to have had a four-blade

The de Havilland C.24 fixed-spindle cabin Autogiro with the original tail unit.
(Philip Jarrett)

rotor 50 ft (15.24 m) in diameter and a mechanical rotor starter. Four passengers were to be carried in a cabin in front of the pilot's cockpit. The design was submitted on August 1, but not proceeded with.

Cierva C.23. Design study for which no details are known, but which was probably overtaken by the development of direct control.

Cierva C.24. (120-hp de Havilland Gipsy III). A neat fixed-rotor spindle Autogiro intended to carry three people in a cabin of the same layout as the de Havilland D.H.80A Puss Moth light airplane. In practice, it was unable to lift more than two people, and was, therefore, usually flown solo, the cabin being extremely cramped. The C.24 was built at Stag Lane by students at de Havillands during 1931. It had a part-welded steel tube and part-wooden fuselage, a folding 34 ft (10.36 m) three-blade cantilever rotor that was also adopted for the production C.19 Mk.IV. The engine drive to the rotor required a modification to the de Havilland Gipsy III engine. This was undertaken by Major Frank Halford, designer of the Gipsy engines, who had also designed the A.D.C. Airdisco engine that had been fitted experimentally with a rotor drive in the Parnall C.11 Autogiro nearly two years earlier.

The C.24 rotor drive would spin-up the rotor to flying speed (200 rpm) in 45 seconds. The C.24 was flown initially by Cierva at Stag Lane in September 1931. It was at first fitted with a single fin and rudder but this proved inadequate, and a dorsal fin plus end-plate fins on the stabilizer were added in October to improve the directional stability. In this form, the aircraft is said to have been renamed C.26, although this seems doubtful and, in any case, it continued to be generally referred to as the C.24. It has been reported that it was fitted at one stage with a two-blade rotor but this, too, seems unlikely. A water ballast tank was provided at the rear end of the fuselage for trimming purposes. Another unusual feature was the nosewheel landing gear. Bendix wheel brakes were fitted as on the C.19.

Only one C.24 (G-ABLM) was built, at a cost of £10,000 (about $275,000 now). Detail design was largely by C.T. Wilkins of de Havillands, who was detached to Ciervas for the task. C.24 proved to be about 10 mph slower than the Puss Moth and its performance was generally disappointing. It was demonstrated in its modified form at Hanworth by Arthur Rawson alongside the C.19 Mk.IV prototype (G-AAHM) on November 19, 1931, and was issued with a C of A on April 23, 1932.

In January 1932, the C.24 was flown and favorably commented upon by Lucien Bourdin, chief test pilot of the French Lioré-et-Olivier company. (At that time, Lioré had acquired a license to manufacture and sell C.19 Mk.IV Autogiros, a license not taken up.) Between May 27 and June 9, 1932, Cierva made a 1,430 mile (2,360 km) European tour in the C.24 during which he stopped off in Bremen to fly the first German-built C.19 Mk.IV. On August 6, 1932, Brie flew the C.24 in the Brooklands-Newcastle Air Race and averaged a speed of 103.5 mph (167 km/h). On October 18 he had an accident in G-ABLM at Castle Bromwich, then the Birmingham Airport. This Autogiro was presented to the Science Museum in London in about 1935 and has recently been reconditioned and been put on public display in the Mosquito Museum at Salisbury Hall near London.

Cierva C.25. (80-hp Pobjoy R Cataract). A small single-seat fixed-spindle Autogiro (G-ABTO), proposed in March 1931, and built by Comper Aircraft Company Limited, at Hooton Park near Liverpool. It was the first Autogiro to use the light and compact Pobjoy Cataract seven-cylinder radial engine that first appeared in 1929. The fuselage and engine installation resembled that of the same firm's Swift light sporting monoplane. The C.25 had a three-blade cantilever rotor with mechanical-drive starting, stub wings and a tail unit initially with a

The C.24 and C.19 Mk.IV flying together at Stag Lane, the former piloted by Cierva and the latter by Arthur Rawson.
(O. Reder)

The Comper C.25 fixed-spindle light single-seat Autogiro with original tail unit at Hooton Park, Liverpool.
(A.J. Jackson)

single vertical surface. Control was by conventional ailerons, elevators, and rudder. The C.25 was registered on January 25, 1932, completed in February, and tested by Cierva at Hooton Park on March 20. The rotor blades incorporated a lot of balsa wood and are believed to have had unidentified manufacturing defects. There may also have been stability and control deficiencies. During his test flight, Cierva became airborne prematurely and the aircraft fell back heavily and was seriously damaged.

The Autogiro was repaired, fitted with new rotor blades and a larger stabilizer before being again tested by Cierva and Rawson on April 20/21. It was then found to be directionally unstable like the C.24, and the tail unit was accordingly similarly modified to incorporate three vertical surfaces. It was next tested by Rawson and Nicholas Comper in June 1932. Comper later flew it down to Heston and then to Hanworth where it was publicly displayed alongside the new C.30 direct-control prototype on April 27, 1933. The one and only C.25 was damaged when a blade broke during a demonstration at Heston later in 1933, and it was struck off the British Register at the end of the year when it was dismantled at Heston. No performance figures or other data on the C.25 seem to have survived but it was claimed to be the fastest Autogiro built up to that time.

Cierva C.26. (Two 80-hp Pobjoy R Cataract). This was a 1931 design study for a single-seat twin-engined Autogiro-helicopter. This machine was to have had two 80-hp Pobjoy R Cataract engines mounted on fixed wings and driving variable-pitch tractor propellers—one engine was to be modified so that the propellers would have been contra-rotating. The starboard engine would have driven the rotor through a free-wheel drive with torque compensation partly by rudder in the slipstream. The C.26 was to have had a rotor 34 ft (10.36 m) in diameter, empty

163

A *Cierva C.19 Mk.IV and the C.24 and C.25 with revised tail units.*
(*Author's Collection*)

weight would have been 900 lb (408 kg) and loaded weight 1,200 lb (544 kg).
This aircraft would have had full hovering capability, when standing on its tail
with the propeller axes vertical, while the maximum speed was estimated at 130
mph (209 km/h). Needless to say, such an ambitious project was not pursued, and
Cierva from then on moved toward less radical Autogiro designs. Also in 1931,
Pitcairn in the United States undertook a design study of a twin-engine Autogiro
which carried the designation PCA-4. It was not built either. (See Chapter 5.)

Cierva C.27. Cierva-Lepère C.L.10. (85-hp Pobjoy R Cataract). Following
Lepère's departure from Weymann and his joining Lioré-et-Olivier, Cierva proposed in March 1932 that the Cierva design license for France be transferred to
Lioré who, late in 1931, had acquired a license to build and sell the C.19 Mk.IV
in France. Weymann agreed to transfer of the license but retained his interest in
the CTW.200 program. The new arrangement took effect from February 1933.
The C.L.10 was a small two-seat side-by-side direct-control cabin Autogiro built
in France by Lioré-et-Olivier to the order of its controlling shareholder "La Participation Mobilière et Immobilière." At a meeting in September 1932, this company's board authorized expenditure of 300,000 francs on two Autogiros to be
built by Lioré-et-Olivier at Argenteuil using rotor blades and engines supplied
from England. The Autogiros were to be built to the designs of Cierva and
Georges Lepère, who by now had become chief engineer of Lioré-et-Olivier.
Lepère spent the last three months of 1932 in England collaborating with Cierva
on the design. With a three-blade cantilever rotor 9.8 m (32 ft 2 in) in diameter,
the C.L.10 was the first new design of Autogiro to incorporate direct control. This
worked on a different system to that developed on the C.19 Mk.V in England. It
also had, for the first time, a hanging stick control column suspended from the
rotor hub. This moved fore-and-aft for pitch control while lateral control was by a
wheel attached to the end of the control column.

The second of two C.L.10's was first test flown by Cierva at Orly near Paris,
on November 24, 1932. The take-off run was measured at 20 m (66 ft) and the
maximum rate of vertical descent at 4 m/s (13.1 ft per second). Later, Cierva flew
the first aircraft after it had been displayed at the XIIIth Paris Aeronautical Salon

Bouché, Cierva, and Lepère with the C.L.10.
(Musée de l'Air et de l'Espace)

held from November 18 to December 4. The two aircraft were flown successfully by Cierva for a total of about six hours, although they proved to be unstable. Control, by means of the tilting rotor head, was oversensitive. The former Weymann test pilot, Pierre Martin, who had joined Lioré-et-Olivier in November 1932, was killed while flying the second aircraft at Villacoublay on December 19, 1932. Cierva believed that Martin attempted to take off with the control column locked. However, it may be that the oversensitive hanging-stick control, to which some pilots had difficulty in adapting, had something to do with the accident.

It seems that Martin, who had already had between 30 and 40 hours of experience on fixed-spindle Autogiros, flew twice as passenger in the C.L.10 with Cierva on the morning of December 19. He was then briefed by Cierva, who had made ten short flights in the aircraft that morning, before going off solo on his first flight in a direct-control Autogiro that afternoon. Following a somewhat unusual take-off, the C.L.10 climbed sharply to about 200 ft (60 m) before diving into the ground. According to some reports, a rotor blade became detached at about 150 ft (45 m) from the ground.

This was the first Autogiro fatality. Up to this time, more than 120 Autogiros had been built (including more than 30 prototypes), 30 to 40 pilots had been trained on them, and well over 100 pilots had flown Autogiros in the United States alone. About 35,000 hours had been flown over a total distance of about 2½ million miles. This represented a remarkable safety record. For comparison, General Aviation in the United States had an accident rate of about one fatal accident every 5,000 hours in 1939. This had improved to about one every 40,000

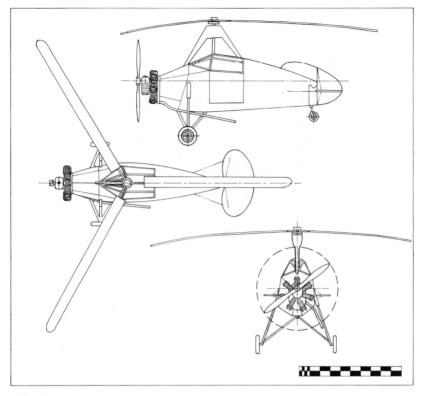

C.L.10 Autogiro.

hours by 1969—a rate not attained by General Aviation in the United Kingdom until 1974. Autogiros were therefore remarkably safe during this early period, even while engaged in experimental and development flying, their safety record being comparable to General Aviation 40 years later.

In May 1934, a C.L.10 was reported at Hanworth. This was presumably the first aircraft which had been on exhibition at the 1932 Paris Salon just before the second aircraft crashed. In modified form, this aircraft may have been known as the C.L.10A.

Cierva-Lepère C.L.10B. (80-hp Pobjoy R Cataract). It seems that a modified version of the original C.L.10 was produced in France during 1933, presumably by Lioré-et-Olivier, and that this Autogiro was later taken to England where it was tested by Cierva and Marsh at Hanworth in April 1934. The C.L.10B was extensively modified from the original C.L.10. The rotor pylon, which had previously been a tripod, was now enclosed within a single large fairing above the cabin roof, while the cabin glazing was considerably extended. However, like the other C.L.10s, the C.L.10B had a rather unsatisfactory wheel control, linked through the cabin roof to the universally tilting direct-control rotor hub. The most notice-

French Cierva-Lepère C.L.10B direct-control cabin Autogiro at Hanworth.
(O. Reder)

able external change was in the empennage which was now similar to that tried on the American Pitcairn PA-22 the previous year. (See Chapter 8.) It featured a braced stabilizer mounted above the rear fuselage with twin fins and rudders suspended from it. The dorsal fin of the C.L.10 was removed. A later version of the C.L.10, the C.L.11 with a 100-hp Renault 7B seven-cylinder radial engine, was projected and, according, to some sources, built in 1932. No details are available.

Cierva-Lepère C.L.20. (90-hp Pobjoy S Niagara III). This was a prototype whose construction was started by Westlands at Yeovil in August 1934 under the supervision of W.E.W. Petter (later famous as designer of the English Electric B-57 Canberra jet bomber) and Arthur Davenport. The C.L.10B was sent to Yeovil to help with this new project. The C.L.20 design was a development of Georges Lepère's C.L.10 and followed the unsuccessful Westland C.29. The C.L.20 prototype (G-ACYI) was a side-by-side cabin two-seater, also with direct control, designed to use the new Pobjoy Niagara engine. It has sometimes been referred to as the C.31, although this designation was also used for a projected high-speed Autogiro in April 1934. The C.L.20 had a 34 ft (10.36 m) folding rotor with three untapered cantilever blades and a gross weight of 1,400 lb (635 kg). First flown at Hanworth on February 4, 1935, by Cierva and Alan Marsh, it proved to be underpowered and deficient in lift, but was pleasant to fly despite oversensitive lateral control. With a passanger it had a ceiling of only a few hundred feet. The fuselage structure was of welded seamless steel tubing, fabric covered. The type never gained a C of A and the prototype was scrapped in 1938. Construction of six production aircraft had been started in March 1935 but was not completed. However, as late as September 1936 Lepère was considering completing and marketing these aircraft. His plans came to nothing.

Cierva C.28. Weir W.1. (40-hp Douglas Dryad). Although James Weir, personally, and Lord Weir, indirectly, had been much involved in the development of the Autogiro since 1925, their family company in Scotland, G. and J. Weir Ltd., had

*The Westland-built Cierva-Lepère C.L.20 direct-control cabin Autogiro.
(Avia Press)*

not been financially associated with the project up to this time. By the summer of
1932, however, the affairs of the Cierva Company had reached a crisis. Cierva's
development of direct control on the C.19 Mk.V at Hamble and Hanworth was
proving to be a major undertaking and was costing more than had been anticipated. Direct control also discouraged sales of earlier technology Autogiros.
James Weir accordingly proposed, at a meeting of the family company's board on
July 6, 1932, that they should themselves obtain a license from the Cierva company to develop an Autogiro. At the time, the company was suffering from the
effects of the worldwide depression. This had caused a major slump in shipbuild-
ing upon which the firm's main buisness depended. It is a tribute to James Weir's
powers of persuasion, as well as to the board's enterprise, that expenditure of
up to £8,000 (about $180,000 in today's values) was duly authorized for this proj-
ect. The new Autogiro was to be a small single-seater which would act as a test
vehicle for a Cierva-designed direct-control rotor and would also be suitable as a
personal flying machine—an application for which James Weir had a special
enthusiasm.

The W.1 had a two-blade folding rotor only 28 ft (8.53 m) in diameter. It had
a 1,200cc Douglas Dryad two-cylinder horizontally opposed air-cooled engine
specially designed and built by Douglas Motors (1932) Ltd. to Weir's order.
Although Douglas got into financial difficulties toward the end of 1932 and dis-
missed most of their staff, canceling other projects, the Autogiro engine was completed and delivered to the Weir works at Cathcart, near Glasgow. A possibly
apocryphal story then has it that the engine refused to start because the original
camshaft was of the wrong hand.

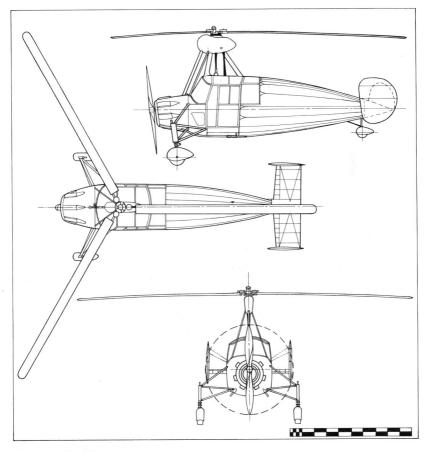

Westland C.L.20.

The W.1 itself was built by Weirs at Cathcart, starting in the latter part of 1932. Design was in the hands of Cierva, and of F.L. Hodgess and R.F. Bowyer in Scotland. Completed in the spring of 1933, the W.1 was taken South and first flown by Cierva at Hanworth in May. Alan Marsh was probably responsible for most of the subsequent test flying but it is recorded that Cierva was flying it again in September. The W.1 was demonstrated to Harold Pitcairn and some of his colleagues who were on a visit to England at this time. Unfortunately the W.1 suffered from excessive vibration, while the rotor spin-up drive was unsatisfactory and the lateral control unacceptable.

The W.1 returned to Scotland in autumn 1933 and was flown there by Marsh in November. In December it was back at Hanworth and Marsh overturned it in landing on the twenty-first.

Weir W.2. (45/50-hp Weir flat-twin). This was aerodynamically similar to W.1 but with structural modifications and a more powerful geared 1,504 cc Weir air-

The W.1 being run-up by Juan de la Cierva.
(Weir Group, Gillies Collection)

cooled engine designed from July 1933 by C.G. Pullin and G.E. Walker. They had joined Weirs from the Douglas Company, where they had been responsible for the original Dryad engine—with Pullin as chief designer. Design of the W.2 airframe and rotor system continued to be in the hands of the Weir team under Fred Hodgess, which by now also inlcuded Ken Watson and J.A.J. Bennett. (Bennett later succeeded Cierva as chief designer of the Autogiro Company.)

As with W.1, the fuselage of the W.2 was a plywood monocoque of oval section. W.2 was first flown by Alan Marsh in June 1934 at Hanworth, where subsequent flight testing was also based. It is believed that Marsh did about ten hours flying on this aircraft. Stability and control proved to be markedly better than W.1, but performance was still disappointing. There was, moreover, a lot of engine-induced vibration and the rotor pylon had to be stiffened with additional struts. A vibration-absorber, designed by Ken Watson, was also subsequently fitted to the propeller boss. Plans, which did not materialize, were made to market this Autogiro for the private owner at £355 (equivalent to about $1,800 then). Design work on the W.2P production version was started and a sales brochure was issued in August 1934. The W.2 prototype was stored for many years by the Science Museum at Knockholt near London, but has now been handed over to the Royal Scottish Museum at East Fortune near Edinburgh.

Although W.2 was not put into production, and a decision was taken on February 5, 1935, to discontinue further Weir Autogiro development, two other small single-seat Weir Autogiros were later built in Glasgow to the designs of the

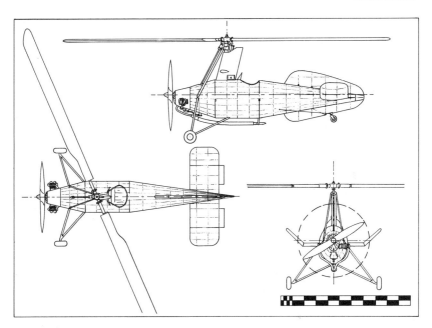

Weir W.2.

The W.2 with enlarged pylon fairing.
(Charles E. Brown)

171

Weir team now under Pullin. These were the jump take-off W.3 and W.4. The W.2 was apparently used to test a number of different rotor heads including the jump take-off head for the W.3. It was also retrospectively fitted with a new design of tail unit later used on the W.3. Weirs developed a form of metal blade construction with plywood covering for W.3 and W.4.

Weir W.3. (55-hp Weir Pixie). The new design was started in June 1935. It was again a single-seater with a two-blade rotor but with a new inverted four-cylinder inline two liter air-cooled engine, also of Pullin and Walker design and Weir manufacture, which developed 50 bhp at 2,550 rpm for a weight of 112 lb (50 kg). W.3 incorporated a new design of Autodynamic head that permitted direct take-off, that is it had the jump take-off capabilities of the final form of Autogiro, which will be discussed in greater detail in Chapter 9. Airframe and engine were designed and built in about twelve months with a design team of only six people.

The direct take-off development enabled the Autogiro to overspeed its engine-driven rotor in flat pitch while on the ground (to about 20 percent above normal flying revolutions) and then suddenly to take on sufficient positive pitch, as the engine was declutched, for it to leap up to about 20 ft (6 m) into the air. It

The Weir W.3 making a jump take-off from Hounslow Heath on July 23, 1936. (British Airways)

*Close-up of the W.3 showing the hanging stick, cockpit,
and rotor head.*
(D.R. Shepherd)

then climbed away in forward autorotational flight under the thrust of its tractor airscrew. The flat pitch of the blades, while the rotor was under power, was achieved in the W.3 rotor by inclining the axis of the drag hinges slightly from the vertical and the axis of the flapping hinges from the horizontal. During rotor spin-up, the blades were held in negative pitch against the forward stop by a driving pin arrangement. When the engine was declutched, the blades were allowed to swing back in relation to the hub and take on sufficient positive pitch to jump the aircraft smartly into the air. The rotor then assumed normal autorotative incidence and continued to turn of its own accord in the airflow as the aircraft climbed away in translational flight.

The Weir W.3, first flown by Alan Marsh at Abbotsinch (now Glasgow Airport) on July 9, 1936, had its first public demonstration at Brooklands on August Bank Holiday. It had been flown for the press on Hounslow Heath alongside the C.30 jump take-off prototype on July 23. It proved to have excellent flying characteristics although the engine gave a good deal of trouble. At one stage, it was planned to market the W.3 at a price of £500, of which the 55-hp Weir engine was to cost £100.

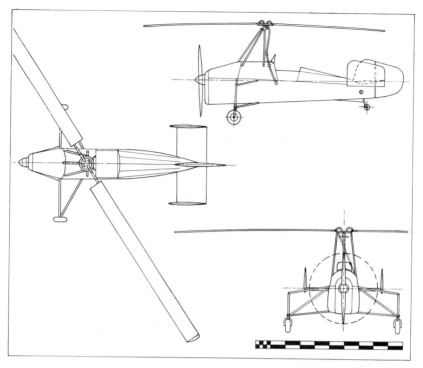

Weir W.3.

Weir W.4. (55-hp Weir Pixie). A refined version of the W.3, fitted with a two-blade Autodynamic rotor for jump take-off, was known as the W.4. The Autodynamic rotor on the W.4 was similar to that fitted to the W.3 and to the C.30 Mk.III (G-ACWF) direct take-off development aircraft (see Chapter 9).

The W.4 had the developed, Type-Tested version of the Pixie engine, later taken over by Aero Engines Ltd. The W.4 apeared in the latter part of 1937 but overturned and was seriously damaged at Abbotsinch during taxi tests by Alan Marsh and did not fly. The rotor was mounted on a streamlined pylon, instead of the multiple strut structure of the W.3, and was fitted with a manually controlled device for spilling the lift on landing. Although he did not get W.4 into the air, Marsh did most of the test flying of the other Weir Autogiros because both Cierva and Brie were too large to be comfortable in these small aircraft. The W.4 was not proceeded with after the accident. This was because the Weir board decided at a meeting on December 28, 1937, to transfer its design team's efforts to helicopters. (See Appendix 5.)

By this date, the Weir designers[22] had acquired a complete rotary-wing capability independent of the Cierva Company. They were, indeed, one of the very few groups in the world with this experience and the Weir directors shrewdly judged that the success of the Bréguet and Focke helicopters showed that it was time to transfer to helicopters. Later the Weir designers and their colleagues from

Weir Autogiro personalities in front of the W.3. Left to right: G.E. Walker, F.L. Hodgess, J.G. Weir, C.G. Pullin, J.A.J. Bennett, and H.A. Marsh. (Flight International)

The Weir W.4 at Cathcart, Glasgow, December 1937. (Weir Group, Gillies Collection)

Cierva were to provide the nucleus of Britain's post-War helicopter design capability. G. and J. Weir Ltd. apparently spent a total of about £60,000 (equivalent to nearly $2 million today) on Autogiro development up to the time when they switched to helicopters.

The Westland C.29 five-seat cabin direct-control Autogiro which did not fly because of ground resonance.
(Avia Press)

Cierva C.29. (550-hp Armstrong Siddeley Panther IIA). Design of the largest and most powerful Autogiro built in Britain started at Westland early in 1933 under the supervision of R.A. Bruce and Arthur Davenport. This machine (K3663) was a five-seat cabin aircraft, with a 50 ft (15.24 m) three-blade direct-control cantilever rotor. Control was by a hanging stick.

Athough built for the British Air Ministry, the Spanish airline, LAPE, is reported to have been interested in the C.29's commercial possibilities. It was designed to have a gross weight of 4,150 lb (1,882 kg) later increased to 5,000 lb (2,268 kg), and although completed and extensively ground tested by Cierva at the Westland Aircraft Works at Yeovil through the Spring of 1934, it could not be flown because of violent swaying as the rotor was spun-up to speed on the ground. On December 11, the C.29 was sent to the Royal Aircraft Establishment for further experimental ground running. However, the rotor vibration could not be overcome and take-off was not attempted. The trouble was said at the time to be due to a spring drive in the 100-hp transmission system for spinning up the rotor. However, it was probably due to ground resonance. The designed maximum speed was as high as 162 mph (260 km/h), the cruising speed 130 mph (209 km/h), and the minimum speed 21 mph (34 km/h). The fuselage structure was of square-section steel and duralumin tubing, fabric covered. If it had been successful, the C.29 would have been a direct-control equivalent to the American PA-19, which had appeared in 1932. The first comparable large direct-control Autogiro to fly—rather unsatisfactorily—was the French C.34 of 1939. (See Chapter 9.)

Cierva C.19 Mk.V

105-hp Armstrong Siddeley Genet Major I. Rotor diameter probably 34–37 ft (10.36–11.28 m); rotor blade section probably Gö 606; fuselage length 19 ft 9¾ in (6.03 m). Empty weight 940 lb (426 kg) maximum take-off weight probably 1,450-1,550 lb (657–

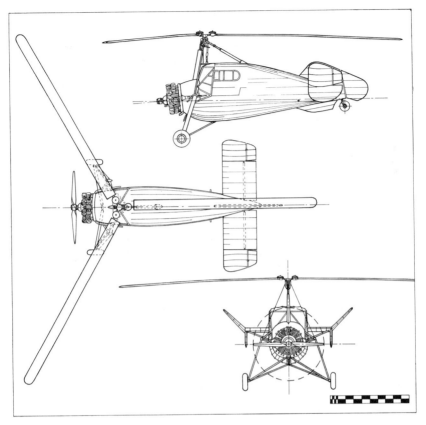

Westland C.29.

703 kg). Fuel 16 Imp gal (72 liters). Maximum speed about 100 mph (160 km/h); rotor speed 180 rpm.

Cierva C.24
120-hp de Havilland Gipsy III. Rotor diameter 34 ft. (10.36 m); overall length blades folded 23 ft 8 in (7.21 m); rotor blade section RAF 34; span of fixed wing 19 ft 6 in (5.94 m). Empty weight 1,280 lb (580 kg); maximum take-off weight 1,800 lb (816 kg). Fuel 21 Imp gal (95 liters). Maximum speed 110–115 mph (177–185 km/h); minimum speed 25 mph (40 km/h); initial climb 600 ft/min (3.04 m/sec); service ceiling 9,150 ft (2,788 m); range 350 miles (563 km) at 97 mph (156 km/h); rotor speed 200 rpm.

Cierva C.27, Cierva-Lepère C.L.10
85-hp Pobjoy R Cataract. Rotor diameter 9.8 m (32 ft 2 in); overall length 6.17 m (20 ft 3 in). Empty weight 280 kg (617 lb) C.L.10, 289 kg (637 lb) C.L.10A, 324 kg (716 lb) C.L.10B; maximum take-off weight 490 kg (1,080 lb) C.L.10, 498 kg (1,099 lb) C.L.10A, 534 kg (1,178 lb) C.L.10B. Maximum speed 164 km/h (102 mph); minimum speed 40 km/h (25 mph); initial climb 4 m/s (787 ft/min); range 500 km (310 miles) at 135 km/h (84 mph); rotor speed 210–235 rpm.

177

Cierva-Leperè C.L.20

90-hp Pobjoy S Niagara III. Rotor diameter 32–34 ft (9.75–10.36 m); overall length 20 ft 4 in (6.19 m). Empty weight 840–920 lb (381–417 kg); maximum take-off weight 1,400–1,426 lb (635–646 kg). Fuel 14.6 Imp gal (66.6 liters). Maximum speed 106 mph (179 km/h); minimum speed 25 mph (40 km/h).

Cierva C.28, Weir W.1

40-hp Douglas Dryad. Rotor diameter 28 ft (8.53 m): rotor blade section Gö 606; overall length 15 ft (4.57 m). Maximum take-off weight 500–600 lb (225–272 kg). Maximum speed 80–100 mph (128–160 km/h); cruising speed 75 mph (120 km/h); rotor speed 200 rpm.

Weir W.2

45-hp Weir 1,500 cc Fiat-twin. Rotor diameter 28 ft (8.53 m); rotor blade section Gö 606; overall length 15 ft (4.57 m). Empty weight 395 lb (180 kg); maximum take-off weight 610 lb (276 kg). Fuel 5.5 Imp gal (25 liters). Maximum speed 90–96 mph (145–154 km/h); minimum speed 28 mph (45 km/h); range 180–200 miles (290–320 km) at 80–90 mph (129–145 km/h); rotor speed 200 rpm. Price £300--400.

Weir W.3

55-hp Weir Pixie (2000 cc). Rotor diameter 28 ft (8.53 m); rotor blade section Gö 606; overall length 14 ft 4 in (4.36 m). Maximum take-off weight 650 lb (294 kg). Maximum speed 100 mph (160 km/h). Range 200 miles (321 miles) at 80 mph (128 km/h); rotor speed 200 rpm. Price £500.

Weir W.4

55-hp Weir Pixie (2000 cc). Rotor diameter 28 ft (8.53 m); rotor blade section Gö 606; overall length 15 ft 4 in (4.67 m); rotor speed 200 rpm. No other data available.

Cierva C.29

550-hp Armstrong Siddeley Panther IIA. Rotor diameter 50 ft (15.24 m); rotor blade section Gö 606; overall length 38 ft (11.58 m). Empty weight 3,221 lb (1,461 kg); maximum take-off weight 4,150–5,000 lb (1,882–2,268 kg). Maximum speed 162 mph (260 km/h); minimum speed 21 mph (33 km/h); initial climb 1,500 ft/min (7.62 m/sec). Range 280 miles (450 km) at 130 mph (209 km/h).[23]

Chapter 7

The C.30 Series

The Cierva C.30 was the most successful Autogiro ever built. About 180 were manufactured in Britain, France, and Germany and they were operated in many parts of the world.

The C.30 represented a major advance in Autogiro practicability. Direct control through the rotor made possible a rotary-wing aircraft that, for the first time, was a truly practical flying machine. Moreover, like other direct-control Autogiros of like size, the C.30 offered an acceptable level of vibration with flying controls which, although not as pleasant as those of some earlier fixed rotor spindle types when flying at cruising or higher speeds, were at least not too heavy or unsatisfactory in feel.

Most important of all, operating procedures could now be laid down which would enable the average pilot, and even one with little experience, to fly the Autogiro without difficulty under most conditions. In his 1934 book, *The Autogiro and How to Fly It*, Reginald Brie was able to spell out the techniques of take-off and landing in the C.30 in the following straightforward terms.

Taking-off
"With the machine head into wind, the right hand holding the handle of the control column in its locked position and the quick release on, apply the wheel brake lever with the left hand. Open the throttle slightly so that the engine is ticking over at about 1,000 rpm and have the feet on the rudder bar which should be in a neutral position, or slightly to the right. With the left hand and in as continuous a movement as possible, release the rotor brake lever, push it to the bottom of its quadrant, slide inwards, and gently ease up on the inner quadrant notch by notch.

"The continued upward movement of the clutch lever for a further two or three notches will result in the clutch plates being brought together and the blades will commence to rotate. Continue the upward movement in a smooth and progressive manner, pausing slightly between the engagement of each notch so as to allow the rotor time to accelerate until, without forcing, any further upward travel is checked.

"The clutch is now fully engaged and the rotor stabilized, from which stage the take-off is accomplished by—

(a) Releasing the control column from its locked position with the right hand and easing back about two inches.

(b) Opening the throttle lever in a smooth manner with the left hand, until the appropriate number of rotor revolutions have been obtained.

(c) Releasing the quick release lever with the fingers of the left hand.

"The clutch and wheel brakes are now disengaged and the machine will commence to move forward. The throttle should be fully opened immediately and the feet kept firmly on the rudder bar, with a slight pressure to the right to keep a straight course over the ground. Allow the machine to accelerate for about three seconds and then ease the control column back. When airborne, in order to obtain the best climbing speed and rate of ascent, the column MUST be eased forward.

Landing

"Under all normal conditions, the approach to land is made with the engine throttled right back, the range of gliding angles varying between vertical descent at an indicated air speed of 0 mph and approximately 1 in 7 at 65 mph. Whatever initial method is employed with the object of losing height, whether gliding turns or the steep angle of descent, at not less than 100 ft above the ground the final approach under normal conditions should consist of a steady glide dead into wind at an indicated air speed of approximately 40 mph.

"At about 10 ft above the ground, the control column is eased progressively backwards to enable the flight path of the machine to become parallel to the ground at about 2 ft above its surface. This results in the ground speed decreasing rapidly owning to the efficient braking action of the rotor disc, and with the easing of the control column right back as the machine again sinks, the tail is depressed, and a perfect three-point landing results with negligible forward run.

"It should be noted that, whether the pilot prefers to keep his feet on or off the rudder bar whilst flying, is of no consequence, but, in order to have adequate ground control (by means of the steerable tailwheel) it is essential that his feet should be on it during the final approach and landing. In addition, as soon as the machine ceases to be airborne, the control column must be pushed forward. This has the immediate effect of spilling air out of the rotor—thus reducing the lift."

Cierva C.30 prototype. (105-hp Armstrong Siddeley Genet Major I). This was the prototype two-seat direct-control Autogiro (G-ACFI) erected early in the spring of 1933 by National Flying Services Ltd., at Hanworth, largely from modified C.19 components, incorporating experience gained with the C.19 Mk.V during the first direct-control experiments. The engine, which had also been used on the C.19s (except for the Mark I), proved to be inadequate. The welded steel tube fuselage was converted from that of a standard Hamble-built C.19 by Airwork Ltd. at Heston (some reports say from the fuselage of the C.19 Mk.V). The rotor blades were made by Oddie, Bradbury and Cull Ltd. at Eastleigh and the rotor hub, clutch, etc. by the Mollart Engineering Company of Kingston-upon-Thames. None of this work was done at Hamble. Air Service Training began to take over the old Avro factory there in April 1931, and Cierva moved out by the spring of 1932.

The famous "Autogiro outpaced by a running man" demonstration. O. Reder on the ground with Cierva piloting the C.30 prototype.
(O. Reder)

From about 1932, Dr. Adolf K. Rohrbach, the well-known German aircraft designer and pioneer of stressed-skin metal aircraft construction, was working on his Cyclogiro, a form of rotary-wing aircraft in which the blades moved like paddle wheels. He joined the Weser Flugzeugbau Gesellschaft in 1934 to pursue this development but it was unsuccessful. However he did suggest that the performance of rotary-wing aircraft could be improved by using the Göttingen 606 aerofoil section for rotor blades instead of Gö 429 or RAF 34 profiles used previously. Cierva accordingly went over to this section on the C.30 and the Americans later followed suit on their direct-control Autogiros. Although the Gö 606 aerofoil improved performance, its marked camber unfortunately produced large periodic pitching moments on the blades as they rotated. Blades of this section therefore feathered and unfeathered elastically during each rotation in response to the dissymmetric loads in forward flight. As forward speed increased, the blades twisted more and more, instead of flapping. This had the effect of reducing the backward tilt of the rotor and of making the aircraft increasingly nose-heavy. As we shall see, this phenomenon could lead to loss of control at high speeds.

The Gö 606 section also caused vibrations that contributed to the stick-shake experienced in the C.30. Substitution of blades of NACA 230 series aerofoil section, which has a substantially zero pitching moment, in later Autogiros contributed materially to reduced vibration.

The cantilever rotor blades of the C.30 weighed 39 lb (17.7 kg) each and the hub 14 lb (6.3 kg). Thus, the hub weighed about 1.15 percent of the aircraft's empty weight. This compares with about 11.5 percent for the hub of the C.8 and 3.5 percent for the PCA-2. The C.30 blades were built up on a tubular steel spar, bolted and sweated at the hub end to a forked fitting. Spruce ribs were attached to the spar by special clips and there were light wooden leading- and trailing-edge members. The whole blade was plywood-skinned and covered in fabric.

The C.30 prototype was a two-seater with a hanging stick for the pilot directly linked to the freely tilting 37 ft (11.28 m) rotor. This hanging stick control, suspended from the top of the rotor pylon, had been first tried in a rather different form on a French-built Autogiro, the Cierva-Lepère C.L.10 in November 1932, and two months later on the C.19 Mk.V in a form adopted for the C.30 series. It was an important part of the new design and was, in due course, to become a characteristic feature of British direct-control Autogiros. RAE pilots who flew the C.30 made some interesting comments on the hanging stick: "Some pilots have an instinctive desire to move the control column in the wrong direction at first. This is because though the hand moves the same way as in an aeroplane the control column tilts in the opposite direction. This desire is soon overcome. It is natural that the rudder is missed."

Excessive shake of the hanging stick was an early problem which was effectively overcome on the C.30 prototype, C.30P, and later models as it had been on the C.19 Mk.V by the simple expedient of ballasting the handgrip with a lead weight.

There were no control surfaces on the C.30's, even the rudder being discarded. There was a differential stabilizer to counter engine torque—that is to say, the left hand stabilizer was cambered on its lower surface and the right hand on its upper surface (generating a rolling tendency to the left). The prototype's rotor was supported on a three-legged pylon mounted ahead of the tandem cockpits. A brake was provided for stopping the rotor after landing. Cierva himself first flew this aircraft in April 1933 and publicly demonstrated it at Hanworth on April 27, so revealing the most important development of his invention in the eight years since he had first brought the Autogiro to the United Kingdom. He was awarded the FAI Gold Medal that year for his development of the direct-control Autogiro and the Wakefield Gold Medal in 1934.

Later in 1933, Cierva, assisted by Alan Marsh, used G-ACFI with a modified rotor for early experiments in jump take-off and achieved the first successful jumps at Hanworth in August of that year. G-ACFI was well-suited for these experiments because it was lighter than the later C.30's. These early jump take-offs were kept secret at the time because of control difficulties that were not completely overcome for another year. Work on jump take-offs had started at the end of 1932 and one-foot jumps followed by a climb-away were being made by October 1934 with the so-called phi-bell head installed in G-ACFI in July. This development was not made public until March 1935 by which time G-ACFI had been repaired, following an accident in October. Jumps were not publicly demonstrated until July 1936. (See Chapter 9).

Close-up of a C.30P showing the hanging stick.
(Author's Collection)

Cierva C. 30P. (140-hp Armstrong Siddeley Genet Major IA). The first of these pre-production machines (G-ACKA) was built by Airwork at Heston. As with the C.30 prototype, the rotor blades were supplied by Oddie, Bradbury and Cull Ltd. and the rotor hub and clutch by Mollart Engineering. The first C.30P—apparently somewhat confusingly known as the C.30P Mk.II—was completed and flown in mid-October 1933. Subsequently, three other pre-production C.30P Autogiros (G-ACIM, G-ACIN, and G-ACIO) were built in the latter part of 1933 by Avro in Manchester, the first gaining its C of A on December 12. All these aircraft were fitted with the more powerful 140-hp seven-cylinder Genet Major IA engine in place of the five-cylinder 105-hp Genet Major I of the C.30 prototype. The landing gear was modified and the folding 37 ft (11.28 m) three-blade rotor was mounted on a four-legged pylon straddling the front cockpit. A Townend ring engine cowling was fitted at first to G-ACKA but later removed. This cowling was also tried on G-ACIO.

In October 1933, Harold Pitcairn and his test pilot, James Ray, visited the United Kingdom to see the prototype C.30 and the first C.30P and to learn to fly direct-control Autogiros. Ray's conclusions on his C.30 flying were that, while acceptable as a prototype, the aircraft was hardly, if at all, better than the PA-22 and was not ready for production. It had a marked bouncing characteristic, similar to the PA-22; its controls were heavy and snatched and jerked; it was unstable in all flight regimes; it rolled one way or the other with changes in power, and it had serious ground resonance problems, evident in both take-off and landing. Production C.30s were to retain some of these undesirable characteristics in less obvious form.

On November 8 and 15, Cierva publicly demonstrated the C.30P at Hanworth. His rapid development of the Autogiro in Britain had outdated the American Autogiros which, at this time, had still not adopted the cantilever rotor. The direct-control feature was obviously even more significant, and Pitcairn made arrangements to make use of both these developments in future American Autogiros. About eighty of the earlier types of Autogiro had been built in the United States up to January 1934 when, for lack of sales and in the face of these rapid new developments, Pitcairn suspended production of his earlier models. Up to September 1933, twenty-four people (aged seventeen to fifty-four) had been granted U.S. Department of Commerce pilot's licenses to fly Autogiros.

Larsen and Stanley both visited the United Kingdom at this time and made comparative performance measurements of the C.19 and C.30. Pitcairn was, however, disappointed in the amount of cooperation Larsen and Stanley received from the British Company at this time. It seems that relations between Bennett and the American engineers were not good. Cierva himself was increasingly preoccupied with political developments in Spain so that he could not give them as much time as they would have liked. Another factor may have been a reluctance by Cierva and his British colleagues to help Pitcairn develop a competitor to the C.30, which they had hopes of putting into large-scale production.

Pitcairn and his engineers therefore returned to the United States in a disappointed mood. Ray stayed on for a time. Early in 1934, Cierva flew a C.30P (G-ACIO) to France and Spain and then used it to tour his native country in February and March—covering a total distance of 2,500 statute miles (4000 km).[24] A notable non-stop flight by a C.30P (G-ACIM) was made by Reginald Brie between London (Heston) and Paris (le Bourget) in 2 hr 20 min on January 5, 1934. The aircraft was being delivered to the French Air Ministry. On May 20-21, 1934, Brie demonstrated a C.30P at the Sixth Fête Aérienne de Vincennes near Paris. He also demonstrated a C.30P to the Belgian Air Force at Evère, near Brussels, in February 1935 and had been responsible for another historic performance in a C.30 a month earlier. This was a series of take-offs and landings on a small (49 ft by 115 ft; 15 m by 35 m) platform erected on the Italian cruiser *Fiume*. The take-offs and landings were made on January 5, 1935, with the ship at anchor and while steaming at 12, 15, 21 and 24 knots in the open sea off the Italian coast near La Spezia.

The Royal Navy conducted deck landing trials with a C.30A Rota on HMS *Courageous* during the 1935 Summer Cruise after Brie had made the first Autogiro deck landings on a British naval vessel on HMS *Furious* on September 9, 1935. The Autogiro (K4230) used for these experiments was specially fitted with Walter Kidde and RFD flotation gear.

C.30A *Rota with flotation gear for carrier trials with the British Royal Navy.* (*Flight International*)

Cierva had himself made the first Autogiro landings on a ship in Europe ten months before Brie, when he landed a C.30P (G-ACIO) on a 52 ft (16 m) by 170 ft (52 m) platform on the Spanish navy's 10,800 ton seaplane tender *Dédalo* moored off Valencia on March 7, 1934. The first-ever Autogiro landings on a ship—in that case an aircraft carrier—had been made by the Americans two-and-a-half years earlier. (Chapter 5.)

In April 1935, Reginald Brie patented a spring cradle device for the landing of Autogiros on ships. This was intended to receive, and hold down, the Autogiro on landing, particularly in rough weather. It also had the potential advantage of eliminating the need for an undercarriage on the aircraft.

The C.30P's were used for a great deal of experimental flying. In March 1934, Marsh tested G-ACIN with rotor blades of various torsional characteristics. In May, he flew G-ACIO with metal rotor blades.

In 1936-37 at Hanworth, the C.30P (G-ACIO) was flown experimentally by Alan Marsh and Max Stoker with a two-position Fairey-Reid propeller.

Cierva C.30A. (140-hp Armstrong Siddeley Genet Major IA). By August 1934, about 150 Autogiros had been built in Spain, Britain, the U.S. and France, (including 44 prototypes,) and a total of nearly 50,000 hr had been flown. Despite James Weir's doubts about the C.30's "lack of controlled stability" and Ray's criticisms, the Autogiro was emerging from the experimental stage. This was becoming clear in the summer of 1933 but Sir John Siddeley, chairman of the Armstrong Siddeley Development Company Ltd, which controlled A.V. Roe and Company Ltd, delayed three months before finally deciding to take a license

Juan de la Cierva takes off in a C.30P (G-ACIO) from the Spanish navy's seaplane tender Dédalo *off Valencia, March 7, 1934.*
(Author's Collection)

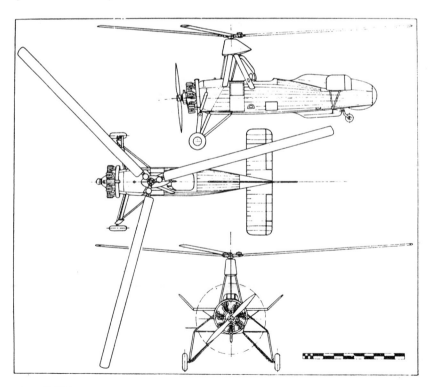

Avro C.30A.

from the Cierva Autogiro Company Ltd. for Avro to manufacture the C.30A in quantity at their Newton Heath works in Manchester. The license was signed early in 1934 and a hundred of these aircraft were laid down as a production batch, although not all were to be completed. Production deliveries started in July 1934. The production C.30A, built by Avro as its Type 671 was identical to the C.30P except for the landing gear. The top of the oleo leg was carried to an outrigger and compressed with less spread of the wheel track—an important improvement for landing with no ground speed because it reduced side loads on the tires.

Orders for this direct-control open-cockpit two-seater—at a price of £1,250 equivalent to $44,000 today—were received from operators in many parts of the world. A total of twenty-six had been ordered by the end of March 1934. The order book had increased to fifty-six by June and, by the end of the year, Avros were turning them out at a rate of nearly twenty per month. However, the market was soon satisfied and sales tailed-off sharply so that production had to be cut back early in 1935, long before the one hundred laid down had been completed. Manufacture in Manchester continued at a low rate until seventy-eight C.30A's had been built. Production ceased in June 1938.

About a dozen C.30A's were sold to private owners. In addition, in the United Kingdom, C.30A's were supplied to the Airwork Flying School at Heston, to Air Service Training at Hamble, to the Lancashire, Bristol and Wessex, and Redhill Flying Clubs and to the Cierva Autogiro Flying School at Hanworth. The Cierva company operated a C.30A for London's Metropolitan Police who were conducting experiments in controlling and studying road traffic from the air. In mid-August 1934, a C.30A, flown by S.J. Chamberlin and fitted with two-way radio, was used for several weeks by the Metropolitan Police for this purpose. An Autogiro was used for actual traffic control on Derby Day for several years.

In October 1934, a C.30A was exported to Western Australia, intended for use in New Guinea, as had been proposed eight years before when the goldfields

Avro production line of C.30A Autogiros at Manchester.
(John Stroud)

were being first exploited and the Autogiro itself was in its infancy. The original intention had been to fly the Autogiro all the way to New Guinea, but prudence prevailed and it was shipped to Perth. From there, it was to be flown to its intended destination. Leaving Perth early in 1935, the C.30 covered 150 miles (240 km) before fracturing a rotor blade at Merredin. After a long delay, while a replacement blade was obtained, the flight continued but got no further than another 200 miles (320 km) to Kalgoorlie, reached in May. The C.30 never got to New Guinea but is reported to have been leased to N.G.A. Mendham in late 1936. Its ultimate fate is unknown.

The Hon. Mrs. Victor Bruce left Lympne on November 25, 1934, on an attempt to fly to Cape Town in a C.30A. She covered 370 miles (600 km) and reached Dijon in France on the first day. However, three days later and another 240 miles (390 km) on, a crash in landing at Courbessac airfield near Nîmes in the south of France damaged the Autogiro and slightly injured Mrs. Bruce, thus ending her plucky attempt and demonstrating once again the Autogiro's unsuitability for long-distance flying. The direct-control C.30 had not got as far toward the Cape as had Young's C.19 two and a half years earlier.

Nevertheless, flying time on direct-control Autogiros was accumulated much more rapidly than on previous types: more than 4,000 hours had been flown on C.30s by March 1935.

In September 1934, flights were made with a C.30A by Reginald Brie between Hanworth and the Mount Pleasant Post Office in central London to see whether the Autogiro could save time by carrying mail between city-center post offices and airports. These experiments anticipated the Eastern Air Lines Autogiro mail service in America in 1939–40 but did not include landings in central London. (See Chapter 8.)

Avro-built C.30A Autogiros were bought for experimental purposes by the Royal Navy and by the French and Spanish navies. The latter service was the first to use an Autogiro on military operations—in Asturias during a rebellion in October 1934. One Autogiro was supplied to the Soviet government, which later used a small number of home-produced A-7-3a autogyros for night reconnaissance and leaflet dropping during World War II. The French had limited numbers of C.30 and C.301 Autogiros in service with both air force and navy at the outbreak of war. Some of these flew a few operational reconnaissance missions toward the end of the Battle of France. As we shall see, the Royal Navy later ordered small numbers of British C.40 and American PA-39 Autogiros just before the war but neither type was used operationally. However, some of the British military C.30's discussed below, together with requisitioned civilian C.30's were used by the RAF during the war.

Cierva C.30A Rota. (140-hp Armstrong Siddeley Civet I). The RAF was one of several air forces which adopted the British-built C.30 Autogiro. The RAF had been tentatively interested in Autogiros since 1925 and this was undoubtedly one of the factors which induced the Air Ministry to provide such limited support as it had to development during the late 1920s. However, after tests with two C.19

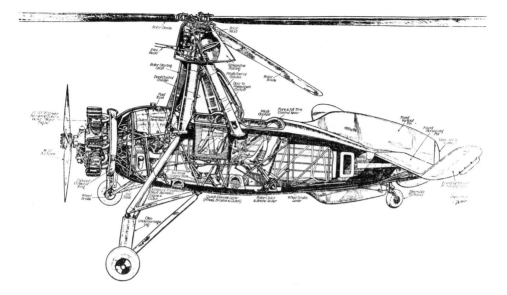

Sectional drawing of the Avro C.30A.
(Flight International drawing)

Mk.IIIs, interest had largely faded by 1932. In September 1933, Reginald Brie took a C.19 Mk.IV to the RAF station at Netheravon and from there, during the following few days, made about forty flights during the Army's maneuvers on Salisbury Plain. A number of senior officers were given flights, including Generals Wavell and Jackson. These demonstrations and the introduction of direct control led to another change in the official attitude. It seemed in 1933 that the new type might be useful for both army cooperation and, possibly, for certain maritime uses.

Two forms of the C.30A, named by the Air Ministry on July 9, 1934, as Rota I (to Specification 16/35) and Rota II (to Specification 2/36), were decided upon for Army cooperation and naval duties and ten (K4230 to K4239) were ordered under Requisition 99/33 for the former role on February 12, 1934. Two other Rotas were supplied later (K4296 and K4775), the former on floats. The Armstrong Siddeley Genet Major IA engine used in the RAF aircraft was known in the service as the Civet I but an uprated 160/180-hp version, known as the Civet Major, was experimentally installed in the last Rota (K4775) and extensively tested at RAE from July to November 1935. This engine was apparently the military version of the geared Genet Major IV. It was later to be proposed for the C.40 Autogiro.

This Rota (K4775) was originally delivered to the RAE in the latter part of 1934 when it was fitted with the standard Civet I engine and it may have reverted to this engine after the tests with the Civet Major. Before conversion, K4775 was extensively tested at RAE, as recorded in R. and M. 1859 (of March 1939). C.N.H. Lock, in his introduction to this report, reviewed ten years of progress which can be summarized as follows:

The importance of the advance represented by the introduction of direct control was acknowledged, but the RAE had reservations about the lack of separate rudder and elevator surfaces. Indeed, the latter was thought to be essential for safety in a high-speed dive.

From C.6 to C.30, the other main improvement had been the fitting of a drive to start-up the rotor, thus reducing take-off time and distance. Blade solidity had been reduced from 0.19 to 0.047, the original symmetrical blade section being changed to a cambered one and the blade angle increased from 1.75 to 5.5 degrees. The thickness/chord ratio of the blades, which were now cantilever, had gone up from 11.4 to 17.1 percent.

After 1928, there had been little official research in gyroplanes in the United Kingdom, although considerable progress had been made in the United States. Eventually in 1934, a C.30 had been acquired for experimental research at RAE. Soon afterward (early 1935) an inquiry was instituted into an accident to a C.30 attributed to loss of control in a steep dive caused by differential twisting of the blades on each side of the aircraft. The inquiry led to detailed theoretical investigation of blade twisting and to flight measurements of blade motion by means of a cine camera mounted on the rotor hub.

Estimates of top speed showed that there was a serious uncertainty about the drag of the C.30's fuselage. This led to wind-tunnel tests of a model at the National Physical Laboratory. Several years later (between April 22 and May 14, 1937) a C.30A was tested by the French in their large Chalais-Meudon wind tunnel.

Performance measurements on the C.30A at RAE showed that it required a ground run of 450 ft (137 m) to take-off in still air (and 1,510 ft, 460 m to reach 50 ft, 15 m) and a 70 ft (21 m) landing run (300 ft, 91 m from 50 ft, 15 m). The maximum level speed was 94 mph (151 km/h) and the minimum 32 mph (51 km/h) at the full load of 1,900 lb (862 kg), dropping to 23½ mph (38 km/h) at 1,560 lb (708 kg). The steepest angle of controlled glide was 45 degrees although the maximum angle of descent measured was 68½ degrees. The latter was, however, only possible by skillful and vigorous use of the controls, and the aircraft pitched and rolled considerably and was quite uncontrollable laterally. The lowest gliding speed was 22 mph (35 km/h) when the Autogiro was descending at 30 ft/sec (9.14 m/s). The minimum rate of descent was 13 ft/sec (3.96 m/s) and the minimum angle of glide 11 degrees. The maximum rate of climb was 355 ft/min (1.8 m/s) and the service ceiling 6,600 ft (2000 m), reached in 33 minutes.

In September 1934, two RAF instructors (Flight Lieutenants W. Humble and R. H. Haworth-Booth) were given a course on C.30's at the Autogiro school at Hanworth. They were then posted to the RAF School of Army Cooperation at Old Sarum to train RAF pilots on the Rotas for service with the five home-based army cooperation squadrons.

Six Rotas had been delivered to the School of Army Cooperation by November 22, 1934. It was reported on December 24 that the War Office had decided to abandon captive observation balloons in favor of the Autogiro. In September 1935, six Rotas took part in combined Army/RAF exercises. The Rota proved, in the event, to be of only limited use for army duties in the three roles envisaged—intercommunication, artillery observation, and reconnaissance. The Autogiro's poor take-off performance and a tendency to ground resonance when landing on rough surfaces were serious handicaps and the type was used only sporadically up to 1939.

During the Second World War, neither the conventional short take-off and landing army cooperation airplane (such as the British Westland Lysander) nor the Autogiro was found, in practice, to meet the army's requirements over the battlefield. Instead, liason or air observation post (AOP) light airplanes (such as the L types in the United States, the Auster series in the United Kingdom, and the rather more powerful Fieseler Storch in Germany) were found to be the best solution. As a result, Autogiros were little used during the war. The French had sizeable numbers in service in 1940 for artillery observation but they were rendered ineffective by the war of movement and soon disappeared after the French defeat. Small numbers of C.30s were employed by the RAF on radar calibration and communications duties and there was a limited amount of operational flying by the Japanese Ka-1A and Ka-2, but the Autogiro's contribution to the war as a whole was very small. A few C.30s were used for coastal patrol and rescue by a Swedish company during the war. In six years their pilot, Rolf von Bahr, flew 2,000 hours on C.30's.

Requisitioned C.30s and a few surviving Rotas remained in service with the RAF until October 1945 but Rotas served with the School of Army Co-operation at Old Sarum only until the outbreak of war. In the early stages of the war, R.A.C. Brie flying a C.30A, almost single-handed, played a vital role in calibrating the United Kingdom's new radar chain which was soon to play such a large part in the Battle of Britain. The success of these little-known operations led, in July 1940, to the few surviving Rotas and requisitioned civilian C.30's being used to equip eight Radio Servicing Units. These later became 1448 Flight based at Hendon, Odiham and Duxford, where they were employed mainly for radar calibration, a role in which the French navy also employed a few Autogiros. The Flight was commanded first by Flight Lieutenant M.J.B. Stoker and later by Squadron Leader (later Wing Commander) R.A.C. Brie. Finally, the RAF's only Autogiro Squadron, No. 529, was formed in June 1943 and continued to operate the type from Halton and Crazies Hill near Henley-on-Thames until the end of the war. The squadron at one time had as many as seventeen C.30s in service. When disbanded on October 20, 1945, it had accumulated a total of 9,141 hours of Autogiro flying. It had been commanded throughout by Squadron Leader Alan Marsh.

The C.30 was thus the first gyroplane to be built and operated in numbers over a protracted period—it remained in service for more than ten years. As was to be expected, structural and other problems, which had not appeared previously

Rota in service with 529 Squadron, RAF, during World War II. The pilot is Flying Officer Norman Hill.
(Norman Hill)

on Autogiros, now revealed themselves. However, these were few in number: one of the most important was fatigue-cracking, occurring at the blade roots near holes through which bolts or rivets held the blade spar to a surrounding sleeve. The problem was cured by a new type of lead-lag hinge damper and by altering the spar so that it ended in an integral collar. Cracking of the rotor head hinge pins required a 100-hour check of this component.

The first fatal accident to an Autogiro in Britain, referred to earlier, occurred to a Rota of No. 2 (Army Co-operation) Squadron at Old Sarum on January 21, 1935. The pilot, Flying Officer L.W. Oliver, was killed when he lost control of his aircraft while flying in cloud and got into a high-speed dive from which he was unable to recover before he hit the ground.

This was the second fatal Autogiro accident. It followed that of the French C.L.10s in 1932. A third was to occur in the United States in August 1935, when Robert Swenson was killed and John Miller injured in an accident to a Pitcairn PA-18 fixed-spindle Autogiro at Willow Grove, Pennsylvania. There is believed to have been a fourth fatal accident at Étamps in Northern France just before World War II. A military pilot, Captain Barbotin, lost his life when a LeO C.30 shed a blade in flight. Another French pilot, Vautier by name, was killed in a landing accident to a C.30A (F-AOIO) at Rouen on May 29, 1938.

It was announced in March 1935 that the British Air Ministry had recently required a modification to the root structure of existing Autogiro rotor blades,

A *Rota with twin floats.*
(R.T. Riding)

presumably as a result of investigations following Flying Officer Oliver's accident. An Air Ministry Order in March 1936 required RAF pilots to wear parachutes while flying Autogiros, although this practice seems to have been discontinued later. Parachutes were not worn by the RAF when flying Autogiros during the War.

Cierva C.30A Rota seaplane. (140-hp Armstrong Siddeley Civet I). Following test-flying by Cierva and Marsh from the River Medway at Rochester between April 13 and 26, 1935, Marsh ferried the Rota seaplane (K4296) mounted on Short F.61 type twin floats from Rochester to Felixstowe. At Felixstowe, this aircraft was tested for the Air Ministry at the Marine Aircraft Experimental Establishment. During these tests, Marsh had a most unpleasant experience. On the evening of April 29 he started a test dive at about 5,000 ft (1500 m) and at 110–115 mph (177–185 km/h) suddenly experienced a violent nose-down pitching moment that he was unable to arrest with the control column. The machine bunted onto its back and Marsh found himself flying upside-down at 3,000 ft (900 m) with the rotor below him. At this point some lead ballast in the front cockpit fell out of the aircraft, fortunately missing the revolving blades as it passed through the rotor disc. The machine then righted itself of its own accord and Marsh, who had meanwhile switched off the engine, force-landed on the open sea immediately beneath. He climbed onto a float, swung the propeller, and taxied back to Felixstowe. An eyewitness recorded that Marsh's only comment when he reached the slipway after this ordeal was "When's the next blankety-blank train back to London?"

This experience of Marsh's was attributed at the time to partial unsticking and lifting of the plywood skinning of the Avro-manufactured blades. It was said that this altered the blade profile at high-speeds and caused the nose-down pitching moment. Brie had experienced a similar phenomenon while diving a landplane C.30 during its Certificate of Airworthiness tests at Martlesham Heath some time before. He also had found, during a gentle dive, that the nose suddenly dropped more and more and that he was unable to prevent it. He throttled back and the machine leveled out before reaching a dangerous attitude.

It seems from these incidents that the C.30 had a tendency to pitch nose-down uncontrollably when dived above a certain speed (apparently about 115 mph, 185 km/h). This was, in fact, due to twisting of the highly cambered blades of Gö 606 aerofoil section, as confirmed by the NACA in the United States about three years later, during tests on a Kellett YG-1B, which had blades of the same section. (See Chapter 8.) In some circumstances, such as loss of control in cloud, this characteristic could be dangerous. However, it does not alter the fact that, as the Autogiro's accident record clearly indicates, this type of aircraft was fundamentally safer than contemporary conventional fixed-wing airplanes.

That the C.30 had such a good safety record seems to have been at least partly thanks to the good sense of its pilots in not diving at excessive speeds. Certainly, a Notice to Airmen (No. 46 of 1935) issued by the Air Ministry in the United Kingdom seems to have provided somewhat inadequate warning. It advised pilots not to exceed a speed equivalent to the "normal horizontal speed" (defined as 85 mph, 137 km/h) by more than 50 percent. This 127 mph (205 km/h) limitation would appear to have been inadequate despite the fact that the notice also warned that a height loss of 300/400 feet (90/120 m) was required to recover from a 130 mph (209 km/h) dive.

The Rota seaplane made one further flight in the following year (1936) after being fitted with a new rotor with blades of different torsional characteristics. Tests were not continued because the Rota, handicapped by the drag and weight of the large floats, which increased the empty weight by 275 lb (125 kg), was too slow (96–98 mph, 154–157 km/h) for useful service application.

Focke-Wulf C.30. (160-hp Siemens Sh 14a). Following their license agreement with Cierva in 1931 relating to the C.19 Mk.IV, Focke-Wulf Flugzeugbau A.G. negotiated an extension of their license in July 1935 to cover production of the C.30. Professor Heinrich Focke had by this time formed his separate rotary-wing development company, Focke-Achgelis G.m.b.H., but production, which started in December 1935, remained with Focke-Wulf Flugzeugbau A.G. Forty C.30's were planned to be built under license in Germany and about thirty (some reports say thirty-six) of these were actually completed between 1935 and 1938. They were named Heuschrecke (Grasshopper) and were mainly sold to private owners. The Focke-Wulf C.30 was very similar to the British Avro-built C.30A except that it had a German engine and a different arrangement of trim tabs on the tailplane. It is not known whether any C.30's were operated by the Luftwaffe either before or during World War II. It is likely that the German-built C.30's

A German-built Focke-Wulf C.30 with 160-hp Siemens Sh 14a engine. (Author's Collection)

French Lioré-et-Olivier LeO C.30 with 175-hp Salmson 9Ne engine. (Musée de l'Air et de l'Espace)

would have been requisitioned on the outbreak of war, like other private aircraft. However no record of this appears to have survived.

Lioré-et-Olivier LeO C.30. (140-hp Armstrong Siddeley Genet Major IA or 175-hp Salmson 9Ne). As already noted, Reginald Brie flew a C.30P to Paris on January 5, 1934. On February 8 Cierva ferried another (G-ACIM) from London to le Bourget and then demonstrated it to the French military and naval authorities at Villacoublay. Some of the flying on this occasion was done by Lucien Bourdin of the Lioré-et-Olivier company, which two years before, late in 1931, had taken a license to build, develop, and sell C.19 Mk.IVs in France. This license had not, in the event, been taken up at that time. However, it was now extended to cover production and development of the C.30.

To handle the new license, Fernand Lioré established a rotary-wings department in his company under the management of Ingenieur Pierre Renoux. Roger Lepreux was made responsible for flight testing French-built Autogiros and for this purpose obtained a gyroplane pilot's license on July 12, 1935.

Rotary wing licenses had been introduced in January of that year and were evidence of increasing French interest in the Autogiro. Another sign was the formation in Paris at this time of the Club Autogire de France with Cierva as chairman.

Under the terms of the license agreement, during 1934, Lioré ordered from the Cierva company four Avro-built C.30As (three with Genet Major IA engines and one with a Salmson). The first of these (C/n 709, G-ACWG) was ferried from Manchester to Paris by Lepreux in July and, painted in military markings, was handed over to the French authorities under the designation C.30-01.

During September, this Autogiro was evaluated in army exercises held at Le Val d'Alion and Mourmelon. Early in October Lepreux ferried a second C.30A (C/n 776, G-ACYC) to France. On November 23, Lepreux made a spectacular landing in this aircraft on the Champs Elysées, in front of the Grand Palais in the heart of Paris, where the XIVth Salon de l'Aéronautique was being held. Another much publicised landing by a C.30 in a similarly restricted space, the Plaza de Cataluna in Barcelona, was to be made in the following year.

Before the end of 1934, a third C.30A (C/n 711, G-ACWI) had been delivered to the French, while the fourth (C/n 733, G-ACWT) arrived in April 1935. This last aircraft was designated C.30S being fitted with a French 203-hp Salmson 9Nd engine and Ratier propeller as a trial installation for the French-built aircraft which were to follow. An order (Contract No. 994/4 in Aircraft Plan I) placed with Lioré-et-Olivier on December 28, 1934, provided for the purchase by the government of the four Autogiros delivered from England. These four were based at St. Cyr and obtained their Certificats de Navigabilité during 1935–36. Given the French registrations F-AOHY, F-AOHZ, F-AOIO and F-AOLK, they were used by the Flight Test Center at Villacoublay until they passed to l'Armée de l'Air in 1939.

The French government placed an order for twenty-five Autogiros (Contract no. 277/5) with Lioré-et-Olivier on April 25, 1935. The first five aircraft were C.30As, manufactured in Manchester (as C/ns 800 to 804), probably as kits of components for assembly in France. Subsequent aircraft were to be completely built in France. L'Armée de l'Air were to use these aircraft for artillery observation and reconnaissance. The first aircraft was due to be delivered on June 24, 1935, but was delayed six months until January 8, 1936, partly so that a modification, which the French company favored, could be incorporated. The modification was expected to give the LeO C.30's almost jump take-off and zero landing run capabilities. Another cause of delay to French-built aircraft was said to be Avro's inadequate C.30A production drawings. The French claimed that, on inspecting the airframe of one of the British-built C.30's that had crashed at Villacoublay and been returned to the factory for repair, they found so many discrepancies in the drawings that they were forced to manufacture many of the components for the new aircraft using the crashed aircraft as a pattern.

Some of the French-built C.30s had Genet Majors and some had Salmson engines—the latter required enlarged tailplanes. The French navy was also interested in Autogiros and four of the initial batch of twenty-five were passed on to l'Aéronavale which received its first (C.30-2) in October 1935. Because the navy had been first in seeking authorization to purchase, it received delivery before the air force. The last Armée de l'Air aircraft (C.30-25) was handed over on July 25, 1936. The C.30s were not to be a great success with the French air force. After a period of debate which lasted about three years—that is until nearly the outbreak of World War II—it was agreed that the Autogiro's primary role should be to replace the artillery observation balloons of World War I. The main French criticisms of the C.30 seem to have been low speed, poor climb, lack of stability, unsatisfactory landing gear, and the frequency with which rotor blades were damaged in the rough and tumble of operations in the field.

Nevertheless, despite this debate, the French were to be the largest users of Autogiros for military purposes. In 1939, l'Armée de l'Air had a sizeable force of Autogiros in the front line for artillery observation. If the war had been static, with the opposing sides dug in along the Maginot and Siegfried lines, as the French generals expected, Autogiros might have served a useful purpose. As it was, blitzkrieg limited their use and defeat of the French army brought with it eclipse of the Autogiro, no longer relevant in unforeseen military roles.

The extent of French military and naval use of the Autogiro should be considered. Under Aircraft Plan II of 1937, forty-six Autogiro flights were envisaged to work with the army, each with three aircraft. However, this proposal was dropped in Plan V of 1938 in favor of thirty flights, also with three aircraft each. Six flights were to be formed in 1938 and eight each in 1939, 1940, and 1941. Meanwhile, on December 21, 1936, Lioré-et-Olivier became part of the nationalized Société Nationale de Constructions Aéronautiques de Sud-Est (SNCASE). At the end of 1936, the new company received an order (Contract no. 377/7) for thirty more C.30s for the air force. Another order (Contract no. 390/7) covered an additional four for the navy.

Delivery of these thirty-four Autogiros did not start until January 1938, a delay of more than four months on the planned date. Despite the late start, deliveries were completed by September. This time the delay was attributed to action recommended by the Cierva Company. Tabs were to be fitted to the tailing edges of the rotor blades to reduce the risk of uncontrollable dives caused by blade twisting at speeds of over 115 mph (185 km/h).

By November 16, 1938, eighteen C.30s equipped the air force units (GAO2/506, 517, 1/520, 2/520) designated to work with the 19th Army Corps Division of Artillery, based in Nancy, Metz, and Reims. By December 16, fifty-five Autogiros had been delivered to l'Armée de l'Air of which twenty-four were serviceable, eleven temporarily out of use mainly because of blade damage and twenty in storage. By the end of the year, a total of sixty-four LeO C.30s had been delivered to the air force and navy.

On September 1, 1939, just before the outbreak of World War II, the following eight French air force first line units were equipped with C.30 Autogiros.

Unit	Station	Autogiros in Service	Autogiros under repair	
GAO 504	Chatres	3	1	
GAO 2/506	Etain-Buzy/Metz	4	0	
GAO 1/514	Gap-Tallard/Lyon	5	0	
GAO 517	Nancy/Toulouse	6	0	
GAO 1/520	Chateau-Salins-Delme	1	1	
GAO 2/520	Nancy	2	0	
GAO 4/551	Saint-Simon-Clastres/Orly	4	0	
GAO 552	Mourmelon/Reims	3	3	
	Totals with operational units:	28	5	= 33

Totals with CIOAA training units at Sommesous   3
Total in storage with EAA301[25]   16
Total in air force service   52

In October 1939, Adjudant de Zimmer of GAO 1/514 (flying LeO C.30-38) made three reconnaissance flights over enemy territory. Later in 1939 GAO 1/508 was formed at Dijon.

The navy used Autogiros primarily to track the trajectory of torpedoes fired during exercises by French submarines and destroyers—a role in which a C.30A was also used by the Royal Australian Navy. The French also calibrated the gunnery director radars on their big warships (*Strasbourg, Dunkerque,* and *Richlieu*). L'Armée de l'Air Autogiros were also sometimes hired by the navy for this task. On September 1, 1939, the following French naval units were equipped with C.30 Autogiros.

Unit	Station	Autogiros in Service
3S-2 Squadron	Cuers-Pierrefeu	4
In reserve		2
Autogiro School	Hyères-le-Palyvestre	2
Total in naval service		8

In February 1940, the French navy had four C.30s and four C.301s—discussed later—on charge. They were soon supplemented by four more Autogiros (including one C.301) transferred from the air force. On March 20, nine of these aircraft equipped a single squadron (3S-2) and three were with the Autogiro school at Hyères.

198

On March 20, 1940, there was a total of forty-seven C.30s with air force units as follows:

23 in squadrons or flights

8 in reserve and for training with CIOAA

16 in storage with EAA 301

(plus 4 damaged awaiting write-off)

Between February and June 1940 the CIOAA, which had moved to Mailly and was commanded by Captain Guy Briand, flew about 1,700 hours and trained some thirty artillery observation pilots.

On May 9, 1940, on the eve of the German assault in the West, there were still forty-seven C.30s on charge with the air force made up as follows:

22 with five squadrons or flights (GAO 2/520, 4/551, 1/506, 2/506, 1/514)
    and the CIOAA, of which 18 were serviceable.

25 in storage with EAA 301.

On the same date, the navy had thirteen Autogiros as follows:

9 in one squadron (3S-2)

2 in reserve

2 in the Autogiro school at Hyères-le-Palyvestre

As the war situation deteriorated, the air force units moved back to Tonneins. The force was by then down to eighteen Autogiros. In the days preceding the Armistice on June 25, 1940, the survivors of the Autogiro units were withdrawn to Biard near Poitiers in central France where twelve Autogiros remained in the hands of the training unit, the squadrons having dispersed.

A notable reconnaissance mission was flown by an Autogiro at this time. Captain Guy Briand of the training unit undertook to determine the position of the advancing German formations, information urgently required by the headquarters of l'Armée de la Loire. At one tense moment on this mission, Briand's C.30 was machine-gunned, by a formation of nine Dornier Do 17s which passed 330 ft (100 m) overhead. Fortunately, it escaped.

A rather similar incident occurred to a British C.30 pilot, Flying Officer Norman Hill, while he was on a radar calibration flight over the English Channel on July 14, 1943. Near the coast, he was engaged by a pair of Focke-Wulf Fw 190's and was lucky to escape undamaged.

The naval 3S-2 Squadron (under Lieutenant de Vaisseau Chatel), with eight Autogiros, moved from its peace-time station at Cuers-Pierrefeu to le Havre and Deauville in late March/early April 1940 to patrol the approaches to le Havre harbour. It proceeded to Cherbourg-Querqueville on May 22 where it undertook patrols of the Seine estuary. On June 3, under threat from the German advance, it withdrew to Lanveoc-Poulmic and there the seven surviving Autogiros were burned on June 18 to prevent them falling into enemy hands. The squadron's personnel were evacuated by sea.

After the Armistice of June 25, 1940, seven Autogiros were still on charge in unoccupied France. Six were later captured by the Italians when the Axis overran Vichy France in November 1942. These survivors were soon grounded by unserviceability. The seventh was successfully hidden until after the war when it flew again and is today preserved in the Musée de l'Air et de l'Espace at Le Bourget.

The test pilot, Stackenburg, with characteristic French élan, is reported to have looped a LeO C.30, at Sommesous thus achieving what was claimed to be the first such maneuver by a rotary-wing aircraft—in fact the first Autogiro loops had been performed in the United States in PCA-2's eight years before in 1931. Nevertheless, Stackenburg's may well have been the first loop by a direct-control Autogiro. As early as 1925, Cierva had predicted that loops in Autogiros were possible. However, in view of the C.30s known dangerous characteristics in high speed dives, the Frenchman's feat may have been more hazardous than he realized. On the other hand, he may have wanted to demonstrate the effectiveness of the new blade tabs in reducing blade twisting and the resulting dangerous nose-down change of trim at high speed.

Lioré-et-Olivier C.30S (175-hp Salmson 9Ne). One LeO C.30 (F-AOLL) was completed in Lioré's old Lavallois factory in March 1936 as the C.30S (S for "Special", not to be confused with the earlier Avro-built C.30S, S for "Salmson"). Fitted with the more powerful Salmson 9Ne engine and a special long-travel landing gear able to absorb rates of descent up to 4.5 m/s (15 ft/sec), this aircraft gained its Certificat de Navigabilité (No. 9762) on July 11, 1936. Known as "Le Sauteur," it was first flown by Louis Rouland and was to be used for jump take-off development.

SNCASE C.301 (175-hp Salmson 9Ne). This was an improved version of the C.30 of which the first of two prototypes first flew in April 1938 piloted by Rouland. Built by SNCASE, the first production version appeared late in 1938. The C.301 differed from the basic C.30 in a number of important respects. These included the more powerful 9Ne Salmson engine and a Chauvière propeller, a modified tail unit, a Messier long-travel landing gear similar to that tested on the C.30S, tabs on the rotor blades, pneumatic rotor clutch, rotor brake and wheel brakes, trimming device on the control column, tripod (instead of four-legged) rotor pylon, an ER-40 radio, and pivoting observer's seat.

Most important of all, the C.301 is reported to have had irreversible controls. This feature was highly regarded by French military pilots. They feared that, in the event of blade damage by enemy action, the C.30's hanging stick, violently oscillated by the feed-back from an unbalanced rotor, would incapacitate the pilot, preventing escape by parachute.

The C.301 was considered by the French to be a marked improvement on the basic C.30. This aircraft could approach in near-vertical descent to a landing without flare. Longitudinal instability at high speeds was said to be completely cured by the tabs on the rotor blades, making safe instrument flying possible. In December 1938, the first production C.301 (C.301-1) was fitted experimentally with a new vertical fin and a stabilizer with marked dihedral.

Manufacture of the C.301 (to Contract no. 767/8) was under way at Peronne in mid-1940 but was stopped by enemy bombing and the French defeat. This marked the end of Autogiro production in France. C301 rotor blades were

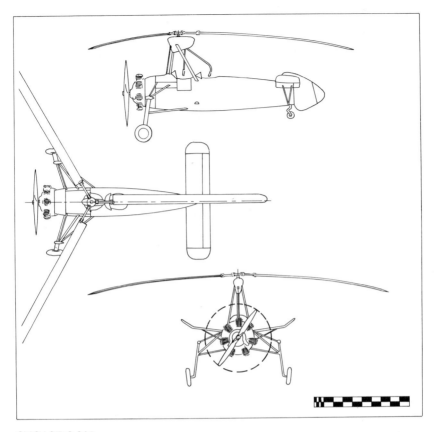

SNCASE C.301.

being manufactured in Norway but none were delivered. Only five C.301s were completed of the hundred ordered in 1938. Presumably these were fitted with blades made in France. An order in 1939 for a further one-hundred aircraft was cancelled. The intention had been to re-equip all the artillery observation squadrons with C.301's. In October 1940, after the French defeat, a C.301 was demonstrated at Marignane before a German armaments commission. The pilot was Henri Déricourt, later alleged to have worked for both the Allies and the Germans as a double agent.

It has been reported (in a recent lecture by General Canet) that after the French liberation two C.30's operated with the French forces in Germany in the last months of World War II. The identity of these aircraft has not been established.

Of all the belligerents, only Japan with its Kayaba Ka-lA and Ka-2 Autogiros, achieved large-scale wartime production of this type of aircraft—British production of the C.30 by Avro having ended in June 1938. Some 95 Ka-lA and Ka-2's were built by the Japanese for artillery spotting with the army. They were, in the

SNCASE C.301.
(Musée de l'Air et de l'Espace)

event, used almost entirely, but still only on a limited scale, for inshore antisubmarine patrols in Japanese home waters. (See Chapter 11.)

SNCASE C.302. (175-hp Salmson 9Ne or 203-hp Salmson 9Ng). In 1938, after flying a total of 68 hours, the C.30S jump take-off development aircraft,F-AOLL, was returned to the factory to be converted into the prototype C.302. This Autogiro initially had a lower-power engine (the 9Nc) substituted for its earlier 175-hp 9Ne, but the former was later replaced by the new more powerful 9Ng. Other changes were a Chauvière Type 308M propeller, a tail unit similar to the modified C.301, and an automatic rotor pitch-charge mechanism that made possible jump take-off. Flown by Stackenburg, the C.302 gave spectacular demonstrations of jump take-offs, according to some reports first in 1940 at Marignane, near Marseilles, and then at both Marignane and Rognac in December 1944. It seems that two other C.302's (also with the more powerful 9Ng engine) were built from C.30 components and completed in 1939. One of these (C.302-3) did not fly until after the war in 1946. This aircraft was probably a conversion of C.30-15 (F-BDAD) used by the Aéro Club Louis Rouland at Marignane and now preserved in the Musée de l'Air et de l'Espace at Le Bourget.

About seventy C.30-type Autogiros seem to have been built in France while Autogiros flown in France had probably accumulated a total of between 5,000 and 6,000 hours by mid-1940. Only a limited amount of experimental and demonstration flying was to be undertaken there during, and immediately after, the war.

SNCASE C.302.
(Musée de l'Air et de l'Espace)

Cierva C.30 Prototype
105-hp Armstrong Siddeley Genet Major I. Rotor diameter 37 ft (11.28 m); rotor blade section Gö 606. Empty weight 1,261 lb (572 kg); maximum take-off weight 1,450–1900 lb (657–862 kg). Fuel 16 Imp gal (72 liters) unconfirmed. Maximum speed 100–109 mph (160–177 km/h); minimum speed 15 mph (25 km/h); initial climb 750 ft/min (3.8 m/s); service ceiling 13,100 ft (4,000 m); range 285 miles (459 km) at 85 mph (137 km/h); rotor speed 180–210 rpm.

Cierva C.30P
140-hp Armstrong Siddeley Genet Major IA. Rotor diameter 37 ft (11.28 m); rotor blade section Gö 606, overall length 19 ft 8 1/2 in (6 m). Empty weight 1,200 lb (544 kg); maximum take-off weight 1,800 lb (816 kg). Fuel 23 Imp gal (104 liters). Maximum speed 116–120 mph (186–193 km/h); minimum speed 15–17.5 mph (24–27.6 km/h); initial climb 902–985 ft/min (4.6–5 m/s); service ceiling 15,250–15,750 ft (4,648–4,800 m), range 300 miles (482 km) at 97–99 mph (156–160 km/h); rotor speed 180 rpm. Original design figures with 105 hp Genet Major I engine were: Maximum take-óff weight 1,530–1,700 lb (694–771 kg); maximum speed 100 mph (160 km/h); cruising speed 85–90 mph (136–145 km/h).

Cierva C.30A (Avro 671)
140-hp Armstrong Siddeley Genet Major IA. Rotor diameter 37 ft (11.28 m); rotor blade section Gö 606; overall length 19 ft 8 1/2 in (6 m). Empty weight 1,210–1,464 lb (548–664 kg); maximum take-off weight 1,800–1,900 (816–861 kg). Fuel 23 Imp gal (104 liters). Maximum speed 94–110 mph (131–178 km/h); minimum speed 15–32 mph

(24–51 km/h); initial climb 355–750 ft/min (1.97–3.8 m/sec); service ceiling 6,600-8,000 ft (2,011–2,438); range 285 miles (458 km) at 75–95 mph (120–152 km/h); rotor speed 180–210 rpm. Price £1,250. Rota floatplane figures were: empty weight 1,495 lb (678 kg); maximum take-off weight 2,088 lb (947 kg). Maximum speed 96–98 mph (154–158 km/h). Price £1,250.

Focke-Wulf C.30 Heuschrecke

160-hp Siemens Sh 14a. Rotor diameter 11.28 m (37 ft); rotor blade section Gö 606; overall length 5.91 m (19 ft 4 3/4 in). Empty weight 574 kg (1,265 lb); maximum take-off weight 820 kg (1,807 lb). Fuel 104 liters (23 Imp gal). Maximum speed 160 km/h (100 mph); minimum speed 32 km/h (20 mph); initial climb 3.17 m/s (623 ft/min); ceiling 2,400 m (7,874 ft); range 350 km (217 miles) at 137 km/h (85 mph); rotor speed 190 rpm.

Lioré et Olivier LeO C.30

156-hp Salmson 9Nc or 175 hp Salmson 9Ne or 140 hp Armstrong Siddeley Genet Major IA. Rotor diameter 11.28 m (37 ft); rotor blade section Gö 606; overall length 6 m (19 ft 8 1/4 in). Empty weight 567–607 kg (1,250–1,338 lb); maximum take-off weight 861–886 kg (1,900-1953 lb). Fuel 110 liters (24 Imp gal). Maximum speed 165–180 km/h (102–111 mph); minimum speed 30 km/h (19 mph); initial climb 4.57 m/sec (900 ft/min); service ceiling 3,000–4,000 m (9,840–13,125 ft); range 300–400 km (186–248 miles) at 136 km/h (85 mph); rotor speed 180 rpm. (Weights and performance with 9Ne engine.)

SNCASE C.301

175-hp Salmson 9Ne or 156 hp Salmson 9Nc. Rotor diameter 11.28 m (37 ft); rotor blade section Gö 606; overall length 7.4 (24 ft 3 3/8 in). Empty weight 586 kg (1292 lb); maximum take-off weight 886 kg (1,953 lb). Fuel 110 liters (24 Imp gal). Maximum speed 170–180 km/h (105–11 mph); minimum speed 30 km/h (19 mph); absolute ceiling 4,000-4,400 m (13,123–14,435 ft); range 420 km (260 miles) at 152 km/h (95 mph). (Weights and performance with 9Nc engine.)

SNCASE C.302

156-hp Salmson 9Ne or 203-hp Salmson 9Ng. Rotor diameter 11.28 m (37 ft); rotor blade section Gö 606; overall length 7.4 m (24 ft 3 3/8 in). Maximum take-off weight 889 kg (1,940 lb). Fuel 110 liters (24 Imp gal). Maximum speed 185 km/h (115 mph); minimum speed 30 km/h (19 mph); service ceiling 3,000 m (9,850 ft); range 465 km (290 miles) at 157 km/h (98 mph). (Weights and performance with 9Ng engine.)

Chapter 8

Direct Control in the United States

Cierva achieved a workable system of direct control in Britain in March 1932. Later that spring, the C.19 Mk.V, incorporating this development, was demonstrated to Harold Pitcairn, James Ray, and Agnew Larsen of the American Autogiro Company who had come to England specially to study this new development. Pitcairn and Ray later flew the C.19 Mk.V. In April 1933, Cierva publicly demonstrated the direct-control C.30 prototype. Early in 1934 the direct-control Avro C.30A entered full production in Manchester and deliveries started in July.

The Americans did not waste time in their attempt to follow suit: the Pitcairn company completed a small prototype direct-control Autogiro of American design (the PA-22) in the spring of 1933 but this machine could not fly in its initial form. Modified, it crashed on its first take-off in March. Many difficulties had to be overcome in its subsequent development both before and after it was first successfully flown by Cierva in the summer of 1933. The PA-22 never reached production; it became instead a most valuable development aircraft and was flown in many forms between 1933 and 1940. Pitcairn did not, in fact, produce a production direct-control Autogiro (the PA-39) until 1941. The first American direct-control Autogiro to go into production was the Kellett KD-1, first deliveries of which were made in early 1935. This aircraft has been described as essentially a scaled-up C.30, but, in fact, it differed in important respects (see below).

In parallel with these developments, the Americans had been making other important contributions to research into rotary-wing flight. The National Advisory Committee for Aeronautics (the NACA) had taken a close interest in Autogiros from 1929. They later purchased a PCA-2 for research and thereafter launched numerous rotary-wing programs. From 1930, Autogiro research had also been undertaken by the U.S. Army at Wright Field.

In 1932, at the instigation of Professor Klemin, Harold Pitcairn endowed a one-year fellowship at New York University. Its objective was wind-tunnel research on Autogiros rotors. The fellowship was awarded to a Mr. Rosen who developed testing techniques that enabled the quantitative performance trends of model rotors to be measured in a wind-tunnel.

In 1934, Pitcairn conducted tests of model rotors mounted on an open motorcar. These tests were directed at measuring the performance of a rotor whose blade area was concentrated at the outer 40 percent of the blade radius. Theoretical studies had suggested that such a configuration would improve performance but this was not borne out by the tests.

In 1935, wind-tunnel tests were conducted at New York University on a series of two-blade rotors specially manufactured by Pitcairn with different distributions of blade area. These experiments confirmed the results of the earlier motorcar tests and of research by NACA. These indicated that removal of blade area inboard reduces the efficiency of rotors. This conclusion had probably been reached by Cierva and the Royal Aircraft Establishment in England as early as 1928 following tests of a rotor with half-length blades on the C.9.

Pitcairn PA-22. (84-hp Pobjoy R Cataract, later replaced by a 90-hp Pobjoy S Niagara). This aircraft, sometimes called the Flying Mock-up, was designed by Agnew Larsen following his visit to England with Pitcairn and Ray in the spring of 1932. During that visit, Larsen had discussions with, and was almost certainly influenced by, Georges Lepère whose C.L.10 direct-control Autogiro was then in design. It was to fly successfully that autumn. Certainly, the PA-22 was like the C.L.10 in weight and size, and bore it a close resemblance. It had a small, side-by-side two-seater cabin with a 32 ft (9.75 m) folding three-blade cantilever direct-control rotor and a British Pobjoy engine. As first conceived, however, the PA-22 was intended to be roadable—that is to say, with its rotor folded, it was to be capable of running on the public roads as a surface vehicle, a scheme strongly advocated by James Ray, the Pitcairn test pilot. However, combining this feature with

The Pitcairn PA-22 Flying Mock-up in its original roadable form.
(O. Reder)

direct control was an ambitious design target as a first step and perhaps not surprisingly the roadable capability was soon abandoned. It was, however, to be revived later in the AC-35 and PA-36 Autogiros. The PA-22 nevertheless had a long and useful career, being flown in a wide variety of configurations, some of the more important being recorded below. (As far as possible, these have been listed in chronological order.)

First (Roadable) Version (84-hp Pobjoy Cataract). As first designed, the PA-22 had an unconventional landing gear consisting of a large central single shock-absorbing engine-driven bull wheel (which did not, however, have its power-drive fitted) mounted beneath the fuselage immediately below the side-by-side two-seat cabin and just aft of the center of gravity. This took the place of a tailwheel. Two forward wheels (which had high-pressure tires) had a more conventional appearance except that they were designed to castor and were intended to be steerable for road use. The cabin was rather narrow for two people, side-by-side, and featured a hanging stick. The tail unit was conventional, consisting of a single central fin, rudder, and straight horizontal stabilizer. As originally completed, the PA-22's three-blade cantilever rotor did not have its spin-up drive installed. The engine drove only a large four-blade wooden propeller.

The PA-22 was first tested early in 1933 but in its first form could not fly because of serious oscillations. When the machine was taxied across the field and the speed of the rotor increased, violent out-of-balance shaking developed. Clearly this could be cured only by major redesign.

Second (Roadable) Version. (84-hp Pobjoy Cataract). Redesign retained the bull wheel landing gear and other features of the first version. Testing was resumed in March 1933 with the rotor spin-up drive still unconnected. Some high-speed taxying was in progress when the aircraft suddenly left the ground unintentionally and went out of control. The PA-22 was badly damaged and the pilot James Ray slightly injured in the subsequent crash. Reasons for the accident may have been several. The pilot's unfamiliarity with the hanging stick, the unduly sensitive lateral control; the lack of asymmetric horizontal tail surfaces (to compensate for propeller torque); and probably some slack in the control system. The previous December, the comparable French C.L.10 had been involved in a similar but, in that case, fatal accident, the first to an Autogiro.

Suggestions have been made that the PA-22 accident was caused by the action of the hanging stick having been deliberately reversed from normal (its stick moved to the left banked the aircraft to the right and vice versa; stick forward raised the nose and vice versa). This seems hardly credible. The hanging stick took a bit of getting used to, even when it operated conventionally. A C.30 was, in fact, modified during the 1939–45 war and flown experimentally with a reversed action hanging stick. Tests showed that the pilot required quite a lot of practice to accustom himself to the change and, in an emergency, unsuppressed instinctive reactions could easily lead to loss of control

A much more likely explanation of the PA-22 accident would seem to be that Ray, like the unfortunate Martin before him, was confused by the unexpected take-off, unfamiliarity with the hanging stick, and excessive sensitivity of the controls. However, if in reality, the PA-22's controls were reversed in the original configuration, this extraordinary design error was presumably corrected in the versions that followed.

Third (Roadable) Version. (84-hp Pobjoy Cataract). Rebuilt in a few weeks after the crash, this version apparently still retained the bull wheel, but control sensitivity had been reduced and there was less slack in the control stabilizer. Perhaps the most important change was the addition of an asymmetric tailplane. The rotor spin-up drive was also connected for the first time. In this form, the PA-22 was successfully flown by Cierva in the mid-summer of 1933. He found that it would take-off in 60 ft (18.29 m) and land without ground run.

Cierva visited the United States for six weeks in summer 1933. In addition to providing help in overcoming Pitcairn's difficulties with the PA-22, as already noted (Chapter 5), he discussed at length his future plans for development of the Autogiro. Cierva had become convinced by 1933 that cyclic and collective pitch control would replace the tilting rotor hub, and he argued that the parent Cierva Company should switch its future development effort in this new direction. Pitcairn, on the other hand, wished to stay with the tilting hub and two-stage collective pitch change for jump take-off. Cierva probably welcomed this as a way of reducing the overlapping of development activity on the two sides of the Atlantic. However, during his visit, Cierva briefed Pitcairn's patent attorney on his new patents relating to cyclic/collective pitch control so that American cover could be arranged.

In the event, the main Cierva effort in the United Kingdom was to continue on the tilting hub right up to the outbreak of World War II, and the prototype Hafner AR III (partly based, with permission, on Cierva patents) became the first autogyro to fly, using the new system, in September 1935.

Fourth (Non-roadable) Version (84-hp Pobjoy Cataract). While Pitcairn, Ray, Larsen and Paul Stanley (Larsen's assistant) were in England during autumn 1933 observing Cierva's first jump take-off experiments with the modified C.30 prototype and the introduction into service of the first direct-control C.30P's, the PA-22 was redesigned and again rebuilt to incorporate suggestions Cierva had made during his visit to the United States earlier in the year. These had included all the latest direct-control ideas and resulted in numerous changes including deletion of the bull wheel. This was replaced by a conventional tailwheel below the stabilizer. The latter had upturned tips inclined at an angle of about 45 degrees. The main landing gear wheels were now given low-pressure tires. Another change was the addition of a large ventral fin and a general strengthening of the fuselage and cabin structure. In this form, with a two-blade propeller replacing the previous four-blade unit, the PA-22 was flown in the latter part of the year after Ray's return from Europe. Testing continued for some months.

Although the direct-control system worked exceptionally well, the PA-22 continued to suffer from serious vibrations, including a persistent and uncomfort-

The PA-22 (fourth variant) as modified into a conventional direct-control Autogiro. (O. Reder)

able three-per-revolution bounce that was in some measure present in all the early Autogiros with cantilever rotor blades.

Fifth (Non-roadable) Version. (84-hp Pobjoy Cataract). This was the same as the previous version but fitted with various different experimental rotors in attempts to reduce vibration. Different blade sections and rotor diameters were tried. The hanging stick was ballasted. The most promising change was the introduction of secondary flapping hinges at about 50 percent of the blade radius which significantly reduced bouncing. Although themselves unacceptable because of their weight and complexity, secondary hinges did suggest that greater blade flexibility in the lifting plane might reduce the kick of blades at the hub in forward flight. This proved to be the case and more flexible blades in later Autogiros resulted in significantly smoother rides. Tests of the PA-22 continued over a period of months extending into 1934.

Sixth (Non-roadable) Version. (84-hp Pobjoy Cataract). The next major changes were to the tail unit. During a rebuild following a crash, the PA-22 was fitted with a raised stabilizer mounted on a central fin. There were two other fins attached some distance in from the stabilizer tips and extending only below it. The ventral fin was removed. This version also had a rotor with secondary flapping hinges and was probably flown sometime during 1934.

Seventh (non-roadable) Version. (84-hp Pobjoy Cataract). Main alteration from the previous version was a changed tail unit. It still had the raised stabilizer but the two outboard fins now projected above and below the stabilizer in an attempt to improve stability. A return was made to a conventional rotor without secondary hinges. This version probably flew in the latter part of 1934. By the end of that year, Pitcairn considered that the PA-22's problems associated with direct-control had been "virtually solved".

The sixth variant of the PA-22.
(S. Pitcairn)

It may have been this version of the PA-22 that was demonstrated at the end of 1934 to the army, navy and civil aviation authorities in Washington. Ray demonstrated direct-control by landing in and taking off from a small field in front of the War College in Washington. Earlier, on November 17,1934, he had made demonstrations along the East River in New York with a view to a possible regular service from the center of the city to Floyd Bennett Field.

Eighth (Non-roadable) Version. (84-hp Pobjoy Cataract). Information on tail area distribution (of both vertical and horizontal surfaces) had been obtained from Lepère by Kellett and had been successfully incorporated in the KD-1. Attempts to duplicate these results in the PA-22 had been responsible for the many changes in tail configuration that had been tried. Directional and lateral stability were still deficient and a further modification to the tail unit was tried in this model. The fins now became outward-tilted end-plates on the stabilizer. The change produced a marked improvement in stability so that this became the definitive tail configuration for Pitcairn Autogiros, and was used on the PA-36, PA-39, and XO-61. First flown early in 1935, the PA-22 in this form gave demonstration landings and take-offs from the roof of the new Philadelphia downtown post office on May 25, 1935. Later in the year, it was demonstrated at the 1935 National Air Races in Cleveland, (August 30–September 2). After the show, during the return trip to Philadelphia, James Ray was forced down by low cloud on the Allegheny Mountains. He landed and taxied ten miles on the road over the mountains before takingoff again and successfully completing his journey by air. The PA-22 had no road drive so that Ray had to depend on his airscrew for propulsion—a somewhat hazardous procedure on the public highway.

Ninth (Jump Take-off) Version. (90-hp Pobjoy S Niagara). A neatly cowled more powerful later-model Pobjoy engine[26] driving a two-blade propeller was fitted in the PA-22 when it was converted for jump take-off in 1935. A wide fairing on the main oleo legs of the landing gear helped to improve its appearance. At the same time, no doubt because this form of tail had been used for the earlier jump take-off

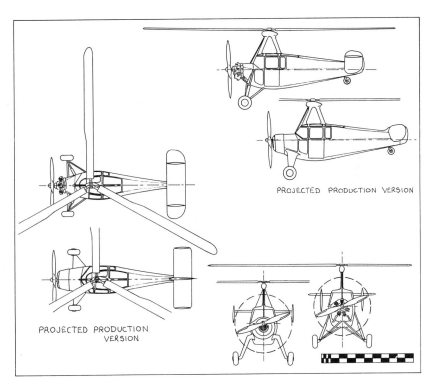

Seventh variant of the PA-22 with scrap views of projected production version.

The ninth (jump take-off) variant of the PA-22.
(O. Reder)

experiments in the United Kingdom, the tail unit was modified back to its earlier form with a lowered differential stabilizer with upturned tips inclined at about 45 degrees. The fin was now somewhat smaller than when this stabilizer had been used previously and there was no ventral fin. The cantilever three-blade jump take-off rotor was mounted on a faired rotor pylon. Its hub incorporated a hydraulic system, holding the blades in zero pitch during rotor spin-up to jump take-off speed. On release of the rotor starter clutch, hydraulic pressure was also suddenly released and centrifugal force drove the blades outward on steep-pitch multi-threaded shanks in each blade root. This had the effect of rotating the blades through 4 3/4 degrees to the flight pitch setting so that, under the impulse of the kinetic energy in the over-speed rotor, the aircraft would jump smartly into the air. This system worked extremely well and, unlike Cierva's Autodynamic head (which could be used only for two-blade rotors—Chapter 9), could be employed with three blades. The same design was later used successfully on the PA-36 and PA-39. In this form, the PA-22 was first flown in autumn 1935 and on November 9 made the first jump take-off in the United States. The jump was to about 10 ft (3 m) followed by a successful climb-away. Tests were continued over a period of several months, investigating the influence on jump take-off of such variables as rotor spin-up gear ratio, rotor blade characteristics, and propeller diameter. However, the PA-22 usually achieved jump heights of only 3 to 4 ft (1–1.8 m) which were of limited practical use because the aircraft usually sank back onto the ground before climbing away.

Tenth (Jump Take-off) Version. (90-hp Pobjoy Niargara). In 1936 the jump take-off PA-22 was fitted with a larger diameter set of blades with secondary flapping hinges similar to those tried previously on the fifth version of the aircraft. Additional reflex was given to the trailing edges of the blades toward the tips. While only a few short flights were made with this rotor, it proved that reflex could be applied to the blade section to a point where the control column reached its forward stop before the aircraft reached dangerously high speeds such as had been experienced in dives with the Kellett KD-1. Tests with the KD-1 had shown that it had a tendency to get into dives in which the pilot seemed to be running out of elevator control as speed continued to increase. This highly dangerous characteristic was due to blade twisting and was cured by fitting reflexed metal tabs on the trailing-edge tips of each blade as suggested by the PA-22 tests.

Eleventh (Jump Take-off) Version. (90-hp Pobjoy Niagara). The PA-22 was also tested during 1936 with a two-blade jump take-off rotor with a hub that permitted variation (in 15-degree increments) of flapping (Delta-3) hinges. Settings were possible from one perpendicular to the blade span axis to a position 45 degrees of the perpendicular, thus causing a decrease of blade pitch as the blades coned upwards.

This rotor was tested in flight between July and September 1936. Ray considered that the PA-22 was now at least as good, if not better, than the C.30 Mk.III. However, Pitcairn decided that it required too much skill for the average pilot to fly safely and he would not agree to its being submitted for certification.

Twelfth (Jump Take-off) Version. (90-hp Pobjoy Niagara). Late in 1938, the PA-22 was tested with a rotor which had Delta-2 tilt of the drag hinges. This was found to be much smoother in flight than rotors with a vertical hinge and friction dampers.

At this point, Pitcairn was still convinced that jump take-off could reverse the U.S. Army's unfavorable conclusions about use of Autogiros reached in 1938 following evaluation of the Kellett YG-1s (see later in this chapter).

Thirteenth (Jump Take-off) Version. (90-hp Pobjoy Niagara). In 1939, the PA-22 was fitted with a two-blade rotor with a hub providing for various inclinations of the drag and flapping hinges. Flight tests showed that while very smooth flight could be achieved at times with certain configurations, the machine was generally very sensitive to gusts with this rotor which was therefore abandoned.

Projected Definitive Jump Take-off Version. (90-hp Pobjoy Niagara). The PA-22 continued to be flown for development purposes until 1940. An improved version—the PA-22A—was projected for production some years earlier but was not built. This model was to have had the same more powerful Niagara motor as all the jump take-off versions. The tail configuration reverted to the lowered stabilizer with end-plate fins, which had proved so successful on the eighth version in 1935. In this case, the fins would not have been mounted vertically. There would have been a new cleaner cantilever landing gear while the jump take-off three-blade rotor would have been mounted on a faired pylon.

Pitcairn PA-23. (420-hp Wright R-975 Whirlwind). Design study undertaken in 1933 of a development of the fixed-spindle PA-19 Autogiro as a flying ambulance. There was provision for pilot, medical attendant, and two stretcher patients. Not proceeded with.

Pitcairn PA-24 (160-hp Kinner R5). This Autogiro was the last Pitcairn design to be built with fixed rotor spindle, that is to say, of pre-direct-control technology. It was a higher-powered version of the PA-20, itself an improved version of the PAA-1. The diameter of the cable-braced four-blade rotor was increased to 40 ft. (12.19 m) like that of the PA-18. There was an optional safety nosewheel and a tailwheel. Two PA-24's were built and about three PAA-1s and two PA-20's were modified to PA-24 standard. The PA-24 gained its U.S. Department of Commerce Approved Type Certificate (no. 507) on May 19, 1933. Like its predecessors, the PA-24 was affected by Pitcairn's decision in January 1934 to stop production of pre-direct-control technology Autogiros. A PA-24 Autogiro (NC11638) is preserved in the Pioneer Museum at Minden, Nebraska.

Pitcairn PA-25. Design Study. No details available.

Pitcairn PA-26. Design study undertaken in 1933 of a six-seat fixed-spindle cabin Autogiro which was a straightforward scaling-up of the PA-19. Not proceeded with.

Pitcairn PA-27 and PA-28. Design studies. No details available.

The Pitcairn PA-24 was the last type of Pitcairn Autogiro of pre-direct-control technology. All PA-24's seem to have been conversions of earlier models. (Peter Bowers)

Pitcairn PA-29. (210-hp Continental W-670 or 240-hp Jacobs L-4). Design study undertaken in 1933 of a four-seat direct-control cabin Autogiro. This was the short fuselage version.

Pitcairn PA-30. (210-hp Continental W-670 or 240-hp Jacobs L-4). Design study, also undertaken in 1933, of a long-fuselage version of the PA-29. Neither version was proceeded with.

Pitcairn PA-31. (420 Wright R-975 Whirlwind). Design study undertaken in 1934 of an ambulance Autogiro, itself a direct-control development of the fixed spindle PA-23 project which, in turn, was a PA-19 variant. Submitted to the U.S. Navy but not proceeded with.

Pitcairn PA-32. (225-hp Jacobs L-4MA). Design study undertaken in 1934 of a direct-control two-seat tandem open cockpit observation Autogiro which was not pursued but which led to the PA-33 and PA-34.

Pitcairn PA-33 (YG-2). (420-hp Wright R-975-9 Whirlwind). In July 1934, the United States armed forces took a new look at the Autogiro. As a result, tenders were invited which led to the YG-2 and XOP-2. Designed and built for the United States Army Air Corps and accepted, following inspection at Wright Field in 1935, the YG-2 (34-279) was a direct-control Autogiro with tandem cockpits for a crew of two. Using a reworked PCA-2 fuselage, it had a 50 ft (15.24 m) three-blade folding cantilever rotor, a gross weight of 3,300 lb, (1497 kg) and, with its powerful 420-hp engine, gave an impressive performance. A maximum speed of 144 mph (232 km/h) at 3,150 ft (960 m) was achieved, equivalent to about 150 mph (241 km/h) at sea level, a record for a rotary-wing aircraft at the time. The PA-33 had a clean cantilever landing gear that significantly reduced drag compared to earlier Autogiros. The PA-34, produced for the U.S. Navy (see below),

The Pitcairn PA-33 was supplied to the United States Army under the designation YG-2. (W. Hannan)

was essentially similar to the PA-33. Both were designed by a team under Paul E. Hovgard.

The PA-33 was not, however, satisfactory as first completed. The control forces were too high and variable to be acceptable for service use. Vibrations, either undetectable or at least unobjectionable in the small PA-22, were not acceptable in an Autogiro of three times the gross weight. The first set of blades tried were rebuilt but showed little improvement. A new set of longer blades—to reduce the disc loading—was therefore designed and built with step-tapered tubular spars. These, together with a redesigned tail unit with large dorsal fin, showed such a marked improvement that the aircraft could be offered to the Air Corps.

The PA-33 went to the NACA at Langley Field, Virginia, in January 1936 for a program of wind-tunnel tests and research flying alongside the Kellett YG-1, which was also there at that time. The PA-33 was destroyed during these tests as a result of rotor blade failure during a speed run at 120 mph (193 km/h) at 3,000 ft (900 m). At the time of the accident on March 30, 1936, the PA-33 was being flown by the chief test pilot of NACA at Langley Field, Bill McAvoy, with a flight test engineer, John Wheatley, as passenger. The accident was caused by one of the fabric covered blades bursting open because of the high air loads generated by the centrifugal force on the air inside the blade. The failure was accompanied by a noise like a steam locomotive while the pilot's control column (with attached stick force recorder) was snatched from McAvoy's hands and rotated violently round the cockpit. Both occupants escaped successfully by parachute coming down in the Back River outside Langley. The Autogiro crashed and was destroyed by fire.

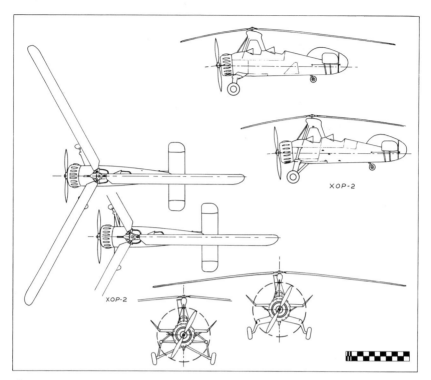

Pitcairn PA-33 (YG-2) and PA-34 (XOP-2).

The PA-33 is reported to have been fitted with the 420-hp Pratt & Whitney R-985 Wasp Junior engine but this seems doubtful.

Pitcairn PA-33B. (420-hp Wright R-975-9 Whirlwind). Design study undertaken in 1939 of a conversion of the PA-33 into a so-called Monorotorplane (or Gyrodyne) which was to have 60/70 percent of the engine's power driving a single main lifting rotor with torque correction. Directional control and a small amount of forward propulsion derived from a single laterally displaced airscrew (taking 30/40 percent of the power) mounted on a pylon projecting to starboard.

Pitcairn PA-34 (XOP-2). (420-hp Wright R-975-9 Whirlwind). Ordered by the U.S. Navy's Bureau of Aeronautics in 1936 and produced in 1937 as the OP-1, in developed form this aircraft was renamed XOP-2. It was a direct-control design, converted from the first of the navy's earlier XOP-1's. As will be remembered, the XOP-1 had been the U.S. Navy's first Autogiro and a variant of the PCA-2. As completed, the XOP-2 was closely similar to the U.S. Army Air Corps' YG-2 (PA-33) except that it had a more conventional open tubular truss landing gear and was fitted with flotation equipment. The high power gave an excellent performance. Like the PA-33, the PA-34 was designed by a team under Paul Hovgard.

216

The Pitcairn PA-34 was similar to the PA-33 but with a redesigned landing gear. It was supplied to the United States Navy under the designation XOP-2. (Author's Collection)

Following the accident to the PA-33 (YG-2) in March 1936, the rotor blades of the XOP-2 were redesigned twice, rebuilt, and tested. The final design, considered satisfactory, incorporated plywood skins, metal leading edges at the tips to withstand abrasion, and step-tapered tubular steel spars. When tested, one set of blades with a built-in reflex at the tips made the aircraft very stable. The PA-34 could be trimmed to fly hands-off and if displaced 5 mph (8 km/h) from the trimmed speed would return to that speed of its own accord.

The designation PA-34 was, apparently, also tentatively applied to a design study for a small Autogiro to be powered by a Warner Super-Scarab. It was not built. Rotor diameter was to have been 43 ft 0 2/16 in (13.11 m) and maximum take-off weight 2,050 lb (930 kg). Maximum speed was estimated at 122 mph (196 km/hr).

Pitcairn AC-35. (90-hp Pobjoy Cascade).[27] Franklin D. Roosevelt's election as president of the United States in 1932 led to the appointment of Eugene D. Vidal as director of the aeronautics branch of the Department of Commerce. Vidal believed that Roosevelt's New Deal should include government help to the United States' aviation industry, and he saw sponsorship of the development of a "poor man's airplane" as a way of providing such help.

In November 1933, a federal government fund of $500,000 (equivalent to $3.4 million today) was accordingly announced and aircraft manufacturers were invited to bid for the development of what was hoped might become the aerial equivalent of Henry Ford's Model T.

The Autogiro, particularly in roadable form, as planned for the PA-22, was seen as one promising way of meeting this requirement. The Autogiro Company of America was therefore contracted in late 1934 to produce a prototype which became the Pitcairn AC-35—AC for Autogiro Company because of its experimental status with the Autogiro Company of America. The Department of Commerce program procured seven aircraft of which the AC-35 was the only entry to meet the Department of Commerce performance requirements without resorting to a larger power-plant. The Department of Commerce requirements

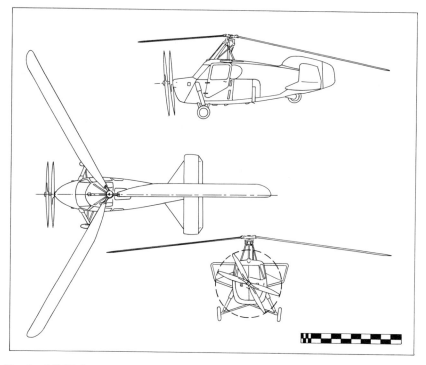

Pitcairn AC-35 first version.

included a speed of 100 mph (160 km/h), take-off and landing in a space 30 ft (9 m) square plus the "roadable" facility.

Developed between 1933 and 1936, the AC-35 was the first roadable Autogiro whose development was pursued, this feature having been dropped from the earlier PA-22. The AC-35 (NX70) was a cabin two-seater with side-by-side seating and a three-blade direct control folding rotor. It was not designed to incorporate the jump take-off feature of the later versions of the PA-22. Of novel layout, but owing much to the PA-22, the AC-35 had a completely buried engine installation with clutching/declutching arrangements to a road drive or to co-axial contra-rotating propellers on the nose of the fuselage.

The design of the AC-35 is said to have owed something to the Cierva-Lepère C.L.20 built by Westland in England in 1934/35 and certainly the two types resembled each other. However, the AC-35 was mainly a development of the PA-22, derived to some extent from the C.L.10, and was designed by the team under A.E. Larsen. Only one of these aircraft was built. It was first flown on March 26, 1936, presumably by Jim Ray.

The AC-35 embodied many ingenious features. The British Pobjoy radial engine was installed behind the seats, within the cabin, where it was aircooled by fan through ducts and louvres. The road drive was taken from the rear end of the engine crankshaft through a clutch and gear to the single rear wheel. An exten-

AC-35 before covering, showing the ingenious layout.
(S. Pitcairn)

sion from the front of the engine crankshaft ran between the seats to a selector box through which it could be coupled either to the rotor (to spin the blades before take-off) or to two co-axial contra-rotating propellers (for take-off and flight), or to run free of either (while the road drive was engaged). The hanging stick, suspended from the cabin roof, had a motorcycle-type twist-grip to operate the throttle. The cantilever rotor blades, mounted on a faired head, folded over the stabilizer when not in use. The maximum road speed was 25–30 mph (40–48 km/h). Had it been put into production, it was planned to sell the AC-35 at a price of $12,500 (equivalent to $90,000 today).

As originally built, the AC-35 had a biplane cellular tail unit, the cell being closed by inclined fin surfaces joining the tips of the unequal-span upper and lower stabilizers. This unusual design was adopted as a result of wind-tunnel tests. However, longitudinal stability at low speeds was very poor with this tail, and it was replaced by a much more satisfactory monoplane unit with inclined tip shields similar to that used on the eighth version of the PA-22.

Although due for delivery in late summer 1935, the AC-35 was not, in fact, handed over to the Department of Commerce until autumn the following year. It was flown to Washington by Jim Ray on October 2 and ceremoniously delivered some weeks later, under its own power and on its own wheels, by road, directly to Secretary Roper at the door of the Department of Commerce in Washington. After extensive tests and demonstrations at Bolling Field by the Experimental Development Section of the Bureau of Air Commerce of the Department of Commerce, the AC-35 was lent back to Pitcairn in 1937 to be used for research and for the AC-35B project (see below). The AC-35B program was abandoned in 1940. The AC-35, restored to its earlier form, was returned to the CAA in 1942.

In 1950, it was finally driven, again under its own power, to the Smithsonian Institution in Washington where it is still preserved at the Silver Hill facility of the National Air and Space Museum.

Both the Bureau of Air Commerce (from August 22, 1938, the Civil Aeronautics Authority) and Pitcairn, to whom the aircraft was lent back for this purpose, undertook extensive testing of the AC-35. During these trials, twelve different combinations of contra-propeller setting and differential stabilizer incidence were tried before the contra-propellers (which proved to be extremely noisy) were removed and replaced with a single large two-blade airscrew that was moved nine inches forward at the same time. Pitcairns reached the conclusion that the contra-propeller complication was unnecessary. At NACA suggestion, tests were also made with fixed contra-propeller surfaces, mounted at the correct angle just aft of the single airscrew disc. These were intended to straighten out the slipstream and provide torque compensation. It was concluded, however, that this could be best achieved with a single propeller and the right size and differential setting of trailing-edge tabs on horizontal tail surfaces. The latter were, in fact, modified from those originally fitted to the PA-22. This confirmed the results of earlier tests on the PA-22. Contra-propellers were therefore not incorporated in the design of the later PA-36.

Many difficult problems were met and overcome by Larsen and his team in the development of this Autogiro. They included those of adequately cooling the aero-engine when running as a road vehicle, overcoming oil-foaming experienced in the transmission, steering on the ground by means of the front wheels and transmitting power either to the rear wheel or to the propellers.

The AC-35 operating as a road vehicle in its third configuration.
(Author's Collection)

The AC-35 proved to have excellent flying characteristics. Several hundred hours of flight testing were completed and the success of this development confirmed the decision to develop the more advanced PA-36 Autogiro.

When Ray went to Europe in autumn 1936, Pitcairn asked him to investigate the possibility of licensing the AC-35 for production by Cierva. The British company was not interested. C.30 production was already tapering off at Avro, and Weir was not convinced of the potential market for a more expensive Autogiro, even one with the increased capabilities of the AC-35.

In 1961, a company in Indiana, Skyway Engineering, considered the possibility of putting a modernized version of the AC-35 into production. They acquired a license from the Autogiro Company of America and built a prototype (N35133) using some components from the original aircraft. However, nothing came of this proposal.

Pitcairn AC-35B. (90-hp Pobjoy Cascade). A program undertaken in 1939 to convert the AC-35 into a gyrodyne. This aircraft was to have been of similar configuration to the PA-33B design study with a power-driven lifting rotor with blades set at about nine degrees incidence and a tractor torque-compensating airscrew offset to starboard. The AC-35 was loaned to Pitcairn for this program by the

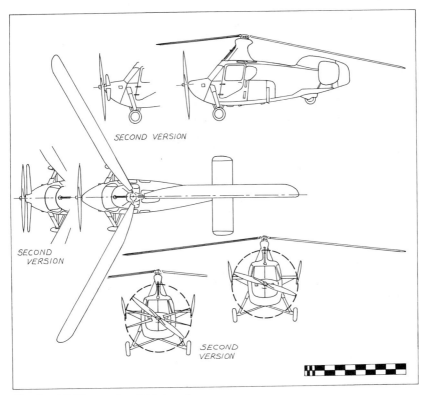

Pitcairn AC-35 second and third versions.

Department of Commerce. Work proceeded well beyond the design stage, a set of blades was completed and modifications to the landing gear started. Design of the rotor hub was 80 percent complete, and design and stress analysis of the tail unit had been completed when the program was abandoned in 1940.

Pitcairn PA-36 Whirl Wing. (175-hp Warner R-500 Super Scarab 165). Developed between 1937 and 1939 by Agnew Larsen's team at the Pitcairn Autogiro Company, which had previously developed the roadable AC-35, the PA-36 was a jump take-off two-seat cabin Autogiro that was planned to be roadable, at speeds of up to 35 mph (56 km/h) in its production version. Two prototypes were laid down but only one was completed and it could not be operated in the roadable mode.

The PA-36 had a three-blade cantilever, folding rotor and was of advanced design with an all-metal stressed-skin fuselage manufactured under sub-contract by the Luscombe Airplane Company of Trenton, New Jersey. The fuselage accommodated a completely buried engine installation amidships, behind the side-by-side seats in the cabin. The tail unit had a large central fin and outward-tilted end-plates on the stabilizer derived from the similar design tried on the eighth version of the PA-22. The PA-36 is claimed to have had outstandingly good flying characteristics, including hands-off stability even in rough air.

At this time theoretical studies were undertaken and mock-ups were made by Pitcairn of possible methods of rotor hub fairing and of suppressing blade root losses. These were intended for possible application to the PA-36 and were a continuation of work done in 1933 on the experimental cantilever rotor for the PA-19.

Other investigations, as design work on the PA-36 progressed, included trials of a pair of single-blade counterweighted counter-rotating propellers (covered by the Tidd patent). There was an undesirable vibration under power that was eliminated by adding a small counterweight to the hub, 90 degrees off the blade-span axis. Possible application to single-blade rotors was also considered.

Larsen and Stanley from Pitcairn had been in England during 1936–37 assisting Cierva with the development of jump take-off. They had moved there with their families in autumn 1936 because experience with the YG-2 and XOP-2 had convinced Harold Pitcairn that the vibration levels of these aircraft were unacceptably high. He, therefore, suspended Autogiro development at Willow Grove and sent the key members of his design team to study developments in the United Kingdom. While there, Larsen and Stanley analyzed the characteristics of the various British types and contributed to development work on jump take-off. The Americans concluded that, taking account of the effects of size (the larger the aircraft, the greater the vibration problems), the generally smaller British autogiros were no better in vibration terms than their bigger American counterparts.

The Americans returned to the United States in February 1937 and started work on the PA-36. Pitcairn put Larsen in sole charge of the program. The latter was confident he could build the prototype for $50,000 (equivalent to about

The Pitcairn PA-36 prototype jump take-off Autogiro. Production PA-36's were to have been roadable but the prototype did not incorporate this feature. (Author's Collection)

$360,000 now, about half the figure originally estimated) and that he could complete it by early 1938, in time for demonstration to Congress during the Dorsey Bill hearings. The hearings took place in April 1938 but the PA-36 was thought to be six to nine months from first flight and was not available even in mock-up form.

By October 1938, the prototype was nearing the ground-running stage. Jim Ray had left the company in September 1937 but visited Europe again in 1938. He returned to the United States in October, convinced that the Autogiro had been overtaken by the helicopter. This issue was discussed at length during an Institute of Aeronautical Sciences meeting on Rotating Wing Aircraft held at the Franklin Institute in Philadelphia on October 28/29. Pitcairn felt there was still a place for the Autogiro and decided to continue the PA-36 program despite a letter from Weir in December announcing the Cierva board's decision to abandon Autogiro development in early spring 1939. Later that year, American official thinking hardened against the Autogiro and at a meeting in Washington, D.C., all the interested United States government agencies decided that helicopter development should receive priority.

Initial test flying of the PA-36 was undertaken by Lou Leavitt, formerly chief test pilot for Kellett, and Alan Marsh who had been loaned by the Cierva Company. Leavitt was unwilling to attempt jump starts and the PA-36 prototype was too heavy for jumps with two up. Marsh was therefore unable to instruct a new pilot in the technique. However, before returning to the United Kingdom in July 1939, after a three month stay in the United States, he briefed a new American pilot (Fred W. Soule) in the jump characteristics of the PA-36. During tests in autumn 1939, Soule experienced severe vibration and was forced to make an emergency landing during which the rotor struck a telegraph pole and the PA-36 was extensively damaged. It was later determined that the accident was due to failure of a rotor blade caused by lack of venting at the blade tip. As with the PA-33 at Langley in March 1936, this had led to a build up of air pressure within the blade under the action of centrifugal force. This caused ribs to fail from end loads and the trailing edge of one blade to become detached. The accident could have been much more serious but for the irreversibility of the PA-36's control system. Development of the PA-36 had cost $200,000 by the end of 1939 (equivalent to about $1.5 m today) compared with the budgeted figure of $50,000.

The PA-36 was repaired and test flying resumed. In the course of testing aimed at achieving adequate jump take-offs, two further accidents occurred caused by the rotor spin-up drive failing to declutch during the jump. After each crash the aircraft was rebuilt with various modifications. These included one to reduce the ground angle and to incorporate a high static thrust four-blade wooden propeller and another to remove the roadability feature and save weight generally.

The PA-36 first achieved sustained jump take-offs on July 8, 1940, when jump heights of up to 35 ft (10 m) were attained. The first jump take-offs publicly demonstrated in the United States were made by this aircraft at Horsham near Philadelphia on July 26, 1940. From November 1935 however, the PA-22, which had been used previously to develop the Pitcairn jump take-off system, had made many experimental jump-starts of limited height without a public audience. The final form of the Pitcairn system employed a two-speed gear through which part of the engine power was used to drive the propeller simultaneously with the spinning of the rotor blades. Full power was transmitted through a higher gear to the propeller when the rotor drive was disengaged.

A pair of wheel segments on push-pull tubes with duplicated rudder pedals provided full dual control. The wheel controls were connected to a pair of Ross cam and lever steering units mounted on the pylon below the hub. Irreversibility was incorporated in the control system so that small vibrations from the rotor would not be felt through the pilot's controls. For jump take-offs, the rotor was over-speeded by 50 percent to 300 rpm. This resulted in a jump of between 15 and 35 feet (4–10 m) depending on the strength of the wind.

In February 1941, demonstrations were given at Bolling Field, Washington, D.C., by Soule to representatives of the army and the press. Jump take-offs were made over an 18-foot (5.5 m) barrier positioned only 5 feet (1.5 m) in front of the Autogiro before spin-up. During a demonstration at New York's recently opened LaGuardia Airport another accident was caused by failure of the rotor spin-up drive to declutch.

In the first half of 1941, on orders from General Arnold, the PA-36 undertook a 5,000 mi (82000 km) tour of U.S. Army bases within the United States (including Forts Bragg, Benning, Knox, and Sill) to investigate possible military applications. While returning from the visit to Fort Sill in Oklahoma, engine failure caused a forced landing near Indianapolis and the Autogiro completed its journey by road.

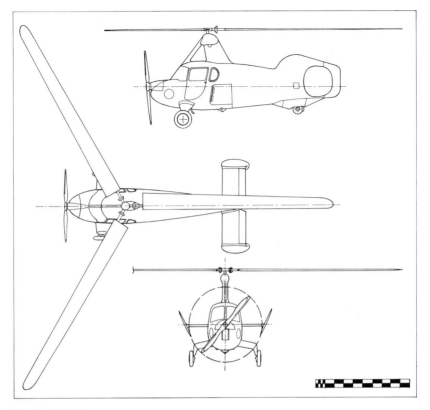

Pitcairn PA-36.

In October 1941, Soule gave a demonstration to the Departments of Commerce and the Interior at College Park, Maryland, in which he made ten perfect jump take-offs. This demonstration was repeated at Bolling Field before General H.H. Arnold and other senior representatives.

Although it had been a logical continuation of the program which had included the PA-22 and AC-35, it is apparent with hindsight that development of the jump take-off potentially roadable PA-36 was a mistake. Pitcairn made various studies of helicopter designs at this time, the most promising of which seemed to be one with a torque-less (tip jet-driven) rotor.

They also designed and built a number of experimental model rotors during 1938/39. These had both single and two blades as well as various hinge arrangements. Twin-rotor configurations were also studied in the so-called Roots blower arrangement, that is a pair of intermeshing rotors with blades synchronized as to relative positions by inter-connecting gearing. Hub centerlines were slightly over one rotor radius apart.

As a result of these helicopter investigations, Pitcairn decided that there was still a place for the Autogiro. The PA-36 therefore went ahead. Much of the technology required for its design, if redirected, might have produced a helicopter contemporaneous with the first practical American helicopters developed by other manufacturers. In the event, the roadable Autogiro, even when capable of jump take-off, did not survive once helicopters entered production. The single PA-36 was withdrawn from service in mid-1941.

Pitcairn PA-37. Design study in 1939 of a tandem two-seat observation jump take-off Autogiro. The cockpits were to be enclosed by sliding canopies. Not proceeded with.

Pitcairn PA-38. Designation of a series of design studies undertaken for a United States Army Air Corps design competition (Spec. XC-417, Circular Proposal 40-260) which closed on April 22, 1940. These were of a large jump take-off Autogiro of 4,200 lb (1905 kg) loaded weight, suitable for military observation or cargo; mail carriage; insecticide-dispensing or forest fire fighting. Kellett submitted studies of two direct-control designs without jump take-off capability. None of the studies was proceeded with. The army contract went to Platt-Le Page for their XR-1 helicopter.

Pitcairn PA-39. (175-hp Warner R-500 Super-Scarab 165). This was a jump take-off Autogiro which employed re-worked fuselages and landing gears of old PA-18 Autogiros, which themselves derived from the PAA-1, one of the earliest American Autogiros. The PA-39 had a three-blade cantilever rotor and incorporated all the latest direct-control and jump take-off improvements. These included a special low pitch setting for the constant-speed airscrew used while the rotor was being speeded-up before jump take-off. It replaced the two-speed trans-

Pitcairn PA-38 project.
(Pitcairn drawing)

mission used on the PA-36. The PA-39 did, however, incorporate the centralized hub and irreversible control features of the PA-36. It also had triple vertical tail surfaces, including a central fin and rudder and outward-tilted end-plate fins on the stabilizer similar to those first tried on the eighth version of the PA-22 and subsequently on the PA-36. Take-off jumps of up to 25 ft (7.62 m) were achieved with the PA-39.

The Pitcairn Autogiro Company, whose name was changed to the Pitcairn-Larsen Autogiro Company in 1940, received a contract from the British Air Purchasing Commission on November 5, 1940 for seven PA-39s for antisubmarine use. Brie visited Pitcairn late in 1940 to see how the program was progressing. The aircraft were delivered in the latter part of 1941. Each was test-flown by Soule and then handed over to Brie. Five were to be shipped to the United Kingdom and two retained in the United States, one for Pitcairn and one for service testing.

In May 1942, by which time the Americans had entered the war, shipboard trials were made by Brie with one of the PA-39's held in America. These took

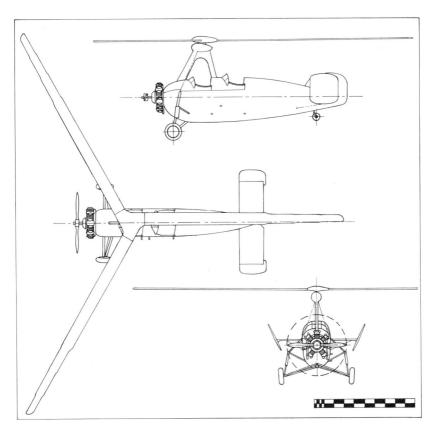

Pitcairn PA-39.

place in Long Island Sound on the British escort carrier H.M.S. *Avenger* and subsequently in Chesapeake Bay off Newport News, Virginia, using a specially constructed stern platform on the British merchant ship, *Empire Mersey*. Take-offs and landings were made with the ship at anchor and under way.

The other PA-39 retained in the United States was lent back to the manufacturer (which by then had become the G. & A. Aircraft Company) for testing a set of rotor blades using laminar flow aerofoils which, when scaled-up in size and strength, were to be used on the XO-61 Autogiro.

The two American-held PA-39s were purchased back from the British. One was given to the Aeronautical Section of Princeton University and its fate is unrecorded, the other was used by the Firestone Tire and Rubber Company (which took over the G. & A. Aircraft Company in 1943) to test the effects of the drag and weight of rocket units at the blade tips of the rotor.

Pitcairn had originally experimented with a tip jet-driven model helicopter as early as 1926. This model was successfully flown in 1927 using compressed carbon dioxide gas as the energising agent. Despite these encouraging results, no full-scale tests were attempted at that time. In 1943, the Autogiro Company of America had discussions with Aerojet of Pasadena in California about a rocket-driven helicopter. A number of studies were made but nothing came of them. However, in 1946, Firestone modified the hub and a set of blades of a PA-39 to accommodate rocket units. This program was terminated before completion and the aircraft sold to the Autogiro Company of America in 1947. Nothing came either of a later plan to develop a rocket-driven rotor in association with Reaction Motors Inc (RMI). This company manufactured the rocket units it was proposed to use. RMI had carried out tests from 1944 under a U.S. Navy contract with an old PA-18 hub and pylon with rocket units running on liquid oxygen and alcohol.

None of the seven PA-39's (BW828 to BW834) were ever employed on actual operations in the intended role. Five were to have been used by the RAF for communication duties but only two reached the United Kingdom and apparently only one (probably BW833) was flown there—initially at Duxford by Alan Marsh

A *Pitcairn PA-39* as supplied to the RAF.
(Author's Collection)

and probably later at Boscombe Down. Three (BW828-BW830) were damaged—according to one account, deliberately sabotaged—in January 1942 in Canada while being loaded for shipment to the United Kingdom and were scrapped together with spares in the same consignment. At the time it was stated that they had been lost at sea when their ship was torpedoed.

Pitcairn PA-40. This was a design undertaken in 1940 that was an unusual one for Pitcairn at this time. It was of a military training airplane which was to have been a derivative of the Pitcairn PA-7 Mailwing biplane of 1929. The project was not proceeded with.

Pitcairn PA-41. This was an Autogiro design study of 1941 which was not proceeded with.

Pitcairn PA-42. (175-hp Warner R-500 Super-Scarab 165). Design study in 1941 for a variant of the PA-39 with a plywood monocoque fuselage. Not proceeded with.

Pitcairn PA-43 (AU-1). Design study in 1942 of a large jump take-off ambulance Autogiro with rear loading doors to the fuselage. Not proceeded with.

Kellett KD-1. (225-hp Jacobs L-4MA). While the Pitcairn Company was busy from 1932 with the development of roadable and later jump take-off Autogiros, the Kellett Autogiro Company had turned its attention in 1934 to production of Autogiros with direct-control. From the mid-1930s there had evidently been a steady decline in the collaboration between the two companies. After Kellett and his chief engineer, Richard H. Prewitt, visited England late in 1933 to see Cierva's latest developments (the C-30A was just coming into production), work started at Kelletts in January 1934 on a direct-control version of the K-2. This led to the KD-1 direct-control model of up to 2,400 lb (1088 kg) gross weight which was first flown on December 9, 1934, by Lou Leavitt and quickly appeared as a production article (with ATC No. 712) on January 1, 1935. Sometimes described as a scaled-up C.30, the KD-1 was a more handsome tandem open-cockpit two-seater which sold in small numbers in its KD-1, KD-1A, and KD-1B civilian variants and as the YG-1, YG-1A, YG-1B and YO-60 to the United States Army Air Corps. The exact number built is not known but it seems likely that about eighteen of all versions were completed, plus 97 of derivatives manufactured under license in Japan. The three-blade 40-ft (12.19 m) rotor was mounted on a neat single streamlined pylon ahead of the front cockpit and the tilting hub was controlled by a conventional floor-mounted control column. The KD-1 had three cantilever folding blades of Gö 606 section that each weighted 61 lb (27.7 kg). The asymmetric stabilizer was of Clark YH section. A new form of friction damper on KD-1 gave trouble at first. Another problem was a lack of stability at speeds above 80 mph (129 km/h). This was corrected by trailing edge tabs on the blades.

The one and only KD-1 was used to make demonstration takeoffs and landings in a Washington street. On May 19, 1939, the KD-1 took off from the street

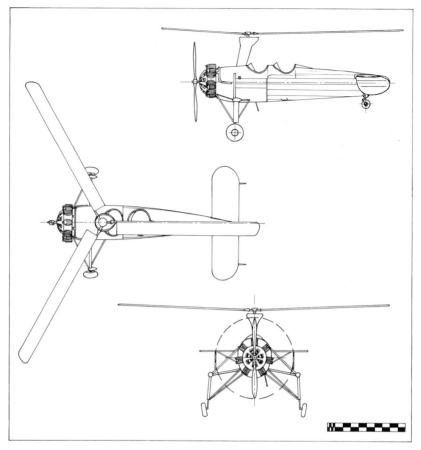

Kellett KD-1 prototype.

in front of the Department of Commerce building in Washington and flew with a load of mail to Hoover Airport. This demonstration helped Eastern Air Lines win a contract for a regular service in Philadelphia (see below). The Philadelphia Police Department used it for directing traffic during the Army-Navy Games and the Pennsylvania State Game Reserve used it for animal count surveys. It was retired in 1943. In 1946, the KD-1 was donated to the Commercial Museum of Philadelphia where it was stored in the basement. It was later restored. Alternative engines offered in the KD-1 were the 250-hp Wright R-760-E Whirlwind or the 225-hp Continental R-670 but, as far as is known, neither was ever fitted.

Kellett KD-1A (225-hp Jacobs L-4MA-7). This was a slightly modified version of the KD-1 which was also offered with the 225-hp Continental R-670 as alternative power plant. The KD-1A had an engine-driven electric generator and an electric engine starter. U.S. Civil Aeronautics Authority Approved Type Certificate no. 712 was obtained on October 31, 1937.

The Kellett KD-1 prototype of the first direct-control Autogiro to go into production in the United States.
(Author's Collection)

A KD-1A was used by the MacGregor Arctic Expedition which, sponsored by the United States Weather Bureau, went to northwest Greenland in the base ship *General A.W. Greeley* in the summer of 1937. Flown by Lieutenant Commander I. Schlossbach, captain of the expedition's ship, the Autogiro made several test flights during November. These were from the expedition's base at Reindeer Point near Utah. In May 1938, R. Johnson, aircraft engineer, had his arm broken by the Autogiro's airscrew while starting the engine. The expedition ended on July 7, 1938. The KD-1A thus made the first Arctic flights by a rotary-wing aircraft and was the second rotary-wing aircraft to fly in polar regions after the Kellett K-3 was taken by Byrd to Antarctica in 1933–35. A Russian autogiro, the TsAGI A-7, was apparently first operated in the Arctic in 1938.

Either another KD-1A was built in 1939 for the Japanese Army Air Force Testing Division or the first aircraft was sold secondhand. This aircraft was later handed over, in damaged condition after an accident, to the Kayaba Company for a Japanese copy to be developed (see Chapter II). The export of the KD-1A to Japan was apparently regarded by Pitcairn as a breach of his license agreement with Cierva. This cannot have helped the already unsatisfactory relations existing between the two American Autogiro companies.

Kellett KD-1B. (225-hp Jacobs L-4MA). A single-seat version of the civil KD series, with a mail compartment of 300-lb capacity in place of the front cockpit, was derived from the military YG-1A. This Autogiro, NC15069, was employed by Eastern Air Lines for a year, from July 6, 1939, to July 5, 1940, to run a scheduled airmail service for the United States Post Office of five round trips a day from Camden Central Airport, New Jersey, to the roof of the central post office in downtown Philadelphia. Eastern had been awarded this mail contract (AM-2001/AM-2002) at a rate of $3.86 per airplane-mile in March 1939. The possibility of such a service had originally been demonstrated by Lou Leavitt in the KD-1 and James Ray in the PA-22 on May 25, 1935, when these aircraft landed on the roof of the central post office building during the opening ceremony. Earlier still, Reginald Brie had, in September 1934, made some experimental flights to the Mount Pleasant Post Office in London but had not landed in the city. More than 90 percent of the Eastern Air Lines scheduled trips were successfully completed. The pilots, J.M. Miller and J.P. Lukens, made some 2300 flights. The original KD-1 (NC14742) was flown by TWA for a time but was not operated on a scheduled basis. The KD-1B was granted an Approved Type Certificate (no. 712) by the CAA in December 1939.

Kellett YG-1/1A/1B. (225-hp Jacobs R-755A1 or R-755A3). The YG-1 series was the military version of the KD-1/KD-1A direct-control Autogiro ordered by the United States Army Air Corps in 1935/36 primarily to equip the Air Corps Autogiro School formed at Patterson Field in Springfield near Dayton, Ohio, on April 15, 1938.

The first service aircraft were delivered to the U.S. Army Air Corps in October 1936 and to the school in 1938, but the first Autogiro of this type purchased by the military was the second civil KD-1 inspected at Wright Field in 1935. It was designated YG-1(35-278). This was followed by one YG-1A (36-352), with military H.F. Radio, and six similarly equipped YG-1B's(37-377/382). One YG-1B (37-378) later became the YG-1C to test an experimental rotor. Later

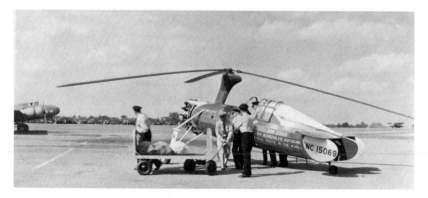

The Kellett KD-1B operated by Eastern Air Lines for a year in 1939–40 on a regular scheduled mail service between Camden Airport and the roof of the Central Post Office in Philadelphia.
(R.E.G. Davies)

232

still, this same aircraft was redesignated XR-2. Other YG-1B airframes were later used for the XG-1B and XR-3.

The first YG-1 went to the NACA at Langley Field, Virginia, early in 1936. In May of that year, service tests started with the Field Artillery Board at Fort Bragg, North Carolina. These comprised directing artillery fire, reconnaissance, and landings in restricted areas. On June 2, 1936, the first telephone conversation from the ground with an airborne Autogiro took place. With the telephone wire extending from a reel, the Autogiro took off and climbed to 1,500 ft (450 m). Communication was maintained for half-an-hour. There were however a number of incidents while testing the YG-1. Damage resulted from resonance effects and from wind gusts forcing rotors into the ground during hovering. The army pilots involved in the tests were Lieutenants H.F. Gregory, Erickson S. Nichols, and G.H. "Bud" Snyder.

The second army YG-1, the YG-1A (36-352), was delivered in October 1936. After brief evaluation at Wright Field, service tests were conducted with it from December 8, 1936, at the Field Artillery School, Fort Sill, Oklahoma. On March 19, 1937, this aircraft was damaged and, after repair, transferred to the NACA at Langley. There it was to be used for full-scale testing in the "30 by 60" wind-tunnel at Hampton to obtain stress measurements of the rotor following the loss of the first YG-1 recorded below. Unfortunately, only preliminary tunnel runs were made before the Autogiro was destroyed on October 26, 1937 by ground resonance. During a wind-tunnel run, violent oscillations set in, disturbing the path of the rotating blades. The rotor was ripped away and wreckage scattered through the test section, damaging the wind-tunnel.

Before this, the first aircraft, YG-1 (35-278), had been temporarily returned to the NACA for flight tests to study the causes of two unexplained accidents. These had been attributed to pilot error but were probably due to unavoidable ground resonance. On April 15, 1937, the aircraft was returned to service testing but on June 16 at Fort Knox, Kentucky, it was destroyed when a hub forging failed in flight and a blade became detached. The out-of-balance rotor ripped the pylon from the fuselage so that it parted from the aircraft at 3,500 ft (1100 m). In this second Autogiro structural failure in flight, both Michaels and his observer were lucky to escape by parachute, although the latter broke his arm when he struck the rear of the fuselage as he jumped.

The first YG-1B was delivered to Wright Field on December 29, 1937, and was used for a flight test program in place of the NACA wind-tunnel tests. The YG-1B had certain structural components strengthened, following the YG-1 accident, and the test program confirmed that the strength was now adequate and that the other YG-1Bs could also be delivered.

The Autogiro school trained nine pilots and nine mechanics during its four months existence in 1938. The YG-1Bs were then dispersed: one going to the NACA, one to Wright Field, and five to various other military establishments. Further service testing established that the Autogiros' more difficult flying characteristics and small payload made them less useful than fixed-wing types, despite their advantage in shorter take-off and landing distances.

Kellett YG-1B supplied to the United States Army Air Corps in small numbers was used to establish an Autogiro training school at Patterson Field, Dayton, Ohio. (Peter Bowers)

The YG-1B used for research by NACA at Langley Field was employed, among other work, on extensive blade-stalling tests and on a comparison between the characteristics of a new set of blades of NACA 230 series section. The latter showed that the rotor with the new blades had improved characteristics, particularly in avoiding control position reversal at speeds above 100 mph (160 km/h). Dangerous stability characteristics had been found near maximum speed when using highly cambered blades (also experienced with the C.30 in England). These characteristics and apparent discrepancies in model tests using blade sections of different camber focused attention on the effect on rotor characteristics of periodic twisting of the blades. An investigation had been made into this problem in 1936 with the Pitcairn PA-22 and a partial solution, applied to the KD-1 rotor, was found by fitting reflexed tabs on the trailing edge tips of each blade. The NACA tests made important contributions to rotary-wing knowledge that soon read across to the design of helicopters. Later Autogiros and some of the first helicopters had blades of NACA 230 series profile.

Kellett YG-1B (Accelerated Take-off) or YG-1C. (225-hp Jacobs R-755A3). Kellett had been working on a collective pitch system for jump take-offs since 1936. This materialized in 1939 and was fitted to a converted YG-1B (37-378), the first Kellett Autogiro with collective pitch control. It had a system (designed by R.H. Prewitt) of tension-torsion rods in the blade fork assembly with centrifugal governor weights and parallelogram links. A cable to a handle in the cockpit gave collective pitch control over the range from zero to four degrees. The 41 ft 7 1/2 in (12.69 m) rotor had blades of NACA 230 series section with step-tapered spars, tapered trailing edge, and fabric covering. A weighted leading edge mass-balanced the blades at 25 percent chord. There was a single box clutch and reduction gear connected to the engine's accessory drive with a torque-limiting release device patented by C.C. Miller. Despite the collective pitch control, this Autogiro was not capable of jump take-offs.

In 1939, W. Wallace Kellett became chairman of the Fellowship Committee for the Juan de la Cierva Memorial Fellowship. The latter was funded with $700 (equivalent to about $5,200 today), contributed by 45 sponsors, to undertake research into rotary-wing aerodynamics at New York University.

Kellett XR-2. (285/300-hp Jacobs R-915A1 or R-915A3). This was a jump take-off development of the YG-1B, fitted with a more powerful engine, a Hamilton Standard constant-speed airscrew, and a long-stroke cantilever landing gear for vertical landings. It was developed for the United States Army Air Forces in 1940 but was destroyed by ground resonance during testing in 1941 and does not seem to have actually achieved jump take-offs. The airframe was a conversion of one of the YG-1B's (37-378), which had been delivered to the United States Army Air Corps in 1938, redesignated YG-1C, and flown in 1939. This aircraft was used for research by the NACA at Langley Field, Virginia.

The XR-2 was said to have had a constant-speed rotor (although what is meant by this is not clear), a shock-mounted pylon, and a form of collective pitch control for jump take-off, similar to that on the YG-1C, but with the pitch range increased to nine degrees. It acted as a development aircraft for the XO-60, of which seven were ordered by the United States Army Air Forces in 1941.

The accident to XR-2 proved to be important to the whole development of rotary wings. During one of the first tests of a jump take-off, ground resonance set in at high rotor speed. This built up so rapidly that the aircraft broke up before

The XR-2 after its destruction in a ground resonance accident.
(C.C. Miller, Jr.)

235

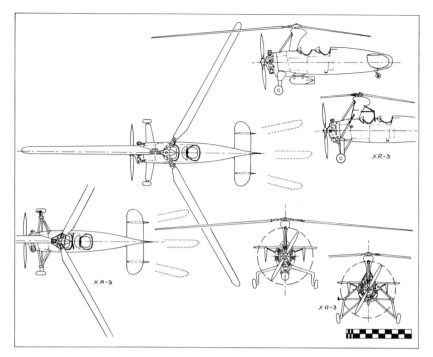

Kellett XR-2 and XR-3.

The Kellett XR-3 jump take-off Autogiro with cyclic pitch control instead of the Cierva tilting rotor hub.
(R.H. Prewitt)

anything could be done to stop it. In less than five seconds, the rotor pylon support structure collapsed and the fuselage broke in two places, between the engine and pylon and pylon and tail. This dramatic further demonstration of a problem that had recurred repeatedly throughout the development of rotary-wing aircraft had an important effect in influencing the United States Army Air Force, the NACA and Kellett into tackling the basic problem of ground resonance. Bob Wagner of Kellett and Prewitt Coleman of NACA came up independently with mathematical solutions for the proper configuration and for damping to prevent ground resonance. This was a major step in the development of rotary-wing aircraft. Paul Stanley of the Autogiro Company of America had also arrived at mathematical and engineering solutions to the problem with the result that Pitcairn Autogiros are claimed to have largely avoided ground resonance.

Kellett XG-1B. (225-hp Jacobs R-755A3). After the accident to the XR-2, another YG-1B was converted to incorporate the former's rotor system. This aircraft was known as the XG-1B. It had a torsionally stiffened pylon and inter-blade friction dampers but suffered from the same severe control column vibration and rotor roughness as had been experienced with the XR-2. This was thought to be due mainly to the rotor hub mounting and the lessons learned were applied to the design of the XR-3.

Kellett XR-3. (225-hp Jacobs R-755A3). A further jump takeoff development of the YG-1B but, unlike the XR-2, the XR-3 did not have a change of engine. It was produced for the United States Army Air Forces in 1941, the airframe (37-380) being a conversion of one of the seven YG-1A/YG-1B's ordered by the Army Air Corps in 1935/36. The rotor hub in the XR-3 was of completely new design, having a fixed spindle with collective and cyclic pitch control instead of the tilting direct-control head. It was thus a radical departure from the Cierva design employed in all previous Autogiros, although Paul Stanley and Richard Prewitt had been associated in 1937/38 in a project for a fixed spindle Autogiro with cyclic pitch control which had come to nothing at the time. Prewitt is also believed to have proposed cyclic and collective pitch control as early as 1932 but by 1934 he was designing the Kellett KD-1 with tilting head. Cierva himself had argued the same way during his visit to the United States in 1933 and even suggested at that time that development of the tilting hub should be abandoned in the United Kingdom and left to his American associates. He had clearly been thinking about what should follow the C.30 which had first flown in the spring of that year.

Jump take-offs were possible with the XR-3 to heights of about 15 ft (4.5 m). Longitudinal trimming was by tilting the rotor axis —rather like the system on the PA-19—while laterally, it was by bungee spring. Control was reported to be very smooth, with low stick loads and reduced shake, but the response was sluggish. The blades were pivoted to the hub with a Delta-3 angle of 30 degrees, considerably improving stability. The landing gear was of conventional truss type. Like the YG-1 and XR-2, the XR-3 had tension-torsion rod blade suspension. This Autogiro, when disposed of by the U.S. Army as surplus was sold to General Electric who used it at their Schenectady research center to develop the rotor for the Kellett XR-8 helicopter.

Kellett XO-60/YO-60. (285/300-hp Jacobs R-915-1 or R-915-3). This jump take-off Autogiro, derived from the KD-1A by way of the YG-1B, XR-2, and XG-1B, was developed during 1942/43 for the United States Army Air Forces by a team under Richard Prewitt. A contract for eight airframes was placed in 1941—seven for flight and one for static test. They were intended for military observation duties, the first being completed in February 1943. After one XO-60 (42-13510), six YO-60's (42-13604/13609) were produced for service test use, the XO-60 being delivered last during 1943. The XO-60 differed from the YO-60 in having a long-stroke cantilever landing gear like the XR-2 while the YO-60s had conventional truss landing gears.

These aircraft all offered jump take-off by means of a form of collective pitch control with a tension-torsion pack at the rotor blade roots. The system, covered by a patent which was subsequently sold to the Autogiro Company of America, was quite different from the Cierva single-Alpha lead-lag hinge or Pitcairn multi-threaded hydraulically controlled systems but proved to be entirely satisfactory. The three-blade rotor folded. Inter-blade damping was hydraulic on the XO-60 and by friction on the YO-60's. Accommodation for the crew of two was in tandem under an exceptionally large transparent canopy. There were also large win-

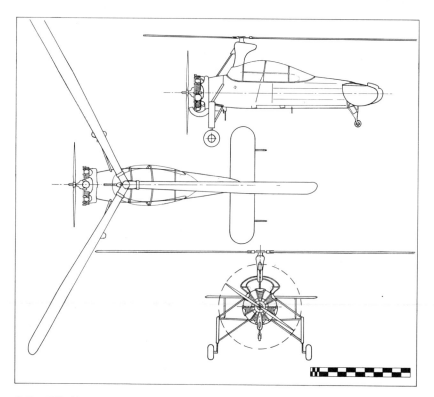

Kellett YO-60.

dows in the floor of the cockpit. The XO-60/YO-60's were the last Autogiros delivered to the United States Army Air Forces. They were extensively tested after delivery but their higher initial cost and greater maintenance demands, as compared with fixed-wing liaison light aircraft, led to their rejection for army cooperation work.

The YO-60's were apparently still susceptible to ground resonance. One (42-13605) was destroyed as a result of this during an attempted jump take-off at Philadelphia airport on June 27, 1943.

The Kellett Autogiro Corporation reverted to its original name of Kellett Aircraft Corporation in June 1943 and turned its attention to helicopters. By then it had built a total of more than forty Autogiros.

Pitcairn (Firestone) PA-44 (XO-61/YO-61). (300/325-hp Jacobs R-915-A4). This jump take-off Autogiro was ordered in 1941, at the same time as the Kellett XO-60, by the United States Army Air Forces Material Command from the A.G.A. Aviation Corporation. (Soon afterward this company became the G. and A. Aircraft Inc. and, from the summer of 1943, was a division of the Firestone Tire and Rubber Company.) A.G.A. Aviation had taken over the activities of the

Group beside a YO-60 (left to right): W. Wallace Kellett, president of the Kellett Autogiro Company; Leslie Cooper, early Autogiro operator and Army Autogiro pilot; Richard H. Prewitt, vice-president and chief engineer of Kellett, and H. Franklin Gregory at Patterson Air Force Base, Dayton, Ohio.
(R.H. Prewitt)

former Pitcairn Autogiro Company. The latter had, for a time from 1940, operated under the name of Pitcairn-Larsen Autogiro Company.

The YO-61 was a pusher cabin tandem two-seater of clean aerodynamic form with central nacelle, twin tail booms, and nosewheel landing gear. The cabin was very similar to that of the Sikorsky R-5 helicopter whose layout was, in fact, probably inspired to some extent by that of this Autogiro.

The Jacobs engine drove a constant-speed propeller, having a special low-pitch setting for rotor spin-up purposes. This was similar to the PA-39 and had originally been proposed by Paul Stanley when commenting on proposals for jump take-off put forward by Richard Prewitt in 1932.

The XO-61 was originally designed with a 42 ft (12.8 m) rotor of NACA 230 series section. This was later increased in diameter to 48 ft (14.63 m).

The YO-61 represented almost the ultimate in development of the Autogiro concept as it had evolved over the preceding twenty years. In addition to one static test airframe, six, (later reduced to one (42-13611)), of the type were originally ordered as XO-61, of which five (42-13612/13616) were to be supplied in YO-61 service test form. However, only two aircraft were completed—the first in the spring of 1943—and these were never submitted to the army for acceptance because the contract was canceled before testing had been completed. The cancellation occurred when the second aircraft had reached the flying stage. Neither went into service because of engineering problems (including ground resonance, said to be due to defective shock absorbers, and engine cooling difficulties); manufacturing delays (G. and A. Aircraft were preoccupied with their involvement in the Waco CG-4A Hadrian troop-carrying glider program); and the appearance of

Pitcairn XO-61 Autogiro ordered by the USAAF from the G. and A. Aircraft Division of Firestone in 1941.
(R.H. McClaren)

the first production helicopters, in the form of the Sikorsky R-4, which entered service early in 1944. Cancellation of the YO-61 order finally terminated American Autogiro manufacture. Pitcairn had by then built rather more than a hundred Autogiros. Of this number, about twenty were rebuilt from earlier models, as if they were new.

Harold Pitcairn progressively withdrew from his aviation interests at this time. However, from 1951 until his death in 1960, he found himself deeply involved in the rotary-wings patents lawsuit against the United States government. He died, accidentally, from a gunshot wound, seventeen years before the lawsuit was finally settled in his favor.

So ended the Autogiro story in the United States. The next chapter looks at developments in Europe where direct take-off (Cierva's term for jump take-off) had evolved much earlier.

Pitcairn PA-22 Flying Mock-Up
80-hp Pobjoy Cataract, later replaced by 90-hp Pobjoy Niagara. Rotor diameter 31 ft 0 7/16 in–32 ft (9.46–9.75 m) later 34 ft 3 1/2 in (10.45 m); rotor blade section probably Gö 606; length 21 ft 3 in (6.47 m). Empty weight 588–600 lb (266–272 kg); maximum take-off weight 1,140–1,350 lb (517–612 kg). Fuel 17 US gal (64 liters). Maximum speed 100–

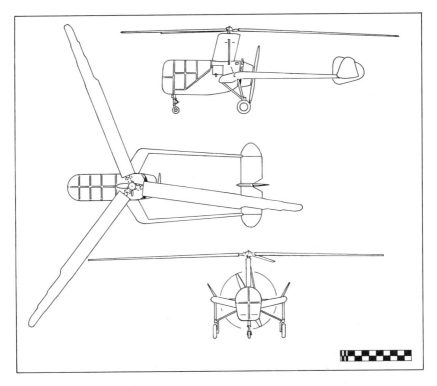

Pitcairn XO-61.

107 mph (160–172 km/h); minimum speed 22 mph (35 km/h); initial climb 900 ft/min (4.57 m/s) range 350 miles (560 km) at 90 mph (145 km).

Pitcairn PA-24

160-hp Kinner R5 or B5. Rotor diameter 40 ft (12.19 m); rotor blade section probably Gö 429; fuselage length 18 ft 7 in (5.66 in); span of fixed wing 22 ft 9 in (6.93 m). Empty weight 1,178–1,257 lb (535–570 kg); maximum take-off weight 1,800 lb (816 kg). Fuel 27 US gal (102 liters). Maximum speed 90–100 mph (145–160 km/hr); minimum speed 20–25 mph (32–40 km/hr); service ceiling 12,000 ft (3,700 m); initial climb 550–750 ft/min (2.79–3.81 m/s); range 235 miles (378 km) at 75–87 mph (120–140 km/hr).

Pitcairn PA-33 (YG-2)

420-hp Wright R-975-9 Whirlwind. Rotor diameter 50 ft (15.24 m); rotor blade section probably Gö 606; fuselage length 22 ft 8 in (6.98 m); overall length 31 ft 5 in (9.57 m). Empty weight 2,300 lb (1,043 kg); maximum take-off weight 3,200–3,300 lb (1,451–1,496 kg). Fuel 66 US gal (250 liters). Maximum speed 140–150 mph (225–241 km/h); minimum speed 22 mph (35 km/h); ceiling 13,700–15,500 ft (4,175–4,724 m); initial climb 870–1,475 ft/min (4.42–7.5 m); range 337–400 miles (542–643 km) at 115–125 mph (185–201 km/h).

Pitcairn PA-34 (XOP-2)

420-hp Wright R-975-9 Whirlwind. Rotor diameter 50 ft (15.24 m); rotor blade section probably Gö 606; fuselage length 22 ft 8 in (6.98 m); overall length 31 ft 5 in (9.57 m). Empty weight 2,300–2,429 lb (1,043–1,100 kg); maximum take-off weight 3,300 lb (1,496 kg). Fuel 66 US gal (250 liters). Maximum speed 140–150 mph (225–241 km/h); minimum speed 22 mph (35 km/h); service ceiling 13,700–15,500 ft (4,175–4,724 m); range 375 miles (603 km) at 115 mph (185 km/h).

Pitcairn AC-35

90-hp Pobjoy Cascade. Rotor diameter 34 ft 3 1/2 in (10.45 m), later 36 ft 2 in (11.07 m); rotor blade section probably Gö 606; overall length 21 ft 8 in (6.4 m). Empty weight 805–828 lb (365–376 kg); maximum take-off weight 1,300–1,450 lb (590–657 kg). Maximum speed 90–115 mph (145–185 km/h); cruising speed 75–100 mph (120–161 km/h); minimum speed 24.5 mph (39.4 km/h); initial climb 355–720 ft/min (1.74–3.66 m/sec); service ceiling 8,500–12,900 ft (2,590–3,930 m). Price $12,500.

Pitcairn PA-36 "Whirl Wing"

175-hp Warner R-500 Super-Scarab #165. Rotor diameter 40–43 ft (12.2–13.1 m); rotor blade section NACA 230 series. Fuselage length 20 ft 5 in (6.22 m). Empty weight 961 lb (436 kg). Maximum take-off weight 1,541–2,050 lb (700–930 kg). Maximum speed 120 mph (193 km/h); cruising speed 100–105 mph (160–169 km/h); rotor speed 200 rpm.

Pitcairn PA-39

175-hp Warner R-500 Super-Scarab 165–D. Rotor diameter 42 ft 3 in (12.87 m); rotor blade section NACA 230 series; overall length 20 ft 6 in (6.24 m). Empty weight 1,340 lb (608 kg); maximum take-off weight 1,946 lb (883 kg). Fuel 20.4 US gal (77 liters). Maximum speed 97–117 mph (156–188 km/h); cruising speed 83 mph (133 km/h); minimum speed 22 mph (35 km/h); initial climb 933 ft/min (4.74 m/s); service ceiling 14,500 ft (4,420 m).

Kellett KD-1

225-hp Jacobs L-4MA. Rotor diameter 40 ft (12.19 m); rotor blade section Gö 606; overall length 26 ft (7.92 m). Empty weight 1,315–1,550 lb (596–703 kg); maximum take-off weight 2,052–2,400 lb (930–1,088 kg). Fuel 48 US gal (181 liters). Maximum speed 120–125 mph (193–201 km/h); minimum speed 16 mph (26 km/h); initial climb 1,000–1,141 ft/min (5.1–5.8 m/sec); range 361 miles (580 km) at 103 mph (166 km/h).

Kellett KD-1A

225-hp Jacobs L-4MA-7. Rotor diameter 40 ft (12.19 m); rotor blade section Gö 606; overall length 25 ft 6 in–25 ft 10 in (7.77–7.87 m). Empty weight 1,345–1,375 lb (610–623 kg); maximum take-off weight 2,075–2,400 lb (941–1,088 kg). Fuel 30 US gal (113 liters). Maximum speed 123 mph (198 km/h); minimum speed 16 mph (25 km/h); initial climb 1,000 ft/min (5 m/sec).

Kellett KD-1B

225-hp Jacobs L-4MA-7. Rotor diameter 40 ft (12.19 m);. rotor blade section Gö 606; overall length 28 ft 10 in (8.78 m). Empty weight 1,630–1,670 lb (739–757 kg); maximum take-off weight 2,250–2,295 lb (1,020–1,040 kg). Fuel 30 US gal (113 liters). Maximum speed 127–130 mph (204–209 km/h); minimum speed 22–24 mph (35–38 km/h); initial climb 800–1,250 ft/min (4.06–6.35 m/sec); service ceiling 14,000 ft (4,267 m); range 200 miles (321 km) at 100–102 mph (160–163 km/h).

Kellett YG-1A and YG-1B

225-hp Jacobs R-755A1 (YG-1A) or R-755A3 (YG-1B). Rotor diameter 40 ft (12.19 m); rotor blade section Gö 606; overall length 28 ft 10 in (8.78 m) YG-1A, 26 ft (7.92 m) YG-1B. Empty weight 1,580–1,586 lb (716–719 kg) YG-1A, 1,375–1,617 lb (623–733 kg) YG-1B; maximum take-off weight 2,254 lb (1,022 kg) YG-1A, 2,240–2,400 lb (1,016–1,088 kg) YG-1B; maximum speed 125 mph (201 km/h) YG-1A, 106 mph (170 km/h) YG-1B; minimum speed 17 mph (27 km/h); initial climb 1,250 ft/min (6.35 m/sec); service ceiling 14,000 ft (4,267 m); range 200 miles (321 km) at 100 mph (160 km/h) YG-1A; 103 mph (166 km/h) YG-1B.

Kellett YG-1B (Accelerated Take-Off) YG-1C

225-hp Jacobs R-755A3. Rotor diameter 41 ft 7 1/4 in (12.68); rotor blade section NACA 230 series. Maximum take-off weight 2,400 lb (1,088 kg). No other data available.

Kellett XR-2

285–300-hp Jacobs R-915A1. Rotor diameter 40 ft (12.2 in) later 41 ft 71/4 in (12.68 m); rotor blade section NACA 230 series; fuselage length 21 ft 5 in (6.5 m); overall length 27 ft (8.22 m). Maximum take-off weight 2,400–2,575 lb (1,088–1,168 kg). Maximum speed 120 mph (193 km/h). No other data available.

Kellett XR-3

225-hp Jacobs R-755A3. Rotor diameter 40–42 ft (12.19–12.8 m); rotor blade section

NACA 230 series; overall length 26 ft (7.92 m). Maximum take-off weight 2,250–2,640 lb (1,020–1,197 kg). Maximum speed 106 mph (170 km/h). No other data available.

Kellett XO-60/YO-60

285–325-hp Jacobs R-915A1 or R915A3. Rotor diameter 42 ft (12.8 m); YO-60, 43 ft 2 1/2 in (13.17 m) XO-60; rotor blade section NACA 230 series; overall length 21 ft 5 in (6.5 m). Maximum take-off weight 2,590–2,800 lb (1,175–1,270 kg). Maximum speed 127 mph (204 km/h); cruising speed 102 mph (164 km/h); minimum speed 15 mph (24 km/h). No other data available.

Pitcairn XO-61/YO-61

300–325-hp Jacobs R-915A3 or R-915A4. Rotor diameter 42–48 ft (12.8–14.63 m); rotor blade section NACA 230 series; overall length 28 ft 6 in (8.68 m). Maximum take-off weight 3,000–3,038 lb (1,360–1,378 kg). Maximum speed 103 mph (165 km/h); minimum speed 29 mph (46 km/h). No other data available.

Chapter 9

Jump Take-off

At a lecture in London before the Royal Aeronautical Society on March 15, 1935, Cierva announced the successful development of direct take-off. The first jump take-offs had been achieved with the C.30 prototype, G-ACFI, fitted with a special rotor head, more than a year and a half earlier than this in August 1933. However, the first experiments were not entirely satisfactory. The rotor tended to wobble during spin-up before reaching maximum revolutions and only low jumps were possible with the aircraft dropping back onto the ground. G-ACFI was eventually damaged when the left landing gear leg collapsed.

Experiments with G-ACFI were resumed in the latter part of 1934 when a developed rotor head was fitted and tested. Marsh achieved jumps of 10 to 12 feet followed by a climb-out on October 28.

These first jump take-offs, some of which were witnessed by Pitcairn and several of his American colleagues, were made with a simple but ingenious modification of the standard direct-control rotor head in which inclined "Phi-bell" drag hinges (no. 7 in the drawing) were angled away from the vertical in such a way that, when the rotor was under power during spin-up, the blades lagged on the hub against the drag stops and in this way acquired a no-lift pitch. As soon as the rotor was up to the correct jump take-off speed, which was well above the normal flying rpm, the engine was de-clutched and the take-off initiated. The blades then overran the hub and moved forward from the drag stops. In so doing, they took on sufficient positive pitch to jump the aircraft smartly into the air. At the top of the jump, at a height of perhaps 15 ft (4.5 m), the Autogiro was intended to accelerate forward under the thrust of the airscrew, the rotor blades being now in normal autorotative pitch and the rotor at normal flying rpm.

The main drawback to this elegantly simple system lay in the fact that unrestricted movement of the blades in the drag plane, required for the jump, meant that it was not possible to provide adequate drag hinge damping to prevent ground resonance. Because of this, the system was found to be only practical for two-blade rotors and, even then, vibration levels were high. Even with two blades, to avoid resonance, it was found that the blades had to be held in flat pitch against the forward stops, instead of being simply allowed to lag during the spin-up. This design was a feature of the Autodynamic rotor which first publicly demonstrated jump take-offs on July 23, 1936.

*The Cierva C.30 Mk.III direct take-off Autogiro, with Autodynamic rotor head,
making a jump take-off from Hounslow Heath near London during a demonstration by
Alan Marsh on July 23, 1936.*
(O. Reder)

Development work on jump take-off over the years 1933 to 1938 was largely directed at overcoming the above problems (see drawing), but this effort had not been brought to a successful conclusion by the time of Cierva's death, late in 1936. Nevertheless, jump take-off even in its early rather primitive forms was Cierva's crowning achievement and marked the culmination of ten years of intensive development in the United Kingdom during which Cierva had himself been not only the mainspring of each technical advance but had also personally done a large part of the often difficult and sometimes dangerous experimental flying.

However, his involvement in this program from late 1933, but particularly during the last year of his life, had suffered from his preoccupation with political developments in Spain. Cierva was a Royalist and a strong supporter of the Nationalists under General Franco. Events leading up to the outbreak of the Spanish Civil War in July 1936 not only gave him many worries about his interests in Spain but also about the safety of his family until he was able to get them to England in September of that year. At the same time he was also much involved in working for the Nationalists under General Franco. He had, for example, organized the clandestine chartering in England of a de Havilland Dragon Rapide transport aircraft to ferry the Nationalist leader from the Canaries, where he was stationed, to Spanish North Africa. This feat enabled Franco to take command of the army and open hostilities against the Popular Front government which had been in power since February 1936.[28]

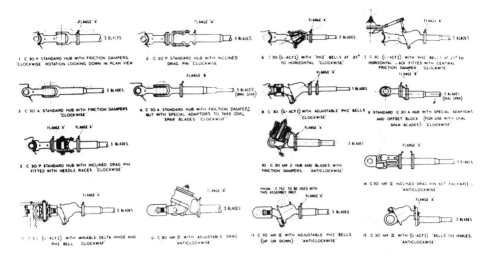

*Some of the rotor-blade hinge designs tested during the development of jump take-off.
(From Dr. J.A.J. Bennett's paper* The Era of the Autogiro, *courtesy Royal
Aeronautical Society)*

It was just at this time that Cierva cabled Pitcairn in the United States suggesting that there should be a joint three-to-four-month effort by the two Autogiro companies to solve the remaining jump take-off problems. Encouraged by an enthusiastic report from Ray (who had traveled to England earlier in the summer) about the C.30 Mk.III's 30-foot (9.1 m) jump take-offs, Pitcairn and Larsen sailed to Europe. However, Cierva's preoccupation with developments in Spain prevented any useful exchanges and Pitcairn soon returned to the United States leaving Larsen and Stanley to stay on until May 1937. Their visit seems to have been largely wasted because of a lack of cooperation between the two teams.

There is little doubt that effective Anglo-American collaboration had depended to an important extent on the personal relationship between Cierva and Pitcairn which had built up in the course of Cierva's four visits to the United States and Pitcairn's fifteen visits to Europe. A new situation developed as Cierva became more and more preoccupied with the war in Spain, and his death ended an alliance that was already faltering.

Cierva C.30 Mk.II and Mk.III (140-hp Armstrong Siddeley Genet Major IA). Public demonstration of jump take-offs was not made until July 23, 1936, when Alan Marsh demonstrated them on Hounslow Heath. Jumps were made up to a height of about 23 ft (7 m) in the C.30 Mk.III with two-blade Autodynamic rotor. This rotor was similar to that on the Weir W.3 (see Chapter 6). Instead of lagging on the drag stops, the blades were held in flat pitch against the forward stops during spin-up. The aircraft, G-ACWF (believed at that stage to be called the C.30 Mk.II) had been flown only experimentally from late 1935 because of what was stated at the time to be bearing trouble. From March 1936, G-ACWF fitted with the Autodynamic head became known as the C.30 Mk.III.

The Autodynamic head, in fact, suffered from serious vibrations, inherent to its design. It had a marked twice-per-revolution bounce which was felt throughout the entire speed range. However, during 1936, G-ACWF with the Autodynamic head proved conclusively that Cierva had at last achieved with the gyroplane the major attributes of a rotary-wing aircraft—the ability to take-off and land without ground run. Only the helicopter could carry this development to its ultimate conclusion and provide full hovering flight in still air. Although the first successful aircraft of this type, the French Bréguet-Dorand 314 and the German Focke-Achgelis Fa 61 had already made their first flights (on June 26, 1935, and a year later on June 26, 1936, respectively), Cierva was not to live to see and participate in the final culmination of his life's work which these aircraft heralded.

On the morning of December 9, 1936, Cierva set off for Amsterdam. The reason for his trip has never been clear but it is supposed that he intended to meet other Nationalist supporters in order to further Franco's cause.

The KLM DC-2 (PH-AKL) flight, due to leave Croydon Airport at 10 a.m., was delayed by thick fog. When Captain Hautmeyer finally taxied out to the end of the fogline (a broad white line used as an initial guide on instrument take-offs), visibility was still only 25 yards. Hautmeyer started his run and apparently swung to the left. Although he must have lost sight of the fogline, he did not abandon take-off but continued on instruments. He did not realise that the DC-2 was now heading directly toward a line of houses on higher ground about a mile from the airport. Enveloped in fog, the aircraft first struck a chimney, then sliced through two roofs, ploughed into a house, and burst into flames. Only two of the sixteen people on board survived the crash. Cierva, at forty-one, perished in the worst-ever airline accident in England up to that time.

There were generous obituaries in the press and Cierva's old friend, Harold Pitcairn, in a specially published tribute, wrote:

> *Juan de la Cierva will be known to enduring fame as the outstanding pioneer in the field of rotary wing aircraft. . . .All helicopters and similar types of craft that have shown promise of practical performance incorporate some of the principles and inventions developed by Cierva.*

On April 26, 1937, the Royal Aeronautical Society posthumously awarded Cierva its Gold Medal.

Cierva C.30 Mk.IV, Mk.V, and C.30J. (140-hp Armstrong Siddeley Genet Major IA or 203-hp by Salmson 9Nd.). Cierva's death did not immediately terminate Autogiro development. Indeed, this continued for about another three years in Britain and another seven in the United States. Effort in Britain was concentrated mainly on developing a satisfactory form of jump take-off rotor. This work was done mostly by the successive testing of a wide variety of rotor head designs on the C.30, G-ACWF. This aircraft was known successively as the C.30 Mk.IV, Mk.V, and C.30J during this program.

Known as the C.30 Mk.III, G-ACWF had been tested until November 1936. Further modifications were then incorporated in December and the aircraft apparently became known as the C.30 Mk.IV. Testing of G-ACWF continued after Cierva's death until March 1937 when the Autodynamic head was finally abandoned.

A production-type jump take-off Autogiro, the C.40 (see later), was produced in Britain in 1938 to the designs of Dr. J.A.J. Bennett, who had taken over the technical direction of Autogiro development at the Cierva company. G-ACWF, probably known from January 1938 as the C.30 Mk.V, was used to flight-test the C.40 rotor hub for three blades which was of a new Delta-three design. This had compound hinging that overcame the faults of the two-blade Autodynamic heads. The final form of G-ACWF had a C.40 pylon and rotor and a Salmson 9Nd engine. It was then known as the C.30J (see later under C.40).

Cierva C.31. (385-hp Napier Rapier IV). This was a design study of a high-speed Autogiro put forward by Cierva in April 1934 and schemed by Bennett. It had a two-seat cabin, a direct-control three-blade 42 ft (12.8 m) rotor, and retractable landing gear. Estimated maximum speed: 206 mph (331 km/h). Empty weight: 2,000 lb (907 kg). Gross weight: 3,000 lb (1360 kg). (See Appendix 10).

Cierva C.32. (200-hp) de Havilland Gipsy Six). A design study of a high-speed Autogiro put forward by Cierva in April 1934, the C.32 was also schemed by Bennett. It had a two-seat cabin, a direct-control three-blade 34 ft (10.36 m) rotor and retractable landing gear. Estimated maximum speed: 180 mph (290 km/h). Empty weight: 1,300 lb (590 kg). Gross weight: 1,900 lb (862 kg). (See Appendix 10).

Cierva C.33. (215-hp Armstrong Siddeley Lynx IVc). This was the Avro 665 design study for a four-seat cabin Autogiro schemed by the Avro drawing office in Manchester in January/June 1934. The 165-horsepower Armstrong Siddeley Mongoose was considered as an alternative engine. The C.33 was to have been a conversion of the Avro 641 Commodore cabin biplane fitted with a direct-control three-blade rotor. This design was discussed with the Spanish airline, LAPE.

Cierva C.34. (350-hp Gnome-Rhône 7 Kg Titan Major). Cabin Autogiro for civil touring or military observation duties built as a prototype in France by Lioré-et-Olivier and taken over by the nationalised SNCASE—the Société Nationale de Constructions Aéronautiques du Sud-Est—which was formed in 1936 incorporating the Lioré-et-Olivier company.

The C.34 was a tandem two-seat Autogiro with enclosed cockpits, designed by Pierre Renoux in collaboration with Cierva. The structure was of welded steel tubes covered with fabric. The rotor blades were entirely of wood. There was a pilot-controlled rudder, but no elevator. The C.34 was to have a fixed forward-firing machine gun and was probably the largest and heaviest Autogiro to fly,

The French SNCASE C.34 Autogiro in its original form. Intended for civil touring or military use, this prototype was one of the largest and heaviest direct-control Autogiros designed.
(Author's Collection)

albeit in an unsatisfactory manner. The three-blade cantilever direct-control rotor was 16.5 m (54 ft 1 9/16 in) in diameter and the maximum take-off weight was 2,300 kg (5,070 lb). The rotor spin-up Spicer drive transmitted 100 hp. The 350-hp Hispano-Suize 9Q, an air-cooled radial based on the Wright Whirlwind, was offered as alternative power plant but was probably never fitted.

Lioré-et-Olivier started designing this Autogiro early in 1936 and it was completed in time to be exhibited at the XV Paris Salon de l'Aéronautique in November of that year. There must, however, have been serious problems when the C.34 was first tested and it seems likely that these were similar to the ground resonance experienced with the almost as large but considerably more powerful C.29 built by Westland in Britain two years before. The C.29 did not fly but it seems that the French were able to do something to overcome their difficulties with the C.34. Apparently, after prolonged testing, a redesigned stabilizer was fitted in 1938 and the C.34 was flown by Louis Rouland at Villacoublay in March 1939. However, handling was not satisfactory and the level of vibration was quite unacceptable—it was reported as "unbearable"! Development was abandoned in 1940 at the time of the German invasion.

Cierva C.35 and C.36. These are believed to have been design studies undertaken during Cierva's lifetime but not built. It is possible, however, that these designations were not used to avoid confusion with the American AC-35 and PA-36.

Cierva C.37. Also known as the Avro 668, this was a twin-engine cabin Autogiro design study schemed in the Avro design office in Manchester in February 1935.

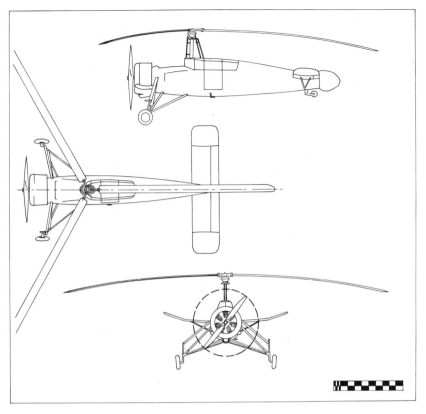

SNCASE C.34.

It had a single three-blade rotor, 54 ft (16.46 m) in diameter. Several different schemes were studied but the type was not proceeded with.

Cierva C.38. Believed to have been a design study only.

Cierva C.39. (600-hp Rolls-Royce Kestrel). This may have been a design study to meet the S.22/38 Specification issued on March 20, 1939 for a fleet spotter for the British Fleet Air Arm. It was to have been a two/three-seater with a three-blade rotor and was probably initially proposed during 1936 to meet Specification 43/36 issued at that time, even if later reconsidered for the 1938 specification.

Cierva C.40. (203-hp Salmson 9Ng or 203-hp Salmson 9Nd). The last British type of Cierva Autogiro, five of which were produced for the Air Ministry to Specification 43/36. They were side-by-side two seaters with partly enclosed cockpits. The order, to contract 649841/37, was announced in August 1937, although it is believed that design work, largely in the hands of Otto Reder, started in July 1936. It was originally announced that the C.40's engine would be the 160–140-hp geared Armstrong Siddeley Civet Major. In the event, the French

251

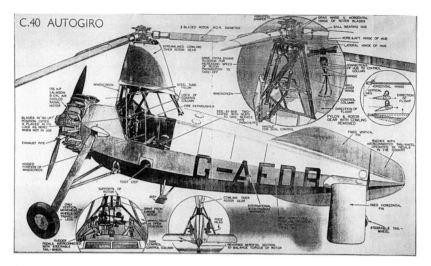

Cierva C.40.
(Flight International drawing)

Salmson was fitted instead. The first aircraft (G-AFDP) was assembled by the British Aircraft Manufacturing Company Ltd. at Hanworth.

Completed early in January 1938 it was first tested on the ground by Alan Marsh on January 4 and 5. While attempting a normal taxying take-off on the seventh, the C.40 broke into ground resonance and was severely damaged, fortunately without injury to the pilot.

As a result of this accident, a decision was taken to convert the C.30 Mk.IV development aircraft (G-ACWF) to take a C.40 pylon and rotor with blades of NACA 230 series section. This modification was quickly made and G-ACWF (probably now designated C.30 Mk.V) was flown successfully by Marsh on January 23. G-ACWF was subsequently fitted with a new pylon with jump take-off mechanism.

On February 25 the repaired first C.40 (G-AFDP) was successfully flown by Marsh with a taxying take-off and circuit. On March 1, Marsh made a jump take-off but there were control problems and the threat of resonance developing.

During March G-ACWF was fitted with a Salmson engine. When tested there were swaying problems as the rotor reached 220 rpm. A set of completely plywood-covered C.40 blades were fitted to G-ACWF which now came to be known as the C.30J. Stiffer rotor blades proved the answer to the resonance difficulty and in May, G-ACWF was flying and jumping satisfactorily.

On June 21, Marsh made four successful jump take-offs in the C.40 (G-AFDP), but on August 23 the C.30J fitted with C.40 blades was nearly wrecked when resonance started. Thereafter, the C.40 was flying and jumping satisfactorily.

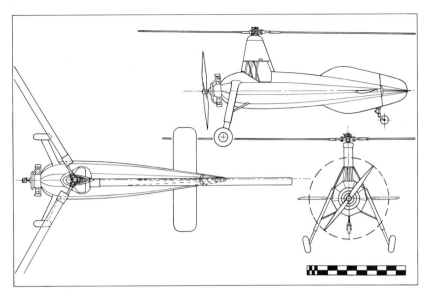

Cierva C.40.

During 1938 the Air Ministry ordered, under Contract 968954/38, two more C.40s. These were allocated serials P9635 and P9636 but only the latter is believed to have been used, applied to the requisitioned G-AFDR.

The C.40's rotor blades, as of most of the later British Autogiros, were made by Oddie, Bradbury and Cull Ltd. of Southampton who also built the wooden monocoque fuselages. This firm actually completed the last six C.40s, the last one after the war had started, the British Aircraft Manufacturing Company having gone out of business in 1938. Seven C.40's were built (L7589 to L7591, L7594, L7595, T1419, and P9636). Two were intended for army use and three were allocated to the navy but were later transferred to the RAF. Two others were initially registered as civil aircraft (G-AFDP and G-AFDR) but were impressed into the services after the outbreak of war. The first of these was lost in France in June 1940. An eighth aircraft, which was to have been allocated to the Cierva Company, was probably not completed.

On February 19, 1939, a C.40 was used by Reginald Brie for a BBC television program about the Autogiro. This was in the early days of public television but resulted in some good publicity. Brie took Miss Jasmine Bligh, the pioneer BBC television announcer, for a flight in the C.40 and she broadcast her impressions.

In anticipation of the delivery of the C.40's to the Royal Navy, two Fleet Air Arm pilots, Lieutenants Illingworth and H.E.H. Torin, each received 50 hours of instruction on Autogiros at the Hanworth school during the first three months of 1939. Two production C.40s were to be delivered to the navy early in 1939 but, in the event, their hand-over was delayed. The two aircraft (L7594 and L7595) were evaluated at Lee-on-Solent between December 1939 and April 1940. The program included a series of simulated deck-landing tests on land but actual sea trials were not attempted.

Before this, the navy's loss of interest had been confirmed when Commanders Couchman and Ermen visited Hanworth on July 6, 1939, the latter flying in the C.40. Royal Navy interest in the Autogiro had been for "night shadowing." It was clearly unsuitable for this role. Two types of small four-engine fixed-wing aircraft—the Airspeed A.S.39 and the General Aircraft GAL.38—were also developed to meet the same requirement. They proved just as unsuitable.

Two RAF army cooperation pilots, Flight Lieutenant B.G. Carroll and Flying Officer J. Weston, took a short training course on the C.30A and C.40 at Hanworth in June 1939. Carroll unfortunately suffered a landing accident on a C.40 (G-AFDP) on June 29.

As a flying machine, the C.40 was claimed to be a most successful design. In particular, its handling characteristics were said to be a marked improvement on the C.30 although most pilots preferred the earlier aircraft. Whatever the C.40's flying characteristics, it had a good pilot's view and the partly enclosed cockpit was comfortable. Its hanging stick followed the design of the C.30.

For the Army's purposes, the C.40 seems to have been a little more successful than the C.30. Two or three C.40s (L7589, probably L7590 and possibly T1419) went to France to join the British Expeditionary Force between October and December 1939. Two more were to have followed them after the army authorities asked for further trials. When British forces were driven out of France,

The Focke-Wulf Fw 186V1 jump take-off Autogiro prototype intended for German army use in the role for which the Fieseler Storch was finally selected. (Author's Collection)

one or two of the C.40's were flown back to England where they served alongside the C.30's in 1448 Flight and 529 Squadron. The other C.40 (possibly T1419) had to be destroyed in France by engineer officers Loder and Dunn to prevent it falling into enemy hands. The army decided at this time to defer further testing of Autogiros until after the war.

The C.40's jump take-off 40 ft (12.19 m) three-blade rotor was of different design from Cierva's Autodynamic head. The new rotor system was designed by James Bennett and avoided the vibration troubles of earlier jump take-off Autogiros. Cierva's Autodynamic rotor system employed inclined drag hinges without friction or hydraulic dampers because damping about these hinges would have slowed down the rate of change of blade pitch and would have spoiled the jump takeoff performance. Only a two-blade rotor at that time was free from ground resonance when fitted with Cierva's inclined drag hinges without dampers. Unfortunately, the two-blade rotor system had an inherent twice-per-revolution vibration which was present throughout the speed range.

The three-blade rotor developed by Bennett for the C.40 was relatively free from vibration and the ground resonance difficulty was overcome by means of hinge dampers which limited the motion of the blades with respect to one another but which allowed symmetrical oscillations of the three blades with respect to the hub to remain undamped. In this way, jump take-offs to a height of about twelve ft (3.66 m) were achieved, by overspeeding the rotor to about 285 rpm, without the undesirable vibrations of the earlier Autodynamic heads.

Focke-Wulf Fw 186. (240-hp Argus As 10c). The Germans also developed a jump take-off Autogiro. This was produced secretly by their Cierva licensees, the Focke-Wulf Flugzeugbau GmbH. of Bremen, to meet an RLM (German Air Ministry) requirement, issued in autumn 1935, for a short take-off and landing army cooperation, liaison and light transport aircraft. After evaluation of the C.30, a decision was taken in 1936 to undertake as a private venture, the development of a direct take-off Autogiro as an alternative to the airplanes being developed to meet the requirement.

By this date, Professor Heinrich K.J. Focke, the former technical director of Focke-Wulf who had been succeeded by Kurt Tank in 1933, had turned his main attention from Autogiros to helicopters. His work resulted in the highly successful Focke-Achgelis Fa 61 helicopter which flew for the first time on June 26, 1936. This aircraft subsequently established a number of world records (see Appendix 1) and led on to Europe's first production helicopter, the Fa 223. Development of the helicopters was undertaken by Focke-Achgelis GmbH. at Hoyenkamp bei Delmenhorst, near Bremen, a company formed by Focke to continue the rotary-wing work he had started at Focke-Wulf.

Meanwhile, the Focke-Wulf company itself (of which Professor Focke was still a director), is reported to have produced about thirty C.30's under license between 1935 and 1938. Development of the Fw 186 Autogiro continued in 1937 and a prototype (D-ISTQ) was flown in July 1938. This two-seat aircraft, with tandem open cockpits, was of similar size to the C.40, but had its three-blade rotor mounted on a single cantilever pylon like the Kellett KD-1. The rotor system was designed by Dr. E. Kosel but the jump take-off feature is believed to have worked on similar principles to that developed by Dr. Bennett in England. The Fw 186 proved to have unsatisfactory flying characteristics and the type was not put into production. The German military authorities, like their counterparts in Britain and the United States, concluded that the battlefield tasks, for which the Fw 186 had been intended, could be more effectively performed by the Fieseler Fi 156 Storch STOL fixed-wing airplane. The latter was, indeed, to prove highly successful and was used in large numbers during World War II. (About 3,000 were built.)

The war, when it came in 1939, led in due course to the stopping of both Autogiro and helicopter development in Britain. By the time work in this field was resumed in that country, toward the end of the war, helicopter developments in the United States and Germany had finally eclipsed the gyroplane. The C.40 was thus the last of its line in Britain just as was the Fw 186 in Germany. A total of some 135 Autogiros had by then been manufactured in Great Britain. (See Appendix 12.)

Cierva C.41. (600-hp Rolls-Royce Kestrel). The last pre-war design study by the Cierva Autogiro Company was Bennett's Cierva Gyrodyne, which incorporated features of the helicopter and Autogiro. No machine of this type was built. It was designed to the S.22/38 Specification issued on March 20, 1939, as a fleet spotter for the Fleet Air Arm and was a step toward James Bennett's Fairey Gyrodyne, which was developed after the war. But it is not clear whether the Cierva Gyrodyne design, which is sometimes referred to as the C.41, was different from the C.39 already mentioned. Pitcairns in the United States were also engaged on their Gyrodyne project at this time. (See Pitcairn PA-33B and AC-35B in Chapter 8).

Cierva C.30 Mk.II to Mk.V, C.30J

140-hp Armstrong Siddeley Genet Major IA (Mk.II-Mk.V). 203-hp Salmson 9Nd (C.30J). Rotor diameter 37 ft (11.28 m) (Mk.II-Mk.IV), 40 ft 1 in (12.21 m) (Mk.V and C.30J); rotor blade section Gö 606 (Mk.II-Mk.IV), NACA 23012 (Mk.V and C.30J); overall length 19 ft 8½ in (6 m) (Mk.II–Mk.IV); rotor speed 210 rpm. No other data available.

Cierva C.34

Gnome-Rhône 7 Kg Titan-Major. Rotor diameter about 16.5 m (54 ft 1 %₁₆ in); rotor blade section Gö 606; overall length 9.8 m (32 ft 1 ⅞ in). Empty weight 1,600–1,650 kg (3527–3,638 lb); maximum take-off weight 2,300 kg (5,070 lb). Fuel 359 liters (79 Imp gal). Maximum speed 220 km/h (137 mph); minimum speed 45 km/h (28 mph); ceiling 4,500 m (14,760 ft); range 750 km (466 miles).

Cierva C.40

203-hp Salmson 9Ng or 203-hp Salmson 9Nd. Rotor diameter 40 ft 1in–44 ft (12.21–13.41 m); rotor blade section NACA 23012; overall length 20 ft 8 in (6.29 m). Empty weight 1,350 lb (612 kg); maximum take-off weight 1,950 lb (884 kg). Fuel 25.5 Imp gal (115 liters). Maximum speed 120 mph (193 km/h); initial climb 1,000 ft/min (5 m/sec); range 200 miles (321 km) at 100–105 mph (160–168 km/h); rotor speed 180 rpm.

Focke-Wulf Fw 186

240-hp Argus As 10c. Rotor diameter about 12.2 m (40 ft); rotor blade section probably Gö 606. No other data available.

Chapter 10

Development in the Soviet Union

Although the program was not heard of in the West until long afterward, the Soviet Union had decided, as early as 1925, that a major research and development effort was necessary in the rotary-wing field. This activity was centered at TsAGI, the main Russian establishment for aeronautical research.

By 1928, the general rotary-wing research undertaken in the Soviet Union up to that time crystalized in the start of design of an actual aircraft, the 1-EA helicopter. By 1929, descriptions of Cierva's early Autogiros had appeared in the technical press and no doubt Autogiros had been inspected and fully reported upon on numerous occasions by Soviet agents abroad.

KaSkr-I (110-hp M-2). This Russian copy of Cierva's Autogiro was sponsored by Osoaviakhim (Society for assistance to aviation and chemical industry), the paramilitary sports organization. It was manufactured without a license but was clearly derived directly from Cierva's design. Named "Red Engineer," it had a U-1 (copied Avro 504K) fuselage, landing gear, and tail unit and was fitted with an M-2 (copied 110-hp Le Rhône) rotary engine. It was, therefore, equivalent to the Cierva C.6 except that its 12 meter (39 ft 4 7/16 in) rotor incorporated paddle blades and flapping and drag hinges like the C.8. This aircraft was the design responsibility of a team under N.I. Kamov and N.K. Skrzhinskii and was first ground-run at the Moscow Central Airport by I.V. Mikheyev on September 1, 1929, 5½ years after the C.6 and 2¾ years after the C.8R. KaSkr-I was not flown because the control system proved ineffective, the aircraft threatening to overturn sideways.

KaSkr-II (230-hp Gnome-Rhône Titan). A larger rudder and 8 kg (18 lb) of offset ballast under the starboard wing tip were tried to cure the KaSkr's problems but the aircraft could not be flown because of lack of power. The overturning problem suggests that the rotor's flapping hinges provided insufficient flapping freedom. Because it was underpowered, the aircraft was re-engined with the much more powerful French Gnome-Rhône Titan air-cooled radial in a helmeted cowling and thus became the KaSkr-II. In this form the Russian aircraft approximated in power and weight to the Cierva C.8L-I. The Russian rotor had always had flapping and drag hinges like that of the C.8 but the flapping freedom may have been increased on KaSkr-II. The re-engined aircraft flew sometime in mid-1930 (about 3¾ years after the C.8L-I) and thereafter, in the hands of D.A. Koshits,

*The KaSkr-II was a Russian copy of the Cierva C.8
Autogiro.
(Jean Alexander)*

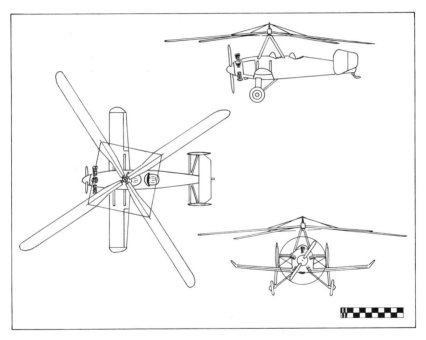

TsAGI 2-EA.

made about 90 flights, the longest of 28 minutes, reaching an altitude of 460 m
(1,500 ft) and a speed of 111 km/h (69 mph). In the winter of 1930–31 the
KaSkr-II was flown on skis. Flying continued until late 1931.

TsAGI 2-EA (230-hp Gnome-Rhône Titan). Another design team under I.P.
Bratukhin and V.A. Kuznetsov was responsible for the second Russian gyroplane
started in the latter part of 1930. It was built at the TsAGI OOK (Department of

259

special construction) under the direction of A.M. Izakson. This new design incorporated a fuselage specially designed for the job and was not an adaptation from an existing airplane. Construction was of welded steel tubes with fabric covering. The 2-EA closely resembled a scaled-up Cierva C.19 Mk.I. The rotor was four-bladed and cable-braced and was of the same 12 m (39 ft 4 $\frac{7}{16}$ in) diameter as that of the KaSkr-I and II. However, it was of more advanced design with parallel chord blades, probably incorporating information obtained about the design of the C.19 Mk.I rotor. Rotor starting was by the deflected slipstream method used by Cierva on the first C.19s. The welded steel tube/fabric tail unit was of box configuration with stabilizer and elevator that could be used to deflect the slipstream onto the rotor. Effectiveness of the method—which was never very great—was still further reduced by the fact that, unlike the C.19s, no wheel brakes were fitted to the 2-EA.

The 2-EA made its first flight on November 17, 1931, piloted by S.A. Korzinshchikov. It was, therefore, about 2⅓ years behind the equivalent C.19. Problems were experienced with what was probably ground resonance but the aircraft is said to have been flown enough to give useful experience in the measurement of gyroplane performance. Take-off distance was 60 m (197 ft) and landing 0–6 m (0–20 ft) depending on the wind.

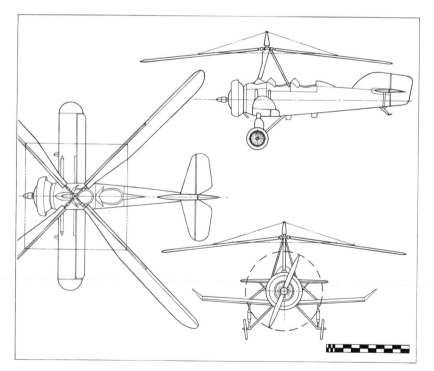

TsAGI A-4.

The TsAGI A-4 taxying. This gyroplane had mechanical rotor spin-up and dual controls. (Author's Collection)

In 1933, the 2-EA was transferred to the Maxim Gorkii Propaganda Squadron but seems to have been little used. It was presented to the Osoaviakim Museum early in 1934.

TsAGI A-4 (300 hp M-26). This autogyro, originally called 4-EA, was significantly larger than the 2-EA, having a bigger four-blade 13 m (42.65 ft) rotor, higher weights, and more power. It was, nevertheless, regarded as a low-risk development of the earlier design but with mechanical rotor starting and dual control added. The A-4 was, moreover, intended for military and civil applications. The fuselage had a structure of welded steel tubes covered with fabric. Design started early in 1932 to meet the requirements of an air force scientific test institute decree under the direction of N.K. Skrzhinskii, A.M. Cheremukhin, and G.I. Solnitsev. Construction was at the TsAGI OOK. In June of that year, it was decided to undertake limited production for military training and observation duties.

The prototype flew for the first time in the hands of S.A. Korzinshchikov on November 6, 1932, followed by the first production aircraft on November 30. The A-4 was thus 2⅔ years behind the American PCA-2, the equivalent Autogiro in the West. The decision to undertake production of the A-4 was premature: problems of heavy and sustained vibration and of low rotor rpm were revealed on the first flight. On the prototype's second flight on November 9, the pilot lost control when heavy rotor vibration developed with loss of lift and the aircraft was badly damaged in the ensuing crash.

The vibration experienced on the A-4 is said to have been eventually overcome by introducing a new design of rotor blade. The original O Type blades weighing 35 kg (77 lb) each were replaced by the UB Type weighing 41 kg (90 lb). However, the A-4 was never produced in quantity, as had been intended at one stage. Rather more than ten are believed to have been built and the type was

The TsAGI A-6 had a cantilever folding three-blade rotor and was of comparable technology to the British C.19 Mk.IV.
(Author's Collection)

briefly evaluated by the military. Take-off distance was 70–100 m (230–328 ft), landing required 3–10 m (10–33 ft). A 360-degree turn could be completed in 15 seconds.

TsAGI A-6 (100-hp M-11). The A-6 was smaller than the A-4 which, although a two-seater, was of similar size, weight, and power to the three-seater American PCA-2. The A-6 was more like the British C.19. It may originally have been known as the 6-EA. With its three-blade cantilever 11 m (36 ft 1 $\frac{1}{16}$ in) rotor, it was designed to a level of technology corresponding to that of the C.19 Mk.IV from which, there is little doubt, the Russian designers drew their main inspiration. The fixed wings with upturned tips folded vertically and the rotor blades folded back for hangarage. Construction was on similar lines to its predecessors. Low-pressure tires were used without shock struts.

Design of the A-6 was the responsibility of V.A. Kuznetsov and his team, who had designed the 2-EA. It was undertaken at about the same time as N.K. Skrzinskii, Cheremukhin, and Solnitsev were busy on the A-4. The A-6 was built at the TsAGI OOK and first flew early in 1933, testing being undertaken by S.A. Korzinshchikov who had earlier flown the A-4's. The A-6 was thus about 1⅔ years behind its Western equivalent, the C.19 Mk.IV.

Ground resonance proved to be a problem with the A-6 but this was eventually overcome by adding dampers to the flapping hinges. Thereafter, flight testing gave satisfactory results. The aircraft proved to have good handling and stability characteristics and was used for various research programs during the winter of 1933. It was demonstrated at the Moscow Aviation Festival on August 18, 1934. However, development of the type did not go beyond the first prototype, attention being diverted to the direct-control A-8 (see later) to which the second and third prototypes of the A.6 were converted before completion. The A-6 was at one stage fitted experimentally with a vee tail unit.

The TsAGI A-7 was of similar technology to the A-6.
It was the best-known Soviet gryroplane.
(Jean Alexander)

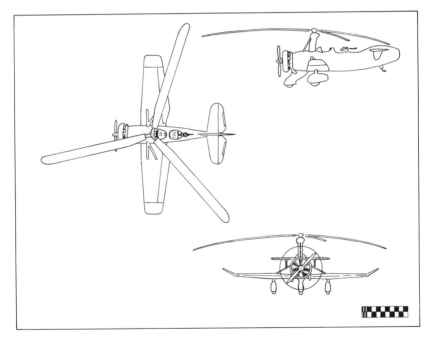

TsAGI A-7.

TsAGI A-7 (480-hp M-22). This was the best known Soviet gyroplane. It was designed to meet an air force scientific test institute demand for a powerful autogyro for front-line duties such as artillery observation, reconnaissance, and liaison. Although still a two-seater, it was a relatively large aircraft of comparable size, weight, and power to the largest Autogiros built in the West. The fuselage was of welded steel tubes with duralumin covering and integral fin. The tail unit was of duralumin with fabric covering and the wing of wood with plywood covering. The engine had a Townend ring cowling. The Russians claimed that the A-7 was the first aircraft in the world to have a steerable nosewheel landing gear. The three-blade cantilever rotor had a diameter of 15.18 m (49 ft 9⅝ in). The blades had stainless steel tubular spars, wooden ribs and stringers, plywood covering of the leading edge, and stainless steel sheet covering the rest. Gross weight was originally 1975 kg (4,354 lb), but was later increased to 2300 kg (5,070 lb). Design started in 1931 and was undertaken by the 3rd Brigade team under N.I. Kamov. The type was of C.19 Mk.IV technology with fixed-wing and control surfaces but a cantilever rotor with engine-powered spin-up drive. By the time the A-7 was flown by S.A. Korzinshchikov on September 20, 1934, the type was out-of-date. It has been claimed that the A-7 was the first autogyro in the world to achieve jump take-offs. Cierva first made such takeoffs in August 1933 with specially modified rotor head on the C.30 prototype G-ACFI. As the A-7 made its first flight a year later, this claim is patently false and, in any case, such take-offs would certainly have been unsatisfactory without direct control, which the A-7 lacked.

The C.30 direct-control Autogiro had been in production in Britain for some months before the A-7 first flew, but it should be noted that the first direct-control Autogiro of comparable size to the A-7, the Westland-built Cierva C.29 of 1934, was not a success and did not fly, although it was completed at about the same date as the A-7 first flew. The first direct-control Autogiro of large size to fly, the French C.34, did not do so until 1939 and, even then, is believed to have had unsatisfactory handling characteristics. The Pitcairn PA-19, of comparable size to the A-7, appeared about 2½ years before the Russian aircraft, but it had a rotor of earlier technology (equivalent to that of the C.19 Mk.III). In any case, in general, direct-control autogyros were not satisfactory in the larger sizes because control forces became excessive, vibration levels were high, and there was increased tendency to ground resonance. Russian experience and that in Western countries seems to have been similar in these respects.

Severe vibration problems dogged the initial flight testing of the A-7. Trouble was also experienced with engine overheating. However, these deficiencies were gradually ironed out so that air force acceptance trials flown by A.A. Ivanovskii were successfully completed in 1936. In the interval, the A-7 prototype was demonstrated at the Soviet Aviation Day Display at Tushino on August 18, 1935.

A second aircraft, the A-7bis, appeared in March 1937 and completed its flight tests in July 1938. It had a modified rotor pylon. Five production aircraft (A-7-3a) were then ordered, these military models being armed with one fixed and two movable PV-1 machine guns. They were put into production in 1939 at a factory at Smolensk. The first was delivered early in 1940. The A-7-3a's had a lighter airframe, improved fuselage, and no spats on the landing gear. Later, during the early days of the war, the A-7's were used operationally for reconnaissance on the Smolensk Front. Before that, in 1938, a prototype had been shipped to Greenland and used in the Arctic, operating from the ice-breaker *Yermak*, on an expedition to rescue Papanin's North Pole station from an ice floe. Another was

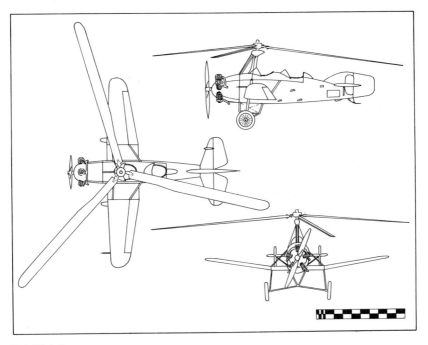

TsAGI A-8.

used in 1938-40 by Aeroflot for forestry patrols during the Tien-Shan expedition in Central Asia.

TsAGI A-8 (100-hp M-11). The second and third A-6 prototypes were converted during manufacture into a new design, the A-8—Russia's first direct-control gyroplane although this operated only for lateral control. Conventional elevators were retained for control in pitch. By the time the A-6 was flying early in 1933, Cierva had been experimenting in England with complete direct control on the C.19 Mk.V for nearly a year and he may have carried out ineffective tests with C.10 and C.11 as early as 1928. Direct control was announced by Cierva and publicly demonstrated by him with the C.19 Mk.V in November 1932. This advance immediately made all earlier designs of Autogiro obsolete and, as was to be expected, the Russians quickly turned to this new development themselves.

Kuznetsov started designing the A-8 early in 1933, and his first prototype flew 16–17 months later on June 29, 1934. The second prototype flew on February 14, 1935. Both aircraft retained the fixed wing and control surfaces of the A-6, but the wings were straight with 5 degrees of dihedral outboard from the center-section and without upturned tips. (This change was similar to that made by Kellett in the United States where, in June 1933, the K-4 with marked dihedral from the wing roots replaced the K-3, which had wings with upturned wing tips.) The control surfaces supplemented lateral control by sideways tilting of the rotor head. The A-8 prototypes are said to have been fitted with the first air/oil shock

One of the TsAGI A-8 prototypes at the Soviet Aviation Day Display in Moscow in 1935. The A-8 was the first Russian direct-control autogyro although it retained a fixed-wing and control surfaces.
(Author's Collection)

struts tried in the Soviet Union. The A-8's were demonstrated at the 1934 and 1935 Soviet Aviation Day displays at Tushino.

TsAGI A-10 (480-hp M-22). This was a 1933 project for a six-passenger cabin gyroplane with a 16 m (52 ft 5 $^{15}\!/_{16}$ ins) three-blade rotor proposed by Skrzhinskii based on experience with the A-4. The type was not built because it was of pre-direct-control technology and became outdated soon after it was proposed. The A-10 designation was later used for another project studied in 1937–39, which was not built. This was for a small two-seat direct-control gyroplane with a 140-hp MV-4 engine (Renault license).

TsAGI A-12 (670-hp Wright Cyclone F-3). Experience with the A-8 direct-control prototypes, with the A-14 wingless conversion of the A-8 (see later), and with the Avro-built C.30A ordered from Britain in 1934, and delivered to the Soviet Union early in the following year, convinced the Russian designers that a high-performance direct-control wingless gyroplane was feasible and might have important military applications. It is interesting that their thinking seems to have been along similar lines to that of Cierva in England. (See Appendix 8.) Following project work in 1934, which included study of various high-performance designs, the OOK 6th Brigade team under N.K. Skrzhinskii started designing the A-12 early in 1935. This was a high performance gyroplane fitted with a 14 m (45 ft 11 $^{3}\!/_{16}$ in) three-blade folding cantilever rotor with spin-up drive. Direct control was provided in roll but not in pitch, the latter being dependent on a conventional elevator. The rotor was mounted on a fuselage of similar shape but different construction to that of the Polikarpov I-16 single-seat fighter. The latter's standard

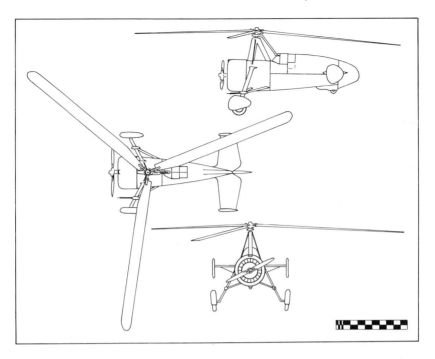

TsAGI A-12.

630-hp M-25 engine (Wright Cyclone built under license) was replaced by an original American-built Wright Cyclone F-3 of 670-hp, perhaps because it had a better power-to-weight ratio. It was estimated that, driving a controllable-pitch propeller, this engine would give a maximum speed of 333 km/h (207 mph) at 2300 m (7,500 ft). The minimum speed was to be 39 km/h (24 mph) at 1000 m (3,300 ft) and the ceiling 7500 m (24,600 ft). Unlike the I-16, the A-12 had a fixed landing gear with the wheels enclosed in spats similar to those on the I-15 fighter. Toe-operated wheel brakes were provided. While the fuselage of the I-16 was a wooden monocoque, that of the A-12 was of steel tubes faired with stringers and covered with fabric.

This formidable aircraft, considerably more ambitious than any other gyroplane built, was completed and first flown by A.P. Chyernavskii on two short straight hops on May 10, 1936. At first badly unstable in flight, the A-12 also suffered from serious vibration of the rotor head. This had to be dampened by a system of springs. Alterations also had to be made to the inclination of the rotor axis and to the design of the main bearing. However, during the twelve months following the first flight, the aircraft was extensively flight tested in the course of 43 flights and for a total flying time of just under 18 hours. The performance envelope was measured up to a maximum speed of 246 km/h (153 mph) at 2200 m (7,200 ft), to an altitude of 5600 m (18,200 ft) and down to a minimum speed of 51 km/h (32 mph) at 900 m (3,000 ft). It was concluded that a maximum speed of

300 km/h (186 mph) should be achievable rather than the 330 km/h (207 mph) originally hoped for.

The maximum speed actually measured for the A-12 was probably a record for rotary-wing aircraft at that time. Nevertheless, it was only slightly faster than the lower-powered and lighter American Pitcairn PA-33 of 1935. Moreover, the PA-33 had a rotor of 1.2 m (4 ft) greater diameter and had flown 16 months earlier.

Unfortunately, on May 23, 1937, while being flown by I. Kozyrev, the A-12 suffered structural failure when a rotor blade became detached in flight following fatigue fracture of the blade's spar. The aircraft crashed and was destroyed, the pilot losing his life.

TsAGI A-13 (100-hp M-11). The Kuznetsov 2nd Brigade team had been responsible for the A-6 and A-8, the latter incorporating makeshift addition of direct-control to a gyroplane with fixed wings and conventional controls. In 1935, the same designers made further extensive modifications to the first A-8 proto-type to improve performance, which was deficient because it was underpowered. Redesignated A-13, the new version also had a direct-control rotor, this time 11.5 m (37 ft 8¾ ins) in diameter, and fixed wings, and control surfaces. Wings and rotor blades could be folded. The motor had a self-starter and rotor spin-up drive. A-13 made its first flight, piloted by Korzinshchikov, on March 13, 1936. The lightening and cleaning-up of the airframe resulted in some improvement in per-formance. At one stage skis were fitted. However, serious vibration was experi-enced which could not be overcome and development was abandoned.

TsAGI A-14 (100-hp M-11). This was a conversion of the second A-8 prototype undertaken by Kuznetsov in August 1935. Modifications included substitution of a redesigned rotor head, removal of the fixed wings and control surfaces, and addi-tion of a new wide-track landing gear. The A-14 was first flown by Korzinshchikov on September 13, or 17, 1935, and was thus the first Russian wingless gyroplane. It appeared 3½ years after the equivalent first flights in Britain of the C.19 Mk.V. Although the A-14 proved to have better take-off and landing performance than the A-8 and was longitudinally more stable, lateral control was unsatisfactory. Nevertheless, it was widely used for research purposes.

Early in 1936, the A-14 prototype was used to flight test a new type of rotor head for the A-12.

TsAGI A-15 (700-hp M-25V). In 1935, M.L. Mil (later to become a well-known helicopter designer) undertook the design of a new powerful direct-control wingless gyroplane for military use—specifically for tactical reconnaissance and artillery observation. The pilot had a fixed forward-firing SHKAS machine gun and the observer, two similar weapons, freely mounted. The new design had a cantilever three-blade rotor no less than 18 m (59 ft 0⅔ in) in diameter. The gross weight came to 2560 kg (5,643 lb). Construction was under the management of A.A. Kuznetsov. The prototype was completed in April 1937 but ground reso-nance seems to have been experienced, as with comparable large Autogiros in the

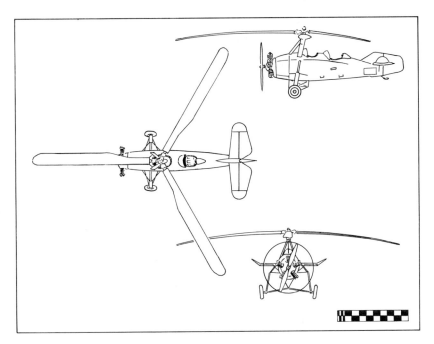

TsAGI A-14.

West. The A-15 was thus completed some 2½ years after the British C.29 of comparable weight and power, which had also been unsatisfactory. Taxying tests were made by Chyernavskii and Ivanov but it is not clear whether the A-15 was actually flown—probably not. Testing was, in any case, interrupted after the A-12 crash on May 23, 1937. It was resumed in February 1938 but abandoned shortly afterward.

TsAGI AK (225-hp MV-6). This was a new design started by N.I. Kamov in 1940 at Smolensk. It was to have been a side-by-side two-seat direct take-off gyroplane with a pusher engine and nosewheel landing gear. The three-blade rotor had a hydraulic mechanism to change the pitch of the blades during jump takeoffs. This feature was probably based on the Pitcairn system. It is interesting that the pusher configuration of the AK was also similar to that of the last American Autogiro, the Pitcairn YO-61. Construction of the AK prototype was interrupted in July 1941 by the evacuation of the Soviet aircraft factories to the East in front of German advances of 1941. Work re-started at a new facility in the Lake Baikal area but was terminated in 1943 thus ending Soviet gyroplane development until after World War II. In the early 1950's, the Russians seem to have produced some rotary-wing gliders intended for the initial training of helicopter pilots. One of these, the Smolensk, resembled the German Fa 330 but had an enclosed cockpit. In 1967 Soviet interest in gyroplanes revived again and experimental examples are reported to have been built at Kharkov, Kubyshev, and Riga.

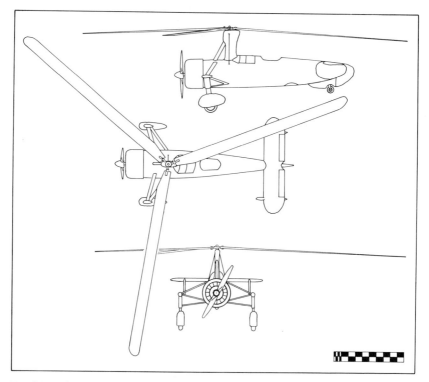

TsAGI A-15.

A rotary-wing kite, the Ch-1, Chaika (Seagull), is believed to have been flown in 1970 but no more recent developments are known.

The story of Soviet gyroplane development, which was clearly inspired by Cierva's work in the West, is an interesting example of illicit technology acquisition. Instead of seeking engineering information directly from Cierva by way of a license—as did companies in the United States, Germany, France, and Japan—the Russians relied almost entirely on published information, supplemented presumably by reports from agents. No doubt, there were many opportunities for interested observers to inspect Autogiros in the West. Autogiros were frequently displayed publicly and there were probably many other occasions when they could be clandestinely examined, sketched, and photographed. The Soviets sought Autogiro information openly only once when they purchased a direct-control C.30A in 1934. By that time, no doubt, Cierva considered this model's technology to be obsolescent.

The Soviets completed their first gyroplane, a direct copy of the C.6 using Avro 504K components, some 5½ years after Cierva's first truly practical prototype had flown in Spain. Design of the rotor of this first Russian gyroplane seems to have been based on that of the C.8R which had drag as well as flapping hinges following the accident to Courtney at Hamble. At this point, the Soviets were some three years behind Cierva. (See table at end of chapter.)

The next important step was to adopt Cierva's rather ineffective deflected-slipstream rotor starting system. The Russians copied this in about 2½ years from the date Cierva started work on the C.12 in Spain.

The first satisfactory engine-powered rotor spin-up drive was an American development appearing early in 1930. The Russians took 2⅔ years to adopt this essential improvement. The French and British took about 1½ years, although the British had an unsatisfactory prototype drive about three months before the Americans.

Cierva's next big advance was to switch from rotors with four cable-restrained blades of symmetrical Gö 429 section to three-blade rotors with cantilever folding blades of RAF 34 cambered section. The improved rotor originally appeared on the C.19 Mk.IV prototype in June 1931 and was revealed to the public in November of that year. The Russian cantilever rotor appeared (on the A-6) fourteen months after Cierva's first public demonstration of his latest development. This short lead time suggests that the Russians may, in this case, have obtained information before the public demonstration—perhaps even as early as the secret flight tests at Hamble six months before.

The most important improvement of the Autogiro was the introduction of direct-control. This was first achieved by Cierva in March 1932 and reported in the newspaper soon afterward. It was not publicly demonstrated until November but the Kay 32/1 gyroplane with laterally tilting head was publicly flown in August 1932. The Russians took 1¾ years to partially follow this step—the A-8, retaining fixed-wings and conventional controls, had only supplementary lateral control through the rotor. The first wingless Russian gyroplane (the A-14) did not appear until 3½ years after direct control had been publicly demonstrated in the West. This was also nine months after a C.30A (C/n 779) had been delivered to the Soviet Union, which suggests that the Russians had despaired of obtaining, in any other way, all the information they required on direct control. The first large Russian direct-control autogyro, the A-15, failed just 2½ years after the failure of the comparable large Cierva Autogiro, the C.29 in Britain.

Starting 5½ years behind the West in gyroplane development, the Russians were able to copy Cierva's successive steps with delays of between 1½ and 3¾ years. However, they failed altogether to take the final step to jump take-off. Significantly, this development was still giving trouble in the West up to the time when the gyroplane was finally eclipsed by the helicopter.

KaSkr-I

110-hp M-2. Rotor diameter 12 m (39 ft 4½ in); rotor blade section probably Gö 429; fuselage length 9.3 m (30 ft 6 in); span of fixed wing 8 m (26 ft 3 in). Empty weight 750 kg (1,653 lb); maximum take-off weight 950 kg (2,094 lb); maximum speed 90 km/h (56 mph); range 135 km (84 miles) at 90 km/h (56 mph). Rotor speed 115 rpm.

KaSkr-II

230-hp Gnome-Rhône Titan. Rotor diameter 12 m (39 ft 4½ in); rotor blade section probably Gö 429; span of fixed wing 8 m (26 ft 3 in). Empty weight 865 kg (1,907 lb); maximum take-off weight 1,100 kg (2,425 lb). Maximum speed 110 km/h (68 mph); ceiling 450 m (1,476 ft); range 51 km (32 miles) at 110 km/h (68 mph); rotor speed 120–135 rpm.

TsAGI 2-EA

230-hp Gnome-Rhône Titan. Rotor diameter 12 m (39 ft 4½ in); rotor blade section probably Gö 429; fuselage length 6.29 m (20 ft 7½ in); span of fixed wing 6.72 m (22 ft 0¾ in). Empty weight 765 kg (1,686 lb); maximum take-off weight 1,032 kg (2,275 lb). Maximum speed 160 km/h (100 mph); minimum speed 58 km/h (36 mph); absolute ceiling 4,200 m (13,779 ft); range 240 km (149 miles) at 140 km/h (87 mph); rotor speed 146 rpm.

TsAGI A-4 (4-EA)

300-hp M-26. Rotor diameter 13 m (42 ft 7¾ in); rotor blade section Gö 429; overall length 7.22 m (23 ft 8¼ in); span of fixed wing 6.73 m (22 ft 1 in). Empty weight 1,020–1,065 kg (2,248–2,347 lb); maximum take-off weight 1,265–1,320 kg (2,347–2,910 lb). Fuel 165 liters (36 Imp gal). Maximum speed 176 km/h (109 mph) at 3,000m (9,842 ft); minimum speed 40–45 km/h (24–28 mph); absolute ceiling 4,500 m (14,763 ft); service ceiling 4,100 m (13,451 ft); range 230 km (142 miles) at 140 km/h (87 mph); rotor speed 140–150 rpm.

TsAGI A-6

100-hp M-11. Rotor diameter 11 m (36 ft 1 ⁄₁₆ in); rotor blade section probably Gö 429; fuselage length 6.17 m (20 ft 3 in); span of fixed wing 6.6 m (21 ft 7¾ in). Empty weight 562 kg (1,239 lb); maximum take-off weight 815 kg (1,796 lb). Fuel 93 liters (20.5 Imp gal). Maximum speed 142 km/h (88 mph); minimum speed 53 km/h (33 mph); ceiling 2,000 m (6,561 ft) rotor speed 180 rpm.

TsAGI A-7, A7bis, A-7-3a

480-hp M-22. Rotor diameter 15.18 m (49 ft 9½ in); rotor blade section probably Gö 429; fuselage length 8.38 m (27 ft 6 in); span of fixed wing 10.4 m (34 ft 1½ in). Empty weight 1,300–1,550 kg (2,866–3,417 lb); maximum take-off weight 1,975–2,300 kg (4,349–5,070 lb). Fuel 459 liters (101 Imp gal). Maximum speed 210–221 km/h (130–137 mph); minimum speed 46 km/h (28 mph); absolute ceiling 4,800 m (15,748 ft); range 400–600 km (250–375 mi) at 150–160 km/h (94–100 mph); take-off distance 60–75 m (197–246 ft); landing distance 18–20 m (59–66 ft); rotor speed 195–200 rpm.

TsAGI A-8

100-hp M-11. Rotor diameter 11 m (36 ft 1 ⁄₁₆ in); rotor blade section probably Gö 429; fuselage length 6.17 m (20 ft 3 in); span of fixed wing 6.5 m (21 ft 4 in). Empty weight 595 kg (1,311 lb); maximum take-off weight 837 kg (1,845). Maximum speed 142 km/h (88 mph) at sea level; minimum speed 48 km/h (29 mph); absolute ceiling 2,260–3,000 m (7,414–9,842 ft).

TsAGI A-12

670-hp Wright Cyclone R-1820 F-3. Rotor diameter 14 m (45 ft 11¼ in); rotor blade section Gö 429/Stek 0009–63; fuselage length 6.74 m (22 ft 1¼ in). Empty weight 1,343 kg (2,960 lb); maximum take-off weight 1,687 kg (3,719 lb). Fuel 229 liters (50.4 Imp Gal). Maximum speed 300 km/h (186 mph) (est); maximum measured speed 243 km/h (152 mph); minimum speed 40 km/h (25 mph); absolute ceiling 6,500 m (21,325 ft); take-off distance 25 m (82 ft); landing distance 5–10 m (16–32 ft); rotor speed 160–260 rpm.

TsAGI A-13

100 hp M-11. Rotor diameter 11–11.5 m (36 ft 1 in–37 ft 8¾ in); rotor blade section probably Gö 429; fuselage length 6.6 m (21 ft 7¾ in); span of fixed wing 6.5 m (21 ft 4 in). Empty weight 559 kg (1,232 lb); maximum take-off weight 798 kg (1,759 lb). Fuel 69.5 liters (15 Imp gal). Maximum speed 151 km/h (94 mph); minimum speed 45 km/h (28 mph); absolute ceiling 3,000 m (9,800 ft); range 250 km (156 miles) at 125 km/h (78 mph); take-off distance 40 m (131 ft); landing distance nil.

TsAGI A-14

100-hp M-11. Rotor diameter 11 m (36 ft 1 ⅟16 in); fuselage length 6.17 m (20 ft 3 in). Empty weight 576 kg (1,270 lb); maximum take-off weight 815 kg (1,797 lb). Fuel 69.5 liters (15 Imp gal). Maximum speed 167 km/h (104 mph); minimum speed 45 km/h (28 mph); take-off distance 50 m (164 ft); landing distance nil.

TsAGI A-15

700-hp M-25V. Rotor diameter 18 m (59 ft 0¾ in); rotor blade section TsAGI Sr.B.Stek; fuselage length 8.64 m (28 ft 4 in). Empty weight 1,695 kg (3,736 lb); maximum take-off weight 2,560 kg (5,643 lb). Fuel 535 liters (118 Imp gal). Maximum speed 260–283 km/h (162–175 mph) at 2,900 m (9,514 ft) (est); minimum speed 48 km/h (30 mph); ceiling 6,750 m (22, 145 ft); take-off distance 35–60 m (115–197 ft); landing distance nil; rotor speed 160–200 rpm.

Main Advances in Technology

	Western Autogyro	First Flight Date	Interval Years	USSR Autogyro	First Flight Date
Autorotation and flapping hinges	C.6	Feb. '24	5½	KaSkr-I	Sep. '29
Stub wings and wide track landing gear	C.6D	Aug. '26	3	KaSkr-I	Sep. '29
New paddle-blade rotor of better blade section	C.8V	Aug. '26	3	KaSkr-I	Sep. '29
Drag hinges and satisfactory inter-blade bracing	C.8R	Apr. '27	2¾	KaSkr-I	Sep. '29
More power	C.8L-I	Aug. '27	3¾	KaSkr-II	Jun. '30
Upturned wing tips	C.17/II	Apr. '29	2½	2-EA	Nov. '31
Deflector tail for rotor spin-up	C.12	May '29	2½	2-EA	Nov. '31
Design for production	C.19/I	Jul. '29	2⅓	2-EA	Nov. '31
Engine-powered spin-up drive	PCA-2	Mar. '30	2⅔	A-4	Nov. '32
Cantilever folding three-blade rotor	C.19/IV	Jun. '31	1⅔	A-6	Feb. '33
Direct control by tilting head	C.19/V	Mar. '32	3½	A-14	Sep. '35
Large size, with fixed spindle	PA-19	Apr. '32	2½	A-7	Sep. '34
Lateral tilting head and elevator for pitch control	Kay 32/1	Aug. '32	1¾	A-8	Jun. '34
Jump take-off	C.30 (Mod)	Aug. '33	1†	A-7	Sep. '34†
Large size, direct control	C.29	Oct. '34*	2½	A-15	Apr. '37*
High speed	PA-33	Jan. '35	1⅓	A-12	May '36
Cyclic and collective pitch control	A.R.III	Sep. '35	—	—	—

† *Unconfirmed*
* *Completed, not flown*

Chapter 11

Japanese Autogiros

Japan bought three British-built C-19 Mk IV Autogiros (G-ABXD, 'XE and 'XF) through Okura and Company in August 1932. One of these fixed-spindle, pre-direct-control technology Autogiros (G-ABXF) was registered J-BAYA and was operated by the Asahi Shimbun newspaper until August 1945. The intention was to use the Autogiro for aerial photography and to collect news stories from places where no proper airfield existed but where a short Autogiro strip might be available. In practice, the C.19 proved inadequate for these tasks and it was used primarily to advertise Asahi Shimbun. This Autogiro is reported to have flown a total of about 250 hours by 1940. After 1940, although flights were few, there were at least two or three every year for demonstrations or airworthiness test purposes.

The other two C.19s were evaluated by the navy but were presumably found unsuitable for the roles envisaged. One was soon damaged and was cannibalized for spare parts to keep the other flying. It is curious that the army should have become interested within a few months in Kellett K-3 Autogiros which, with cable-braced rotors, were of earlier technology than the C.19 Mk.IV with its cantilever rotor. Perhaps the side-by-side seating of the Kellett was preferred.

For whatever reason, in December 1932, two American K-3 fixed-spindle Autogiros were ordered through Okura and Company for evaluation by the army. They were paid for by public subscription. In a ceremony in Tokyo on April 16, 1933, they were named *Aikkoku 81* and *82* and were then demonstrated before a crowd of 20,000 people. One of the K-3's was seriously damaged in an accident on June 28, 1933. The fate of the other is not known. Despite this interest, the Japanese do not seem to have done anything about acquiring a manufacturing license for Autogiros at this time.

However, about five years later, in August 1939, an American Kellett KD-1A direct-control Autogiro (probably NC15684) was imported from the United States through Okura and Company by the Japanese military aviation authorities and handed over to the Army Air Force Research Division for evaluation. Unsatisfactory experience of the use of captive balloons for artillery observation during the Manchurian–Mongolian "Border Incidents" in 1939 (many were shot down) suggested that Autogiros might be more effective in this role.

Three Cierva C.19 Mk.IV fixed-spindle Autogiros were exported to Japan in August 1932, two for evaluation by the Japanese navy, and a third (registered J-BAYA) which was flown for some years by the Asahi Shimbun newspaper.
(Asahi Shimbun photograph)

Two Kellett K-3 Autogiros were delivered to Japan for evaluation by the army in April 1933. This was the naming ceremony in Tokyo, April 6, 1933.
(O. Reder)

As a result of the evaluation, the Japanese apparently obtained a license to manufacture the KD-1A, presumably from the Autogiro Company of America through Kellett. However, while flying with the Army Air Force at Tachikawa airfield in February 1940, the sample Autogiro was seriously damaged in an accident.

Six months later, in August 1940, the Imperial Army's Air Force Technical Command transferred the wreck to Osaka University where its design was studied by Professor Miki. On December 4, the Technical Command invited K.K. Kayaba Seisakusho (the Kayaba Industrial Co., Ltd.) to repair and modify the American Autogiro. This company was a small aircraft vendor equipment supplier and sub-contractor founded by Shiro Kayaba. Its main activity was the manufacture of landing gears for many types of Japanese aircraft. However, it was also engaged in rotary-wing research and so was an obvious choice for the Autogiro assignment.

Kayaba accepted an informal order from the Technical Command to repair the KD-1A and to develop a Japanese version for artillery observation and liaison duties. No doubt this was behind the request for spares sent by the Japanese to Kellett in 1941. The request was refused by the U.S. State Department.

Meanwhile, the wreck of the KD-1A was passed to Kayaba's Tokyo factory at Shibaura. Three Kayaba engineers were briefed on the Autogiro at Osaka University by Professor Miki and Goro Obara, Kayaba's chief engineer.

Repair and modification of the KD-1A was completed in April 1941 and the aircraft was first flown at Haneda (later Tokyo International Airport) on May 26, 1941, by Masaaki Iinuma.[29] The modified Autogiro proved to have exceptional handling characteristics, taking off in only 30 m (100 ft) at light weights and being capable of almost full hovering flight when the nose was pulled up to maximum angle of about 15 degrees at full throttle. It was reported that, in these conditions, the modified Autogiro could even complete a turn of 360 degrees without serious loss of height. Testing continued at Tamagawa near Tokyo until July 1943, much of the flying and maintenance being undertaken by former Asahi Shimbun pilots and mechanics.

The test program included artillery observation on a range at Nashino in Chiba Prefecture (February 1943) and air raid rescue and evacuation work (April 1943). On June 4, take-offs and landings were made on the 9,190 ton light aircraft carrier/landing ship *Akitsu Maru*. With the ship under way, the Autogiro required 12 m (40 ft) for take-off. There was no ground roll in landing. Most of this flying was done by Zenji Nishibori formerly of the Asahi Shimbun. Testing was moved to Oitsu airfield in Toyohashi City in November 1943. Nishibori then undertook depth charge dropping trials to investigate the possible use of Autogiros in anti-submarine warfare. A high level of bombing accuracy was achieved. In this role, the KD-1A was modified to carry a 60 kg (132 lb) depth charge and flown as a single-seater.

Kayaba Ka-1. (240-hp Kobe-built Argus As 10c). Some eighteen months earlier, in June 1941, an order had been placed with Kayaba for two experimental Ka-1 Autogiros for artillery observation duties. These were manufactured at Shibaura

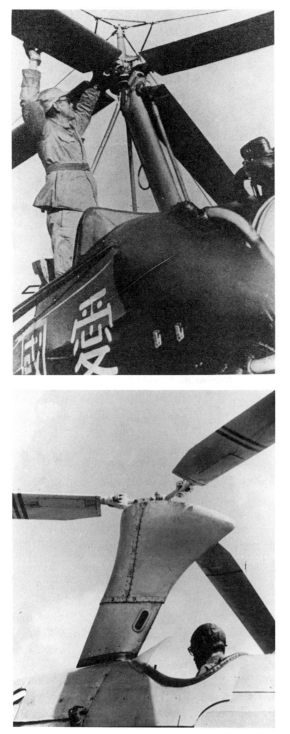

Comparison of rotor pylon and hub: K-3 and Ka-1. (Wide World Photos)

Kellett KD-1A operating from Akitsu Maru.
(Zenji Nishibori)

and differed from the KD-1A in having, instead of the Jacobs radial, the same German air-cooled inverted-vee Argus engine as had been used on the Focke-Wulf Fw 186 Autogiro in Germany. This engine was built under license in Japan by Kobe Seisakusho (Kobe Steel Company) at Ogaki City in Aichi Prefecture. The wooden propeller was manufactured by Nihon Gakki.

The two Ka-1's were completed in November 1942, nearly a year after Japan entered World War II. However, they were apparently not flown until June 1943, probably at least partly because of overheating problems with the Argus engine. The first flights were made at Tamagawa by Nishibori.

Kayaba Ka-1A (240-hp Kobe-built Argus As 10c). Also in November 1942, an order for quantity production of 300 Autogiros was placed on Kayaba by the Army Ordnance Administration Command. Sixty aircraft were to be delivered in the 1943 fiscal year and 240 in 1944 at a rate of 20 per month. (The same rate as Avro achieved in the United Kingdom in 1934/35 on C.30's.)

Production Argus-powered Autogiros were designated Ka-1A. The first of these was completed at Kayaba's Sendai factory in the Miyagi Prefecture on June 17, 1943, seven months after the order was placed. Production Autogiros were test

Kayaba Ka-1A direct-control Autogiro manufactured in Japan under Kellett license.
About thirty-five of this version were built.
(Cierva Rotocraft Ltd.)

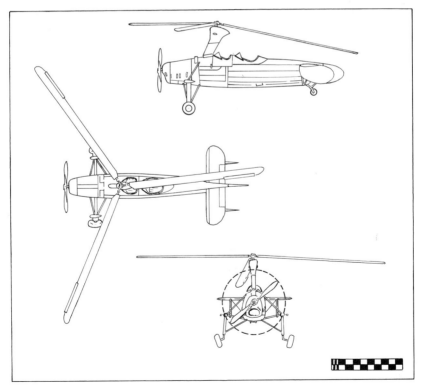

Kayaba Ka-1A.

279

flown at Kasuminome airfield. About 35 Ka-1A's seem to have been manufactured, but ten or more of these, hidden in a forest, were destroyed by American B-29 bombing.

Kayaba Ka-2. (240-hp license-built Jacobs L-4MA-7). Meanwhile, because of continued difficulties with the Argus engine, the Ka-2 with an air-cooled Jacobs radial was put into production alongside the Ka-1A. The first of this new model appeared in summer 1944. The Jacobs engine was built under license in Japan by the Tokyo Gasu Denki. Weights and performance of Ka-1A and Ka-2 proved to be closely similar. Production of both models ceased after about 95 had been delivered to the army. Almost 60 of these were Ka-2s, the remainder being Ka-lA's. About 30 nearly completed Autogiro airframes, without engines, were still held in the factory when production ceased. Apparently about 50 Autogiros entered service with the Japanese forces, some with artillery units. However, it is probable that none were used operationally in this role.

As the war progressed, the Japanese became increasingly concerned about the successes of Allied submarines in Japanese home waters. Tests with the KD-1A had suggested that gyroplanes might be suitable for short-range anti-submarine patrols over coastal waters. Production Autogiros were accordingly equipped like the KD-1A to carry a depth charge and were based at about half a dozen selected coastal sites to cover the Korean, Tsugara, and Eastern Channels and other Japanese inshore waters.

Kayaba Ka-2. This was a re-engined version of the Ka-1A. About sixty were built. (J.S. Shapiro)

Kayaba Ka 1KAI (240-hp Kobe-built Argus As 10c). This was an experimental version of the Ka-1 fitted with powder rockets near the tips of the rotor blades. Each rocket weighed 1.5 kg (3.3 lb) and developed a thrust of 16 kg (35 lb). This method of over-speeding the rotor for jump take-off provides an interesting contrast with that employed earlier in other countries. The latter all depended on shaft-drive from the engine which was de-clutched before take-off. With rocket propulsion, the rotor could continue under power during the jump because there was no torque-reaction, such as there would be with shaft-drive to the rotor. It is not known how successful these Japanese experiments were but during a test in April 1945, just before the end of the war, the rotor (after being partly spun-up with the engine) came up to a speed of 300 rpm in five seconds and generated a lift of 1,400 kg (3,086 lb). The Autogiro was tethered for this trial but the results were equivalent to a take-off run of 10 m (33 ft) and an initial climb angle of 45 degrees. The Ka-1 normally required a take-off roll of 60 m (200 ft) in still air.

At the end of the war, similar tests were to have been made in the United States with a PA-39 fitted with liquid fuel rockets, but these were discontinued when the U.S. Navy contract covering this program was cancelled.

The Japanese defeat at the end of World War II (on August 15, 1945) also marked the end of gyroplane development in Japan. Although the Ka-1A and Ka-2 were probably at least as widely used operationally as any aircraft of this type produced anywhere in the world, their employment remained peripheral. Indeed, the use of gyroplanes for anti-submarine work in Japanese coastal waters was not on a large enough scale and was not sufficiently successful to suggest defective evaluation of their potentialities by either British or Americans. The tests performed by the British with the Pitcairn PA-39 on the *Empire Mersey* in 1942 seem to have correctly shown the likely operational limitations of the Autogiro in this role.

The tactical use of gyroplanes over the battlefield, particularly for artillery observation—which was their main intended military application, anticipated in every country before World War II—did not materialize in Japan any more than it did elsewhere. Gyroplanes proved, in practice, to be as unsuitable for this work as large specially developed army co-operation fixed wing airplanes. The brief and limited use of A-7 gyroplanes by the Russians for night reconnaissance and the dropping of leaflets in the desperate days of 1941, when every sort of equipment was pressed into service, does not contradict this conclusion.

Thus, by the end of World War II, the gyroplane had shown itself to be unsuitable as a weapon of war. It was not just that it was eclipsed by the helicopter that was starting to emerge as a much more satisfactory rotary-wing aircraft. Whatever military roles the helicopter was to win for itself in the future—and these were, in time, to prove remarkably widespread and important—the gyroplane had shown itself to lack the essential characteristics required. The same must be said for its record in the civil field.

Kayaba returned briefly to rotary-wing developments after the war. In March 1952 he converted a Cessna 170 light airplane into a helicopter with a tip-drive rotor. In July 1954, this machine was wrecked during a trial ground run and the project was abandoned.

The first Japanese helicopter was a tandem rotor design, the "Tokushu Choban Re," produced at the Yokohama Industrial College in 1944 while the war was still in progress. In July of that year it lifted clear of the ground but was over-turned by a gusty wind and seriously damaged. A second helicopter was nearly complete when the war's end stopped further development.

Kayaba Ka-1 and Ka-1A

240-hp license-built Argus As 10c. Rotor diameter 12.2 m (40 ft ¼ in); rotor blade section Gö 606; overall length 9.2 m (30 ft 2¼ in). Empty weight 750–775 kg (1,653–1,709 lb); maximum take-off weight 1,170 kg (2,579 lb). Fuel 113 liters (30 US gal). Maximum speed 165 km/h (102 mph); initial climb 5.3 m/sec (1,050 ft/min); service ceiling 3,000–3,245 m (9,840–10,645 ft); range 280–360 km (174–224 mi) at 115–120 km/h (71–75 mph).

Kayaba Ka-2

240-hp license-built Jacobs L-4MA-7. Rotor diameter 12.2 m (40 ft ¼ in); rotor blade section Gö 606. No other data available but performance similar to Ka-1A

Chapter 12

Autogyros During and Since World War II

Cierva Autogiros and their derivatives gradually disappeared from the scene during World War II under the twin influences of the rapidly developing helicopter and the Autogiro's failure to provide a capability matching any large or important requirement. By the end of the war, the Autogiro, as Cierva had originally conceived it, was dead even though a few of the prewar and wartime machines survived in flying condition for some years. Sixteen serviceable C.30's had, in fact, been flown to Kemble for disposal in October 1945 by the pilots of the RAF's 529 Squadron.

Yet this was not the end of the gyroplane story. Some investigation continued throughout the war on unpowered rotors and was quite distinct from that associated with the emerging helicopter. These developments led after the war to the appearance of small autogyros that still survive in limited numbers. Some are used as aerial motor bikes, mainly for pleasure flying.

We saw in Chapter 6 that, chiefly at the instigation of James Weir, Cierva cooperated with the Weir Company in the 1930s in the development of several small single-seat direct-control and jump take-off Autogiros intended for the private aircraft market. At about the same time the Cierva Company experimented with models of an Autogiro kite that had been brought over from the United States in 1937. They were a product of Captive Flight Devices of Abingdon, Pennsylvania.

Early in the war a proposal was made to the British authorities that larger versions of an unmanned autogyro kite should be used to raise barrage cables above ships in convoy as a defense against low-flying aircraft. In the event, balloons were found to be more suitable and the concept of an autogyro kite was not pursued. However, this was by no means the end of the idea.

From early in 1942, the Germans developed the Focke-Achgelis Fa 330, which they called the Ubootsauge (U-boat's eye), or Bachstelze (Water Wagtail). This was essentially a quickly dismantled man-carrying gyroplane kite for use for observation purposes from submarines. FA 330s were also occasionally used to hoist a radio antenna. About 200 of these rudimentary aircraft were built from 1942, under the direction of Fritz Kunner, by Focke-Achgelis G.m.b.H., at Hoyenkamp bei Delmenhorst near Bremen. The company was by this time a subsidiary of the Weser Flugzeugwerke of Bremen.

The German Focke-Achgelis Fa 330, Bachstelze, autogyro kite used on a limited scale during World War II by U-boats for lookout purposes while on the surface. (Musée de l'Air et de l'Espace)

An unknown number of Fa 330s were embarked on Type IX U-boats but it is believed that they were used operationally (in the South Atlantic and Indian Ocean) to only a very limited extent. This seems to have been because of the U-boat commanders' reluctance to risk giving away their presence by flying the kites.

The Fa 330 closely followed Cierva practice in having a tilting hub and three-blade flapping rotor, 7.31 m, later 8.53 m (24 ft, later 28 ft) in diameter. The empty weight was 82 kg (180 lb), loaded weight 150 kg (330 lb) and towing speed 40 km/h (25 mph). The rotor normally turned at about 200 rpm. The single-seat Fa 330 was said to be capable of lifting its pilot-observer to a maximum height of between 150 and 300 m (500 ft to 1,000 ft), but the normal operating height was about 120 m (400 ft). The pilot was provided with a parachute and a method of jettisoning the rotor, should he wish to descend in a hurry if the submarine had to crash-dive. A powered version of the Fa 330 with 60-hp engine, known as the Fa 336, was projected but not built.

Another wartime German autogyro experiment was the Fa 225. This was a transport gyroplane glider, consisting of one of the 12 m (39 ft 4½ in) three-blade rotors of the Fa 223 helicopter mounted on a pylon above the fuselage of a DFS 230 transport glider. A prototype, which had a loaded weight of 2,000 kg (4,410 lb) was designed and built in 1942 and successfully flown in 1943, towed by a Junkers Ju 52/3m. Development was completed in the remarkably short time of seven weeks. However, the type was not proceeded with.

Manned rotary-wing parachutes, gliders, or kites (the three are really indistinguishable) were also developed by the British. From October 3, 1940, the A.R.III Construction (Hafner Gyroplane) Company undertook work in this field.

In December 1941, the work was taken over by the development section of the Central Landing Establishment at Ringway, now Manchester Airport. This unit was later renamed the Airborne Forces Experimental Establishment (AFEE) and moved to Sherburn-in-Elmet near Leeds and then to Beaulieu near Southampton. The first British aircraft of this type was the Rotachute which was developed, after tests with a series of models, by Raoul Hafner, Dr. J.A.J. Bennett, and O.L.L. Fitzwilliams. The models were launched from an obsolete Boulton Paul Overstrand bomber over Tatton Park, their rotors starting turning only after being dropped. The Rotachute was originally intended—at Hafner's suggestion—to be a one-man rotary-wing parachute capable of being launched from a suitably modified aircraft, as a means of landing agents in enemy territory. The first full-size machine, the H.8 designed in November 1940, had an empty weight of only 48 pound (22 kg) and a two-blade rotor of 15 ft (4.51 m) diameter with conventional free flapping blades but without drag hinges. The hanging stick control column, which operated a tilting head, worked in the reverse sense to normal, and the test pilot first had to learn the special techniques required on a C.30

The German Focke-Achgelis Fa 225 troop-carrying glider autogyro was flown experimentally in 1943 but not adopted for service.
(Author's Collection)

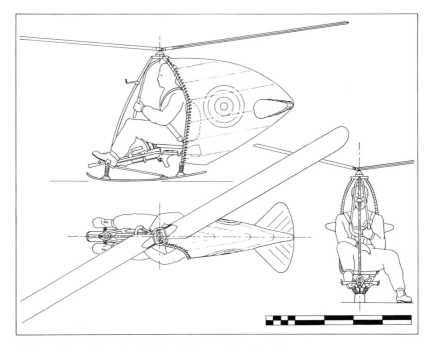

Airborne Forces Experimental Establishment Rotachute I.

Autogiro, which was fitted with a control system specially modified for this purpose. Although never launched in the manner originally intended the full-size Rotachute was extensively tested as a towed glider pulled by a Jeep at Ringway and along a long runway at Chelveston. It was first flown in this mode by Flight Lieutenant (later Squadron Leader) Ian Little on February 2, 1942, and was progressively improved (see Appendix 6), untimately becoming the Mark IV, to Specification 11/42, first flown on April 29, 1943.

The ability of this machine to land in confined spaces suggested a number of applications for rotary-wing gliders. On tow at low speeds, the drag of a rotary-wing glider was rather optimistically estimated to be of the same order as that of a fixed-wing glider of the same useful load while, potentially, it should have the advantage in take-off and climb as well as in short landing. The rate of vertical descent was expected to be less than that of a parachute, of the same diameter as the rotor, when carrying the same load. In the event, the performance of the Rotachute was found to be significantly worse than had been estimated.

Five of the more than twenty Rotachutes built by F. Hills and Sons of Manchester and the Airwork General Trading Company of Hounslow were modified to Mark IV Standard (see Appendix 6). During flight tests, tows by a de Havilland Tiger Moth and Avro Tutor were made up to heights of nearly 4,000 ft (1,200 m) and at speeds of up to 93 mph (150 km/h). This development work, which was directed at investigating the characteristics of towed rotary-wing glid-

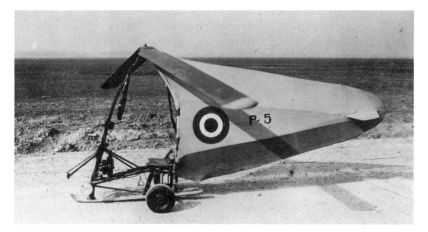

AFEE Rotachute III of 1942. Originally intended to be a rotary-wing parachute, the
Rotachute was used for experiments with towed autogyro gliders.
(Author's Collection)

ers, was terminated in 1943, the last aircraft-towed flight of a Rotachute being on
October 18.

Several other rotary-wing projects were studied at AFEE after the move to
Sherburn-in-Elmet in July 1942. These included examples to transport large airborne lifeboats and light two-man submarines. Detailed proposals were made for
designs to carry the 3,000 lb (1360 kg) S-Type vehicle, popularly known as the
Jeep (in April 1942), and a 14-ton (14,225 kg) Vickers Valentine tank (in November 1942).

Development of the Jeep carrier started in August 1942 with the design of
the Malcolm Rotaplane or Rotabuggy to Specification 10/42. As finally built by
M.L. Aviation at White Waltham, this aircraft incorporated a modified Willys ¼
ton "four-by-four" military truck. Unlike the Rotachute, it had controls which
operated in the normal sense. It was first tested by Ian Little on November 16,
1943, and first flown on the twenty-seventh of that month. It subsequently made
about sixty flights, towed by a motor vehicle along a 6,000 ft (1,830 m) runway at
speeds of up to 72 mph (116 km/h). On one horrific occasion, on September 11,
1944, it was towed to a height of 1,700 ft (500 m) behind an Armstrong
Whitworth Whitley V bomber, subsequently landing on tow. Despite this extraordinary feat, there were considerable vibration difficulties which could not be overcome. Development of the Rotaplane was therefore abandoned soon
afterward.

A program similar to the Rotaplane was started in Australia. "Project Sky-
wards," to develop the "Fleep" or flying Jeep, began in 1943. However it was terminated before the flying stage was reached.

The Rotaplane was notable because, as originally designed, it was one of the
earliest applications of the seesaw or teetering rotor, in which the two blades, inte-

gral with a fixed coning angle, rock on a common hinge at the rotor head. (A see-saw rotor had been first tried by Gerard Herrick in the United States in 1931, and in the United Kingdom on a Rotachute on September 21, 1942.) The two--blade seesaw rotor of the Rotaplane was 46 ft 8 in (14.22 m) in diameter. It proved unsatisfactory and was replaced by a 48 ft (14.63 m) rotor with separate blades with flapping and drag hinges. Seesaw rotors were subsequently adopted for most small autogyros and are also widely used for helicopters.

Dr. Bennett visited the United States in October 1942 and there cooperated with the Autogiro Company of America. The latter was associated with the G. and A. Aircraft Company, which in turn had taken over the former Pitcairn Autogiro Company. This association led to the design and construction of a Rotachute that unfortunately crashed on test injuring a member of the Autogiro Company's engineering staff.

Six of the Rotachutes manufactured in the United Kingdom were eventually sent to the United States. There they may have provided a starting point for the development of the so-called Gyro-glider at General Electric's Schenectady

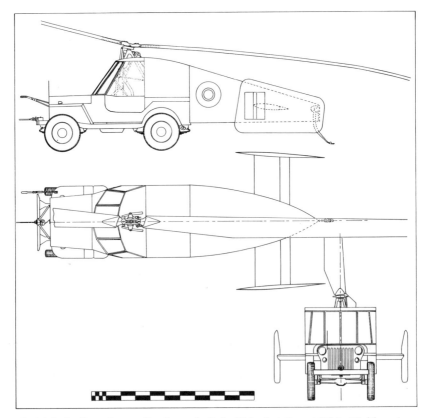

The Malcolm Rotaplane or Rotabuggy built by M.L. Aviation at White Waltham in 1942–43.

Malcolm Rotaplane in flight.
(Author's Collection)

The Bensen B-8M Gyrocopter of 1957 is typical of the glider and powered ultra-light autogyros developed and widely marketed (usually in kit form) by the Bensen Aircraft Corporation. More than four thousand B-8M Gyrocopters had been built by 1977. (Author's Collection)

289

Flight Test Center. G.E. also ran a research program using the war-surplus XR-3 Autogiro which had a fixed spindle rotor with collective and cyclic pitch control. Dr. Igor B. Bensen, who worked for General Electric some years after the war, started developing his series of Gyro-gliders. These differed from the Rotachute notably in having teetering rotors. The Bensen Aircraft Corporation was formed in 1953 to market Gyro-gliders, primarily in the form of kits for home-construction by amateurs. Later Bensen added an engine to his basic design and thus began to market the Gyrocopter, a small motorbike type of open frame autogyro that has since enjoyed widespread popularity, primarily for sporting fly-ing. By 1977, Bensen was able to claim that more than 4,000 Gyrocopters had been built throughout the world and that about 2,000 were flying. A number of derivatives have also appeared in various countries, including the Grudieaire, Saalfeld, Russel, Wigal, and Bannick in the United States, and the Wallis, McCandless, and WHE in the United Kingdom. A number have also been built in the Soviet Union. Some of these aircraft incorporate important design changes, as compared with the Bensen, but they all represent an extension of the aerial motorbike open-frame autogyro concept initiated by him.

In 1945, the French SNCASE flew a large three-seat autogyro of its own design called the SE.700, but development did not proceed beyond the prototype.

The Beagle-Wallis WA-116 ultra-light autogyro of 1962, a small batch of which were built and delivered to the British army by Beagle Aircraft Ltd.
(W/Cdr. K. H. Wallis)

One of the most ambitious programs since the war was the British Fairey Rotodyne of the 1950s. This was a 35/40-passenger transport compound helicopter that operated as an autogyro in cruising flight but employed tip-jets to power its large four-blade rotor in take-off and landing as a helicopter. Its development, which did not proceed beyond the prototype, owed much to experience gained with the smaller Fairey Gyrodyne in 1947–48 (see Chapter 9), which established a world speed record for rotary-wing aircraft.

Attempts have continued at intervals since World War II to revive the gyroplane in sizes similar to those of the Cierva designs of between the wars. Perhaps the most notable post-War projects have been the American Umbaugh of 1958 (certificated and built in some numbers), the Canadian Avian of 1960, the Australian Victa of 1962, the British Thruxton Gadfly of 1964, the American McCulloch J-2 of 1968 (certificated and built in small numbers), and the Spanish AISA GN of 1982. However, despite all these attempts, and others, the autogyro has failed to reestablish itself on any significant scale and it seems that, even in the aerial motorbike application, possibilities are limited.

It is interesting to speculate on the reason for this. The probable answer is that the better take-off and landing and safer slow-flying capabilities of the gyroplane, as compared with the fixed-wing airplane, have proved insufficiently attractive to military and civilian operators to compensate for the gyroplane's higher cost and reduced performance and payload/range capabilities. The helicopter, on the other hand—which probably suffers even greater operating cost, payload/range, and performance penalties but which offers full hovering capability—has been able to establish itself in both the military and civilian fields and has now become an extremely useful, widely used vehicle, second in importance only to the fixed-wing airplane, with the gap between them partly bridged by the V/STOL jet-lift airplane.

From an historical point of view, the story of the gyroplane has something in common with that of the airship. Both vehicles achieved limited service for a few years but have now largely faded from the scene, except for small numbers in limited nontransport applications. The important difference is that the gyroplane led straight to the successful helicopter, while lighter-than-air development has made only minimal contributions to subsequent aviation progress.

Time will show whether the gyroplane's failure to establish itself contains lessons for the future. Current enthusiasm for short take-off and landing may be similarly questioned. All airplanes until the 1930s were what would now be termed STOL but, except for a relatively small number of specialized types, short field capabilities have been largely sacrificed since then in the interests of better payload/range, higher performance, and superior economics. Except for a limited number of special applications, perhaps the majority of future military and civil operators will, in time, show little more interest in STOL than those of the thirties did in the Autogiro.

Whether or not the story of Juan de la Cierva's Autogiro teaches this lesson, it remains in its own right a remarkable episode in the history of technology, testimony to a man of genius who was truly the father of practical rotary-wing flight.

Development of the Helicopter
A Short History

The helicopter solution to the problem of powered human flight surprisingly enough received more attention from early thinkers and experimenters than the much simpler fixed-wing concept until the Englishman Sir George Cayley first expounded the principles of the airplane at the end of the eighteenth century. Even after that date, the helicopter continued to attract the attention of many would-be pioneers and, as a result, the first helicopter to lift off the ground in free flight did so within four years of the first flight of an airplane.

In considering the pattern of development of the helicopter both before and since that date it is convenient to split up the story into five phases. These are:

Phase I (Up to 1922). Solution of the problem of generating sufficient lift for a man-carrying helicopter to leave the ground.

Phase II (1907–35). Solution of the problem of stability and control.

Phase III (1924–55). The influence of the gyroplane.

Phase IV (1935–55). The first practical helicopters.

Phase V (After 1943). Refinement of the practical helicopter.

Phases I and II overlap by about fifteen years because of the variety of helicopter types developed as solutions to the problem and the span of time over which they achieved success. Phases II and III overlap by about ten years because the solving of the problems of stability and control went on concurrently with the development of the gyroplane, which also made valuable contributions to the solutions adopted. Phases III and IV overlap because the gyroplane had a period of utility before the helicopter emerged as a practical vehicle and because of the contribution it made to the potential future of the compound helicopter. Phases IV and V overlap because some helicopter configurations reached the practical stage quicker than others.

The Achievement of Helicopter Flight

The Chinese were probably the first to demonstrate the principle of the helicopter with their "flying tops" in about the first century A.D., although the Greek philosopher, Archimedes, had proposed vertical flight by the screw principle in the third century B.C. A Flemish manuscript of 1325 shows the first known illustration of a whirligig toy which may have demonstrated the helicopter principle. It was powered by pulling a string. The first man to illustrate a full-size helicopter design was almost certainly that unique genius of the fifteenth century, Leonardo da Vinci. Details of his work were not, however, to be published for nearly 300 years and Leonardo was probably not the anonymous inventor. Shortly before his ideas became generally known, in 1768, a Frenchman, A. J. P. Paucton, put forward his man-powered Pterophore design which was the first practical proposal for the application of the helicopter principle. Two other Frenchmen, Launoy and Bienvenu, produced the first working model helicopter. This had two co-axial superimposed two-bladed silk-covered rotors and flew successfully in Paris in 1784 under the power of a bent whalebone. Sir George Cayley copied this design in about 1792 using feathers as rotor blades.

Numerous other experimenters, including Cayley, put forward helicopter designs during the nineteenth and early twentieth centuries but mention need be made only of W. H. Phillips who demonstrated tip-drive for rotors on a successful model in 1842; C. Renard who put forward a design in 1904 which first incorporated articulated rotor blades; and G. A. Crocco who suggested cyclic pitch control in 1906 (it was first applied to a flyable helicopter by the Dane J. C. H. Ellehammer in 1912). Crocco also suggested that a windmilling rotor could provide helicopters with a means of safe descent and landing following engine failure. The majority of other designs during this period contained little which made any real contribution to the solution of the problem of controlled full-scale rotary-wing flight.

The first helicopter to lift a man off the ground—it was really just a tethered test rig—was the French Bréguet-Richet Gyroplane No. 1, which did so on September 29, 1907, under the power of a 45-hp Antoinette petrol engine driving four 8 m (26 ft 3 in) biplane rotors. The "flight" was tethered and, lacking stability or any means of control, the aircraft became unmanageable when moving translationally. However, the first free helicopter flight is believed to have been achieved soon afterward, also in France on November 13 of the same year, by Paul Cornu with a tandem-twin rotor design with two-blade 6 m (19 ft 8 ¼ in) rotors. This machine is reported to have achieved durations of about 20 seconds in free flight and made flights of up to about a minute while tethered. Control and propulsion were by means of vanes in the down-wash of the rotors, although this method proved of limited effectiveness. Stability was also deficient. Power was provided by a 24-hp Antoinette. Control difficulties—the great bugbear of all early helicopters—prevented this design from being developed further.

The Bréguet-Richet Gyroplane No. 2bis appeared in the following year. It had twin 7.6 m (24 ft 11 ¼ in) rotors, with flapping blades, tandem fixed biplane surfaces, and was powered by a 55-hp Renault engine. On July 22, 1908, it took off vertically and was flown unsteadily for a distance of 19.5 m (64 ft) at a height of up to 4.5 m (15 ft), but was wrecked on landing. Among the other projects of that period were two unsuccessful attempts to build a helicopter by Igor Sikorsky who was later to play such a big part in the development of the successful helicopter.

Stability and Control Problems

The first helicopter flights of 1907 and 1908 were not strictly comparable to the first airplane flights by the Wrights a few years earlier. During the period 1903-05, the Wright Flyers were shown to be capable of sustained flight under the complete control of their pilot. This was not the case with any of these early helicopters. Their historical significance lies in that they showed that power-driven rotors could support man-carrying machines off the ground. The problems of control and stability were still unsolved, as was the question of a safe landing in the event of engine failure. Many years were to pass before these difficulties were to be fully resolved. Indeed, the first helicopter flights comparable to the airplane flights made by the Wrights in 1903–05 did not take place until 1935–36.

During the intervening years, many helicopter designs were produced which progressively increased the time that a man-carrying machine was supported in the air by rotors, while the problems of stability and control were gradually completely overcome (see Table 1). The first steps toward success in providing satisfactory control were taken by G. de

Table 1
The Evolution of Systems of Control

				Means of Control in			
Year	Type	Configuration	Translational Flight	Vertical Flight	Yaw	Pitch	Roll
1907	Cornu	Tandem	vanes in downwash	throttle	vanes in downwash	vanes in downwash	vanes in downwash
1922	de Bothezat	Four rotors	diff. coll. p.	throttle	diff. coll. p.	diff. coll. p.	diff. coll. p.
1922	Oemichen No. 2	Four rotors	airscrew	throttle	airscrew	v.p. airscrew	v.p. airscrew
1923	Berliner	Side-by-side	helicopter tilt	throttle	rudder	elevator + v.p. airscrew	vanes in downwash
1923	Cierva C.4	Gyroplane	airscrew	—	rudder	elevator	ailerons
1924	Pescara No. 3	Co-axial	cyclic p.	coll. pitch	diff. coll. p.	cyclic p.	cyclic p.
1930	Ascanio	Co-axial	cyclic p.	throttle	v.p. airscrew	cyclic p. + v.p. airscrew	cyclic p. + v.p. airscrew
1931	Wilford	Gyroplane	airscrew	—	rudder	cyclic p. + elevator	cyclic p.
1932	Kay 32/1	Gyroplane	airscrew	coll. p.	rudder	elevator	tilt head
1932	Cierva C.19 Mark V	Gyroplane	airscrew	—	tilt head	tilt head	tilt head
1933	Florine Type II	Tandem	diff. coll. p.	coll. p.	tilt heads	diff. coll. p.	cyclic p.
1933	TsAGI 3-EA	Single-rotor	cyclic p.	coll. p.	2 airscrews	cyclic p.	cyclic p.
1933	Cierva C.30 Mark II	Gyroplane	airscrew	"Autodynamic" head	tilt head	tilt head	tilt head
1935	Hafner A.R. III	Gyroplane	airscrew	coll. p.	rudder	cyclic p.	cyclic p.
1935	Bréguet-Dorand 314	Co-axial	cyclic p.	coll. p.	diff. coll. p.	cyclic p.	cyclic p.
1936	Focke-Achgelis Fa 61	Side-by-side	cyclic p.	coll. p.	diff. cyclic p.	cyclic p.	diff. coll. p.
1938	Weir W-5	Sid-by-side	cyclic p.	coll. p.	diff. cyclic p.	cyclic p.	cyclic p.
1939	Flettner Fl 265	Intermeshing	cyclic p.	coll. p.	diff. coll. p. + rudder	cyclic p.	cyclic p.
1939	Sikorsky V.S.300	Single-rotor	cyclic p.	coll. p.	v.p. rotor	cyclic p.	cyclic p.
1940	Sikorsky V.S.300 mod.	Single-rotor	helicopter tilt + coll. p.	coll. p.	v.p. rotor	v.p. rotor	v.p. rotor
1941	Sikorsky V.S.300A	Single-rotor	cyclic p.	coll. p.	v.p. rotor	cyclic p.	cyclic p.
1945	Doblhoff WNF 342V-4	Tip-drive	airscrew	coll. p.	rudder	cyclic p.	cyclic p.
1945	Piasecki XHRP-1	Tandem	cyclic p.	coll. p.	diff. cyclic p.	diff. coll. p.	cyclic p.

Note: *Reference to control by pitch change or tilting head in this table applies to main rotor or rotors.*   Abbreviation p.   blade pitch.

Bothezat and E. Oemichen. Starting in 1921, de Bothezat produced a four-rotor helicopter for the U.S. Army that consisted basically of a large framework in the form of a horizontal cross with the rotors mounted at the ends of the arms. It proved moderately stable and partly controllable and was flown for the first time, for 1 min 42 sec, at McCook (now Wright) Field by Major T. H. Bane on December 18, 1922. This helicopter was powered by a 180-hp Gnome-Rhône engine (later replaced by an engine of 220 hp) and weighed 3,585 lb (1626 kg). The six-blade 22 ft (6.7 m) rotors had individual collective pitch control and, at first, there were two horizontal "steering airscrews," but these were later removed as unnecessary. About 100 flights were made up to heights of about 15 ft (4.6 m) and on one occasion five people were lifted together. Development of the de Bothezat helicopter cost over $200,000 (say $1 million now).

Oemichen started experimenting in France in 1920. In 1922 he produced, as his second design, a fantastically complicated four-rotor machine which, like de Bothezat's, was in the form of a horizontal cross. Two rotors were 7.6 m (24 ft 11 ¼ in) and two 6.4 m (20 ft 11 ¹⁵⁄₁₆ in) in diameter. They were driven by a 120-hp Le Rhône rotary engine (later replaced by a 180-hp Gnome-Rhône) and had two propulsive airscrews, another screw for directional control, and five variable-pitch auxiliary propellers for control in pitch and roll. The gyroscopic action of a large flywheel was claimed to contribute to stability. On April

14, 1924, this aircraft established the first helicopter record to be recognized by the Fédération Aéronautique Internationale. The distance flown was 360 m (1,181 ft), which was increased to 525 m (1,722 ft) on April 17. On May 4, 1924, the same machine won a French Air Ministry prize of 90,000 francs for the first circular kilometer to be flown by a helicopter. A distance of 1692 m (5,550 ft) was covered, at a maximum height of 15 m (50 ft), and an endurance of 14 minutes, with a useful load of 200 kg (440 lb) in addition to the pilot. In all, Oemichen's machine made more than a thousand flights. It represented the first serious attempt to solve the problem of control about all three axes and, for this reason, marks an important step in the development of the practical helicopter.

On April 18, 1924, an Argentine, Raul de Pateras Pescara, took the world record from Oemichen with a flight in France of 738 m (2421 ft) in 4 min 11 sec at a height of 2 m (6 ft). He had started experimenting in 1919 and this success was his third design which had previously made a flight of 10 min 10 sec in January 1924. It had two co-axial superimposed six-blade biplane 7.2 m (23 ft 7⅞6 in) rotors driven by a 180-hp Hispano-Suiza engine and weighed 1,000 kg (2,200 lb.) For control, the blades could be warped to alter the pitch of the rotors cyclically and collectively, but the design lacked satisfactory stability—a major difficulty with all co-axial designs. Pescara, however, deserves more credit than de Bothezat and Oemichen for his development of control systems. He was the first to demonstrate reasonably effective control by rotor-blade pitch variations, a method since adopted for all successful helicopters. He is said to have achieved a maximum endurance of 12 minutes and to have successfully demonstrated how forward propulsion could be achieved by means of the main lifting rotors. Pescara was, moreover, among the first helicopter designers to make provision for, although he did not make use of, the principle of autorotation by which a helicopter can descend still supported by its free-wheeling rotor after engine failure. (See British Patent No. 146265 of June 1919.)

Another experimenter in the early 1920s was H.A. Berliner who built co-axial and side-by-side twin-rotor designs in the United States. Both were unstable but had sufficient control to achieve short flights. The Brennan helicopter, developed at the RAE, Farnborough, between 1919 and 1925, was flown for about 10 hours on about 200 short flights in 1924–25 until it crashed on October 2, 1925. It proved reasonably controllable but was unstable in translational flight. This aircraft had a 60 ft (18.29 m) two-blade rotor driven by a 230-hp Bentley B.R.2 rotary engine and weighed 3,300 lb (1500 kg) loaded. The rotor was driven by airscrews at the tips of two of the blades and its pitch was controlled by auxiliary flaps. An Italian, V. Isacco, working in various countries, developed a series of designs between 1929 and 1934 which he called Helicogyres. These were similar to the Brennan machine in having single torqueless rotors, but they had small power units driving airscrews mounted on the blades. No real success was achieved and this type of helicopter has not been developed further. However, since then single torqueless rotors have been tried successfully with jet—instead of airscrew—tip drive.

On October 8, 1930, an Italian, M. Nelli, flying a helicopter designed by C. d'Ascanio, raised the world record to 8 min 45 sec and on October 10 flew 1079 m (3,540 ft) in a straight line. The Ascanio helicopter had two co-axial 13.0 m (42 ft 7¹⅜6 in) rotors, with articulated blades, powered by a 95-hp Fiat A.50 engine. The loaded weight was 798 kg (1,760 lb). Control was by three variable-pitch propellers—one for pitch, one for roll, and one for yaw—and by a form of cyclic pitch control of the rotor blades. Stability, although an advance on earlier co-axial designs, remained inadequate. A significant design developed between 1924 and 1930 was due to a Dutchman, A. G. von Baumhauer, who made use of an anti-torque tail rotor—albeit driven by an unnecessarily powerful separate engine—and thus originated the later successful single-main rotor layout. The aircraft achieved brief hovering flights. On October 31, 1935, a helicopter designed by N. Florine, a Russian émigré in Belgium, and flown by R. Collin, increased the world record to 9 min 58 sec. The Florine Type II was a tandem-rotor design with 7.2 m (23 ft 7 7⁄16 in) four-blade rotors. Powered by a 200-hp Renard engine, it weighed 950 kg (2,095 lb). Lack of adequate margins of stability and control remained the big obstacle to further development with this as with previous designs.

A Hungarian, O. von Asboth, developed four co-axial type helicopter designs between 1924 and 1930. These had control vanes in the rotor down-wash. The first, the AH-1, achieved hovering flight on September 9, 1928. The fourth, the AH-4 with a 110-hp Clerget rotary engine, climbed to a height of about 30 m (100 ft) on August 27, 1930, and covered a distance of about 2750 m (9,000 ft) at about 20 km/h (12 mph). It was relatively stable but difficult to control and had no provision for a safe landing in the event of engine failure. Asboth's helicopters flew more than 29 hours in 182 flights.

In Russia, the Central Aero-Hydrodynamic Institute (TsAGI) produced a series of three interesting designs of single-rotor helicopters from 1930. These aircraft had small anti-torque rotors at the nose and tail of their open framework fuselages, together with both collective and cyclic pitch control. The two small rotors were provided in the mistaken belief that one would not provide the required anti-torque couple. The first machine, known as the TsAGI 1-EA, made a number of notable flights, including a climb to 600 m (2,000 ft) before being damaged in an accident. A similar machine, the 3-EA, appeared in 1933 and made several successful flights of 10–15 min duration and of up to 120 m (400 ft) in height. A circuit of about 3 ¼ km (2 mi) and a maximum speed of 21 km/h (13 mph) is also said to have been achieved. The 3-EA, like the 1-EA, lacked stability but control was quite satisfactory. Power in both aircraft was from a 120-hp M-2 rotary. A further development in 1934, the 5-EA, is claimed to have shown a high degree of stability.

Influence of the Gyroplane

Long before the above developments, in the early 1920s, Juan de la Cierva had evolved his Autogiro. The Autogiro is not a helicopter because its rotor is not power-driven in flight, but experience with this form of intermediate rotary wing aircraft contributed much to the development of the first successful helicopters that appeared in the mid-1930s. Cierva's two big initial contributions were the practical demonstration of autorotation and of the use of flapping hinges for rotor blades. Autorotation seems to have been suggested by Hodgson in 1915 and Pescara in 1919, while articulated blades had previously been proposed by C. Renard to reduce stresses in rotor blades. However, in 1922 Cierva first showed how flapping blades would enable a single-rotor aircraft to fly forward without rolling sideways because of the unbalanced lift resulting from the different speeds through the air of the advancing and retreating blades. A later contribution by Cierva was the drag hinge on the rotors which enabled the blades to move slightly in relation to each other in their plane of rotation and thus relieve the stresses induced in the blade roots.

Other developments by Cierva were direct control, first tried on the C.19 Mk.V in 1932, by which the Autogiro was controlled entirely by tilting the rotor head—a far more effective method at low speeds than that employed on earlier designs which had depended on conventional fixed control surfaces—and jump take-off, first achieved with the C.30 prototype in 1933, by which vertical take-offs to a limited height became possible by overspeeding the rotor on the ground—by means of an engine drive—and then declutching the drive and simultaneously automatically giving the blades extra pitch to lift the aircraft vertically into the air. These developments helped to make the Autogiro into a completely practical aircraft which was used on a limited scale in the 1930s and early 1940s until superseded by the true helicopter. Some 480 Autogiros were built plus about 25 Russian derivatives.

Four other exponents of the gyroplane were a Scotsman, David Kay, two Americans, E. Burke Wilford and Gerard P. Herrick, and an expatriate Austrian, Raoul Hafner, who came to England and later became a British subject. In 1927, Kay proposed a design which combined collective pitch with a tilting head for lateral control. The latter feature was, as we have already seen, later adopted by Cierva for his direct-control designs. In this connection, it is significant that Cierva had in 1922 tried and discarded a sideways tilting head for lateral control on one of his first unsuccessful Autogiros. Kay built prototypes with articulated rotors in 1932 and 1935 which confirmed the practicability of his designs. Wilford's work was based on the theories of two Germans, W. Kreiser and W. Rieseler (whom he contacted in 1928), and featured cyclic pitch control on a rigid four-blade rotor. At first this control was used only in the rolling plane but it was later also applied in pitch. Herrick pioneered the convertiplane in 1931/33. His second design successfully made repeated conversions from fixed-wing to gyroplane flight. Hafner had built two unsuccessful helicopters in Vienna, in 1930 and 1931, before he developed his A.R.III gyroplane in England. This had both collective and cyclic pitch control and used flapping blades. The Hafner gyroplane first flew in September 1935.

The First Practical Helicopters

The first successful helicopters appeared in 1935–36. Louis Bréguet, who had been responsible in 1907 for the first helicopter to lift a man off the ground, and René Dorand evolved the Bréguet-Dorand 314 Gyroplane Laboratoire between 1931 and 1935. The first flight piloted by Maurice Claise was made on June 26 of the latter year but performances were, at first, quite modest and difficulty was experienced because of inadequate stability while hovering. On December 14, 500 m (1,640 ft) were flown in a closed circuit at heights exceeding 10 m (33 ft). A week later it achieved 99 km/h (61 mph). By the latter part of 1936 the 314 had made a flight of over an hour, reached a speed of 105 km/h (65 mph), flown 44 km (27 miles) over a closed circuit and reached a height of 158 m (518 ft). It continued to fly up to the outbreak of war. By 1938, it was making successful landings in autorotation with the engine throttled back. The Bréguet-Dorand had two superimposed, co-axial two-blade, freely articulating 16.4 m (54 ft) rotors which were provided with cyclic and collective pitch control. It weighed 1,950–2,049 kg (4,279–4,517 lb) loaded and was powered by a 240-hp Bréguet-Bugatti engine later replaced by a 350-hp Hispano-Suiza 9Q.

Bréguet's helicopter did not remain unchallenged for long. Exactly a year later, on June 26, 1936, the German, H.K.J. Focke, who had been experimenting with rotary wings since 1931 and whose company, Focke-Wulf Flugzengbau A.G., had built Autogiros under license, flew his Focke-Achgelis Fa 61 helicopter (D-EKRA). It was built by a new company, Focke-Achgelis G.m.b.H. specially formed in 1933 to continue Focke's rotary-wing development following disagreements on the Focke-Wulf board. The pilot on the first flights was Edwald Rohlfs. Within a year, this aircraft had established a series of new world records: an endurance of 1 hr 20 min, a closed-circuit distance of 80 km (50 miles), a height of 2440 m (8,000 ft), and a speed of 122 km/h (76 mph). The Fa 61 had two side-by-side articulated three-blade 7 m (23 ft) rotors with cyclic/collective pitch control hubs designed under licence from Cierva. It was powered by a 160-hp Bramo Sh14A radial and weighed 950–1040 kg (2,100–2,300 lb) loaded. Longitudinal and direction control was by cyclic pitch change, lateral control by differential collective-pitch change of the two rotors.

Neither the Bréguet-Dorand 314 nor the Fa 61 proceeded beyond the prototype stage, but both were flown extensively and later gave rise to further successful developments of their two distinct configurations. The Bréguet superimposed co-axial rotor layout has been used on several helicopters since World War II including further experimental designs by Bréguet. The Fa 61 configuration was closely followed by the Weir W-5 helicopter in Great Britain, development of which started in October 1937, as a culmination of four years previous experience of autogyro development by the company. The British Air Ministry and Weir negotiated unsuccessfully for a licence from Focke-Achgelis in spring 1938, although Focke was already a licencee of Cierva which was associated with the Weir Company.

The W-5 had two side-by-side 15 ft (4.57 m) two-blade rotors, weighed 860 lb (390 kg), and had a 50-hp Weir engine. It was the first successful British helicopter and made its first flight at Dalrymple on June 6, 1938, piloted by R. A. Pullin, son of its designer C. G. Pullin. The W-5 completed nearly 80 hrs' flying up to July 1939, and achieved speeds up to 70 mph (113 km/h). It was followed by the similar but larger W-6 which had 25 ft (17.62 m) two-blade rotors, weighed 2,360 lb (1070 kg), and had a 205-hp Gipsy Six II engine. The W-6 (which bore the serial R5269) first flew on October 20, 1939, also piloted by Pullin. On October 27, it became the first successful helicopter to carry a passenger and then, on the following day, carried two passengers. Problems were experienced with blade breakages and development was discontinued in July 1940, after about 70 hrs of flying, because of the war situation.

In the United States, the Platt Le Page Aircraft Company was given a $335,000 contract by the U.S. Army in July 1940, for the XR-1, a design also inspired by the Fa 61. This aircraft had side-by-side 30 ft (9.14 m) rotors, a 450-hp Pratt & Whitney radial engine, and weighed 5,200 lb (2360 kg) loaded. It first flew on June 23, 1941, and was extensively tested but not developed further because it was sluggish on the controls and suffered from pylon resonance and longitudinal instability—the latter was also a failing of the Focke helicopters.

Helicopters with widely spaced side-by-side rotors have not survived as a popular type but the configuration may find favor for compound helicopters and convertiplanes. It is convenient at this point to refer to two further historically significant designs of this layout. These were both twin-engined and were, in fact, the first successful multiengined helicopters.

The Russian TsAGI Omega I and II were designed by I. P. Bratukin and the first aircraft was originally tested in 1941, although extensive flying was not undertaken until after the end of the war. The Omega II had AI-26 radial engines of 420 hp each, a loaded weight of 4000 kg (8,820 lb), and an aerodynamically cleaner airframe than the first aircraft. It appears to have been first flown in 1948 and was intended to carry six passengers at a cruising speed of 145 km (90 mph). This design was apparently not developed further.

Returning now to Germany and the story of the Fa 61, Focke-Achgelis themselves continued the development of their basic design up to and throughout the war. Late in 1937, the famous American pilot Colonel Charles Lindbergh, on an official visit to Germany, was shown the Fa 61. From February 1938, all publicity restrictions on the Fa 61 were removed by the German authorities and Hanna Reitsch gave spectacular demonstrations before large crowds inside the Deutschlandhalle in Berlin—the helicopter was clearly on its way in Europe. Inconclusive discussions about possible collaboration took place between the Cierva Company and Focke and Bréguet, as they did also between Focke and the Americans, Havilland H. Platt and W. Lawrence Le Page.

In 1938, Focke-Achgelis undertook the development of a six-passenger transport helicopter for Lufthansa, the German airline, which was simply a scaled-up version of the Fa 61 with 11.9 m (39 ft) rotors, a loaded weight of 3200 kg (7,055 lb), and an 800-hp BMW 132 radial engine. The prototype of the Fa 266 was completed in September 1939 but was then taken over for military use. Renamed Fa 223, it made its first free flight in August

1940, and the type was later ordered into production with a 1,000-hp Bramo 323 radial and a maximum loaded weight increased to 4300 kg (9,500 lb). The first examples were delivered to the German forces in 1942 but, although a total of 121 were ordered, the Fa 223 never went into widespread service because its production was twice disrupted by Allied bombing of the manufacturer's factory. Only twelve aircraft were completed and flown. The type was, however, revived experimentally after the war in France and Czechoslovakia.

While these developments were taking place in Europe, Igor Sikorsky had started work in the United States in 1937, on a single-rotor configuration which he had been thinking about since 1929, patented in 1935, and which, in the event, was to lead to the first widely used production helicopters. Sikorsky's design, as first flown by its designer on September 14, 1939, featured a single 28 ft main rotor with collective and cyclic pitch control and a single small anti-torque tail rotor. Power was from a 75-hp Lycoming engine. Contrary to most published references, this initial version of the VS-300 is believed to have made short free untethered flights on September 14.[30] Only later was the aircraft restrained by cables as a safeguard during development flying. The cyclic pitch control gave trouble and was moreover covered by Cierva patents. It was soon replaced by a variety of different combinations of auxiliary control rotors at the tail. A configuration with three tail rotors was finally decided upon which gave satisfactory control and the aircraft made its first free flight in this form on May 13, 1940. Although satisfactory from the control aspect, the three tail rotors were heavy, complicated, and ungainly. They were therefore progressively eliminated and a return was made to an improved cyclic and collective pitch control with a single anti-torque tail rotor. The aircraft was first flown again in this form on December 8, 1941. Sikorsky's V.S.300 design thus finally crystallized in a form closely similar to its first flight configuration.

The V.S.300 was only a development aircraft. However, an enlarged and more powerful, but similar design, with a 38 ft (11.58 m) rotor and a 185-hp Warner radial engine, the VS-316 (soon to be known as the R-4), was ordered by the U.S. Army Air Corps early in 1941 and made its first flight in January 14, 1942. This aircraft went into production, together with two still further improved Sikorsky designs, the R-5 and the R-6. Some 400 of these three types were built and saw service with the American forces, the RAF, and the Royal Navy before the end of the war.

The success of the Sikorsky helicopters inspired other American companies, as well as manufacturers in other parts of the world once the war was over, to enter the field so that the construction of helicopters soon became a major activity of the world's aerospace industries. The majority of helicopter manufacturers have adopted Sikorsky's configuration of a single main rotor with small torque-compensating tail rotor, but a few have tried and stayed with other layouts. The most notable are the tandem twin-rotor series originated by F. N. Piasecki and now built principally in the United States by Boeing-Vertol, and the Russian Kamov types with co-axial superimposed contra-rotating rotors.

Piasecki's first tandem-rotor helicopter made its initial flight in March 1945, and was the first successful helicopter of this type. The configuration was later adopted by, notably, the Bristol Company in England for their Bristol 173/192 series (1952) and by the Russians for their large Yak-24 helicopter (1954). Both these types were twin-engined, as are the latest Boeing-Vertol aircraft of this configuration.

Kaman in the United States produced for a time helicopters with twin intermeshing side-by-side two-blade rotors (the first, the K-125, first flew on January 15, 1947). These followed a pattern pioneered by A. Flettner in Germany between 1938 and 1940. The idea of closely intermeshing synchronized rotors had previously been suggested by J. A. J.

Bennett of the Cierva Company, but the Flettner Fl 265 was the first helicopter of this type to be built and successfully flown. The first aircraft crashed on its first flight in May 1939 because of fouling of the rotors, but this difficulty was subsequently overcome and the Fl 265 then flew well. Six were built.

The first design was succeeded by the generally similar Fl 282 Kolibri developed in the period 1940–45, which was highly successful and was ordered into large-scale production but, due to Allied bombing, only twenty-two aircraft were completed. The intermeshing layout was first used in America with three-blade rotors by the Kellett Aircraft Corporation, which had previously built Autogiros since it was formed in 1929. Work started on the first Kellett helicopter, the XR-8, in 1943 and its first flight was made on August 7, 1944. Early in 1945, Kellett undertook the development of a larger twin-engined helicopter, the XR-10, also with intermeshing rotors. The XR-10 had two 525-hp Continental engines, a loaded weight of 15,000 lb, and 65 ft rotors. It was first flown on April 27, 1947. This aircraft later crashed because of control failure and further development of the type was discontinued because it was considered that there was a risk of the three-blade rotors fouling each other during certain maneuvers.

The co-axial superimposed twin-rotor configuration was tried by Hiller toward the end of the war and also, again, by Bréguet after peace returned. Neither of these developments was, however, continued. The Russians later became the only users, on any scale, of this configuration which they adopted for the Kamov series.

Tip-drive single-rotor helicopters, on the principle originally suggested by W. H. Phillips, were pioneered in practical form in Germany by F. Doblhoff from 1942. By 1945 he had produced four successively improved prototypes employing an engine-driven compressor in the fuselage which fed an air/fuel mixture through the hollow rotor blades to their tips, where it was burnt in combustion chambers which rotated the blades by jet propulsion. No anti-torque provision is required with this form of rotor drive, but Doblhoff employed an airscrew in his later designs to give yaw control by means of the slipstream over tail surfaces and to propel the aircraft in translational gyroplane flight while cruising with the tip-drive not operating.

Doblhoff also studied ramjets and pulse jets for rotor drives and after the war the ramjet system, in particular, was extensively tested but did not gain any wide acceptance.

Tip-drive by means of a central compressor also had its advocates. The first production tip-drive helicopter was the French Sud-Aviation SO 1221 Djinn, the prototype of which first flew on January 2, 1953. This aircraft did not employ tip combustion chambers, the rotor being driven by the so-called warm-air system whereby compressed air from the central source is simply ducted through the blades and ejected from the tips. The type has not survived.

Cierva's work with Autogiros in the 1920s and '30s led to the compound helicopter, which may eventually emerge as an important type. Compound helicopters have rotors that are power-driven for take-off and landing and allowed to autorotate, like those of gyroplanes, while cruising. Rotor lift may be supplemented by a fixed wing in cruising flight. The first compound helicopter seems to have been produced in Russia by the Central Aero-Hydrodynamic Institute in 1938. The TsAGI 11-EA had a main rotor that was shaft-driven for vertical take-off and landing and declutched for autorotation in cruising flight when a fixed wing unloaded the rotor and supplemented its lift. Forward propulsion was by two forward-facing variable-pitch propellers that also provided control in yaw and main rotor torque compensation.

Mention has already been made of Doblhoff's wartime tip-drive helicopters, some of which were designed to cruise in autorotation. After the war, McDonnell in the United

The Fairey Rotodyne prototype. This thirty-five-to-forty-passenger transport compound helicopter of 1958 had a tip-driven rotor for take-off and landing but cruised as an autogyro.
(J. Stroud)

States produced the XV-1 compound helicopter which had tip-drive of the main rotor for take-off and landing and a single horizontal propeller for forward propulsion. On April 29, 1955, this aircraft achieved the first authenticated full transition from helicopter to gyroplane flight with a fixed wing providing some of the lift. It subsequently attained a speed of about 200 mph. The British Fairey Rotodyne twin-turboprop compound helicopter, which also featured tip-drive of the main rotor, made its first transition on April 10, 1958.

All the practical helicopters so far mentioned employed variations of the classic Cierva-type freely articulated rotor with both flapping and drag hinges. However, from November 1941, Arthur D. Young, working for the American Bell Company, developed the two blade seesaw rotor (sometimes called the semi-rigid or teetering rotor) with its two blades rigidly inter-connected and a single central universal joint to the shaft. This type of rotor was tried at about the same time in England on a Rotachute rotary-wing glider. The first seesaw rotors had been flown on the Herrick HV-1 and HV-2A Vertaplanes from 1931. The Bell seesaw rotor, which incorporates certain refinements to increase stability, was first flown on the Bell 30 in the spring of 1943 and has since been used on many thousands of Bell helicopters.

Another kind of rotor, the rigid type with cyclic pitch variation and no teetering freedom, was first flown successfully by Wilford on his gyroplane in 1931. It was later used on a number of early helicopters which proved unsatisfactory. Its first successful application to a helicopter was in the American Landgraf H-2 that first flew on November 2, 1944. The

301

rigid rotor has not so far been much used, although there have been a number of experimental helicopters in the United States with rotors of this type. Rotors of semi-rigid design, in which torsion bars provide flapping and lagging freedom, have also gained acceptance.

Refinement of the Practical Helicopter

After 1942, when Sikorsky started producing the R-4 and its successors in numbers in America, the helicopter rapidly matured as a production article and as a practical vehicle in its smaller sizes. The various configurations that have gained favor (see Table 2) achieved practical status at different dates in the period 1942–53, while other new forms and combinations have been developed since, particularly in the direction of compound helicopters and convertiplanes.

The helicopter was used to a limited extent by the Americans and British mainly for rescue work during World War II. The Germans also employed it on a few occasions. In the immediate post-war years the helicopter found its most useful applications with navies for rescue and communications work and with land forces as an assault, evacuation, and tactical transport, particularly for antiguerilla operations in undeveloped areas. During the Korean War, the helicopter was used on a very much larger scale than ever before, although primarily still in the same roles. In Vietnam, the helicopter really came into its own, becoming a major weapon.

Since the end of World War II, the helicopter has come into increasing use for a wide variety of civil purposes, notably for all kinds of charter and other aerial work such as crop spraying, oil prospecting, power line inspection, police and coast guard patrol, and for communications, oil rig support, etc. Although a high-cost vehicle, the helicopter has clearly established its utility in these and similar fields and there is no doubt that there is a rapidly growing requirement for, mainly, relatively small helicopters for such work. Development has steadily improved their reliability, durability, and economy. The adaptation of turbine power units has made important contributions in this direction and has, in fact, been the most important single step in the development of the modern helicopter. The first single-turbine helicopter was the American Kaman K-225 which first flew on December 10, 1951. The Kaman HTK-1, which first flew in March 1954, was the first twin-turbine helicopter.

Since 1947, scheduled mail services and after 1950, scheduled passenger services have developed on a limited scale. The Russians later also entered this field. Development of such operations on a large scale has been dependent on the provision of bigger helicopters of improved lifting capacity, reliability, and economy, with multi-engines and satisfactory engine-failed performance together with improved all-weather capability. Development in these directions is also required for certain naval and military applications, notably for antisubmarine work and for assault and tactical transport. These requirements have inspired recent progress which has resulted in twin-engined helicopters of about 20,000 lb loaded weight being currently in extensive military and much more limited commercial service and smaller numbers of multi-engined helicopters of 40,000 to 100,000 lb loaded weight being in military service—so far mainly in the United States and the Soviet Union. Normal operating speeds are still in the range 100 to 150 knots and maximum speeds up to about 200 knots.

Table 2

The First Successful Helicopters

Configuration	Twin-rotor Co-axial	Twin-rotor Side-by-side	Twin-rotor Intermeshing	Twin-rotor Tandem	Single-rotor (+ tail rotor)	Single-rotor (Tip-drive)	Miscellaneous
1935	Bréguet-Dorand 314 F						
1936		Focke-Achgelis FA 61 G					
1937							
1938		Weir W-5 B					
1939		Weir W-6 B	Flettner Fl 265 G		Sikorsky V.S.300 US		
1940		Focke-Achgelis Fa 223 G					
1941		Platt Le Page XR-1 US; TsAGI Omega I R			Sikorsky V.S.300A US		
1942			Flettner Fl 282 G		Sikorsky XR-4 US		
1943					Piasecki PV-2 US; Bell 30 US; Sikorsky XR-6 US	Doblhoff WNF 342V-1 G	
1944	Hiller XH-44 US		Kellett XR-8 US			Doblhoff WNF 342V-2 G	
1945		McDonnell XHJD-1 US		Piasecki XHRP-1 US		Doblhoff WNF 342V-4 G	Cierva W-9 B (jet torque compensation)
1946	Bréguet G 11E F		SNAC NC 2001 F	Jovanovich JOV-3 US	Sikorsky S-51 US; Bell 47 US		
1947	Hoppicopter Model 103 US; Kamov Ka-8 R		Kaman K-125 US; Kellett XR-10 US		Doman LZ-1A US; Hiller UH-5 US; Bristol 171 B	McDonnell XH-20 US	Fairey B Gyrodyne (off-set forward facing propeller)
1948		TsAGI Omega II R; SNCASE SE 3000 F		Piasecki XHJP-1 US	Cierva W-14 B	SNCASO SO 1110 F	Cierva W-11 B (Three-rotors); SNCASE SE 3101 F (Twin-tail rotors)
1949	Kamov Ka-10 R		Kaman K-225 US	McCulloch YH-30 US	Sikorsky S-55 US; SNCASE SE 3120 F	American Helicopter Co. XA-5 US; Hughes XH-17 US	
1950	Bréguet III F		Kaman K-240 US	Piasecki HUP-1 US		Hiller HJ-1 US	
Present status	Configuration in limited production in the U.S.S.R.	Configuration fallen out of favor but may be revived for convertiplanes.	Configuration now out of favor	Configuration in production in the U.S.A.	Most common configuration, in large-scale production all over the world.	Configuration now out of favor	Unconventional configurations still appear from time to time.

Appendix 2

Chronology of Autogiro Development

August 27, 1920	Cierva is granted his first Spanish Autogiro patent.
October 1920	C.1 demonstrates autorotation at Getafe but does not fly.
November 18, 1920	Cierva, with brother Ricardo and Pablo Diaz, sets up workshop to manufacture cars, aircraft, and accessories.
June 1921	C.3 with three-blade rotor with cyclic pitch control tested unsuccessfully at Getafe.
January 1922	C.2 with rigid five-blade rotor makes short hops at Getafe.
April 1922	C.4 completed: tested over next few months with pilot-controlled laterally tiltable rotor hub. It is not satisfactory.
January 17, 1923	C.4 is first Autogiro to fly employing flapping blades successfully for the first time. Fixed-spindle rotor.
April (about) 1923	C.5 flies but is destroyed in a crash in July.
November 7, 1923	Cierva is granted a Spanish patent for his successful Autogiro configuration.
February 1924	C.6 flies at Cuatro Vientos. First Autogiro funded by the Spanish government.
December 12, 1924	C.6 is first Autogiro to make a cross-country flight, from Cuatro Vientos to Getafe, piloted by Loriga.
May 1925	Pitcairn and Larsen visit Madrid for talks with Cierva.
June 6 or 8, 1925	First flight of C.6bis, piloted by Loriga at Cuatro Vientos.
October 10, 1925	Courtney starts flying C.6A at Farnborough.
October 14–31, 1925	Demonstrations by Courtney of C.6A at Farnborough lead to British government sponsorship of the Autogiro.
October 22, 1925	Sir Sefton Brancker reads Cierva's paper about the Autogiro to the Royal Aeronautical Society in London.
January 27, 1926	Courtney has crash at Villacoublay during demonstrations of C.6A in France.
March 24, 1926	Cierva Autogiro Company Ltd. formed in the United Kingdom. It is based at Hamble near Southampton.

June 19, 1926	C.6C (J6068) built by Avro flies for the first time, piloted by Courtney at Hamble.
June 30, 1926	C.6C rotor-blade bracing fails during test flight.
July (about) 1926	C.8V (G-EBTX) built by Avro flies for the first time, at Hamble.
July 3, 1926	C.6C demonstrated by Courtney at the RAF Display at Hendon.
July 29, 1926	C.6D (G-EBTW) built by Avro makes its first flight, at Hamble, piloted by Courtney.
July 30, 1926	C.6D first Autogiro to carry a passenger (Cierva himself), piloted by Courtney.
September 5, 1926	Courtney demonstrates C.6D in Berlin.
September 25, 1926	C.6C crashes at Farnborough, piloted by Flying Officer Saint.
October 20, 1926	C.8V and C.6D demonstrated to the Press at Hamble.
November 15, 1926	Loring C.VII first flown, at Cuatro Vientos, by Ureta.
January 1927	C.8V (G-EBTX) fitted with four-wheel landing gear. C.10 completed by Parnall.
	C.6C considerably modified during reconstruction at Hamble.
February 7, 1927	C.6C flown by Courtney at Hamble has accident caused by lack of drag hinges on the rotor blades.
February 28, 1927	Juan de la Cierva gains his pilot's license for airplanes.
about May 1927	C.8R (G-EBTW) converted from C.6D by Avro, first flown at Hamble, by Hinkler; introduces drag hinges.
May 19, 1927	Modified Loring C.VII with drag hinges first flown, in Spain at Carabanchel Alto, piloted by Truelove.
July/August 1927	C.8L-I (J8930) first flown, by Hinkler, at Hamble.
August 2, 1927	Cierva starts flying Autogiros: flies C.8R at Worthy Down.
September 1927	C.9 (J8931) built by Avro first flown, by Hinkler, at Hamble.
September 30, 1927	Cierva makes first cross-country flight by an Autogiro in England: Hamble to Farnborough in C.8L-I.
October 6, 1927	C.8L-I damaged by heavy landing at Farnborough.
October 18, 1927	C.8L-I had flown a total of 5 ¾ hours to this date and had made 34 landings.
October 20, 1927	C.8V makes cross-country flight from Hamble to Croydon and back, piloted by Hinkler.
November 11, 1927	C.11 completed by Parnall at Yate.
December 31, 1927	Cierva makes substantial contribution to the total of 35 hours flying accumulated on C.6D/C.8R, C.7, C.8V, C.8L-I and C.9 in 1927.

January 11, 1928	Accident to C.8L-I due to failure of interblade bracing.
February 1928	Parnall C.11 (G-EBQG) crashes on its first flight at Yate, piloted by Cierva. Has adjustable rotor hub probably for trimming purposes.
	Cierva has accident at Hamble in C.8V.
April 26, 1928	Parnall C.10 (J9038) crashes on taxying trials at Yate, piloted by Flight Lieutenant Hamersley. This Autogiro has adjustable rotor hub probably for trimming purposes.
May 1928	C.9L-II (G-EBYY) flies for first time, piloted by Hinkler.
May 28, 1928	Cierva has accident in C.8L-II at Hampshire Air Pageant at Hamble.
July 1928	Pitcairn on a visit to England has his first flight in an Autogiro (C.8L-II).
	Rawson joins Cierva Company as pilot. Later becomes first pilot to achieve 1,000 hrs on Autogiros.
July 3, 1928	C.8R flown from Hamble to Farnborough by Rawson.
July 31, 1928	Following flight by Cierva in C.9, tailplane fittings found to have failed in fatigue.
August 7, 1928	From Northolt, Rawson starts tour of the United Kingdom in C.8L-II.
August 1928	Pitcairn orders C.8W.
September 18, 1928	Cierva flies C.8L-II from London to Paris, with Bouché as passenger.
September 1928	C.8L-III first flown, by Rawson, at Hamble.
September 21, 1928	Cierva crashes C.8L-II during demonstration in Paris.
October 1928	Reconstructed C.11 retains adjustable rotor hub probably for trimming purposes.
October 23, 1928	C.17 Mk.I (G-AABP) first flown, by Cierva, at Hamble. Was to have been first production Autogiro but superseded by C.19.
November 1928	C.8W makes its first flight in the United Kingdom.
November 5, 1928	Parnall C.10 crashes at Andover during taxying trials, piloted by Rawson.
December 19, 1928	C.8W is first Autogiro to fly in the United States, piloted by Rawson, at Bryn Athyn.
January 1929	Cierva demonstrates C.8L-III at Monte Cello near Rome in Italy.
January 12, 1929	Pitcairn orders the PCA-2-30 (X759W) from Alfaro.
January (about), 1929	Weymann-Lepère Company formed in France. Acquires Autogiro design license for France.
February 14, 1929	Pitcairn-Cierva Autogiro Company of America formed as Cierva licensee in the United States.

April 1929	C.17 Mk.II (G-AAGJ) first flown, by Cierva, at Hamble.
	Pitcairn, Larsen, and Nicol visited United Kingdom and France for discussions with Cierva and Lepère.
May 23, 1929	Loring C.XII is first flown, by Cierva, at Cuatro Vientos. Introduces deflected slipstream rotor spin up.
June 1929	Weymann-Lepère C.18 (G-AAIH) completed in France and given UK registration.
July 1929	Autogiro manufacture in the United States starts at Pitcairn's new Willow Grove plant.
July 11, 1929	Rambaud makes a nonstop flight (350 mi) from Madrid to Lisbon in C.XII.
July 12/27, 1929	C.19 Mk.I (G-AAHM) exhibited at the Aero Show at Olympia in London.
July 1929	C.19 Mk.I (G-AAGK) first flown by Cierva, at Hamble.
August 1, 1929	C.19 Mk.I tested at Hamble by Flight Lieutenants Rogenhagen and Rawson.
August 2, 1929	C.19 Mk.I gains United Kingdom Certificate of Airworthiness.
August 12, 1929	Weymann-Lepère C.18 first flown at Villacoublay, probably by Cierva. First all-metal and cabin Autogiro.
August 13, 1929	Cierva leaves for his first visit to the United States in the *Majestic*, taking the first C.19 Mk.II (G-AAKY) with him. He returns to Europe in November.
August 20, 1929	C.19 Mk.II (NC311V ex G-AAKY) first flown in the United States, by Cierva, at Willow Grove.
August 22, 1929	C.19 Mk.II demonstrated at Cleveland National Air Races by Cierva. This continued until end of Races on September 2.
September 1929	Weymann-Lepère C.18 first flown in the United States at Willow Grove, probably by Cierva.
October 7 (about), 1929	Pitcairn PCA-1 (X94N) first flown, by Cierva. First American Autogiro. Crashed on an early flight.
October (late), 1929	Pitcairn PCA-1A (X95N) first flown.
November (early), 1929	Pitcairn PCA-1B (X96N) first flown.
November 18, 1929	Pitcairn's old plant at Bryn Athyn destroyed by fire. PCA-1 wreck destroyed in blaze.
November 30, 1929	30/35 Autogiros flown up to this date.
January 1930	C.19 Mk.IIA (G-AAUA) first flown, by Cierva, at Hamble.
January 8, 1930	Engine-powered rotor spin-up drive on C.11 demonstrated on ground to RAE representatives. Not satisfactory.

February 13, 1930	Cierva lectures to the Royal Aeronautical Society in London about progress with the Autogiro.
March 1930	Pitcairn PCA-2 prototype (X760W) makes its first flight, at Willow Grove, piloted by Ray. First Autogiro with satisfactory mechanical-drive rotor spin-up.
April 25, 1930	Cierva performs water tests with C.17 Hydrogiro seaplane. May not have flown on this occasion.
May 1930	French navy issues requirement for two CTW.200 Autogiro floatplanes.
July (early), 1930	C.19 Mk.III (G-AAYN) first flown, by Cierva, at Hamble. This was first true production Autogiro and is shipped to Pitcairn in United States.
August 18, 1930	Alfaro PCA-2-30 makes its first flight, at Willow Grove. Plastics extensively used in its construction.
August 23, 1930	C.19 Mk.III (X3Y ex G-AAYN), PCA-2 prototype (X760W) and PCA-1B (X96N) demonstrated at Chicago National Air Races until September 1.
October 30, 1930	Pitcairn announces PCA-2 going into production. It has a fixed rotor spindle with engine-driven rotor spin-up.
November 1, 1930	First production PCA-2 (NR784W) makes its first flight, at Willow Grove. Has larger 300 hp R-975 engine.
November 1930	Cierva makes his second visit to the United States returning to Europe in December. Sees rotor spin-up drive incorporated in PCA-2.
	Brie joins Cierva as pilot. He flies 2,150 hrs on Autogiros during following 12 years. Becomes Chief Pilot and Flying Manager of company in 1933.
December 31, 1930	Two thousand hours flown on Autogiros in the United States up to this date. (In two years since December 1928.)
February 7, 1931	French navy orders two CTW.200 Autogiros from Weymann.
February 1931	Pitcairn PAA-2 prototype makes first flight, at Willow Grove.
March 1931	Pitcairn PAA-1 prototype makes its first flight, at Willow Grove.
	Cierva starts development of three-blade cantilever folding rotor, first used on C.19 Mk.IV and later on C.24.
April (early), 1931	Weymann CTW.200 first flown, by Cierva in France.
April 2, 1931	Pitcairn PCA-2 is first Autogiro to be certificated in the United States (ATC No. 410).
April 17, 1931	First Weymann CTW.201 (F-ALLA) being flown at Villacoublay, by Martin.
April 1931	Seventy Autogiros flown up to this date.

April (about) 1931	New 34 ft three-blade cantilever folding rotor tested on C.19 Mk.III (G-AALA).
April 22, 1931	Pitcairn is awarded Collier Trophy. Ray lands PCA-2 on White House lawn.
April 24, 1931	Kellett K-2 makes its first flight, at Philadelphia Municipal Airport, piloted by Ray.
May 1931	Weymann CTW.210 (F-ALQX) flying at Lille-Ronchin.
June 1931	Pitcairn XOP-1 delivered to the U.S. Navy.
	C.19 Mk.IV prototype (G-AAHM) flies with three-blade cantilever rotor and engine-powered rotor spin-up drive.
	Pitcairn PAA-1 is first flown, at Willow Grove.
July 17, 1931	Kellett K-2 is certificated in the United States (ATC. No 437).
August 5, 1931	Wilford WRK in the United States is first gyroplane with rigid rotor to fly successfully. Has cyclic pitch variation instead of flapping blades.
August 7, 1931	Pitcairn PAA-1 is certificated in the United States (ATC No. 433).
August 1931	Pitcairn PCA-3 is first flown, at Willow Grove.
September 23, 1931	Pitcairn XOP-1 makes first Autogiro landings on an aircraft carrier (USS *Langley*).
September 1931	C.24 (G-ABLM) cabin Autogiro makes its first flight, piloted by Cierva.
November 19, 1931	Public demonstration at Hanworth of C.19 Mk.IV prototype and C.24—both with three-blade cantilever folding rotors.
December 1931	Focke-Wulf in Germany and Lioré-et-Olivier in France sign C.19 Mk.IV license agreements.
December 16, 1931	Cierva applies for direct-control patent.
December 22, 1931	Cierva makes third trip to the United States to be picked up from the New York jetty by Ray in a PCA-2. Returns to Europe February 10, 1932.
December 31, 1931	Total of about 7,700 hours flown on Autogiros in 1931 in the United States (9,700 hours since December 1928).
January 1932	On this visit to the United States, Cierva explains direct-control concept and possibility of jump take-off to his Pitcairn American licensees.
February 1932	Kellett K-3 in the United States makes its first flight.
	About 50 fixed-spindle Autogiros built in the United States up to this date.

March 1, 1932	Pitcairn PA-18 makes its first flight, at Willow Grove.
March 5/12, 1932	C.19 Mk.V (G-ABXP) direct-control development aircraft has its first flight tests, at Hamble.
March 20, 1932	Comper C.25 makes its first flight, at Hooton Park, piloted by Cierva. Aircraft damaged on landing.
March 22, 1932	C.19 Mk.IV production version makes its first flight, at Hamble.
March 23, 1932	Cierva proposes to Weymann that French design license for Autogiros be transferred to Lioré-et-Olivier.
March 26, 1932	Kellett K-3 in the United States is certificated (ATC No. 471).
March 27, 1932	Report of wingless direct-control Autogiro appears in the *Sunday Express* London newspaper.
April 5, 1932	Marsh joins Cierva Company as pilot.
April 1932	C.19 Mk. V flown by Pitcairn and Ray in England, Larsen discusses C.L.10 direct-control design with Lepère.
April 12, 1932	Cierva gives details of direct-control in lecture to Aero-Technical High School in Madrid.
April 20, 1932	Repaired C.25 again tested by Cierva and Rawson at Hooton Park. Found to be directionally unstable. Fins added.
May 14, 1932	Brie wins second place in C.19 Mk.III (G-AAYP) in Skegness Air Race.
May 27, 1932	Cierva starts 1,430 miles European tour in C.24. Ends June 9.
June 1932	Focke-Wulf C.19 Mk.IV (D-2300) flies in Germany: believed to be only one built under Cierva license.
July 1932	Japanese navy buys two C.19 Mk.IVs (G-ABXD, and 'XE) through Okura & Co. A third (G-ABXF) goes to the *Asahi Shimbun* newspaper as J-BAYA.
July 4, 1932	Pitcairn PA-18 in the United States is certificated (ATC No. 478).
July 6, 1932	Board of G. and J. Weir Ltd. decide to undertake direct-control Autogiro development.
August 2/5, 1932	C.19 Mk.V first direct control Autogiro tested at RAE.
August 1932	Kay 32/1 is the first gyroplane to fly with collective pitch control with flapping blades. Laterally tiltable hub. Control in pitch by normal elevators.
August 6, 1932	Brie competes in Newcastle Air Race in C.24.
September 3, 1932	Weymann agrees to transfer Cierva design license in France to Lioré-ey-Olivier.
September 1932	Pitcairn PA-19 flies in the United States. Fixed-rotor spindle but tiltable for trimming.

October 1932	Lepère comes to England for three months to collaborate with Cierva on design of C.L.10 (C.27).
November 14, 1932	C.19 Mk.V publicly demontrates direct control, at Hanworth, for first time. Has floor mounted control column.
November 18, 1932	Lioré-et-Olivier C.L.10 (C.27) direct-control Autogiro exhibited at XIII Paris Salon de l'Aéronautique. Ends December 4.
November 24, 1932	C.L.10 direct-control Autogiro first flown, by Cierva, at Orly.
December 1932	Japanese army buys two K-3's through Okura & Co.
December 19, 1932	C.L.10 piloted by Martin suffers first fatal Autogiro accident, at Villacoublay. First Autogiro to have hanging stick control.
December 31, 1932	More than 120 Autogiros (including 30 prototypes) built up to this date. Had flown about 30,000 hours—13,276 hours flown in 1932.
January 1933	Pitcairn PA-22 roadable direct-control Autogiro (X13198) undergoes ground testing but does not fly. Design changes required.
January 11, 1933	Cierva receives FAI Gold Medal.
January (late), 1933	Hanging stick control to tiltable rotor hub introduced into C.19 Mk.V development aircraft. It previously had a floor-mounted stick.
February 1933	A Kellett K-3 flies 500 hours at an average speed of 92 mph and cost of less than $4.00 per hour for fuel, oil, and repairs.
February 13, 1933	Weymann confirms to French Air Ministry that Cierva design license has been transferred to Lioré-et-Olivier.
March 1933	Modified PA-22 crashes on attempted first flight, piloted by Ray.
March 12, 1933	Tests completed on C.19 Mk.V. Aircraft to be dismantled.
April 1933	C.30 prototype (G-ACFI) makes its first flight, piloted by Cierva. Has hanging stick.
April 27, 1933	C.30 prototype publicly demonstrated by Cierva at Hanworth. C.25 also demonstrated.
May 1933	Weir W.1 (C.28) first flown, by Cierva, at Hanworth. Numerous problems with this direct-control Autogiro.
May 16, 1933	Cierva makes fourth visit to the United States. Returns in July. During this visit Cierva proposes that Pitcairn should continue with tilting head developments while the U.K. company shifts to cyclic and collective pitch control on a fixed spindle.
May 19, 1933	Pitcairn PA-24 is certificated in the United States (ATC No. 506).

June 28, 1933	Cierva receives Daniel Guggenheim Gold Medal.
June 1933	Kellett K-4 first flown, in United States.
July (about), 1933	Pitcairn PA-22 makes its first successful flights, at Willow Grove, piloted by Cierva.
August 1933	C.30 prototype (G-ACFI) with modified rotor, used for first experimental jump take-offs. Some witnessed by Pitcairn and some of his American colleagues. High levels of vibration and only low jumps.
	There were at this time 68 fixed-spindle Autogiros with current licenses in the United States. Twenty-four pilots licensed only on Autogiros.
September 18–23, 1933	C.19 Mk.IV (G-ABUG) piloted by Brie with Squadron Leader Baker takes part in British Army maneuvers on Salisbury Plain. Showed promise in the intercommunication role.
October 15 (about), 1933	C.30P Mk.II preproduction direct control Autogiro (G-ACKA) makes its first flight. Assembled by Airwork at Heston.
October 1933	Pitcairn, Larsen and Ray in United Kingdom to evaluate C.30P's direct-control characteristics. Pitcairn and Ray learn to fly C.30P.
November 8, 1933	C.30P Mk.II preproduction direct-control Autogiro (G-ACKA) publicly demonstrated at Hanworth.
December (about), 1933	Pitcairn PA-22 in its first non-roadable form flies successfully. High levels of vibration.
December 21, 1933	First C.30P (G-ACIM) gains its Certificate of Airworthiness. Built by Avro in Manchester.
	C.28 (W.1) crashes at Hanworth, piloted by Marsh.
December 27, 1933	Kellett K-4 is certificated (ATC No. 523).
December 31, 1933	About 80 fixed rotor-spindle Autogiros with non-cantilever blades built in the United States up to this date. In the world as a whole about 150 Autogiros had been built including 44 prototypes: 22 in Britain, 12 in the United States, 8 in Spain, and 2 in France. Between 40,000 and 50,000 hours flown.
January 1, 1934	Pitcairn closes down U.S. production of his fixed-spindle Autogiros until satisfactory direct-control Autogiros can be substituted.
January 1934	Lioré-et-Olivier extend their Cierva license to cover manufacture and development of the C.30 in France.
	Kellett and Prewitt visit the United Kingdom to study direct control.
March 7, 1934	Cierva lands C.30P (G-ACIO) on a platform on the Spanish navy seaplane tender *Dédalo*.

April 1934	C.L.10B flown several times by Cierva, at Hanworth.
May 20/21, 1934	Brie demonstrates C.30P at the Fête Aérienne de Vincennes near Paris.
June 1934	Weir W.2 direct-control Autogiro makes its first flight, at Hanworth, piloted by Marsh.
July 1934	Deliveries start of production C.30A's manufactured by Avro in Manchester (78 built).
September 1934	Brie makes experimental C.30 flights to Mount Pleasant post office in central London. Does not land on post office roof.
October 1934	C.30A in Spain first used on military operations by the Spanish navy in Asturias.
October 28, 1934	C.30 prototype (G-ACFI), piloted by Marsh, achieves first successful jump take-off followed by climb-away (with Phi-Bell rotor head).
November 1934	Kellett KD-1 (X14742) direct-control Autogiro in the United States makes first flight, piloted by Leavitt.
November 14, 1934	Cierva makes jump take-off in C.30 prototype (G-ACFI).
November 23, 1934	Lepreux lands C.30 (G-ACWG) on the Champs Elysées during XV Paris Salon de l'Aéronautique.
January 1935	Kellett KD-1 direct-control Autogiro in the United States goes into production.
January 21, 1935	Fatal accident to RAF Rota (C.30A) at Old Sarum. Loss of control in high speed dive.
February 4, 1935	C.L.20 direct-control Autogiro makes its first flight, piloted by Cierva. Built by Westland at Yeovil.
February 5, 1935	Weirs decides to terminate Autogiro development but in the event continue until 1937.
February 18, 1935	First flight of Kay 33/1, piloted by Rawson. Had collective pitch control, laterally tilting head, and normal elevator and rudder.
March 15, 1935	Cierva announces the achievement of jump take-off in lecture to the Royal Aeronautical Society.
March 1935	A total of 4,000 hours flown on C.30's up to this date.
April 13/26, 1935	Rota (C.30A) first flown on floats, by Cierva and Marsh, at Rochester. Marsh ferries the aircraft (K4296) to Felixstowe.
May 25, 1935	Demonstration landings on Philadelphia central post office by Pitcairn PA-22 and Kellett KD-1.
June 22/26, 1935	C.30 with Salmson trial installation (G-ACWT) tested by Marsh.
June 26, 1935	Bréguet-Dorand 314 in France is the first helicopter to fly successfully, piloted by Claisse.

June 1935	Design of W.3 jump take-off Autogiro started at Weirs.
July 1935	Focke-Wulf C.30 enters production in Germany (about 30 built).
July 12, 1935	C.30A with Salmson trial installation (G-ACWT) delivered to Villacoublay, by Marsh.
August 10, 1935	Fatal accident to Pitcairn PA-18 at Willow Grove, Pennsylvania.
September 1935	Hafner A.R.III in United Kingdom is first gyroplane with cyclic and collective pitch to fly successfully. Uses some Cierva patents.
September 9, 1935	C.30A (K4230) flown by Brie makes first Autogiro landings on Royal Navy vessel—HMS *Furious*.
October 1935	First flight of first French-built C.30.
November 9, 1935	Pitcairn PA-22 makes the first jump take-offs in the United States. Limited jump heights.
December 31, 1935	Total of 7,797 hours flown on Autogiros worldwide (except USA) during preceding two years. At Hanworth, 144 pupils trained and 4,147 hours flown.
March 26, 1936	Pitcairn AC-35 (NX70) roadable direct-control Autogiro in the United States makes its first flight piloted by Ray. Built for Department of Commerce.
March 30, 1936	Pitcairn YG-2 (PA-3) (35-279) crashes under test at NACA Langley. Sheds blade during high speed test. Crew parachute safely.
June 26, 1936	Focke-Achgelis Fa 61 in Germany is the second helicopter to fly successfully, piloted by Rohlfs.
July 9, 1936	W.3 jump take-off Autogiro makes its first flight, at Abbotsinch, piloted by Marsh.
July 23, 1936	C.30 Mk.III (G-ACWF) and W.3 development Autogiros with two-blade Autodynamic rotor hubs give first public demonstrations of jump take-offs, piloted by Marsh. There are still vibration difficulties.
October 1936	Kellett YG-1A (36-352) delivered to the United States Army Air Corps.
October 2, 1936	Pitcairn AC-35 roadable direct-control Autogiro delivered to the United States Department of Commerce.
November 1936	Pitcairn Autogiro design activity in the United States suspended. Larsen and Stanley from Pitcairn go to work in the United Kingdom until February 1937.
December 1936	C.30 Mk.IV with two-blade rotor tested by Marsh.
December 9, 1936	Cierva killed in Douglas DC-2 accident at Croydon Airport.
January/March 1937	C.30 Mk.IV with two-blade rotor under test by Marsh. Autodynamic hub abandoned.

April 26, 1937	Cierva posthumously awarded Gold Medal of the Royal Aeronautical Society.
July 24, 1937	Herrick HV-2A in the United States is first aircraft to translate in flight from fixed-wing to gyroplane flight. Had seesaw rotor.
August 1937	British Air Ministry announces order for C.40 Autogiro.
October 31, 1937	Kellett KD-1A in the United States is certificated (ATC No. 712).
December 28, 1937	Board of G. and J. Weir Ltd. decides to switch development from Autogiros to helicopters.
January 7, 1938	First C.40 (G-AFDP) wrecked by ground resonance at Hanworth during attempted first taxy take-off.
Jan. 23/March 16, 1938	C.30 Mk.V (G-ACWF) development aircraft with three-blade Delta-3 rotor hub achieves jump take-offs with satisfactory levels of vibration.
February 1938	Pitcairn makes trip to Europe to study developments.
February 25, 1938	Rebuilt first C.40 makes successful taxy take-off and circuit.
April 1938	SNCASE C.301 in France makes its first flight, piloted by Rouland.
May 17/24, 1938	C.30J performing quite satisfactory jump take-offs with three-blade rotor.
June 7, 1938	W.5 helicopter flies successfully, at Dalrymple in the United Kingdom, piloted by Pullin.
June 21, 1938	C.40 jump take-off Autogiro makes its first jump take-offs, at Hanworth, piloted by Marsh. Max. height of jump: 10 ft.
September 21, 1938	C.40 making jump take-offs consistently. Jump heights modest in no-wind conditions.
November 2–4, 1938	Cierva team (including Brie, Marsh, and Ellis) visit Paris to evaluate C.301.
February 1939	Pitcairn makes trip to the United Kingdom and Europe to witness C.40 and W.5 flying.
February 19, 1939	Jasmine Bligh of BBC visits Hanworth and flies in C.30 and C.40. Autogiros are subject of a television program.
March 1939	SNCASE C.34 direct-control Autogiro in France flies but handling proves unsatisfactory.
June 29, 1939	Flight Lieutenant B.G. Carroll has landing accident at Hanworth on C.40 (L7589).
June (about) 1939	Pitcairn PA-36 jump take-off Autogiro makes its first flights, at Willow Grove, piloted by Marsh and Leavitt.
July 6, 1939	Eastern Air Lines operates scheduled mail service with Kellett KD-1B Autogiro between Philadelphia Airport and central post office. Service maintained until July 5, 1940.

July 17, 1939	C.40 (G-AFDP) awarded permit to fly.
August 1939	Kellett KD-1A delivered to Japanese army.
September 14, 1939	Sikorsky V.S.300 helicopter in the United States makes successful free flights in its original configuration.
October 20, 1939	W.6 (R5269) helicopter flies successfully in the United Kingdom, piloted by Pullin. Testing continues until July 1940 when stopped by the war.
December 1939	Kellett KD-1B in the United States is certificated (ATC No. 712).
February 1940	Kellett KD-1A crashed in Tachikawa in Japan.
July 8, 1940	Pitcairn PA-36 in the United States achieves successful jump take-offs, piloted by Soule.
October (about), 1940	James Weir visits the United States for discussions with Pitcairn and Stanley. Weir leaves notes about Aerodynamically Stable Rotor (ASR) derived from tests on W.6. Later used on XR-9 helicopter.
February 1941	Pitcairn PA-39 Autogiro in the United States makes its first flight.
April 15, 1941	Sikorsky V.S.300 helicopter (in its intermediate form) flies for over one hour.
May 26, 1941	Repaired KD-1A Autogiro in Japan makes its first flight.
June 1941	Two experimental KA-1 Autogiros ordered from Kayaba in Japan.
(date unknown) 1941	Kellett XR-3 Autogiro flies with fixed spindle and cyclic and collective pitch control.
August 12, 1941	Sikorsky V.S.300A helicopter in the United States makes its first flight in its definitive configuration.
September 27, 1941	Pitcairn PA-39 Autogiro: first of six delivered to the British Air Purchasing Commission.
December 8, 1941	Sikorsky V.S.300A helicopter makes its first satisfactory free flights.
February 10, 1942	AFEE Rotachute I flies for first time, in the United Kingdom.
May 1942	PA-39 Autogiro deck landing trials conducted by Brie in Long Island Sound and Chesapeake Bay.
May 29, 1942	Rotachute II makes its first flight.
June 2, 1942	Rotachute III makes its first flight.
October 1942	Bennett visits United States to discuss Rotachute. One constructed and tested but involved in accident.
November 1942	Kayaba Ka-1A ordered into production at Sendai (about 35 built).
April 29, 1943	Rotachute IV makes its first flight.

June 4, 1943	Kellett KD-1A makes take-offs from and landings on *Akitsu Maru* in Japan.
June 17, 1943	First flight of Ka-1A, at Kasuminome.
November 27, 1943	Malcolm Rotaplane makes its first flight.
January 1944	Sikorsky R-4 helicopter in the United States enters service.
Summer 1944	First flight of Ka-2. About 60 of this re-engined version built at Sendai.
October 1944	W.9 helicopter (PX203) first tested, at Thames Ditton near London.
October 20, 1945	No. 529 (Autogiro) Squadron of the RAF disbanded. Had flown a total of 9,141 hours.

Kay Gyroplanes and Helicopters

(Prototypes and design studies by David Kay and Kay Gyroplanes Ltd.)

Kay 32/1 Gyroplane. (Prototype) One 40-hp ABC Scorpion. Rotor diameter 22 ft (6.7 m); four blades; gross weight 550 lb (249 kg). Control system: collective pitch, laterally tilting head, and normal elevator and rudder. Experimental single-seat gyroplane completed in 1932. First flown in August 1932, probably at Perth. Damaged in a heavy landing at Leuchars in April 1933 and not rebuilt. This aircraft is believed to have originally been fitted with a 24-hp Blackburne engine. Development financed by Lt. Col. M. Ormand Darby.

Kay 33/1 Gyroplane. (Prototype) One 80-hp Pobjoy R Cataract. Rotor diameter 22 ft (6.7 m); four blades; empty weight 624 lb (283 kg); maximum weight 850–920 lb (385–417 kg); cruising speed 85 mph (136 km/h); maximum speed 97 mph (156 km/h). Control system: collective pitch, laterally tilting head, and normal elevator and rudder. Capable of jump take-offs to 10–20 ft (3–6 m). Experimental single-seat gyroplane (G-ACVA). Designed 1933; built 1934 by Oddie, Bradbury and Cull Ltd. First flown on February 18, 1935, at Eastleigh. Pilot A.H.C.A. Rawson. This aircraft was tested at RAE from September 23, 1935, to March 1936. Further official handling tests were made on September 18, 1936. Preserved in the Glasgow Museum of Transport.

Kay 35/1 Gyroplane. (Design Study) Single engine. Control system: collective pitch, laterally tilting head, and normal elevator and rudder. Proposals for a three-seat gyroplane made to the Air Ministry on January 21, 1936. Not built.

Kay 36/1 Gyroplane. (Design study) Twin engines. Control system: collective pitch, laterally tilting head, and normal elevator and rudder. Proposals for a twin-engine gyroplane made to the Air Ministry on March 10, 1936. Particulars of this design believed submitted to the Air Ministry on March 30, and to the Admiralty and Police Commissioners on June 20. Not built.

Kay 37/1 Gyroplane. (Design study) Single engine. Control system: collective pitch, laterally tilting head, and elevator and rudder. Proposals made to the Air Ministry during the visit of Air Commodore Verney to Eastleigh on February 24, 1937. This aircraft was to meet an Air Ministry Specification (possibly 43/36) for a three-seat gyroplane for the Fleet Air Arm which had been put forward by Commander Graham at a meeting at the Admiralty on January 21, 1936. Not built.

Kay 39/1 Gyroplane. (Design study) One 450-hp Alvis Leonides. Rotor diameter 50 ft (15.24 m); three blades; empty weight 3,460 lb (1,569 kg); maximum weight 4,600 lb (2,086 kg); cruising speed 94 mph (151 km/h); maximum speed 112 mph (180 km/h).

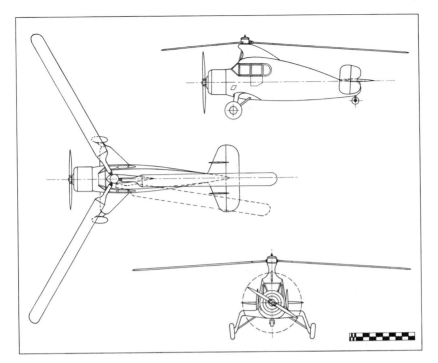

Kay Type 39/1.

Control system: collective pitch and fully tilting head linked with conventional elevator for fore-and-aft control. Proposals for a three-seat cabin gyroplane set out in a brochure dated 1939. Alternative engine installations were for the Pratt & Whitney Wasp Junior and the Wright Whirlwind. In appearance the Kay 39/1 would have looked very much like a direct control development of the American Pitcairn PA-19. Not built.

Kay 42/1 Helicopter. (Design study) Control system: collective pitch control and fully tilting head. Proposals for a helicopter with tip jet driven rotor. Not built.

Kay 46/1 Helicopter. (Design study) One 450-hp Rolls-Royce gas-turbine. Control system: collective pitch and fully tilting head, with tail rotor for torque compensation and yaw control. Proposals for a two-seat helicopter made in 1946. Not built.

Hafner Gyroplanes and Helicopters

(Prototypes built and design studies by Raoul Hafner and A.R. III Construction (Hafner Gyroplane) Company)

R.I Helicopter Revoplane I. (Prototype) One 30-hp ABC Scorpion. Single-seat wood fuselage. Torque reaction by twin wood and fabric aerofoils mounted in down-wash from rotor. Three-blade wire-braced, rigid rotor. Design start in 1929. Designed in collaboration with Nagler and Novotny. Tested in 1930 at Aspern Airport, Vienna. Development financed by Major J.A. Coates who provided £10,000 (then $49,000). Rotor diameter 10 m (32 ft 9¾ in).

R.II Helicopter Revoplane II. (Prototype) One 40-hp Salmson AD.9. Single-seat steel tube fuselage. Torque reaction by twin wood and fabric airfoils mounted in down-wash from rotor. Three-blade, cable-braced, rigid rotor. Designed and flown in 1931 at Aspern Airport, Vienna. Airborne for 1–2 minutes, but very unstable and difficult to fly. Taken to England, 1933. Modified at Heston to three-blade flapping rotor and used mainly as rotor hub test bed. Development also financed by Major Coates. Rotor diameter 10 m (32 ft 9¾ in).

R.III Helicopter. (Design study) Two contra-rotating rotors. Not built.

A.R.III Gyroplane Mk.1, Revoplane III. (Prototype) One 80-hp Pobjoy R Cataract. Single-seat, steel tube fabric-covered fuselage. Variable-incidence tailplane. Three-blade cantilever rotor with flapping blades, spider control (cyclic and collective) and tie-bar suspension. Engine-powered rotor starting and direct take-off. Designed at Hanworth by A.R.III Construction (Hafner Gyroplane) Company, 1934. Built by Martin-Baker Aircraft Ltd. and first flown at Heston in September 1935, piloted by Captain V.H. Baker. Registration G-ADMV. Development also financed by Major Coates. Rotor diameter 32 ft 5¾ in (9.9 m).

A.R.III Gyroplane Mk.II. (Prototype) One 90-hp Pobjoy S Niagara III. After a landing accident at Farnborough while being flown by A.E. Clouston, G-ADMV was rebuilt by Martin-Baker with minor modifications as Mk.II. First flown 1937. Rotor diameter 32 ft 5¾ in–33 ft (9.9–10.06 m); length 18 ft ½ in (5.49 m); empty weight 640 lb (290 kg); maximum take-off weight 890 lb (403 kg); maximum speed 115–120 mph (185–193 km/h). A.R.III was damaged three times while under test at RAE—at least one of these accidents being due to ground resonance. After the last accident on March 22, 1938, the aircraft was fitted (in March 1939) with a new landing gear which, however, proved unsatisfactory. Another landing gear was designed and built by Dowty and had been fitted by January 1940. Following further modifications, A.R.III was flown again by Clouston on April 25, 1940, but further trials were suspended at the end of the month when RAE work on rotary

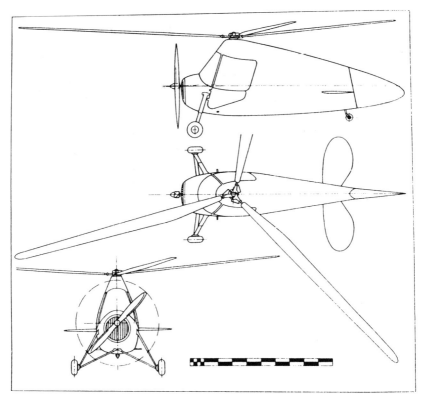

Hafner AR.IV.

wings ceased. A.R.III was sold to the Air Ministry (serialed DG670) in April 1941. It remained at RAE until struck off charge on April 11, 1942, after an accident.

A.R.IV Gyroplane. (Under construction) One 90-hp Pobjoy Niagara III or 125-hp Niagara IV. Two-seat side-by-side cabin gyroplane. Variable-incidence tailplane. Three-blade cantilever rotor with flapping blades. Designed in 1938 to Specification S.29/37 when Hafner collaborated with Pobjoy Airmotors and Aircraft Ltd. at Rochester. Two or three reported ordered from Short Brothers in 1939. Under construction at Rochester but not completed. Projected price £1,200 (then $5,300). Rotor diameter 32 ft 2¼ in (9.81 m); length 19 ft 3 in (5.86 m); tare weight 847 lb (384 kg); gross weight 1,330 lb (603 kg); maximum speed 115 mph (185 km/h).

A.R.Vg Gyroplane. (Under construction) One 210-hp de Havilland Gipsy Six II. Three-seat. Pilot's open cockpit; two-passenger cabin. Variable-incidence tailplane. Three-blade rotor with flapping blades. A 1937 project for fleet spotter and night shadower for Fleet Air Arm to Specification S.22/38. Two prototypes ordered from Short Brothers in January 1940. Construction started but ceased in May 1940. Serials V8906, V8909. Rotor diameter 49 ft 2½ in (15 m); gross weight 3,500 lb (1587 kg).

A.R.Vn Gyroplane. (Design study) One 350-hp Pobjoy Nile. Alternative engine installation to A.R.Vg.

P.D.6 Helicopter. (Under construction) One 90-hp Pobjoy Niagara III or 125-hp Niagara IV. Single-seat with airfoil fuselage for torque reaction. Three-blade steel rotor. Designed in 1938. One (EA No. 115) ordered under contract 972103/38 to Specification A.10/39 from Short Brothers. Under construction at Rochester in 1939/40 but not completed. Serial T3005. Rotor diameter about 30 ft. (9.14 m); maximum speed 150 mph (240 km/h) (est.); rate of climb: 1500 ft/min (7.6 m/s) (est.); gross weight 1000 lb (454 kg).

P.D.7 Helicopter. (Design study) One 400-hp Pobjoy Nile. Two-seat naval reconnaissance amphibian with airfoil fuselage for torque reaction. Three-blade steel rotor. Armed with one movable Oerlikon cannon. 1938 project. Rotor diameter 52 ft 2 in (15.9 m); maximum speed 210 mph (338 km/h) (est.).

Weir Autogiros and Helicopters

(Prototypes built and design studies by G. & J. Weir Ltd. and, from 1943, by the Cierva Autogiro Co. Ltd.)

Weir C.28, W.1. (Prototype) One 40-hp Douglas Dryad. Built by G. & J. Weir Ltd. at Cathcart, near Glasglow, to the design of Cierva and F.L. Hodgess. Experimental single-seat Autogiro with direct-control two-blade 28 ft (8.53 m) rotor. First flown, at Hanworth by Cierva, in May 1933.

Weir W.2. (Prototype) One 45-hp Weir flat-twin. Weir-built development of W.1 to the design of F.L. Hodgess. Direct-control two-blade 28 ft (8.53 m) rotor. Single-seat. Tried later with Autodynamic head. First flown, by Alan Marsh at Hanworth, in June 1934. Markings: W-2.

Weir W.3. (Prototype) One 55-hp Weir Pixie. Weir-built Autogiro to the design of C.G. Pullin. Two-blade jump take-off rotor. Single-seat. A 28 ft (8.53 m) rotor mounted on pylon of struts. First flown, by Alan Marsh at Abbotsinch, on July 9, 1936. Publicly demonstrated on Hounslow Heath on July 23, 1936. Markings: W-3.

Weir W.4. (Prototype) One Weir 55-hp Pixie. Weir-built Autogiro (1937) to the design of C.G. Pullin. Two-blade Autodynamic jump take-off rotor. 28 ft (8.53 m) rotor mounted on single streamlined pylon. Device for manually spilling rotor lift on landing. Single-seat. Wrecked on ground before it was flown. Markings: W-4.

Weir W.5. (Prototype) One 55-hp Weir Pixie. Weir-built side-by-side twin-rotor single-seat helicopter. Designed by C.G. Pullin. Two-blade 15 ft (4.6 m) rotors on outriggers. First flown, by Raymond A. Pullin at Dalrymple, on June 7, 1938.

Weir W.6. (Prototype) One 205-hp de Havilland Gipsy Six II. Weir-built side-by-side twin-rotor open cockpit tandem two-seat helicopter. Designed by C.G. Pullin to Specification W.28/38 of March 6, 1939. Three-blade 25 ft (7.6 m) rotors on outriggers. First flown by Raymond Pullin, at Thornliebank, on October 20, 1939. (Serial R5269.) Development stopped July 1940. A second W.6 (Serial Z2130) may have been ordered by the Ministry of Aircraft Production in 1940.

Weir W.7. (Design study) One 600-hp Rolls-Royce Kestrel. Weir helicopter proposal (1940). Side-by-side feathering rotors mounted on folding fixed lifting surfaces. Fleet spotter for Fleet Air Arm to Specification S.22/38.

Weir W.8. (Design study) One 205-hp de Havilland Gipsy Queen II. Weir helicopter proposed (1943). Single 40 ft (2.2 m) rotor with tip jets supplied by engine-driven Rolls-Royce Vulture supercharger plus heat exchanger using engine exhaust heat. Single-seat.

Cierva W.9. (Prototype) One 210-hp de Havilland Gipsy Queen II. Cierva-built at Thames Ditton, Middlesex, for Ministry of Aircraft Production to Specification E.16/43. Cabin side-by-side two-seat helicopter with single three-blade 36 ft (10.97 m) rotor and anti-torque jet. First tested in October 1944 with upswept tail pipe and faired fuselage. Manual tilting hub found to be impractical. Wrecked ground running. (Serial: PX203.)

Cierva W.9. (Prototype) One 210-hp de Havilland Gipsy Queen II. Rebuilt and lightened version. Fully powered controls for tilting hub. Tested by Alan Marsh in June 1945 at Henley-on-Thames. (Serial: PX203.)

Cierva W.9A. (Prototype) One 210-hp de Havilland Gipsy Queen II. Modified version of same basic design with collective pitch and combined cyclic control and tilting hub. Straight tailpipe and unfaired fuselage. Yaw control by variable-pitch fan instead of by baffles. Tested by Alan Marsh, at Eastleigh, early 1946. (Serial: PX203.)

Cierva W.9B. (Prototype) One 210-hp de Havilland Gipsy Queen II. Later version of W.9A (1947) with vertical tail surface added. Later had dual controls added. (Serial: PX203.)

Cierva W.10, Air Horse. (Design study) One 1,600-hp Rolls-Royce Merlin 32. Cropsprayer proposal for Pest Control Ltd. Three 46 ft (14 m) three-blade rotors. Gross weight: 15,000 lb (6,800 kg).

Cierva W.11, Air Horse. (Prototype) One 1,620-hp Rolls-Royce Merlin 24. Ciervabuilt at Eastleigh. Two prototypes of 24-passenger transport helicopter built for Ministry of Supply to Specification E.19/46. Three 47 ft (14.32 m) three-blade rotors. Gross weight: 17,500 lb (7,937 kg). First flown, by Alan Marsh, at Eastleigh, on December 8, 1948. Demonstrated at the S.B.A.C. Show at Farnborough in September 1949. The first prototype (VZ724) crashed at Eastleigh on June 13, 1950, having flown a total of 69 hours. Alan Marsh, F.J. Cable and J. Unsworth were killed. Serials and registrations: VZ724, WA555, G-ALCV, G-AKTV.

Cierva W.11T. (Design study) Two 1,620-hp Rolls-Royce Merlin 502. 1948 proposal to Ministry of Supply for twin-engine development of W.11 to Specification E.10/48. Three 54 ft (16.46 m) three-blade rotors. Gross weight: 25,000 lb (11,340 kg).

Cierva W.12. (Design study) Two 475-hp Armstrong Siddeley Cheetah, or two 500-hp Alvis Leonides. 1948 proposal for transport helicopter with three three-blade rotors. 12/14 passengers. Gross weight: 10,000 lb (4,536 kg).

Cierva W.13. This designation was not used.

Cierva W.14, Skeeter 1. (Prototype) One 106-hp Jamieson F.F.1. Cierva-built at Eastleigh. Cabin side-by-side two-seat helicopter. Single 29 ft 5 in (8.97 m) three-blade rotor and tail rotor. Prototype with welded-tubular framework fuselage and composite metal and wood rotor blades. First flown, by Alan Marsh, at Eastleigh, on October 8, 1948. (Registration: G-AJCJ.)

Cierva W.14, Skeeter 2. (Prototype) One 142-hp de Havilland Gipsy Major 10. Second prototype built as private venture with redesigned stressed-skin metal fuselage and metal tail rotor. Single 32 ft (9.75 m) three-blade rotor. First flown, by Alan Marsh, on October 20, 1949. Broken up during ground running: ground resonance. Target production price: £3,000 (then $11,000). (Registration: G-ALUE.)

Cierva W.14, Skeeter 3. (Prototype) One 150-hp de Havilland Gipsy Major 8. Development taken over by Saunders-Roe Limited. Two military aircraft to Specification A.13/49 ordered (1950) by Ministry of Supply (Serials: WF112, WF113.)

Cierva W.14, Skeeter 3B. (Prototype) One 180-hp Blackburn Bombadier 702. Converted Mk.3s. Development taken over by Saunders-Roe (1951). Ordered by Ministry of Supply to Specification A.13/49. (Serials: WF112, WF113.)

Saunders-Roe took over the Cierva Autogiro Co. Ltd. on January 22, 1951, and continued development of the Skeeter, which was later put into production. Some further development work was also undertaken on the W.11.

Appendix 6

Central Landing Establishment and Airborne Forces Experimental Establishment Rotary-Wing Parachute/Gliders

Work on Rotachutes started late in 1940 at Ringway, Manchester, in the hands of A.R.III Construction (Hafner Gyroplane) Co. This was taken over by Central Landing Establishment, at Ringway, in December 1941. In July 1942, the Establishment moved to Sherburn-in-Elmet. Later still, it became Airborne Forces Experimental Establishment, finally at Beaulieu. Most of the flying of these rotary-wing gliders was undertaken by Flight Lieutenant (later Squadron Leader) Ian Little.

Rotachute Mk.I. Single-seat. Tail of rubberized fabric, its shape maintained by ram air pressure. Two-blade rotor of 15 ft (4.5 m) diameter. Tare weight: 38 lb (17.25 kg). Intended to carry one Sten or Bren gun and 300 rounds of ammunition. First flown at Ringway, towed by a car on February 10, 1942. Skid landing gear. Aircraft was directionally unstable. Designed rate of vertical descent about 20 ft/sec (6.1 m/s). Minimum sinking speed in a glide 8 ft/sec (2.4 m/s).

Rotachute Mk.II. Single-seat. Semi-rigid tail lengthened by 50 percent. Skid and wheels landing gear. Two-blade rotor of 15 ft (4.5 m) diameter. First flown May 29, 1942.

Rotachute Mk.III. Single-seat. Rigid tail. Skid and wheels landing gear. Two-blade rotor of 15 ft (4.5 m) diameter. First flown June 2, 1942.

Rotachute Mk.IV. Specification E.11/42. Single-seat. Rigid tail. Skid and wheels landing gear. Two-blade rotor of 15 ft (4.5 m) diameter. Tare weight: 85 lb (38.5 kg); gross weight 285 lb (130 kg). Twin endplate fins on tailplane. Instrument panel. First flown April 29, 1943.

The Rotachutes were developed by Raoul Hafner, Dr. J.A.J. Bennett, and O.L.L. Fitzwilliams. All marks had flapping blades but one was flown experimentally with a seesaw rotor (on September 21, 1942). James Bennett visited the United States in October 1942 and cooperated with the Autogiro Company of America (who were working with the G. & A. Aircraft Company, which by then had taken over the activities of the former Pitcairn Autogiro Company) in the development of a Rotachute, which subsequently crashed under test. Six of the United Kingdom manufactured Rotachutes were later sent to the United States, possibly leading to the General Electric Gyro-glider and later Bensen types (see Chapter 12).

Rotabuggy: Design study for Rotachute for Blitz Buggy: April 1942. Two-blade 44 ft (13.4 m) rotor. Gross weight: 2,700 lb (1,225 kg).

Rotatank: Valentine tank design study, November 1942.

Malcolm Rotaplane or Rotabuggy: Specification E.10/42. Two-seat Army vehicle with wood and fabric tail and initially a two-blade seesaw rotor of 46 ft 8 in (14.22 m) diameter. This was later replaced by a 48 ft (14.6 m) rotor with two separate blades with flapping and drag hinges. Cable and pulley rotor starting. First flown November 27, 1943, at Sherburn-in-Elmet. Modified to increase fin area. Made about sixty low-level short flights and one longer flight to 1,700 ft (518 m) on September 11, 1944.

Rotacub: Proposal for a powered Rotachute which could be launched from a long-range fixed-wing aircraft. It would be capable of then landing in enemy territory and taking off again so as to return to its "mother aircraft" in flight.

Cierva Type Numbers

Type Number	Other Designation	Designer and/or Manufacturer	Remarks
C.1	Autogiro No. 1	Cierva/Diaz workshop	Did not fly. Possibly based on Deperdussin.
C.2	Autogiro No. 2	Cierva/Diaz workshop	Did not fly. Possibly based on Spanish biplane.
C.3	Autogiro No. 3	Cierva/Diaz workshop	Did not fly. Possibly based on Sommer Type E.
C.4	Autogiro No. 4	Cierva/Diaz workshop	First Autogiro to fly. Possibly based on C.3.
C.5	—	Cierva/Industrial College	Prototype only. Possibly based on C.2.
C.6	—	Military Aircraft Works	Based on Avro 504.
C.6bis	C.6A	Military Aircraft Works	Based on Avro 504. First Autogiro demonstrated in England.
C.6C	Avro 574, 3/26	Avro	First Autogiro built in England.
C.6D	Avro 575, 3/26	Avro	First Autogiro to carry a passenger.
C.7	Loring C. VII	Loring	Prototype only.
G.8R	Avro 587	Avro	Converted from C.6D.
C.8V	Avro 586	Avro	Development Autogiro.
C.8L-I	Avro 611, 11/26	Avro	Prototype for Air Ministry.
C.8L-II	Avro 617	Avro	Ordered by James Weir.
C.8L-III	Avro 617	Avro	For Italian government.
C.8 Mk.IV	C.8W	Avro	First Autogiro demonstrated in United States
C.9	Avro 576 4/26 (See note 9)	Avro	Prototype only.
C.10	Parnall 4/26	Parnall	Prototype only. Did not fly.

C.11	Parnall Gyroplane	Parnall	Prototype only.
C.12	Loring C.XII	Loring	Last Spanish-built Autogiro. Prototype only.
C.13	Short 31/26	Short	Design study—flying boat Autogiro.
C.14	—	—	Design study.
C.15	—	—	Design study.
C.16	—	—	Design study.
C.17 Mk.I	Avro 612	Avro	Prototype only.
C.17 Mk.II	Avro 620, Hydrogiro	Avro	Prototype only. Converted to first Autogiro seaplane.
C.18	—	Weymann-Lepère	First Autogiro built in France.
C.19 Mk.I	—	Cierva/Avro	First production Autogiro.
C.19 MkII	—	Cierva/Avro	Production Autogiros.
C.19 MkIIA	—	Cierva/Avro	Special demonstration model.
C.19 Mk.III	—	Cierva/Avro	Production Autogiros.
C.19 Mk.IV	—	Cierva/Avro	First production Autogiros with cantilever rotor and engine spin-up drive.
C.19 Mk.IVP	—	Cierva/Avro	Preproduction Autogiros.
C.19 Mk.V	—	Cierva/Avro	Experimental direct control Autogiro.
C.20	—	Cierva	Design study for Air Ministry.
C.21	—	Cierva	Design study of pusher Autogiro.
C.22	—	Cierva	Design study for Air Ministry.
C.23	—	Cierva	Design study.
C.24	—	de Havilland	Prototype only.
C.25	Comper G.31/1	Comper	Prototype only.
C.26	—	Cierva	Design study of Autogiro-helicopter.
C.27	Lepère C.L.10	Lioré-et-Olivier	Built in France.
C.28	W.1	Weir	Prototype only.
C.29	—	Westland	Did not fly.
C.30	—	National Flying Services	Prototype of first production direct-control Autogiro.
C.30P	Avro 671	Avro	Preproduction Autogiros.

C.30P Mk.II		Airwork	Preproduction Autogiro.
C.30A	Avro 671, Rota, 16/35,2/36	Avro	First production direct-control Autogiro.
C.30 Mk.II	—	Avro	Jump take-off development Autogiro.
C.30 Mk.III	—	Cierva	Jump take-off development Autogiro.
C.30 Mk.IV	—	Cierva	Jump take-off development Autogiro.
C.30 Mk.V	—	Cierva	Jump take-off development Autogiro.
C.31	—	Cierva	Design study.
C.32	—	Cierva	Design study.
C.33	Avro 665	Avro	Design study. Based on Avro Commodore.
C.34	—	Lioré-et-Olivier	Prototype only.
C.35	—	Cierva	Design study.
C.36	—	Cierva	Design study.
C.37	Avro 668	Avro	Design study of twin-engine Autogiro.
C.38	—	Cierva	Design study.
C.39	S.22/38	Cierva	Design study.
C.40	43/36	British Aircraft, Oddie, Bradbury, and Cull	Last British production Autogiro.
C.41	S.22/38	Cierva	Design study.

Pitcairn Type Numbers

Airplanes, Autogiros, and helicopters built and design studies undertaken from 1923 by the Pitcairn Aircraft Company, the Pitcairn Autogiro Company, the Autogiro Company of America, the Pitcairn-Larsen Autogiro Company, the AGA Aviation Corporation, G. & A. Aircraft Inc., and the Firestone Tire and Rubber Company. Chief designers were Agnew E. Larsen, Walter C. Clayton, R.B.C. Noorduyn, and Paul H. Stanley. Firestone withdrew from rotary-wing activity in 1947.

PA-1	Fleetwing		1925
PA-2	Arrow		1926
PA-3	Orowing		1926
PA-4	Fleetwing 2		1927
PA-5	Mailwing	Fixed-wing aircraft	1927
PA-6	Super Mailwing		1928
PA-7	Super Mailwing		1929
PA-8	Super Mailwing		1930
9			
10			
11	These numbers may have been reserved to cover		
12	PCA-1, PCA-1A, PCA-1B, PCA-2, XOP-1, PAA-2 and PAA-1.		
13			
14			
15			
PA-16	Autogiro design study by Heraclio Alfaro		1931
PA-17	Autogiro design study		1931
PA-18	Autogiro, development of PA-17		1932
PA-19	Autogiro, 4–5-seat cabin		1932
PA-20	Autogiro, development of PAA-1		1932
PA-21	Autogiro, development of PCA-2		1932
PA-22	Autogiro experimental prototype		1932
PA-23	Autogiro, design study development of PA-19		1933
PA-24	Autogiro, development of PAA-1		1933
PA-25	Autogiro design study		1933
PA-26	Autogiro design study: six-seat scaled-up PA-19		1933
PA-27	Autogiro design studies		1933
PA-28	Autogiro design studies		1933
PA-29	Autogiro design study: four-seat direct-control		1933

PA-30	Autogiro design study: long fuselage version of PA-29	1933
PA-31	Autogiro design study: direct-control ambulance development of PA-23	1934
PA-32	Autogiro design study	1934
PA-33	Autogiro, YG-2 for USAAC	1935
PA-34	Autogiro, XOP-2 for USN	1936
AC-35	Autogiro for Bureau of Air Commerce	1936
PA-36	Autogiro experimental prototype	1937
PA-37	Autogiro design study	1939
PA-38	Autogiro design study for USAAC	1940
PA-39	Autogiro for RAF	1941
PA-40	Fixed-wing military trainer design study based on PA-7	1940
PA-41	Autogiro design study	1941
PA-42	Autogiro design study: development of PA-39	1941
PA-43	Autogiro design study: AU-1 for USAAF	1942
PA-44	Autogiro, XO-61 for USAAF	1941
GA-45	Helicopter: civil version of XR-9B (NX58457)	1946

Autogiro Development Dates and Times

Dates in parentheses indicate that the aircraft was not flown.

Type	Start	First Flight	Certification or First Delivery	Development Time to First Delivery (Months)	Number Built
Spain					
C.1	early 1920	(Oct.'20)	—	—	1
C.2	Mar.'21	(Jan.'23)	—	—	1 + (4)
C.3	Apr.'21	(Jun.'21)	—	—	1 + (9)
C.4	Mar.'22	(Jun.'22)	—	—	1 + (14)
C.4 (Modified)	—	Jan. 17,'23	—	—	(1)
C.5	Feb.'23	Apr.'23	—	—	1
C.6	late 1923	early Feb.'24	—	—	1
C.6A	early 1925	Jun. 6 or 8,'25	—	—	1
C.7 (C.VII)	mid-1926	Nov. 15,'26	—	—	1
C.7. (Modified)	Feb.'27	May 19,'27	—	—	(1)
C.12 (C.XII)	mid-1928	May 23,'29	—	—	1
C.12 (Modified)	Jan.'29	Jun.'29	Jul. 11,'29	6	(1)
France					
C.18	early 1929	Aug. 12,'29	Sep.'29	9	1
CTW.200	Jun.'30	Mar.'31	—	11	1
CTW.201	Jun.'30	Apr.'31	—	—	1
CTW.210	Feb. 7,'31	May'32	—	—	1
C.27, C.L.10	Apr.'32	Nov. 24,'32	—	7	2
C.L.10B	early 1934	1935	—	—	(1)
LeO C.30	Feb.'35	Oct.'35	Jan.'37	22	about 70
LeO C.301	—	Apr.'38	mid-1940	—	5
LeO C.302	1938	1938	—	—	(3)
C.34	1936	Mar.'39	—	—	1

Germany

C.19	Dec.'31	Jun.'32	—	—	1
C.30	1934	1935	—	—	30
Fl 184		1936	—	—	1
Fw 186	1937	1938	—	—	1

Japan

Ka-1	Jun.'41	Jun.'43	—	—	2
Ka-1A	Nov.'42	Jun. 27,'43	1943	—	35
Ka-1 KAI	1943	1943	—	—	(1)
Ka-2	1941	summer 1944	1944	—	60

United Kingdom

C.6C	Jan.'26	Jun. 19,'26	—	—	1
C.6D	Jan.'26	Jul. 29,'26	—	—	1
C.8V	spring 1926	summer 1926	Sep. 9,'27	17	1
C.8R	Feb.'27	about May'27	Sep. 9,'27	7	1 + (3)
C.8L-I	late 1925	Jul./Aug.'27	Sep. 30,'27	10	1
C.8L-II	late 1927	May'28	Jun. 21,'28	7	1
C.8L-III	early 1928	Sep.'28	Jan.'29	12	1
C.8W, C.8MIV	Aug.'28	Nov.'28	Dec. 18,'28	4	1
C.9	late 1926	Sep.'27	Jul.'28	20	1
C.10	late 1926	(Apr. 26,'28)	Apr.'28	16	1
C.11	mid-1927	Oct.'28	—	—	1 + (2)
C.17 Mk.I	1928	Oct. 23,'28	—	—	1
C.17 Mk.II	late 1928	early 1929	—	—	1
C.17 Hydrogiro	late 1929	Apr. 25,'30	—	—	(1)
C.19 Mk.I	late 1928	Jul.'29	Aug. 2,'29	10	3
C.19 Mk.II	Jul.'29	Aug.'29	Sep. 26,'29	2	3
C.19 Mk.IIA	Dec.'29	Jan.'30	Aug. 1,'30	8	1
C19 Mk.III	Late 1929	early Jul.'30	Sep. 10,'30	9	9
C.19 Mk.IV Prototype	Mar.'31	Jun.'31	—	—	1
C.19 Mk.IVP	mid-1931	Nov.'31	Mar. 22,'32	9	(4)
C.19 Mk.IV	mid-1931	May'32	May 24,'32	11	12 + (1)
C.19 Mk.V	Dec.'31	Mar 5,'32	—	—	(1)
C.24	early 1931	Sep.'31	Apr. 23,'32	15	1
C.25	Mar. 20,'31	Mar. 20,'32	—	—	1
C.L.20	Aug.'34	Feb. 4,'35	—	—	1
C.28,W.I	Aug.'32	May'33	—	—	1
W.2	Jul.'33	Jun.'34	—	—	(1)
W.3	Jun.'35	Jul. 9,'36	—	—	1
W.4	1936	(1937)	—	—	(1)
C.29	early 1933	(Dec. 11,'34)	—	—	1
C.30 Prototype	late 1932	Apr.'33	—	—	1
C.30P Mk.II	1933	mid Oct.'33	—	—	1
C.30P	spring 1933	Dec.'33	Dec. 21,'33	8	3
C.30A	Jan.'34	Jul.'34	Jul.'34	6	78
C.30 Mk.II	1935	Dec.'35	—	—	(1)
C.30 Mk.III	1935	Mar.'36	—	—	(1)
C.30 Mk.IV	1936	Dec.'36	—	—	(1)
C.30 Mk.V	1937	Jan. 23,'39	—	—	(1)
C.30J	Mar.'38	May 22,'38	—	—	(1)
C.40	Jul.'36	Feb. 25,'38	1939	20	7

United States

PCA-1	Apr.'29	about Oct. 8,'29 —		—	1
PCA-1A	mid-1929	late Oct.'29	—	—	1
PCA-1A (Modified)	late 1929	early Nov.'29	—	—	(1)
PCA-1B	Aug.'29	early Nov.'29	—	—	1
PCA-2 Prototype	late 1929	Mar.'30	—	—	1
PCA-2 Production	Mar.'30	Nov. 1,'30	Apr. 2,'31	4	21
XOP-1	1930	early 1931	Jun.'31	—	3
PCA-3	—	Aug.'31	Aug. 25,'31	—	2
K-2	late 1930	Apr. 24,'31	Jul. 17,'31	6	19
K-3	—	early 1932	Mar. 26,'32	—	5+(2)
K-4	—	Jun.'33	Dec. 27,'33	—	(2)
PCA-2-30	Jul. 17,'29	Aug. 18,'30	—	—	1
PAA-2	spring 1931	Feb. 11,'31	—	—	1
PAA-1	spring 1931	Mar.'31	Aug. 7,'31	4	17 + (1)
Buhl	Apr.'31	Dec. 15,'31	—	—	1
PA-18	—	Mar. 1,'32	Apr. 7,'32	—	19 or 23
PA-19	Feb.'32	Sep.'32	Jun. 23,'33	—	5
PA-20	—	Aug.'33	1933	—	2
PA-21	—	1932	—	—	(about 5?)
PA-22 (Roadable)	late 1932	spring 1933	—	—	1
PA-22 (Non-Roadable)	spring 1933	late 1933	—	—	(1)
PA-22 (Jump Take-off)	mid-1935	autumn 1935	—	—	(1)
PA-24	—	Aug.'33	May 19,'33	—	2
PA-33 (YG-2)	1935	1935	early 1936	—	(1)
PA-34 (XOP-2)	mid-1936	late 1936	1937	—	(1)
AC-35	late 1934	Mar. 26,'36	Oct. 26,'36	about 23	1
PA-36	May'37	Apr.'39	1941	—	2
PA-39	1939	mid-1941	late 1941	about 24	(7)
KD-1	early 1934	Dec. 9, '34	Jan. 1, '35	about 12	1
KD-1A	—	1937	Oct. 31,'37	—	1 or 2
KD-1B	—	1939	1939	—	1
YG-1	1934	1935	early 1936	—	1
YG-1A	1936	1936	Oct.'36	—	1
YG-1B	1937	1937	Dec.'37	—	7 + (1)
YG-1C	—	—	—	—	(1)
XR-2	—	1941	—	—	(1)
XG-1B	1941	1941	—	—	(1)
XR-3	1941	1941	—	—	(1)
XO-60/YO-60	1941	1942	1943	—	1 + 6
XO-61/YO-61	1941	1942	—	—	2

		Soviet Union			
KASKR-I	1929	(Sep. 1,'29)	—	—	1
KASKR-II	—	mid-1930	—	—	(1)
TsAGI 2-EA	late 1930	Nov. 17,'31	1933	about 18	1
A-4	early 1932	Nov. 6,'32	—	—	11
A-6	—	early 1933	—	—	3
A-7	1931	Sep. 20,'34	1936	about 60	7
A-8	early 1933	Jun. 29,'34	—	—	(2)
A-12	early 1935	May 10,'36	—	—	1
A-13	Aug.'35	Mar. 13,'36	—	—	(1)
A-14	1935	Sep. 13,'35	—	—	(1)
A-15	1935	(Apr.'37)	—	—	1
AK	1940	not completed	—	—	—

High Speed Autogiros

(Extract from Cierva CAC Report No. 56, April 9, 1934)

Continuing the policy which this company has followed in its technical development, it appears that now that all the secondary problems of the direct-control system seem to be satisfactorily solved, the time is ripe to take a definite step in one of the directions more promising for the utilization of the peculiar high speed-range qualities of the Autogiro.

If a machine with a top speed of the order of 200 mph could be produced that retains substantially the slow flying characteristics of our existing machines, there is no question that such a machine will have tremendous practical possibilities.

There are two problems present in the design of a high speed-range Autogiro. One is the cleaning up of the design so as to reduce the possible drag to a minimum figure which should be comparable to that of an equivalent high-speed airplane. The other is to design a rotor having a minimum solidity, allowing in consequence a large rotor disc area in comparison with the actual blade area.

The latest Autogiro, the C.30P, has a rotor whose solidity is unnecessarily small for the top speed of the machine, since the tip speed to forward speed ratio at top speed is between 2.5 and 3, while previous experiments have illustrated the fact that it could be as low as 1.7 or so, with advantage from the efficiency point of view and without appreciable vibration being developed.

This means that if the C.30 were clean enough or had power enough to have a top speed of the order of 160 mph, its rotor should be satisfactory without modification, assuming the weight of the machine unchanged, its low-speed characteristics should be approximately equivalent to the present.

The solidity of the C.30 rotor is approximately 0.047 and while extremely low it cannot be considered by any means as the lowest possible in practice. By building the blades in the metal type of construction which this Company, in conjunction with Messrs. G. and J. Weir, is developing at present, it is considered as perfectly feasible lowering solidity by some 20 percent if necessary. As the top speed depends on the loading per square foot of blade area while the slow-speed characteristics depend almost exclusively on the loading per square foot of disc area, it is easy to reach the conclusion that top speeds of the order of 200 mph could be obtained with rotors of solidities of some 0.038 and disc loadings of 2 to 2.1 lb/sq ft (9.7–10.2 kg/sq m) which is not more than the disc loading of some Autogiros which have proved very satisfactory on their slow speed characteristics. As the loading of C.30 is approximately 1.7 lb/sq ft (8.3 kg/sq m), it means that a loading of 2.1 lb/sq ft (10.2 kg/sq m) means an increase of only about 10 percent in the minimum horizontal speed, in the vertical speed of descent, and in the landing.

In order to increase somewhat the tip speed for a given blade loading it would be possible to decrease either the chord of the blade toward the tip or the thickness of the section, or both. Decrease of the chord will probably not contribute anything toward increased efficiency at high speed, but decrease in the relative thickness of the section probably would, considering in particular the very high relative air speeds which will be attained by the tip of the blade which advances, and so it is proposed to give the blades of the high speed-range machines taper in thickness toward the tip.

In order to obtain the lowest possible figure for a parasite drag, it will be advisable to use air-cooled inline or H engines, to retract the undercarriage during flight into the fuselage, to use a single-strut pylon of minimum section inside of which will be contained the mechanical transmission for the rotor starter and all the rotor controls, to design rotor hub and articulations with a minimum of frontal area, and to build cantilever tails with perfect streamlined attachments to the fuselage.

In view of the preceding considerations, the following preliminary specifications for two machines designated as C.31 and C.32 respectively are proposed.

C.31 Two-seat coupé machine.

One 385-hp sixteen-cylinder Napier Rapier IV. (Note—Gears must be altered to allow for maximum airscrew rpm of not less than 2,200).

Estimated empty weight 2,000 lb (907 kg), useful load 1,000 lb (454 kg), (one pilot, one passenger, 7 Imp gal (32 l) oil, 60 Imp gal (273 l) petrol, leaving 120 lb (54 kg) for disposal)

Parasite drag with undercarriage folded—estimated at equivalent of 75 lb (34 kg) at 100 mph (161 km/h) non-corrected for airscrew slipstream interference. Number of rotor blades—three; rotor diameter—42 ft (12.8 m); rotor rpm at top speed, at sea level =234; load/sq ft of disc area =2.15 lb (10.5 kg/sq m); peripheral rotor speed at sea level =515 ft/sec (157 m/s).

Estimated performance. Top speed at sea level 206 mph (332 km/h); minimum horizontal speed at sea level 22 mph (35 km/h); vertical speed of disc at about 10 mph (16 km/h) forward speed 15/17 ft/sec (4.6/5.2 m/s); landing when flattening out—about 10 percent faster than C.30; take-off run—about 20 percent longer than C.30; steep climb for slow forward speeds—about equivalent to C.30; rate of climb at about 100 mph (161 km/h) is 1,700 ft/min (8.64 m/s); practical ceiling 25,000 ft (7,620 m).

If a variable-pitch airscrew is incorporated, take-off could be made after a run from 10 percent to 20 percent shorter than that of C.30, and the climb at slow forward speeds would be about 75 percent better.

Maximum relative air speed at top speed, sea level, will attain about 0.75 speed of sound. No appreciable compressibility effects are anticipated.

At ceiling peripheral speed will increase to 0.65 to 0.7 of speed of sound, but forward speed will have diminished to about 200 ft/sec (136 mph or 219 km/h).

Compressibility effects should not be of any importance since speed of sound is not reached, and it is only the extreme tip of the blades that will have a small thickness ratio that will be affected and that only for a very short time per revolution.

C.32 Two-seat coupé machine.

One 200-hp de Havilland Gipsy Six. Empty weight 1,300 lb (590 kg); useful load 600 lb (272 kg). Rotor diameter 34 ft (10.36 m); rotor rpm top speed at sea level 270; load/sq ft disc area 2.06 lb (10.06 kg/sq m); rotor solidity 0.047.

Estimated parasite drag with undercarriage folded equivalent to 55 lb (25 kg) at 100 mph (161 km/h) non-corrected for airscrew slipstream interference.

Estimated performance. Top speed at sea level 180 mph (290 km/h); minimum horizontal speed 20 mph (32 km/h); vertical speed of disc at 10 mph (16 km/h) forward speed 14/16 ft/sec (4.3/4.9 m/s); landing about 8 percent faster than C.30; take-off run about 10 percent longer than C.30's; rate of climb at slow forward speed—same as C.30; rate of climb at about 90 mph (145 km/h) 1,200 ft/min (6.1 m/s); practical ceiling =16,000 ft (4,880 m).

By using a variable-pitch airscrew take-off and the steep climb at slow forward speeds could be considerably increased.

Autogyro Production List

(In sequence used in text)

Type Number	Constructor's Number	Markings	Remarks
Cierva			
(Built by Avro unless otherwise stated)			
C.1			Built in Diaz workshop at Getafe. Completed October 1920. Did not fly. Possibly employed fuselage of 1911 Deperdussin monoplane.
C.2			Built in Cierva/Diaz workshop. Completed early 1922. Did not fly. Possibly employed fuselage of biplane built by Military Aircraft Works.
C.3			Built in Cierva/Diaz workshop. Completed June 1921. Did not fly. Employed fuselage of 1911/12 Sommer Type E monoplane.
C.4			Built in Cierva/Diaz workshop. First flight Getafe, January 17, 1923. Possibly employed fuselage of C.3.
C.5		C.5	Built in Cierva/Diaz workshop. First flight Cuatro Vientos, spring 1923. Employed C.2 fuselage.
C.6			Built by Military Aircraft Works. First flight Cuatro Vientos February 1924. Employed Avro 504K fuselage, tail, landing gear, and engine.
C.6bis, C.6A		C.6A	Built by Military Aircraft Works. First flight Cuatro Vientos, June 1925. Employed Avro 504K fuselage, tail, landing gear, and engine.
C.6C		J8068	First flight Hamble, June 19, 1926. Crashed Hamble, February 7, 1927.
C.6D	C/n 5114	G-EBTW	First flight Hamble, July 29, 1926. Rebuilt 1927 as C.8R.
C.7, C.VII			Built by Loring. First flight Cuatro Vientos November 15, 1926. Employed Loring T-1 fuselage.
C.8V	C/n 5113	G-EBTX	First flight summer 1926. Formerly Avro 552A G-EAPR. Reg. September 9, 1927, reconverted to Avro 552A in 1930 as G-ABGO.

C.8R	C/n 5114	G-EBTW	First flight about May 1927. Formerly C.6D. Reg. September 9, 1927. Scrapped 1929.
C.8L-I		J8930	First flight mid-September 1927. To RAE September 30, 1927. Written-off at Andover mid-1930.
C.8L-II		G-EBYY	First flight May 1928. Reg. to J.G. Weir, June 21, 1928. Sold in France, April 1930. Preserved in the Musée de l'Air et de l'Espace, Paris.
C.8L-III			For Italian government. First flight September 1928.
C.8 Mk.IV C.8W		NC418	First flight in November 1928. To H. Pitcairn. First flight in U.S., December 19, 1928. Flown in a variety of configurations. Preserved in Smithsonian Institution, Washington, D.C.
C.9		J8931	First flight Hamble, September 1927. Fitted with half-length untapered blades, September 1928. To Science Museum, London, January 1930.
C.10	C/n P.1/5280 (unconfirmed)	J9038	Built by Parnall. Wrecked on first flight attempt April 26, 1928 at Yate. Another unsuccessful attempt at Andover, November 5, 1928.
C.11	C/n P.1/5281	G-EBQG	Built by Parnall. Wrecked on first flight attempt February 1928. Rebuilt. First flight October 1928. Dismantled 1931.
C.12, C.XII			Built by Loring. First flight Cuatro Vientos, May 23, 1929. Flown in several different configurations.
C.17 Mk.I		G-AABP	First flight October 23, 1928. Dismantled Hamble, December 1931.
C.17 Mk.II	C/n 5129	G-AAGJ	First flight April/early May 1929. Reg. April 19, 1929. Converted to Hydrogiro, spring 1930.
C.17 (Hydrogiro)	C/n 5129		C.17 Mk.II converted. First flight April 25, 1930. Converted to Avro Avian II G-ADEO in 1935.
C.18	C/n 18	G-AAIH	Built by Weymann-Lepére. Completed June 1929. First flight Villacoublay, August 12, 1929. Flown in U.S., September 1929.
CTW.200	C/n 01		Built by Weymann-Lepére. First flight March 1931.
CTW.201	C/n 1	F-ALLA	Built by Weymann-Lepére. First flight April 1931.
CTW.210		F-ALQX	Built by Weymann. First flight May 1931.
C.19 Mk.I	C/n 5130	G-AAGK	First flight July 1929. C of A August 2, 1929. Sold abroad January 1930.
C.19 Mk.I	C/n 5131	G-AAGL	C of A August 1929. Crashed Haldon, September 21, 1929.
C.19 Mk.I	C/n 5132	G-AAHM	Exhibited at Olympia, July 1929. Converted to C.19 Mk.IV.

C.19 Mk.II	C/n 5133	G-AAKY	Taken to U.S., August 1929. Sold to H. Pitcairn December 1929. Believe re-reg. NC311V.
C.19 Mk.II	C/n 5134	G-AAKZ	C of A September 26, 1929. Crashed Sherburn-in-Elmet, May 21, 1931.
C.19 Mk.II	C/n 5135	G-AALA	C of A December 24, 1929. Converted to C.19 Mk.III. Crashed May 1932.
C.19 Mk.IIA	C/n 5136	G-AAUA	First flight January 1930. C of A August 1, 1930. Sold abroad March 1931, to Spain.
C.19 Mk.III	C/n 5137	G-AAYN	First flight July 1930. Sold abroad October 1930. To U.S. as X3Y.
C.19 Mk.III	C/n 5138	G-AAYO	C of A September 10, 1930. On RAF charge November 6, 1930, as K1696. Struck off February 21, 1931.
C.19 Mk.III	C/n 5139	G-AAYP	C of A September 10, 1930. Converted to C.19 Mk.IV. Scrapped 1932.
C.19 Mk.III	C/n 5140	G-ABCK	C of A October 14, 1930. To New Zealand December 1930 as ZK-ACL. Crashed at Oamaru, May 1931 and wreck shipped back to United Kingdom.
C.19 Mk.III	C/n 5141	G-ABCL	C of A October 20, 1930. Crashed November 29, 1930.
C.19 Mk.III	C/n 5142	G-ABCM	C of A December 23, 1930. Delivered Hamble-Farnborough, January 5, 1931. RAF charge January 16, 1931 as K1948. Struck off March 14, 1934.
C.19 Mk.III	C/n 5143	G-ABFZ	C of A March 24, 1931. Converted to C.19 Mk.IVP. Scrapped 1937.
C.19 Mk.III	C/n 5144	G-ABGB	C of A April 2, 1931. Converted to C.19 Mk.IVP.
C.19 Mk.III	C/n 5145	G-ABGA	C of A March 26, 1931. Converted to C.19 Mk.IVP. Withdrawn from use, 1931.
C.19 Mk.IV	C/n 5132	G-AAHM	First flight June 1931. C of A March 22, 1932. Converted from C.19 Mk.I. Crashed Wembley Stadium, London, September 29, 1932.
C.19 MK.IVP	C/n 5143	G-ABFZ	C of A April 1932. Converted from C.19 Mk.III. Scrapped 1937.
C.19 Mk.IVP	C/n 5144	G-ABGB	To South Africa December 1933. Converted from C.19 Mk.III. Crashed Cape Town, February 17.
C.19 Mk.IVP	C/n 5145	G-ABGA	Withdrawn December 1931. Converted from C.19 Mk.III
C.19 Mk.IV	C/n 5139	G-AAYP	Converted from C.19 Mk.III.
C.19 Mk.IV	C/n 5148	G-ABUC	C of A May 24, 1932. To Singapore, November 1936, as VR-SAR.
C.19 Mk.IV	C/n 5149	G-ABUD	C of A May 26, 1932. Crashed March 1933. Repaired.
C.19 Mk.IV	C/n 5150	G-ABUE	C of A May 26, 1932. To Germany, May 1932. Registered D-EKOT.

C.19 Mk.IV	C/n 5151	G-ABUF	C of A June 25, 1932. Scrapped May 1935.
C.19 Mk. IV	C/n 5152	G-ABUG	C of A June 16, 1932. To Sweden, December 1935, as SE-ADU.
C.19 Mk.IV	C/n 5153	G-ABUH	C of A July 12, 1932. To Australia, December 1934, as VH-USO. Crashed June 15, 1935.
C.19 Mk.IV	C/n 5154	G-ABXD	C of A July 6, 1932. To Japan, August 1932. Evaluated by Japanese navy.
C.19 Mk.IV	C/n 5155	G-ABXE	C of A August 6, 1932. To Japan, August 1932. Evaluated by Japanese navy.
C.19 Mk.IV	C/n 5156	G-ABXF	C of A August 25, 1932. To Japan, August 1932, as J-BAYA. Operated by Asahi Shimbun.
C.19 Mk.IV	C/n 5157	G-ABXG	C of A September 15, 1932. Crashed Hanworth, April 25, 1937.
C.19 Mk.IV	C/n 5158	G-ABXH	C of A October 4, 1932. To Spain, December 1932, as EC-W13. Re-reg. EC-ATT/EC-CAB/EC-AIM.
C.19 Mk.IV	C/n 5159	G-ABXI	C of A October 4, 1932. To Spanish air force, December 1932, as 49-1.

Focke-Wulf

C.19 Mk.IV	C/n 122	D-2300	Believed one aircraft only "Don Quichote." First flight June 1932. Reg. August 1932. Evaluated by DVL. Crashed Berlin, 1934.

Pitcairn

PCA-1	C/n A-1	X94N	First flight October 1929. Crashed same month; not repaired. Burned at Bryn Athyn.
PCA-1A	C/n A-2	X95N	First flight late October 1929. Now stored at NASM, Silver Hill.
PCA-1B	C/n A-3	X96N NC96N	First flight early November 1929.
PCA-2	C/n B-4	X760W NC760W	First flight March 1930. Prototype.
PCA-2	C/n B-5	NR784W NC784W	First flight November 1, 1930. ATC No. 410 awarded on April 2, 1931.
PCA-2	C/n B-6	NR799W NC799W	Detroit News. Now in Ford Museum at Dearborn (stored).
PCA-2	C/n B-7	NC10761	C.E. Haines. Earl T. Vance. Crashed July 26, 1931.
PCA-2	C/n B-8	NC26 NC2624	Standard Oil, later Sealed Power Corp. Autogiro Sales and Industrial Service. Fred W. Soule. Connecticut Aero Historical Assn. Canadian National Collection.
PCA-2	C/n B-9	NC10768	Horizon Company. Destroyed by fire 1934.
PCA-2	C/n B-12	NC10780	Amelia Earhart, Beech-Nut Packing, S.S. Pike, Jr. Gyro Ads Inc.

PCA-2	C/n B-13	NC10781	J.M. Miller. Giroflyers Ltd. J.R. Hopkins. Giro Associates.
PCA-2	C/n B-14	NC10785	Standard Oil of Ohio.
PCA-2	C/n B-15	NC10786 CF-ARO	Fairchild Aircraft of Canada. H.M. Pasmore.
PCA-2	C/n B-16	NC10787	Walter Hoffman. Santa Barbara Airports. Destroyed by fire May 3, 1932.
PCA-2	C/n B-22	NC10788	Beech-Nut Packing. Sank in Lake Michigan, September 5, 1933.
PCA-2	C/n B-23	NC10789	Curtiss Wright, Morgan Oil, Coca Cola, Georgia School of Technology.
PCA-2	C/n B-24	NC10790	Tri-State Airways, Gilbert Flying Service. F. Soule, Giro Associates.
PCA-2	C/n B-25	NC10791 NACA-44	NACA
PCA-2	C/n B-26	NC11608	Puget Sound Airways. R.H. Bailey.
PCA-2	C/n B-27	NC11609	Champion Spark Plug. Preserved by A.K. Miller.
PCA-2	C/n B-28	NC11610	Johnson & Johnson Co. Pitcairn Aircraft.
PCA-2	C/n B-29	NC11611	R.W. Johnson.
PCA-2	C/n B-31	NC11613	Pitcairn Aircraft.
PCA-3	C/n E-42	NC11671	United Airports. First flight August 1931. Destroyed by fire September 1931.
PCA-3	C/n E-45	NC11612	United Airports. Jesse K. Fenno. U.S. Dept. of Agriculture.
XOP-1	C/n B-10	8850	First flight June 1931. U.S. Navy.
XOP-1	C/n B-43	8976	First flight September 1931. U.S. Navy.
XOP-1	C/n B-44	8977	First flight September 1931. U.S. Navy.
PAA-2	C/n D-17	X10756	Prototype. First flight February 1931.
PAA-1	C/n F-11	X10770	Prototype. First flight March 1931. ATC 433 awarded August 7, 1931.
PAA-1	C/n F-18	X10771 NC10771	Pitcairn Aircraft. Converted to PA-20 C/n F-18. Swivel landing gear trial installation.
PAA-1	C/n F-19	NC10773	Pitcairn Aviation. Rising Sun Airport
PAA-1	C/n F-20	NC10772	No record.
PAA-1	C/n F-21	NC10769	Autogiro Specialities Company. First flight March 1931.
PAA-1	C/n F-30	NC11612	Not completed. Serial number reassigned to PCA-3.
PAA-1	C/n F-32	NC11625	W.E. Scripps. Wehrhan Aircraft Corp., C.D. Reichard.
PAA-1	C/n F-33	NC11626	F.W. Steere.
PAA-1	C/n F-34	NC11627	Westchester Airport.
PAA-1	C/n F-35	NC11628	J.J. White. Giro Transport & Sales.
PAA-1	C/n F-36	NC11629	Westchester Airport, W.L. Convell, J.C. Rolfe. Standard Aviation Inc.
PAA-1	C/n F-37	NC11630	W.A. Read.

PAA-1	C/n F-38	NC11631	Pitcairn Aviation. Earl S. Eckel. Converted to PA-24 C/n F-38.
PAA-1	C/n F-39	NC11632	J.F. Ballard.
PAA-1	C/n F-40	NC11633	Des Moines Register and Tribune
PAA-1	C/n F-41	NC11634	H.F. Pitcairn. Converted to PA-24 C/n F-41.
PAA-1	C/n F-52	NC11635	W.R. Miller. Pitcairn Aviation. Nathan Pitcairn. U.S. Dept. of Agriculture. Converted to PA-24/C/nF-52.
PAA-1	C/n F-53	NC11636	Pitcairn Aviation. J.K. Fenno. U.S. Dept. of Agriculture. Converted to PA-24 C/n F-53.
PAA-1	C/n F-54	NC11637	New England Giro.
PAA-1	C/n F-55	NC11638	Pitcairn Aeronautical Corp. E.S. Eckel. Converted to PA-20 and later PA-24 C/n F-55. Harold Warp. Preserved in Pioneer Museum, Minden, Nebraska.
PAA-1	C/n F-56	NC11639	Pitcairn Aeronautical Corp. L.S. Wilson.
PAA-1	C/n F-57	NC11640	Atlantic Seaboard Airways. Converted to PA-20 and later PA-24 C/n F-57. Fitted with tail wheel.
PAA-1	C/n F-58	NC11641	Pitcairn Autogiro. B.K. Schaefer. U.S. Dept. of Agriculture. Converted to PA-20 C/n F-58 and later PA-24 C/n F-58.
PAA-1	C/n F-59	NC11642	Converted to PA-20 and later PA-24 C/n F-59.
PAA-1	C/n F-60	NC11643	Converted to PA-20 and later PA-24 C/n F-60.
PAA-1	C/n F-61	NC11644	Converted to PA-20 and later PA-24 C/n F-61.
PAA-1	C/n F-72	NC11648 CF-ASQ	Pitcairn Aviation. Later sold in Canada to Leavens Bros. Air Service. Later converted to PA-24 C/n F-72. Burned May 13, 1948.

Alfaro

PC-2-30	C/n 1	X759W	First flight August 18, 1930. Crashed August 21, 1930.

Kellett

K-1X			First tests October 14, 1930. Seesaw rotor gyroplane. Did not fly.
K-2	C/n 1	X10766 NC10766	First flight April 24, 1931. ATC No. 437 awarded July 17, 1931. Steel Pier.
K-2	C/n 2	NC10767	Modified to K-3. Howard E. Quick.
K-2	C/n 3	NC10666	Modified to K-4. Edward Law.
K-2	C/n 4	NC10667	Modified to K-2-A. Atlantic Gyro Aviation. Gyro Sales and Service.
K-2	C/n 5	NC10668	George M. Pynchon. Crashed October 4, 1931.
K-2	C/n 6	NC11683	Ludington Flying Service.

K-2	C/n 7	NC11685	Modified to K-2-A. Gyro Sales and Service.
K-2	C/n 8	NC11686	Samuel Metzger.
K-2	C/n 9	NC11687	Modified to K-2-A, later to K-4, Kellett Aircraft Corp. Herman Schram.
K-2	C/n 10	NC11691	Modified to K-2-A. Douglas Robinson. Kellett Aircraft Corp.
K-2	C/n 11	NC12603	George B. Wells. Giro Sales and Service.
K-2	C/n 12	NC12605	Modified to K-3. Roger Amory.
K-3	C/n 2	NC10767	Converted from K-2. ATC No. 471 awarded on March 26, 1932.
K-3	C/n 12	NC12605	Converted from K-2. The Pep Boys.
K-3	C/n 14	NC12671	Kenneth H. Woolson.
K-3	C/n 16	NC12691	Hathaway & Mather.
K-3	C/n 17	NC12633	Converted from K-2. Mohawk Giro Inc.
K-3	C/n 18	NR12615 NC12615	Converted from K-2. Pep Boys Automotive Store. Used on Byrd's Second Antarctic Expedition. Crashed September 28, 1934.
K-3	C/n 20	NC13151	Col. Robert L. Montgomery.
K-4	C/n 23	X10666 NC10666	Converted from K-2. ATC No. 523 awarded December 27, 1933. Lincoln Air Services.
K-4	C/n 9	NC11687	Converted from K-2-A.

Pitcairn

PA-18	C/n G-62	NC12663	Pitcairn Autogiro. First flight March 1, 1932. ATC 478 awarded on April 7, 1932.
PA-18	C/n G-63	NC12676	W.A. Read.
PA-18	C/n G-64	NC12677	W.D. Dickey. Pacific Giro Sales.
PA-18	C/n G-65	NC12678	Pitcairn Aeronautical Corp. Anne W. Strawbridge. Preserved by F. Sewerka.
PA-18	C/n G-66	NC12679	Pal-Wankee Airport. Pitcairn Autogiro. W.A. Read.
PA-18	C/n G-67	NC12680	Giro Transport and Sales. Westchester Airplane Sales. A.W. McCurdy.
PA-18	C/n G-68	NC12681	Gilbert Flying Service. U.S. Dept. of Agriculture. Cockpit enclosure.
PA-18	C/n G-69	NC12682	New England Giro. O.R. Kelley.
PA-18	C/n G-70	NC12683	Pacific Giro Sales; Autogiro Advertising Corp.
PA-18	C/n G-71	NC12684	Garden Spot Motor. U.S. Dept. of Agriculture.
PA-18	C/n G-73	NC12685	Giro Transport and Sales. Heart Island.
PA-18	C/n G-74	NC13131	Giro Transport and Sales. Heart Island. A.C. Edgar.
PA-18	C/n G-75	NC13189	Harrisburg Autogiro Sales. C.H. Earle III. U.S. Dept. of Agriculture.

PA-18	C/n G-76	NC13190	J.F. Luesler, J.C. Davis.
PA-18	C/n G-77	NC2435	Horizon Company.
PA-18	C/n G-78	NC2437	Pitcairn Aeronautical Corp.. E.C.T. Bick. Genesse Brewing Co.. C.W. Kopf. A.A. Lombardo.
PA-18	C/n G-79		A.L. Seabra in Brazil.
PA-18	C/n G-80	NC2491	Pitcairn Autogiro.
PA-19	C/n H-84	X13149 NC13149	Autogiro Co. of America. Mohawk Giro.
PA-19	C/n H-85	X13182 NC13182	U.S. Dept. of Agriculture. Club Transportation Service.
PA-19	C/n H-87	NC2503 G-ADBE	Pitcairn Autogiro. A.E. Guinness. British C of A January 11, 1936.
PA-19	C/n H-88	NC2740	R.L. Montgomery. U.S. Dept. of Agriculture.
PA-19	C/n H-89	G-ADAM	A.E. Guinness. British C of A December 27, 1934.
PA-20	C/n F-18	NC10771	Pitcairn Aircraft. Converted from PAA-1 C/n F-18.
PA-20	C/n F-55	NC11638	E.S. Eckel. Converted from PAA-1 C/n F-55. Converted to PA-24 C/n F-55.
PA-20	C/n F-57	NC11640	Atlantic Seaboard Airways. Converted from PAA-1 C/n F-57. Converted to PA-24 C/n F-57.
PA-20	C/n F-58	NC11641	Pitcairn Autogiro. Converted from PAA-1 C/n F-58. Converted to PA-24 C/n F-58.

Cierva

C.19 Mk.V		G-ABXP	Built by Avro at Hamble. First flight March 1932. Scrapped 1935. Direct-control development aircraft.
C.24	C/n 710	G-ABLM	Built by de Havilland. First flight September 1931. Preserved at Salisbury Hall, near Hatfield.
C.25	C/n G31/1	G-ABTO	Built by Comper. First flown March 20, 1932. Dismantled Heston December 1933.
C.27, C.L.10	C/n 01		Built by Lioré-et-Olivier. First flight December 1932. Later converted to C.L.10A.
C.L.10	C/n 02		Built by Lioré-et-Olivier. First flight November 24, 1932. Crashed December 19, 1932.
C.L.10A	C/n 01		Possibly rebuilt, from C.L.10 C/n 01.
C.L.10B	C/n 01		Built by Lioré-et-Olivier. First flight 1935. Probably converted from C.L.10 C/n 02.
C.L.20	C/n WA2351F	G-ACYI	Built by Westland. First flight February 4, 1935. Scrapped 1938.

Weir

C.28, W.1			One prototype. First flight Hanworth, May 1933.

W.2		W-2	One prototype. First flight Hanworth mid-1934.
W.3		W-3	One prototype. First flight Abbotsinch, July 9, 1936.
W.4		W-4	One prototype. Not flown.

Cierva

(Built by Avro unless otherwise stated)

C.29		K3663	Built by Westland. Not flown.
C.30	C/n 1	G-ACFI	Prototype. Built by National Flying Services. First flight April 1933. Scrapped 1938.
C.30P Mk.II	C/n AH1	G-ACKA	Built by Airwork at Heston. First flight mid-October 1933.
C.30P	C/n 658	G-ACIM	C of A December 21, 1933. Preproduction aircraft. Sold abroad, March 1934, to Lioré-et-Olivier, France.
C.30P	C/n 659	G-ACIN	C of A January 2, 1934. Preproduction aircraft. Scrapped 1938.
C.30P	C/n 660	G-ACIO	C of A January 2, 1934. Preproduction aircraft. Scrapped 1937.
C.30A	C/n 705	G-ACUI	C of A July 27, 1934. To HM581, to G-AHTZ. Destroyed in accident March 4, 1958.
C.30A	C/n 706	G-ACVC	C of A July 28, 1934. Sold abroad August 1934.
C.30A	C/n 707	G-ACVX	C of A October 2, 1934. To PH-ASA.
C.30A	C/n 708	G-ACWF	C of A July 31, 1934. To DR624 To G-AHMI. (Became jump take-off aircraft C.30J.) Broken up for spares, c. 1951.
C.30A	C/n 709	G-ACWG	C of A September 11, 1934. To F-AOHY. Delivered to France, July 14, 1934.
C.30A	C/n 710	G-ACWH	C of A September 26, 1934. To DR623, to G-AHLE. Scrapped c.1952.
C.30A	C/n 711	G-ACWI	C of A August 23, 1934. To F-AOIO. Delivered to France, December 1934.
C.30A	C/n 712	G-ACWJ	C of A September 5, 1934. To PH-HHH, to AP508. Crashed off Seaton, Devon, April 16, 1951.
C.30A	C/n 713	G-ACWK	C of A November 3, 1934. To D-EKOM. Evaluated at Rechlin.
C.30A	C/n 714	G-ACWL	C of A November 16, 1934. To D-EKOP. Evaluated at Rechlin. Crashed Alsfeld, July 1935.
C.30A	C/n 715	G-ACWM	C of A April 18, 1935. To AP506. Preserved at the British Rotorcraft Museum, Weston-Super-Mare.
C.30A	C/n 716	G-ACWN	C of A November 12, 1934. Sold abroad, February 1937.

C.30A	C/n 717	G-ACWO	C of A December 21, 1934. To V1187. Sold in Belgium for spares, c. 1949.
Rota	C/n 723	K4230	RAF. Delivered August 1934.
Rota	C/n 724	K4231	RAF
C.30A	C/n 725	G-ACUT	C of A September 18, 1934.
C.30A	C/n 726	G-ACUU	C of A September 14, 1934. To HM580. Displayed at Hendon Exhibition, July 1951. Preserved at Duxford.
C.30A	C/n 728	G-ACWP	C of A November 16, 1934. To AP507. Preserved in Science Museum, London.
C.30A	C/n 731	G-ACWR	C of A August 1, 1934. To V1186. Crashed in sea off Worthing, October 24, 1943.
C.30A	C/n 732	G-ACWS	C of A August 23, 1934. To AP509, to G-AHUC, to SE-AZA.
C.30A	C/n 733	G-ACWT	C of A July 5, 1935. To F-AOLK. Trial installation with Salmson 9Nd engine and Ratier propeller. Delivered to France July 1935.
C.30A	C/n 734	VR-HCT	Exported to Hong Kong.
C.30A	C/n 735	LN-BAD	To SE-AFI. Preserved in the Dutch National Air Museum?
C.30A	C/n 736	G-ACWU	C of A January 10, 1935. To HB-MAB.
C.30A	C/n 737	G-ACXW	C of A October 6, 1934. To BV999. Scrapped c. 1951.
C.30A	C/n 738	PP-TAF	Exported to Brazil.
C.30A	C/n 739	OK-ATS	Exported to Czechoslovakia.
C.30A	C/n 740	SE-AEA	Preserved in the Stockholm Technical Museum.
C.30A	C/n 741	VT-AFF	Exported to India.
C.30A	C/n 742	VT-AFS	Exported to India.
C.30A	C/n 743	G-ACXG	C of A September 19, 1934. To PH-ARA. Crashed June 6, 1937.
C.30A	C/n 744	G-ACXV	C of A January 3, 1935. Sold abroad, December 1935.
C.30A	C/n 745	G-ACYP	C of A November 30, 1934. To SP-ANN to Polish air force, December 1934.
Rota	C/n 746	K4232	RAF. Preserved in the RAF Museum.
Rota	C/n 747	K4233	RAF.
C.30A	C/n 748	VT-AFQ	Exported to India.
C.30A	C/n 749	G-ADKY	C of A July 11, 1935. Delivered to Italy, August 1935.
C.30A	C/n 750	M.1	Danish army, captured by German army, Vaerlose, April 1940, to SE-AKL.
Rota	C/n 751	K4234	RAF. Crashed January 21, 1935. To G-AHMJ.

C.30A	C/n 752	G-ACWZ	C of A December 31, 1934. To British Air Transport Ltd. Withdrawn from use March 1938.
C.30A	C/n 753	G-ACXA	C of A May 8, 1935. To I-CIER, to MM 30030. Preserved in Milan?
C.30A	C/n 754	G-ACXB	Reg. April 4, 1935. To Czechoslovakia as OK-IEA.
C.30A	C/n 755	G-ACXC	Reg. April 4, 1935. (Possibly not completed.)
C.30A	C/n 756	EC-SCA	Exported to Spain.
C.30A	C/n 757	EC-SCB	Exported to Spain.
C.30A	C/n 760	G-ACXR	C of A December 15, 1934. Withdrawn from use May 1938.
C.30A	C/n 771	G-ACYH	C of A January 24, 1935. To DR622, to G-AHRP. Withdrawn from use c. July 1948 at White Waltham.
C.30A	C/n 772	G-ACXP	C of A September 28, 1934. To VH-USQ. Withdrawn from use July 1940.
Rota	C/n 774	K4235	RAF. Preserved in the Shuttleworth Collection.
C.30A	C/n 775	G-ACYE	C of A November 21, 1934. To AP510. Reduced to spares, December 1951, at Eastleigh.
C.30A	C/n 776	G-ACYC	C of A September 21, 1934. To F-AOHZ. Delivered to France October 1934.
C.30A	C/n 777	LY-LAS	Exported to Lithuania.
C.30A	C/n 779		To Soviet Union.
C.30A	C/n 780	G-ADCK	Reg. February 5, 1935. To VH-UUQ.
C.30A	C/n 781	41-2	Spanish air force.
C.30A	C/n 782	41-3	Spanish air force.
C.30A	C/n 791	G-ACZV	C of A January 17, 1935. Sold in France c. April 1937. To F-BDAA.
C.30A	C/n 792	VH-USR	Preserved at Bankstown, Sydney, NSW.
Rota	C/n 793	K4236	RAF.
Rota	C/n 796	K4237 1142M	RAF.
C.30A	C/n 798	G-ADBJ	C of A June 21, 1935. Reg. canceled, April 1, 1940.
C.30A	C/n 800		French Air Ministry. See also note 31.
C.30A	C/n 801		French Air Ministry.
C.30A	C/n 802		French Air Ministry.
C.30A	C/n 803		French Air Ministry.
C.30A	C/n 804		French Air Ministry.
Rota	C/n 805	K4238	RAF.
Rota	C/n 806	K4239	RAF. To G-AIOC.
C.30A	C/n 808		To China.

C.30A	C/n 815	OE-TAX	Exported to Austria. June 1935. Dienst NR63.
C.30A	C/n 818		Belgian air force.
C.30A	C/n 885	M.2	Danish army, captured by German army, Vaerlose, April 1940.
C.30A	C/n 1029		Yugoslav air force.
C.30A	C/n 1030		Yugoslav air force.
C.30A	C/n 1031		To Argentina.
C.30A	C/n 1032		To Argentina.
Rota	Not known	K4296	Seaplane trial installation.
Rota	Not known	K4775	Used for trial installation of 160/180 hp Armstrong Siddeley Civet Major engine.

Total Avro C.30A/Rota Production: 78

Focke-Wulf

Fw C.30		D-EIRO	Built in Bremen 1935 under Cierva license. 40 aircraft planned for production. About 30 completed.
Fw C.30		D-INCR	German-built. Evaluated at DVL. Crashed Travemunde, 1937.
Fw C.30	C/n 1791	F-BDAA?	German-built aircraft acquired by French after WWII.

Lioré-et-Olivier

LeO C.30	C/n 01	F-AOHY	Avro-built as C/n 709, G-ACWG. Registered July 1, 1936.
LeO C.30	C/n 02	F-AOHZ	Avro-built as C/n 776, G-ACYC. Registered November 1935.
LeO C.30	C/n 03	F-AOIO	Avro-built as C/n 711, G-ACWI. Registered October 8, 1935.
LeO C.30	C/n 04	F-AOLK F.401	Avro-built as C/n 733, G-ACWT. Became C.30S.
LeO C.30	C/n 2 to 25	F-402 to 425	Production for l'Armée de l'Air, October 1935/July 1936. Order for 24 aircraft completed.
LeO C.30S	C/n 26	F-AOLL	One from following batch. Delivered March 1936. C of N No. 9762, July 11, 1936. Registered July 27, 1939.
LeO C.30	C/n 26-29	HY-61/64?	Production for l'Aéronavale. 4 aircraft completed.

SNCASE

(From December 21, 1936)

C.30	C/n 30 to 59	F.426 to 455	Production for l'Armée de l'Air. January/September 1938. Order for 30 aircraft completed.
C.301	C/n 01	F-BDAA?	First prototype. First flight April 1938. Converted G-ACZV?
C.301	C/n 02	F-BDAB?	Second prototype.
C.301	C/n 1	HY-65?	First production for l'Armée de l'Air later to Aéronavale. First flight late 1938. Experimentally fitted with modified tail unit December 1938.

C.301	C/n 2 to 5	HY-81/84?	Production of 4 aircraft for l'Aéronavale completed.
C.301	C/n 6 to 100		95 aircraft ordered August 1938 but not built.
C.301	C/n 101 to 200		100 aircraft ordered September 2, 1939. Later canceled.
C.302	C/n 01	F-AOLL	Prototype converted from C.30S.
C.302	C/n 02		Not completed.
C.302	C/n 03	F-BDAD	Converted from 30-15. First flight 1946. Preserved in Musée de l'Air et de l'Espace, Paris.

Total French C.30, C.301, C.302 production: about 70.

Pitcairn

PA-22	C/n J-86	X13198 NX13198	Flown in many different configurations. Crashed on its first flight early March 1933. Destroyed by fire 1951.
PA-24	C/n F-38	NC11631	Pitcairn Aviation. Eckels Air Service Tydol "Triplex X". Converted from PAA-1 C/n F-38. ATC 507 awarded May 19, 1933.
PA-24	C/n F-41	NC11634	H.F. Pitcairn. U.S. Dept. of Agriculture. Converted from PAA-1 C/n F-41, March 1933.
PA-24	C/n F-52	NC11635	Converted from PAA-1 C/n F-52.
PA-24	C/n F-55	NC11638	Converted from PA-20 C/n F-55.
PA-24	C/n F-57	NC11640	Atlantic Seaboard Airways. Converted from PA-20 C/n F-57.
PA-24	C/n F-58	NC11641	Pitcairn Autogiro. Converted from PA-20 C/n F-58.
PA-24	C/n F-59	NC11642	Converted from PAA-1 C/n F-59.
PA-24	C/n F-60	NC11643	Converted from PAA-1 C/n F-60.
PA-24	C/n F-61	NC11644	Converted from PAA-1 C/n F-61.
PA-24	C/n F-72	NC11648	Converted from PAA-1 C/n F-72.
PA-33 YG-2	C/n K-90	X14776 35-279	U.S. Army Air Corps. Crashed at NACA Langley, March 30, 1936.
PA-34 XOP-2	C/n J-10	8850	Rebuilt from XOP-1 C/n B-10.
AC-35	C/n J-91	X70 NX70	Prototype only, for U.S. Dept. of Commerce. Stored at NASM, Silver Hill.
PA-36	C/n L-94	NX20674	Prototype. Broken up 1942.
PA-36	C/n L-95		Not completed.
PA-39	C/n M-98	N3908	Pitcairn-Larsen Autogiro Co. First flight February 1941. Being restored by Stephen Pitcairn.
PA-39	C/n M-99	BW828 (see note 32)	Scrapped January 1942.
PA-39	C/n M-100	BW829	Delivered to British Purchasing Commission, September 1941. Scrapped January 1942.
PA-39	C/n M-101	BW830	Scrapped January 1942.

PA-39	C/n M-102	BW831	
PA-39	C/n M-103	BW833	
PA-39	C/n M-104	BW834	
PA-39	C/n M-105	BW835	Destroyed by fire in United States.

Kellett

KD-1	C/n 101	X14742 NC14742	First flight November 1934. ATC No. 712, January 1935. Retired 1943. Restored 1953. Destroyed and rebuilt 1959.
YG-1 (KD-1)	C/n 102	35-278 (see note 33)	To USAAC in May 1936. Crashed at Fort Knox on June 16, 1937.
KD-1A	C/n 103	NX15684 NC15684	ATC No. 712, October 1937. Sold to Japan 1939?
YG-1A (KD-1A)	C/n 104	36-352 NC13946?	To USAAC in October 1936. NACA Langley wind tunnel accident, October 26, 1937. To United States-Mexico Border Patrol, 1941.
YG-1B (KD-1A)	C/n 105	37-377	To USAAC in December 1937. To United States-Mexico Border Patrol, 1941.
YG-1B (KD-1A)	C/n 106	37-378	To USAAC in 1938. To YG-1C, 1939. To XR-2, 1940. To NACA Langley. Destroyed in ground accident, 1941. XR-2 did not fly.
KD-1B	C/n 107	NC15069	First flight 1939. ATC No. 712, December 1939. EAL Philadelphia postal service, July 6, 1939 to July 5, 1940. Sold to Charles H. Babb Co. December 1941. Became KH-17.
YG-1B (KD-1A)	C/n 108	37-379	USAAC in 1938. To U.S.-Mexico Border Patrol, 1941.
YG-1B (KD-1A)	C/n 109	37-380	To USAAC in 1938. To XR-3, 1941. Sold to General Electric.
YG-1B (KD-1A)	C/n 110	37-381	To USAAC in 1938. To US-Mexico Border Patrol, 1941.
YG-1B KD-1A)	C/n 111	37-382	To USAAC in 1938. To US-Mexico Border Patrol, 1941.
YO-60	C/n 112	42-13604	To USAAF in 1942.
YO-60	C/n 113	42-13605	To USAAF in 1942. Damaged in ground accident. Not repaired.
YO-60	C/n 114	42-13606	To USAAF in 1942.
YO-60	C/n 115	42-13607	To USAAF in 1942.
YO-60	C/n 116	42-13608	To USAAF in 1942.
YO-60	C/n 117	42-13609	To USAAF in 1942.
XO-60	C/n 118	42-13610	To USAAF in 1943. To Wright Field, 1944. Now preserved in NASM, Washington, D.C.

Pitcairn

PA-44, XO-61		42-13611	Prototype. To USAAF.
PA-44, YO-61		42-13612	Service test. To USAAF.
PA-44, YO-61		42-13613 to 42-13616	Not completed.

Cierva

C.30 Mk.III-V C-30J C/n 708		G-ACWF	Development aircraft flown in successive variants. First flight March 1936.

SNCASE

C.34	C/n 01		One prototype. First flight March 1939 at Villacoublay.

British Aircraft/Oddie, Bradbury and Cull

(The sequence in which the following serials were allocated is unconfirmed)

C.40	C/n 1001 OBC265	G-AFDP T1419	Built by British Aircraft. First flight February 25, 1938. Delivered to the RAF September 15, 1939. Lost in France, June 1940. With 26 Squadron.
C.40	C/n 1002 OBC 266	G-AFDR P9636	Built by Oddie, Bradbury, and Cull. Delivered to RAF December 6, 1939.
C.40	C/n 1003	L7589	Built by Oddie, Bradbury, and Cull. Intended for Royal Navy, 1939, but transferred to RAF. Flown to France, October 21, 1939. Crashed at Odiham, April 29, 1940. With 81 Squadron.
C.40	C/n 1004	L7590	Built by Oddie, Bradbury, and Cull. Delivered to RAF. Probably went to France in December 1939. With 81 Squadron.
C.40	C/n 1005	L7591	Built by Oddie, Bradbury, and Cull. Delivered to RAF.
C.40	C/n 1006	L7594	Delivered to RN. At Lee-on-Solent, December 1939 to April 1940.
C.40	C/n 1007	L7595	Delivered to RN. At Lee-on-Solent, December 1939 to April 1940.
C.40	C/n 1008	P9635	Probably not built.

Flettner

Fl184	C/n V1	D-ADVE	Prototype only. First flight November 1936.
Focke-Wulf	WNR 1971		Crashed December 1936.

Fw 186	C/n V1	D-ISTQ	Prototype only. First flight July 1938.
TsAGI			Crashed spring 1939.

KaSkr-I			Completed September 1, 1929. Did not fly.
KaSkr-II			First flight 1930. Prototype only.
2-EA			First flight November 17, 1931. Prototype only.
4-EA A-4			First flight November 6, 1932. 1 prototype and about 10 production aircraft.
A-6			First flight early 1933. 3 prototypes. Second and third converted to A-8.
A-7			First flight September 20, 1934. First prototype.

A-7bis	First flight March 1937. Second prototype.
A-7-3a	First flight 1939. 5 production aircraft.
A-8	2 prototypes converted from A-6. First flight June 29, 1934.
A-12	First flight May 10, 1936. Prototype only.
A-13	First flight March 13, 1936. Conversion of A-8 first prototype.
A-14	First flight September 13, 1935. Conversion of A-8 second prototype.
A-15	Completed April 1937. Not flown.

Kayaba

Ka-1	Two experimental aircraft built at Shibaura. First flight June 1943.
Ka-1A	About 35 production aircraft built at Sendai. First flight June 1943.
Ka-2	About 60 production aircraft built at Sendai. First flight summer 1944.
Ka-1KAI	Prototype only. Jump take-off development.

Total Japanese production Ka-1, Ka-1A, Ka-2: about 97.

Autogyro Production Numbers

Experimental and Prototypes	Years	No. of Types	No. of Aircraft
Spain	1923–29	4	4
United Kingdom	1926–38	13	13
Soviet Union	1929–37	11	10
France	1929–39	5	6
United States	1929–42	9	10
Germany	1932–38	3	3
Japan	1941	1	2
Totals		46	48

Production Series	Years	No. of Types	No. of Aircraft
C.6 (Spain, United Kingdom)	1924–26	4	4
C.8 (United Kingdom)	1926–28	6	6
C.19 (United Kingdom)	1929–32	4	29
Pitcairn PCA-2 (United States)	1930–31	3	25
Pitcairn PAA-1 (United States)	1931–33	4	28
Kellett K-2/4 (United States)	1931–33	3	21
Pitcairn PA-18 (United States)	1932	1	18
Pitcairn PA-19 (United States)	1932	1	5
TsAGI 4-EA (Soviet Union)	1932	1	10◄
C.30 (United Kingdom, France, Germany)	1933–39	10	183◄
Kellett KD-1 (United States)	1934–42	4	18
C.40 (United Kingdom)	1938–39	1	7
TsAGI A-7-3a (Soviet Union)	1939	1	5
Pitcairn PA-39 (United States)	1941	1	(7)•
Kayaba Ka-1A/Ka-2 (Japan)	1943–44	2	96
Totals		46	454

◄ Approximate
• Rebuilds of earlier models

Notes

1. The group of young people who collaborated with the youthful Juan de la Cierva included: José "Pepe" Barcala Moreno, Pablo Diaz Fernández, Tomás de Martin-Barbadillo, Rafael Silvela Tordesillas, and Antonio Hernandez-Ros Murcia Codorníu

It should be noted that it is Spanish practice often to give the mother's family name after the surname, which is of course taken from the father.

2. "Autogiro" was registered first in Spain in 1923 and then in other countries as the Cierva Company's trademark. This word should therefore be spelt with a capital when used for Cierva's products. The generic term "autogyro" (spelt with a y and without a capital) is now widely used to describe all rotary-wing aircraft with unpowered rotors. The original designation gyroplane is, however, sometimes used in this book to reduce confusion with Cierva's trademark. Cierva's Autogiros can therefore be described as autogyros or gyroplanes, but autogyros (and gyroplanes) are Autogiros only if built by the Cierva Company or one of its licensees.

A gyroplane or autogyro differs from a helicopter in that its rotor is not power-driven in flight. The rotor is kept turning only by the passing airstream. Forward propulsion is obtained from a conventional airscrew.

3. The final entry in Cierva's last-known pilot's logbook was made in October 1935 when his flying time as pilot totaled 735 hr 5 min. Because he was preoccupied with events in Spain, Cierva's flying was probably significantly reduced during the last year of his life. It is not known whether this flying is recorded in another logbook.

4. Amalio Diaz had built a fighter, powered by a 180-hp Hispano-Suiza 8Ab and designed by Julio Adaro Tarradillos, for the 1919 Spanish Military aircraft competition. It had won one of the prizes.

5. The closed circuit wind tunnel at the Aeronautical Laboratory at Cuatro Vientos was started in 1919 and commissioned in 1921. It was reported to be the largest in Europe at that time and had a 3 m (10 ft) diameter working section. The 4-blade 4 m (13 ft) diameter fan was driven by a 700-hp Fiat engine and generated 50 m/s (110 mph). (*Janes All The World's Aircraft* 1926). Later the Fiat was replaced by a 500-kw electric motor which increased the speed to 56 m/s (124 mph).

6. It is possible that some of the first tests of C.4 were undertaken by Lieutenant Gomez Spencer who later made the historic first real flights of C.4 in its final form. He was away from Madrid in July/August 1926 during which time the testing was undertaken by Espinosa.

7. Cierva's most important patent was No. 81,406 taken out in Spain on November 15, 1922 covering flapping blades. Cover of the flapping blade concept was granted in other countries as follows:

France: No. 562,756 on September 14, 1923.
United Kingdom: No. 196,594 on June 30, 1924.
Germany: No. 416,727 on July 27, 1925.
United States: No. 1,590,497 on June 29, 1926.

Methods of engine-powered rotor-spin-up were covered by two United Kingdom patents: No. 263,988; No. 265,716

Different blade shapes and, in particular, paddle blades as used by Cierva from 1926 to 1929: No. 264,965.

Folding rotor blades: No. 264,968

Fixed-wings incorporating ailerons: No. 264,286

Limitations on blade flapping: No. 264,963

Provision of cyclic pitch change of a rotor with flapping blades: No. 264,753

8. Reginald Truelove [Folch] was an Englishman. He became a flying instructor in Spain and later was Loring's chief test pilot. He was killed in a flying accident in 1931.

9. The C.9 has also been reported as the Avro 609 but this seems improbable.

10. Strangely enough, only seven months after Rambaud's flight, Arthur Rawson seems to have been completely unaware of it. During the discussion which followed Cierva's second lecture to the Royal Aeronautical Society on February 13, 1930, Rawson stated that 140 miles was the longest distance flown non-stop by an Autogiro up to that time.

11. The nine C.19 Mk.IIIs built from scratch at Hamble were: G-AAYN, G-AAYO, G-AAYP, G-ABCK, G-ABCL, G-ABCM, G-ABFZ, G-ABGA, and G-ABGB.

12. The thirteen C.19 Mk.IVs built from scratch at Hamble were: G-ABUC to G-ABUH, G-ABXD to G-ABXI, and G-ABXP.

13. T.H. White was wrongly informed by Alan Marsh about looping an Autogiro. Actually, the first Autogiro loops had been made three and a half years earlier by Godfrey Dean in the United States. John Miller had made hundreds more since then at flying exhibitions and country fairs (see Chapter 5). It is probably true, however, that nobody tried looping a direct-control Autogiro until the French test pilot Stachenburg did so in a C.30 in 1939.

14. The performance figures quoted for the German C.19 are estimates for the production version powered with the Sh 14 engine.

15. In giving testimony before the U.S. Congress on April 26, 1938, during hearings on the Dorsey Bill, Harold Pitcairn stated that $3.5 million had been spent in the United States up to that time on rotary-wing aircraft research and development plus an equal amount abroad. In the 1930s $3.5 million was equivalent to something like $26 million today.

16. *Hereter Alfaro* 8 (180-hp Hispano-Suiza 8Ab)
        Built by Talleres Hereter S.A., Independencia 113, Barcelona
        Type: single-seat fighter biplane, one built
        First flight: April 1919 at Cuatro Vientos. Crashed.

17. John Scott, a chemist, of Saint Patrick Square in the City of Edinburgh, Scotland, in 1816 bequeathed to the City of Philadelphia the sum of $4,000 (equivalent to perhaps $55,000 today), the income from which was to be "laid out in premiums to be distributed among ingenious men and women who made useful inventions, but no one of such premiums shall exceed twenty dollars [$270] and along with which shall be given a copper medal with this inscription 'to the most deserving.'"

18. Lanchester and Prandtl were distinguished scientists who laid the foundations of modern aerodynamics. Frederick W. Lanchester (1868–1946) put forward his famous vortex theory of flight in 1894. Among other major contributions to aeronautical knowledge, Ludwig Prandtl (1875–1953) developed the vortex theory during the First World War.

19. Established in 1848, the Elliott Cresson Gold Medal is "Awarded for discovery or original research, adding to the sum of human knowledge, irrespective of commercial value; leading and practical utilizations of discovery; and invention, methods or products embodying substantial elements of leadership in their respective classes, or unusual skill or perfection in workmanship."

20. The performance figures quoted for the PCA-2 are for the production version with the 300-hp Wright R-975-E Whirlwind J-6-9 engine.

21. Even experienced Autogiro pilots like Brie and Marsh were having frequent minor accidents—they had four between them in nine months in 1932/33.

22. The Weir design team included Dr. J.A.J. Bennett, C.G. Pullin, K. Watson, G.E. Walker, F.L. Hodgess, R.F. Bowyer, R.A. Pullin, T. Nisbet, L. Pullin, and W. Stein at different times.

23. C.29 performance figures are estimated. The aircraft never flew.

24. This tour of Spain by Cierva may have had objectives other than those of purely technical demonstration—he was actively promoting his political interests at this time.

25. GAO—Group d'Aviation d'Observation (Flight or Squadron)

CIOAA—Center d'Instruction à l'Observation sur Avions Autogyres (Training center)

EAA—Entrepots de l'Armée de l'Air (Storage depot)

26. The Pobjoy Niagara, which first appeared in 1935, differed from the earlier Cataract in having fully enclosed valve gear.

27. The Pobjoy Cascade was a direct-drive version of the Cataract which appeared in 1934.

28. One of Cierva's activities on behalf of the Nationalists during the Spanish Civil War (1936–39) is well known. He and Luis Antonio Bolin Bidwell, London correspondent of the Royalist Madrid newspaper *A B C*, were responsible for the secret chartering in England, from Olley Air Services Ltd., of the de Havilland DH.89 Dragon Rapide (G-ACYR) which transported General Francisco Franco from the Canary Islands to Spanish Morocco at the start of the war. This aircraft is now preserved in the Museo del Aire at Cuatro Vientos near Madrid.

Bolin and Cierva arranged for an English friend, Major Hugh Pollard, his daughter and another girl, accompanied by Bolin, to be flown by Olley's to Casablanca in Morocco and on to Las Palmas in the Canaries, ostensibly on a tourist trip. They departed from Croydon, London's airport, on July 11, 1936, piloted by Captain Cecil W. H. Bebb. Bolin left the aircraft at Casablanca and the English party flew on to Las Palmas, later returning to England by sea. On July 18, Bebb picked up Franco and his ADC in Las Palmas and flew them to Tetuan where they arrived on July 19 after refuelling at Agadir and night-stopping in Casablanca. Franco was thus in a position to launch, from North Africa, the civil war against the Communist Republican government. By coincidence, Bebb had given the author his first flight (in an Avro Cadet, G-ACOZ) some two years earlier, on August 24, 1934.

29. Masaaki Iinuma was well known for his record "Goodwill Flight" from Tokyo to London sponsored by the Asahi Shimbun in the Mitsubishi Ki-15 *Kamikase* (*Divine Wind*) on April 5–9, 1937.

30. Conversation of the author with Igor Sikorsky during visit to Bridgeport, Connecticut, on June 17, 1955.

31. The five Cierva C.30A Autogiros supplied to the French Air Ministry (C/n 800-804) are believed to have been delivered as kits for assembly by Lioré-et-Olivier in France.

32. Six PA-39s were purchased by the British Air Commission (five were shipped to the United Kingdom and two arrived). The PA-39s (C/n M-98 to 104) were all rebuilt from PA-18s and should for consistency have been given their original PA-18 constructors numbers prefixed with M.

33. The C/ns of all the Kellett YG-1, YG-1A, and YG-1B Autogiros delivered to the USAAC are unconfirmed. There are also uncertainties about the C/n of most of the YO-60s delivered to the USAAF.

Glossary

Some terms and abbreviations used in this book

AFEE	British Airborne Forces Experimental Establishment.
Ailerons	Movable flaplike surface hinged at trailing edge of the wings of a heavier-than-air craft to provide lateral control.
Air-oil shock strut	Landing gear strut in which a hollow piston travels in an oil-filled cylinder. Under load oil is forced through a small orifice to provide a shock-absorbing effect. (Same as oleo landing gear.)
Airplane controls	Control surfaces on a rotary-wing aircraft similar to those on a fixed-wing aircraft, as distinct from control exercised through the rotor.
Alpha hinge	Hinge about which an articulated rotor blade trails or advances in its plane of rotation. (Same as drag or lead-lag hinge.)
ARC	The Aeronautical Research Committee appointed to advise the British government on scientific aspects of aeronautics.
Articulated rotor	Rotor with flapping and drag hinges attaching the blades to the hub.
ASI	Airspeed indicator.
ATC	Approved Type Certificate awarded in the United States when an aircraft is officially approved for public use.
Autodynamic rotor	A specific Cierva design of jump take-off rotor head.
Autogiro	Trade name for Cierva's gyroplane (spelt with a capital A).
Autogyro	Rotary-wing aircraft whose support in flight is chiefly from a rotor turned only by air forces resulting from its motion. Propulsion is by conventional engine and airscrew. (Same as gyroplane.)
Autorotation	Rotation of a rotor solely under the effects of a passing airstream.

360

BEA	United Kingdom airline: British European Airways, later absorbed into British Airways.
Box tail	Arrangement whereby the slipstream of a gyroplane can be deflected at will on the ground so as to spin-up the rotor to near flying speed before take-off. (Same as deflector or scorpion tail.)
CAA	Civil Aeronautics Authority, the United States government agency formerly responsible for civil aviation from 1938 to 1959.
Cantilever (blades, wings, tail surfaces)	A member supported at or near one end only without external bracing.
Co-axial rotors	Rotary-wing aircraft with superimposed rotors on a common axis.
Collective pitch control	Changing the blade angle of all the blades simultaneously.
Constructor's number (C/n)	Manufacturer's individual aircraft identification.
Contra-propeller	Propeller that rotates in the opposite direction to another coaxially mounted propeller.
Control column	Lever with which the pilot can control an aircraft in roll and in pitch. (Same as stick.)
Coriolis effect	Oscillation of a rotary-wing aircraft's rotor blade about its drag hinge.
C of A	Certificate of Airworthiness.
Cyclic pitch control	Periodic variation of the blade angle of a blade in a rotor during its cycle of rotation thus tilting the plane of the rotor. (Same as feathering control.)
Deflector tail	Arrangement whereby the slipstream of a gyroplane can be deflected at will on the ground so as to spin-up the rotor to near flying speed before take-off. (Same as box or scorpion tail.)
Delta hinge	Hinge about which an articulated rotor blade flaps. (Same as flapping hinge.)
Direct control	Control of a rotary-wing aircraft exercised by tilting the rotor hub.
Direct take-off	Take-off in which the rotor blades of a rotary-wing aircraft in nonlifting pitch are spun up to a high rpm then suddenly increased in pitch to lift the aircraft into the air. (Same as jump take-off.)
Drag hinge	Hinge about which an articulated rotor blade trails or advances in its plane of rotation. (Same as Alpha or lead-lag hinge.)
Drag hinge offset	Amount the drag hinge of a rotor blade is out of line with the blade axis.
Dual control	A double set of pilot's controls.

361

Elevator	A movable flaplike surface usually hinged at the trailing edge of the stabilizer (or tailplane) which provides control about a lateral axis.
Empennage	Combination of surfaces at the rear of an aircraft for control and stability. (Same as tail unit.)
End-plate fins	Fixed substantially vertical surfaces attached at the tips of the stabilizer (or tailplane).
FAA	Federal Aviation Administration, the United States government agency responsible for civil aviation since 1959.
Feathering control	Periodic variation of the blade angle of each blade in a rotor during its cycle of rotation thus tilting the plane of the rotor. (Same as cyclic pitch control.)
Fixed fin	Fixed vertical surface usually in the tail unit.
Fixed spindle rotor	Gyroplane rotor hub bearing—which is immovably attached to the rotor pylon. (Sometimes referred to as pre-direct-control technology.)
Flapping hinge	Hinge about which an articulated rotor blade flaps. (Same as Delta hinge.)
Float	Buoyant boat-shaped structure which supports or stabilizes a seaplane on the water. (Same as pontoon.)
Flotation gear	Inflatable bags to support an aircraft which comes down in the water.
Frise aileron	Aileron with leading edge projecting ahead of its hinge line but flush with the lower wing surface when neutral. When the aileron is raised the leading edge projects below the lower wing surface increasing drag to offset the increased drag of the opposite lowered aileron.
G	Acceleration equal to the force of gravity (32.2 ft/sec-sec).
Ground resonance	Self-excited mechanical (potentially destructive) vibration on the ground of a rotary-wing aircraft involving a couple between the blade motion and that of the supporting structure or of the whole aircraft.
Gyrodyne	Rotary-wing aircraft whose rotor(s) provide lift only in autorotation in normal flight but are powered for take-off and landing.
Gyroplane	Rotary-wing aircraft whose support in flight is chiefly from a rotor which is turned only by air forces resulting from its motion. Propulsion is by conventional engine and airscrew. (Same as autogyro.)
Hanging stick	Pilot's control column which hangs down from the rotor head instead of being mounted on the floor of the cockpit.

Helicopter	Heavier-than-air craft supported in the air chiefly by one or more power-driven rotors with substantially vertical axes which, if slightly tilted, also provide translational propulsion.
HEU	Helicopter Experimental Unit of British European Airways, now British Airways Helicopters.
Inline engine	Internal combustion engine with its cylinders arranged in a single line.
Instrument flight	Flight using instruments to maintain orientation and to determine position in limited visibility.
Inter-blade bracing	Cables between the blades on a noncantilever rotor to restrain the movements of the blades in relation to each other.
Irreversible controls	Aircraft control system in which the aerodynamic forces acting on the control surfaces or blades of a rotary-wing aircraft are not transmitted back to pilot's controls.
Jump take-off	Take-off in which the rotor blades of a rotary-wing aircraft in nonlifting pitch are spun-up to a high rpm then suddenly increased in pitch to lift the aircraft into the air. (Same as direct take-off.)
Lead-lag hinge	See alpha hinge.
NACA	National Advisory Committee for Aeronautics, the former United States government agency for aeronautical research (now absorbed into NASA).
Nosewheel landing gear	Components, including a wheel under the nose, which support an aircraft on the ground and absorb any landing shocks. (Same as tricycle undercarriage.)
NPL	National Physical Laboratory. British Research Establishment.
Oleo landing gear	Landing gear strut in which a hollow piston travels in an oil-filled cylinder. Under load, oil is forced through a small orifice to provide a shock-absorbing effect. (Same as air-oil shock strut.)
Phi	Change in pitch angle of rotor blades for jump take-off.
Pontoon	Buoyant boat-shaped structure which supports or stabilizes a seaplane on the water (Same as float.)
Pusher	Aircraft with its propeller mounted behind the lateral axis or center of gravity.
Radial engine	Internal combustion aero-engine with cylinders fixed radially around the crankshaft.
RAE	Royal Aircraft Establishment, the United Kingdom government research agency.
RAF	The British Royal Air Force.
RAeS	The British Royal Aeronautical Society.

R&M	Reports and memoranda issued by the British Aeronautical Research Committee.
Rigid rotor	A nonarticulated, nontilting rotor.
Rotary-engine	Internal combustion aero-engine with cylinders disposed radially which rotate around a fixed crankshaft.
Rotary-wing aircraft	Aircraft which in its usual flight attitudes is supported in the air wholly or in part by blades rotating about a substantially vertical axis. (Same as rotorcraft.)
Rotor	Assembly of airfoils and a hub that rotates about a substantially vertical axis to provide lift or lift and propulsion for a rotary-wing aircraft.
Rotor blade	Airfoil surface which is part of a rotor system.
Rotorcraft	Aircraft which in its usual flight attitudes is supported in the air wholly or in part by blades rotating about a substantially vertical axis. (Same as rotary-wing aircraft.)
Rotor head	Rotor hub assembly including control system mounted on the hub.
Rotor hub	Central assembly of a rotor to which the blades are attached.
Rotor pylon	Column or structure supporting the rotor of a rotary-wing aircraft.
Rotor spin-up drive	Provision for the engine of a gyroplane to bring the rotor up to flying speed before take-off.
Rudder	Movable upright flap-like surface which provides control about a vertical axis.
Scorpion tail	Arrangement whereby the slipstream of a gyroplane can be deflected at will on the ground so as to spin-up the rotor to near flying speed before take-off. (Same as box or deflector tail.)
Seesaw rotor	Rotor with blades free to tilt only as a unit. (Same as teetering rotor.)
Semi-rigid rotor	Partly articulated rotor, especially a rotor with blades free to flap but not to lead or lag in the plane of rotation.
SFNA	Société Française de la Navigation Aérienne.
Shock strut	A shock-absorbing landing gear strut.
Slipstream	The stream of air driven backward by a rotating propeller.
Solidity	Ratio of total blade area to disc area of a rotor.
Stabilizer	Fixed or adjustable horizontal aerofoil surface that provides stability for an aircraft. (Same as tailplane.)
STAé	Service Technique de l'Aéronautique—the French aeronautical technical directorate.

364

Stick	Lever with which the pilot can control an aircraft laterally and about a transverse axis. (Same as control column.)
Stick-force recorder	Instrument to measure the force required from a pilot to move the control column.
STOL	Short Take-Off and Landing.
Tailplane	Fixed or adjustable horizontal aerofoil surface that provides stability for an aircraft. (Same as stabilizer.)
Tail unit	Combination of surfaces at the rear of an aircraft for stability and control purposes. (Same as empennage.)
Teetering rotor	Rotor with blades free to tilt only as a unit. (Same as see-saw rotor.)
Tie-bar suspension	Flexible member used in some rotor systems instead of flapping and drag hinges to attach the blades to the hub.
Tilting head	Rotor hub which can be tilted in all directions for control purposes.
Tip-drive rotor	Rotor powered by pressure jets at the tips of the blades.
Torque reaction	Tendency of a rotary-wing aircraft to rotate in the opposite direction to its shaft-driven rotor or propeller.
Towering take-off	Jump take-off in which the gyroplane continues to gain height after the energy in the over-speeded rotor has been dissipated.
Tricycle undercarriage	Components, including a wheel under the nose, which provide support for an aircraft on the ground and absorb any shock in landing. (Same as nosewheel landing gear.)
Turbine helicopter	Helicopter powered by one or more gas turbines.
Type number	Manufacturer's designation for a specific aircraft design.
USAAC	United States Army Air Corps.
USAAF	United States Army Air Forces.
USAF	United States Air Force.
VTOL	Vertical Take-Off and Landing.
Wind tunnel	Tubelike passage, sometimes continuous, in which a high speed wind is generated by a fan so that the aerodynamic effects of the airflow on aircraft or other items, mounted in the tunnel on suitable balances, can be measured.

Bibliography

Books

Adams, F.D. *Aeronautical Dictionary*. Washington: U.S. Government Printing Office, 1959.

Aerospace, 1939–1943. New York: Aerosphere Publishing Company, 1940–44.

Barnes, C.H. *Shorts Aircraft Since 1900*. London: Putnam, 1967.

Bridgman, L. *Aircraft of the British Empire*. London: Sampson Low, 1936.

Brie, R.A.C. *The Autogiro and How to Fly It*. 1933. 2d ed. London: Pitman, 1934.

British Standard Glossary of Aeronautical Terms. (Revised 1933). London: British Standards Institution, June 1933.

Cierva Codorníu, J. de la, and Rose, D. *Wings of Tomorrow*. New York: Brewer, Warren Putnam, 1931.

Cooper, H.J., and Thetford, O.G. *Aircraft of the Fighting Powers*. Vol. 5. Leicester: Harborough, 1944.

Courtney, F.T. *Flight Path*. London: William Kimber, 1972. Also published as *The Eighth Sea*. New York: Doubleday & Co., 1972.

Dorman, G. *British Test Pilots*. London: Forbes Robertson, 1950.

Farley, J.C. *U.S. Army Aircraft, 1908–46*. New York: Ships and Aircraft, 1946.

Faur, P. *Thirty Years in the Service of Aviation: Louis Bréguet*. Paris: Blondel la Rougery, 1944.

Focke-Wulf Flugzeuge. Steinebach: Zuerl, c.1965.

Francillon, R.J. *Japanese Aircraft of the Pacific War*. London: Putnam, 1970.

Francis, D.E. *The Story of the Helicopter*. New York: Coward-McCann, 1946.

Gablehouse, C. *Helicopters and Autogiros*. Philadelphia: J.B. Lippincott Co., 1967, 1969.

García Albors, E. *Juan de la Cierva y el Autogiro*. Madrid: Editiones Cid, 1965.

Gessow, A., and Meyers, G.C., Jr. *Aerodynamics of the Helicopter*. New York: MacMillan, 1952.

Gomá Orduña, J. *Historia de la Aeronáutica Española*. Vol. 1. Madrid: Prensa Española, 1946.

Gregory, Col. N.H. *The Helicopter: Anything a Horse Can Do*. London: George Allen & Unwin, 1948.

Gunston, Bill. *Aircraft of the Soviet Union*. London: Osprey, 1983.

Harlin, E.A., and Jenks, G.A. *Avro: An Aircraft Album*. London: Ian Allan, 1973.

Herrera Linares, E. *Aerotécnica*. Madrid: Gráficas R. Ferry, 1936.

Hubler, R.G. *Straight Up: The Story of Vertical Flight*. New York: Duell, Sloan and Pearce, 1961.

Jackson, A.J. *British Civil Aircraft, 1919–59*. London: Putnam, 1959.

―――. *De Havilland Aircraft Since 1915*. London: Putnam, 1962.

―――. *Avro Aircraft Since 1908*. London: Putnam, 1965.

Jackson, R. *The Dragonflies*. London: Barker, 1971.

Jupner, J.P. *U.S. Civil Aircraft*. Vols. 1–9. Los Angeles: Aero Publishers, 1962–81.

Kingston Smith, F. *Legacy of Wings: The Harold Pitcairn Story*. New York: Jason Aronson, 1981.

Lambermont, P.M., and Pirie, A. *Helicopters and Autogyros of the World*. 1958. 2d ed. London: Cassell, 1970.

Lamé, Lt. Col. *Le Vol Vertical*. Paris: Blondel la Rougery, 1934.

Lukins, A.H. *The Book of Westland Aircraft*. Leicester: Harborough, 1944.

Martín-Barbadillo, T. de. *El Autogiro. Ayer, hoy' mañana. . . .* Madrid: Espasa-Calpe, 1935.

Mead, P. *The Eye in the Air*. London: HMSO, 1983.

Munson, K. *Helicopters and Other Rotorcraft Since 1907*. New York: Macmillan, 1969.

Nelson, H., and Williamson, G.W. *Aeronautics*. Vol. 4. London: Newnes, c. 1939.

Nowarra, H.J., and Duval, G.R. *Russian Civil and Military Aircraft, 1884–1969*. London: Fountain Press, 1970.

Penrose, H. *British Aviation: The Adventuring Years, 1920–29*. London: Putnam, 1973.

_____. *British Aviation: Widening Horizons, 1930–34*. London: HMSO, 1979.

_____. *British Aviation: The Ominous Skies, 1935–39*. London: HMSO, 1980.

_____. *Architect of Wings*. Shrewsbury: Airlife, 1985.

Putnam, G.P. *Soaring Wings*. London: Harrap, 1940.

Reader, W.J. *Architect of Air Power*. London: Collins, 1968.

_____. *The Weir Group Centenary History*. London: Weidenfeld and Nicolson, 1971.

Salas Larrazabel, J. *From Fabric to Titanium*. Madrid: Espasa-Calpe, 1983.

Sanders, C.J., and Rawson, A.H. *The Book of the C.19 Autogiro*. London: Pitman, 1931.

Saville-Sneath, R.A. *British Aircraft*. Vol. 2. London: Penguin, 1944.

_____. *Aircraft of the United States*. Vol. 2. London: Penguin, 1946.

Smith, J.R. *Focke-Wulf: An Aircraft Album*. London: Ian Allan, 1973.

Townson, G. *Autogiro: The Story of the Windmill Plane*. Fallbrook: Aero Publishers, 1985.

Warleta Carrillo, J. *Autogiro: Juan de la Cierva y su Obra*. Madrid: Instituto de España, 1978.

Articles

Alfaro Fournier, H. "New Type of Flying Machine—The Lacierva Autogiro." *Aviation*, April 1923.

"The Autogiro." *Cierva Autogiro Co. Ltd.*, 1930, 1932.

"Autogiro News." *Autogiro Co. of America*, January 1931—September 1932.

"The Autogiro." *Autogiro Co. of America*, c. 1932.

"Autogiro," *Avion*, January 1963.

Bairstowe, L."The Cierva Auto-Gyro." *Nature*, October 31, 1925.

Barcala Moreno, J. "Yo Vi Nacer el Autogiro." *Blanco y Negro*, January 16, 1965.

Bennett, J.A.J. "Rotary-Wing Aircraft." *Aircraft Engineering*, January/August, 1940.

_____. "The Era of the Autogiro (First Cierva Memorial Lecture)." *Journal of the Royal Aeronautical Society*, October, 1961.

Blanco Pedraza, P. "Juan de la Cierva y su contribución al desarrollo de las aeronaves de alas giratorias." *Asociación de Ingenieros Aeronáuticos*, Madrid, September 8, 1958.

Brie, R.A.C. "Rotary Wings at Sea." *Aeroplane*, July 6, 1951.

_____. "The Rise of the Helicopter." *Flight*, January 23, 1953.

_____. "A History of British Rotorcraft, 1865–1965." *Westland Aircraft*, 1965.

Brooks, P.W. "Rotary Wing Pioneer." *Aeroplane*, December 9 and 16, 1955.

_____. "The Development of the Helicopter." *World Helicopter and Vertical Flight*, March 1959.

Capon, P.T. "Cierva's First Autogiros." *Aeroplane Monthly*, April and May, 1979.

Caygill G.E., and Woodward Nutt, A.E. "Wind Tunnel and Dropping Tests of Autogyro Models." *R & M* 1116, November 1926.

"The Cierva Autogiro Type C.30." *Cierva Autogiro Co. Ltd.*, 1933.

Cierva Codorníu, J. de la, "Un Nuevo Sistema de Aviación." *Real Academia de Ciencias, Madrid*, March 5, 1921.

_____. "Comunicación a la Real Academia de Ciencias." *Real Academia de Ciencias, Madrid*, February 15, 1923.

_____. "Ce qu'est l'autogire." *L'Aéronautique*, April 1933.

_____. "El Autogiro." *Alas*, March 15, 1924.

_____. "Essais Aérodynamiques d'un Modèle d'Autogire." *L'Aéronautique*, January, 1925.

_____. "Comment j'ai conçu l'Autogire." *L'Aéronautique*, April 1925.

_____. "The Development of the Autogiro." *Journal of the Royal Aeronautical Society*, January 1926.

_____. "L'Autogire." *L'Aéronautique*, November 1928.

_____. "The Autogiro." Lecture at Cambridge University, November 8, 1928.

_____. "Engineering Theory of the Autogiro." *Cierva Autogiro Co. Ltd.*, 1929.

_____. "A New Way to Fly." *Saturday Evening Post*, November 2, 1929.

_____. "The Autogiro." *Journal of the Royal Aeronautical Society*, November 1930.

_____. "The Theory of the Autogiro." *Fortune*, March 1931.

_____. "Prüfungebericht der abgeänderten C.19." *Cierva Autogiro Co. Ltd.*, August 1931.

_____. "The Autogiro: A Synopsis of Information on the Principles." *Cierva Autogiro Co. Ltd.*, 1931, 1935.

_____. "El Autogiro en el Momento Actual." *Revista de Aeronáutica*, December 1933.

_____. "Rotary-Wing Aircraft." *Proceedings of the Royal Philosophical Society of Glasgow*, vol. 61, 1934.

_____. "Seguridad comparada del alia figa y les sistemes rotativos." *Le Congrese International de la Société Aérienne*, T. III, Madrid, 1930.

_____. "Comparaison de machines volantes." *L'Aéronautique*, February 1934.

_____. "The Evolution of the Autogiro." *Aircraft Engineering*, May 1934.

_____. "Rotary-Wing Aircraft." *Aircraft Engineering*, June 1934.

_____. "Rotary-Wing Aircraft." *Cambridge University Engineering and Aeronautical Society's Journal*, 1934.

_____. "Neuere Fortschritte des Autogiros." *Luftwissen*, May 1935.

_____. "New Developments of the Autogiro." *Journal of the Royal Aeronautical Society*, December 1935.

_____. "Theory of Stresses on Autogiro Rotor Blades." *Cierva Autogiro Co. Ltd.*, 1936.

Cierva Codorníu, J. de la, and Lepère, R. "L'Autogire C.L.10." *L'Aéronautique*, December 1932.

Courtney, F.T. "Note sur le Pilotage de l'Autogire." *L'Aéronautique*, January 1926.

Fair, E.W. "Hopping Helicopters." *American Aviator, Airplanes and Airports*, November 1928.

"The First Fatal Autogiro Accident." *Flight*, December 29, 1932.

"Flying with a Mill on Top." *Shell Aviation News*, no. 108, June 1947.

Focke, H. "German Thinking on Rotary-Wing Development." *Journal of the Royal Aeronautical Society*, May 1965.

Glauert, H. "A General Theory of the Autogiro." *R & M* 1111, November 1926.

_____. "The Theory of the Autogiro." *Journal of the Royal Aeronautical Society*, June 1927.

Hafner, R. "British Rotorcraft." *Journal of the Royal Aeronautical Society*, January 1966.

Hill, N. "Wingless Combat." *RAF Flying Review*, January 1963.

Hodgess, F.L. "The Weir Autogiros." *Helicopter World*, July, August, October, and November, 1964.

Jones, E.T. "Performance of the C.19 Gyroplane." *RAE Report* BA865, May 1930.

Karman, Th. von. "Die Seitenwege der Luftfahrt." *Zeitschrift für Flugtechnik und Motorluftschiffahrt*, vol. 22, 1931.

———. "Aerodinámica." *Temas selecciónados a la luz de su desarrollo historico*, INTA, Madrid, 1954.

"The Kay Gyroplane Type 331." *Aeroplane*, December 26, 1934.

Keith, R. "British Helicopters Were Three Years Ahead." *Canadian Aviation*, October 1944.

Klemin, A. "Principles of Rotary Aircraft." *Journal of the Franklin Institute*, vol. 227, no. 3, March 1939.

Larsen, A.E. "Development of the Autogiro." *Aero Digest*, October 1930.

———. "Progress of Autogiro Development." *Autogiro News*, September 1931.

———. "Engineering Aspects of the Modern Autogiro." *SAE Journal (Transactions)*, 1932.

———. "American Autogiro, Gyroplane and Early Convertaplane Developments." *Journal of the American Helicopter Society*, January 1956.

Liptrot, R.N. "Modern Developments of the Helicopter." *Journal of the Royal Aeronautical Society*, July 1931.

———. "Historical Development of the Helicopter." *Bulletin of the Helicopter Association*, March 1947.

———. "Rotating Wing Activities in Germany during the Period, 1939–45," B.I.O.S. Overall Report No. 8., HMSO, 1948.

Liron, J. "Lioré-et-Olivier—Les Voilures Tournantes." *Aviation Magazine*, September 1 and 15, October 1, 1970.

Llave Sierra, J. de la, "El Autogiro la Cierva." *Iberica*, November 5, 1927.

Lock, C.N.H. "Further Development of Autogyro Theory." *R & M* 1127, March 1927.

"Long Before Sikorsky." *RAF Flying Review*, December 1955.

Loriga, J. "Le Pilotage de l'Autogire." *L'Aéronautique*, January 1925.

"La Machine Volante de la Cierva." *La Revue Maritime*, January 1926.

Maltby, R.L., and Brotherhood, P. "The RAE Contribution to Helicopter Research." *RAE TM Structures Report* no. 885, March 1976.

Mayne R. and Johnson Jr., W.C. "A Simplified Dynamic Stress Analysis of Hinged Rotor Blades." *Proceedings of the Fifth Annual Forum of the American Helicopter Society*, 1949.

Molin, K.G., Bahr, R. von, and Luthander, S. "Autogiron," Stockholm, 1943.

Moreno Caracciolo, M. "El Autogiro." *Ingeniería y Construcción*, March 1923.

———. "El Autogiro Cierva." *Boletín Tecnológico*, 1925.

"A New Type of Flying Machine." *Flight*, October 22, 1925.

Pitcairn, H.F. "The Autogiro: Its Characteristics and Accomplishments." *Smithsonian Report for 1930*, Washington D.C., 1931.

———. "Juan de la Cierva: In Memoriam." *Autogiro Co. of America*, January 9, 1939.

Poulsen, C.M. "British Helicopters." *Flight*, May 11, 1944.

Prewitt, R.H. "Possibilities of the Jump Take-Off Autogiro." *Journal of the Aeronautical Sciences*, November 1938.

"Proceedings of Rotary-Wing Aircraft Meeting." *Franklin Institute*, Philadelphia, October 28 and 29, 1938.

Puig Adams, P. "Sobre la estabilidad del movimiento de las palas del Autogiro." *Revista de Aeronáutica*, September 1934.

Pullin, R.A. "A Rotary-Wing Enterprise." *Aeronautics*, November 1946.

"Rotating-Wing Aircraft." *Flight*, March 26, 1943.

"Some Facts of Interest about Rotating-Wing Aircraft." *Autogiro Co. of America*, October 1934.

Stanley, P.H. "Historical Outline." *Engineering Department, Autogiro Co. of America*, Glenside, Penn., 1952.

Townson, G. "General Information and History of the Autogiro." *Kellett Aircraft Company*, June 1, 1960.

_____. "The History of the Autogiro." *American Helicopter Society Newsletter*, March 1961.

Warleta Carrillo, J. "Siete Etapas de la Historia de Autogiro." *Carrillo XXI Conferencia "Juan de la Cierva." Asociación de Ingenieros Aeronáuticas*, February 9, 1979.

Wright, K.V. "Flight Tests of the C.19 Mk III Gyroplane." *RAE Report BA 881*, November 1930.

Yeatman, H.M. "The Cierva Autogiro." *Aero Digest*, April 1928.

Many other references can be found in: *Aeronautics, L'Aéronautique, Aeroplane, Les Ailes, Alas, L'Année Aéronautique, 1919–1939, Aviation Magazine, Avion, Flight, Interavia, Jane's All the World's Aircraft*.

Index

(Excluding appendices, which are largely self-indexing)

Page numbers in bold indicate illustrations.